OLD ABBEVILLE PRESBYTERIAN CHURCH

THE HISTORY
OF
CAPE MAY COUNTY
NEW JERSEY

FROM

THE ABORIGINAL TIMES

TO

THE PRESENT DAY

EMBRACING

AN ACCOUNT OF THE ABORIGINES; THE DUTCH IN DELAWARE BAY;
THE SETTLEMENT OF THE COUNTY; THE WHALING; THE GROWTH
OF THE VILLAGES; THE REVOLUTION AND PATRIOTS; THE
ESTABLISHMENT OF THE NEW GOVERNMENT; THE WAR
OF 1812; THE PROGRESS OF THE COUNTY; AND
THE SOLDIERS OF THE CIVIL WAR

1638–1897

ILLUSTRATED

Lewis Townsend Stevens

HERITAGE BOOKS
2011

HERITAGE BOOKS
AN IMPRINT OF HERITAGE BOOKS, INC.

Books, CDs, and more—Worldwide

For our listing of thousands of titles see our website
at
www.HeritageBooks.com

A Facsimile Reprint
Published 2011 by
HERITAGE BOOKS, INC.
Publishing Division
100 Railroad Ave. #104
Westminster, Maryland 21157

Copyright © 1997 Heritage Books, Inc.

Entered according to act of Congress, in 1897, by
Lewis T. Stevens
In the office of the Librarian of Congress, at Washington, D.C.

— Publisher's Notice —
In reprints such as this, it is often not possible to remove blemishes from the original. We feel the contents of this book warrant its reissue despite these blemishes and hope you will agree and read it with pleasure.

International Standard Book Numbers
Paperbound: 978-0-7884-0764-2
Clothbound: 978-0-7884-8961-7

PREFACE.

"The History of Cape May County" is the result of many years of research, and the author hopes that it will meet with the approbation of the public. Some ten years ago the author began the keeping of a scrap book of Cape May county history, among other things, and this constant accumulation of facts resulted, about a year ago, in a determination on the part of the author to prepare a history of the county, which would portray its gradual development and the progress of its people from the earliest times. The cause which led to its preparation principally was the fact that no history had ever before been published, excepting the sketch of Dr. Maurice Beesley, in 1857, which contained only fifty printed pages.

The information obtained for this volume was largely supplemented from the collections of the New York Historical Society, the New Jersey Historical Society and the Pennsylvania Historical Society. Many facts were gathered also from the articles of Francis B. Lee, Esq., of Trenton, and the author has also been aided in his work by Colonel J. Granville Leach, of Philadelphia; County Clerk Edward L. Rice, and Mr. Aaron Leaming. The diaries of Aaron Leaming the first, of Aaron Leaming the second, and of Jacob Spicer the second have been perused and liberal extracts made from the same. The work of Dr. Beesley has been woven into this volume and proper credit given to him for every fact for which he is responsible.

The county of Cape May has a most honorable history and the one aim of the author has been to tell the facts as he finds them and yet try to keep away from the dryness which characterizes such works. There may be errors in the volume, but the author has been very careful in the verification of dates and names. The different ways of spelling family names is caused by the literal copying of the records from which they are taken.

If this volume serves to preserve to the people the history of the county, the author will feel that he has been repaid for his efforts.   LEWIS T. STEVENS.

Cape May, May 15, 1897.

ODE TO CAPE MAY.

By Theophilus T. Price, M. D.

Tune: "Dearest May."
(Revised by the author for this work.)

Dear land of my nativity!
And scene of childhood's play,
I fondly sing my love to thee
In humble, fervent lay.
Let others roam who have a mind;
With thee I'd rather stay,
For many ties there are that bind
My heart to thee, Cape May.

CHORUS:—
Cape May! Cape May!
My thoughts to thee will stray
With fond delight, in memories bright,
When I am far away.

Thy sunny skies look down serene
Where warbling woodlands lay;
And fertile fields stretch out between
The ocean and the bay.
And health on every breeze is borne
That o'er thee takes its way;
And plenty pours her teeming horn
Into thy lap, Cape May.
Chorus.

Thy daughters' praise truth gladly speaks,
  While fond emotions rise;
The glow of beauty gilds their cheeks
  And sparkles in their eyes;
And hearts of love and tenderness
  Within their bosoms play;
Their virtues fair adorn and bless
  Thy happy homes, Cape May!
    Chorus.

Thy sons, a generous patriot band,
  Hospitable and brave,
Love loyally their native land,
  Their homes, and circling wave;
Bold are their hearts where duty lies,
  Or honor points the way;
And noble, honest men arise,
  Thy proudest boast, Cape May!
    Chorus.

I love to breathe thy healthful air;
  I love thy sky and sea;
I love thee, for my friends are here,
  And all that's dear to me.
I love thee, for thou art my home,
  And wheresoe'er I stray
The golden chain of memory
  Still binds me to Cape May!
    Chorus: Cape May! Cape May! etc.

Contents.

Chapter I—The Indians and the Dutch Explorers.... 9
Chapter II—Pioneers and Whaling 23
Chapter III—The Settlers and Their New Homes.... 36
Chapter IV—Life Early in the Eighteenth Century... 59
Chapter V—Development of Religious Denominations 70
Chapter VI—Maritime Tendencies and Cattle Owning 79
Chapter VII—Ancient Loans and Taxes............. 90
Chapter VIII—The Religious Controversies......... 98
Chapter IX—West Jersey Society Rights............106
Chapter X—Jacob Spicer and His Sayings..........116
Chapter XI—Aaron Leaming and His Times........132
Chapter XII—John Hatton, the Tory...............143
Chapter XIII—Preparations for War 171
Chapter XIV—The Revolution Begins 183
Chapter XV—Cape May Patriots 195
Chapter XVI—The Ending and Independence.......208
Chapter XVII—The County in 1800................224
Chapter XVIII—The War of 1812.................233
Chapter XIX—Progress After the War.............248
Chapter XX—Noted Men of a Generation..........267
Chapter XXI—The Decade Before the Rebellion....280
Chapter XXII—Opening of the Civil War..........301
Chapter XXIII—First New Jersey Cavalry..........316
Chapter XXIV—The Enlistments of 1862...........328
Chapter XXV—The Campaigns of 1864 and 1865....344
Chapter XXVI—Life Following the Rebellion......355
Chapter XXVII—Fifteen Years of Prosperity.......375
Chapter XXVIII—Distinguished Visitors 393
Chapter XXIX—Cape Island 405
Chapter XXX—Cape May City.....................429

Chapter XXXI—The Boroughs 445
Appendix A—Members of the Legislature 450
Appendix B—Boards of Freeholders 453
Appendix C—County Officials 463
Appendix E—Municipal Officers 472
Appendix D—Postmasters 465
Appendix F—Table of Population 480

ERRATA.

Page 43—For "Thomas Caesar Hoskins" read "Thomas Hand, Caesar Hoskins."

Page 206—For "Daniel Ganetson" read "Daniel Garretson."

Page 338—For "Willoby Snyder" read "Willoby Souder."

Page 360—For "Miss Emma T. Brooks" read "Miss Emma T. Sutton."

Page 393—For "thunpike" read "shunpike."

Page 423—For "Mashel" read "Maskel."

Illustrations.

Cold Spring Presbyterian Church .... Frontispiece
Map of Cape May County 177
Townsend Coat of Arms 37
Steamboat Landing, Cape May Point, in 1859............. 189
Congress Hall, Cape Island, in 1859 211
The Carlton, Cape May Point............................ 235
President Harrison's Cottage, Cape May Point 245
Marine Villa, Cape May 251
Joshua Townsend 254
The Jail of 1829 257
Rev. Moses Williamson 261
Jonathan Hand 268
James L. Smith 270
Joseph S. Leach 280
The Court House 283
Jesse H. Diverty 288
Dr. Maurice Beesley 289
William S. Hooper 291
George W. Smith 313
Henry W. Sawyer 319
William J. Sewell 347
Jonathan F. Leaming 353
Clerk's and Surrogate's Offices 357
Thomas R. Brooks 360
Richard S. Leaming 367
Dr. Alexander Young 368
Joseph E. Hughes 369
William T. Stevens 376
Waters B. Miller 378
Alfred Cooper 381
Thomas E. Ludlam 388
Dr. Walter S. Leaming 390
Eugene C. Cole 391
Dr. Anna M. Hand 397
The Jail of 1894 399
Edmund L. Ross 400
Andrew J. Tomlin 401
The Synagogue, Woodbine 402
Aaron W. Hand 403
Robert E. Hand 404
First Baptist Church, Cape May 421
Dr. James Mecray 430
Joseph Q. Williams 432
Frederick J. Melvin 435
James M. E. Hildreth 441

HISTORY OF CAPE MAY COUNTY.

CHAPTER I.

THE INDIANS AND THE DUTCH EXPLORERS.

The first inhabitants of what is now the county of Cape May, as far as history teaches us, were the red men of the forest. These aborigines were of that great tribe of the Algonquins, which had their first home about Ottawa, Canada, and being of a roaming and nomadic disposition, more so than most other families, they naturally cared little for agricultural pursuits and wandered over the country and were found east of the Mississippi River, through all the Middle, Northern Central and New England States. Of all the tribes who were most unfortunate were the Algonquins. Disease took thousands of them away and the greedy settlers killed them off like birds. The branch of the Algonquins which inhabited New Jersey were the Lenni-Lenapes, who happily were treated honorably and paid for their land by the settlers the prices demanded by their chiefs. Indians, as all know, are fond of game and during the hunting season Cape May had its share of the inhabitants of the forest. Birds of varieties abounded. Wilson, the ornithologist, who did most of his writing and studying at Beesley's Point, said, "If birds are good judges of excellence in climate, Cape May has the finest climate in the United States, for it has the greatest variety of birds."

The last king of the Lenni-Lenapes, King Nummy, is buried on Nummy Island near Hereford Inlet, and it is said that all Indians left the county after the ceremony of burial and journeyed to Indiana, settling on the banks of the Wabash river.

The Lenni-Lenapes were called often the Delawares, and were the most influential tribe in this section, as well as the most peaceable. The name of the particular tribe inhabiting Cape May county, living at Cape May Point, was the Kechemeches. The Delaware river was called the Whittuck, and the province, now New Jersey, was called Skaakbee, or Sheyichbi. The name of Tuckahoe is of Indian origin, and means where deer are shy or difficult to approach. Hunting for deer about the head of that river, which was enjoyed by the Indian, was indulged in by the residents of the county until 1890, since which time very few have been seen there.

It has been supposed by many that the number of aborigines in this State when first visited by Europeans was considerable. That they were very numerous in this county there cannot be any doubt, from the great quantities of shells found contiguous to the seaboard. Many hundreds of bushels are to be seen, in numerous places in one mass, and the soil in many places abounds with them and is enriched thereby. There is a singular, and perhaps, unaccountable fact, respecting these deposits; the shells are, universally, so broken that seldom a piece is found larger than a shilling. Many Indian relics have been discovered, such as isinglass, medals, stone hatchets, arrow heads, earthenware of a rough description, beads, javelin heads, etc.

Dr. Maurice Beesley, in his "Sketch of the Early History of Cape May" (1857), says of the Indians:

"Of the aborigines of Cape May little seems to be known. It has been argued they were very inconsiderable at the advent of the Europeans. Plantagenet in 1648 speaks of a tribe of Indians near Cape May, called Kechemeches, who mustered about fifty men. The same author estimates the whole number in West Jersey at eight hundred; and Oldmixon, in 1708, computes that 'they had been reduced to one-quarter of that number.' It cannot be denied by any one who will view the seaboard of our county that they were very numerous at one time here, which is evidenced by town plats, extensive and numberless shell banks, arrow heads, stone hatchets, burying grounds, and other remains existing with us. One of these burying grounds is on the farm formerly Joshua Garretson's, near Beesley's Point, which was first discovered by the plowman. The bones (1826) were much decomposed, and some of the tibia or leg bones bore unmistakable evidences of syphilis, one of the fruits presented them by their Christian civilizers. A skull was exhumed which must have belonged to one of great age, as the sutures were entirely obliterated, and the tables firmly cemented together. From the superciliary ridges, which were well developed, the frontal bone receded almost on a direct line to the place of the occipital and parietal sutures, leaving no forehead, and had the appearance of having been done by artificial means, as practiced at present on the Columbia among the Flat Heads. A jaw-bone of huge dimensions was likewise found, which was coveted by the observer; but the superstitions of the owner of the soil believing it was sacrilegious, and that he would be visited by the just indignation of Heaven if he suffered any of the teeth to be removed, prevailed on us to return it again to its mother earth.

"In 1630, when sixteen miles square was purchased of nine Indian chiefs, it would infer their numbers must have been considerable, or so numerous a list of chiefs could not have been found on a spot so limited. Yet, in 1692, we find them reduced to fractional parts, and besotted with rum.

"A tradition is related by some of the oldest inhabitants, that in the early part of the eighteenth century the remnant of Indians in the county, feeling themselves aggrieved in various ways by the presence of the whites, held a council in the evening in the woods back of Gravelly Run, at which they decided to emigrate; which determination they carried into effect the same night. Whither they went no one knew, nor were they heard from afterwards. In less than fifty years from the first settlement of the county the aborigines had bid a final adieu to their ocean haunts and fishing grounds.

"Less than two centuries ago Cape May, as well as most other parts of our State, was a wilderness; her fields and lawns were dense and forbidding forests; the stately Indian roved over her domain in his native dignity and grandeur, lord of the soil, and master of himself and actions, with few wants and numberless facilities for supplying them. Civilization, his bane and dire enemy, smote him in a vital part; he dwindled before it as the reed before the flame; and was soon destroyed by its influence, or compelled to emigrate to other regions to prolong for a while the doom affixed to his name and nation.

"The following (synopsis of an) Indian deed, and believed to be the only one that has been handed down, was found among the papers of Jacob Spicer, and is now in the possession of Charles Ludlam, Esq., of Dennisville.

"It was given January 1st, 1687, by Panktoe to John Dennis, for a tract of land near Cape Island, viz.: 'Beginning from the creek and so running up into the woodland, along by Carman's line to a white oak tree, at the head of the swamp, and running with marked trees to a white oak by a pond joining to Jonathan Pine's bounds. All the lands and marsh lying and between the bounds above mentioned and Cape Island.'

"The witnesses were Abiah Edwards and John Carman. Panktoe's mark bore a striking resemblance to a Chinese character."

It is a boast of the citizens of all New Jersey, and especially of the land owners, that not a foot of its soil was ever taken by fraud or force from the red man. The first Dutch settlers purchased theirs, as did the Swedes subsequently, and later the English Friends, or Quakers. And the succeeding proprietors all pursued the same honorable course.

During the period of exploration, in the sixteenth century, Cape May's shores were probably seen by many bold navigators who did not land. Being partially surrounded with water and with long, low marshes between the beaches and the main land, and possessing no natural harbor for vessels, excepting a slight one on the Delaware Bay side, just above the point of the cape, the hardy ocean voyager pressed on to places more promising, where ships could ride at anchor and be safe from the wind and storm.

John Cabot, the loyal Englishman, and son, Sebastian Cabot, who made a voyage to America in 1498, may have seen Cape May and explored it, because it is recorded that he explored the coast of what is now New England and as far south as Cape Hatteras. John de Verrazani, a Florentine navigator, sailing under the flag of France, is also believed to have passed Cape May, and is believed to have rounded the Cape in the spring of 1524 in the "Dolphin." The county was in the territory claimed by Verrazani as New France.

Cape May county, the boundary of which has not been changed to a very great extent since its organization, is bounded on the north by the Tuckahoe river, which rises in the great cedar swamp in the northern part of the county, and which inter-locks with Dennis creek, the latter emptying into the Delaware Bay. This cedar swamp in which they rise stretches for seventeen miles across the county. That portion of the land north of the Tuckahoe river was first known as Gloucester county, but became Atlantic county when the latter political division was formed.

Being a level county, with an alluvial formation, and with the unpromising beaches along the ocean side, the early explorers who were hunting for gold mines had no time to tarry long upon them. They left it for those who wanted to settle down to agricultural pursuits, for which the territory was excellently calculated. The beaches formed excellent places for the pasture of cattle, and the sounds between the beaches and main land were places to fish and gather the clams and oysters which abounded in the waters. The soil of the county was composed generally of sand, loam and gravel, which was covered in many places with oak, while in the northern end much pine was found.

By right of the discoveries of the Cabots the English claimed about all of North America, and in 1584 King James granted a patent to Sir Walter Raleigh, which embraced the provinces of New Jersey and New York, then all one and known under the name of Virginia. This grant he soon ignored, and in 1606 granted a new charter for Virginia in which was included the territory now known as the New England States, New York, New Jersey, Pennsylvania and Maryland, to the Duke of York, afterwards King of England.

By this time New Jersey and adjacent lands were claimed also by the Swedes and Dutch. Previous to this second grant of King James I, about the year 1600, Balthazer Moncheron, of Holland, and several of his associated patrons of discovery, moved by "terrors, sufferings and failures of their explorers, abandoned the then prevailing idea of a northwest route to India, and left this question to the English and Danes for settlement." But the works they had done acted as a sprouting seed, out of which came the Dutch East India Company's determination to make an exploring move. The notion got into the heads of its officers, and against the advice of Moncheron, the Amsterdam directors became jealous of Denmark and England, and decided to seek the route. Having received seventy-five per centum dividend on their stock, they could easily afford the venture. "De Halve Maan" (Half Moon), of forty last or eighty tons, with two masts, was fitted out for an arctic voyage. Sir Henry Hudson, an Englishman, who had already made two voyages to the new world in search of the self-same passage, was tired of by his own country, and happened to be in Amsterdam at the time. It was no trouble for this powerful monopoly, the East India Company, to secure the services of Hudson, whose surname was afterward changed to Hendrick. He was given charge of the ship, assisted by an under skipper and twenty men. Robert Juet was made Hudson's clerk and became historian of the voyage. On the fourth of April, 1609, he set out for the northern coast of Norway. He sailed northward until icebergs drove him to turn the prow of his ship to the south. In July he reached Newfoundland and later he explored the coast of Maine, and in August he found himself in the Chesapeake Bay. Sailing northward, on the 28th of the month, he entered Delaware Bay, which was called South Bay by the Dutch, and when barely escaping shipwreck ran the Half Moon inside the bay and anchored around the point of the Cape, probably opposite Town Bank. He spent a day in exploring about the Cape. Vander Donk says in his account, "The bay of the South river was the first place of which the men of the Halve Maan took possession, before any Christian had been there." No settlement was attempted by Hudson's crew. They sailed up along the bay side of the county for some distance, but encountering flats, which are common there to this day, turned back, and Vander Donk reports "finding the water shoal, and the channel impeded by bars of sand, he did not venture to explore it." The craft then sailed north and into North river, which has since taken the name of its explorer, Hudson.

Hudson's explorations, with others, created a desire among the tradesmen of the Netherlands to seek more business, and in answer to the petition of a number of merchants a general edict was issued by the States-General of Holland on March 27th, 1614, for the encouragement of discovery and promotion and protection of an aborginal trade. The States-General enacted that the discoverers of "any new courses, havens, countries or places," should have "the exclusive privilege of resorting to and frequenting the same for four voyages," and all intruders were to be punished by a fine and a confiscation of their property. A number of merchants, principally of Amsterdam, formed a company for the making of discoveries and to accept the benefit of the edict. They fitted out five vessels to follow in the wake of Hendrick Hudson, with Manhattan Island (now New York) as their objective point, from which to begin their operations. One of these crafts was named the "Fortune," and sailed from Hoorn, a port in Northern Holland, with Cornelius Jacobsen Mey as navigator. Another of the five, also called the "Fortune," was in care of Commander Hendrick Christiansen. The "Tiger," another, was navigated by Captain Aariaen Block. They made a few discoveries and gave up their work.

The natural successors of this company was the Dutch West India Company, which was formed in Holland in 1621. The States-General granted the Dutch West India Company a charter in 1622, by which the company was given possession of the whole of the domain of New Jersey. On the 21st of June of the year following it secured the assent of the States-General to its prepared articles of internal government for its colony. Three ships were fitted out and a party of settlers made up, and all given into the charge of Captain Cornelius Jacobsen Mey. He sailed in the "Blyde Broodschap" (Glad Tidings), well provided with the means of subsistence and with articles of trade. Mey was styled the First Director of New Netherlands. He reached Manhattan Island in May, 1623, and then proceeded to examine the coast where Hendrick Hudson had preceded him fourteen years earlier. Mey encountered the French, who had attempted to take possession, and repulsed them, and a second time he met the French, who had renewed the attempt to take possession of "Zuyt Baai" (Delaware Bay). We are told that the French were driven off by the Dutch settlers and traders.

About four years previous to this Cornelius Hendricksen, in the "Onrest," had been at Cape May and left a lookout there.

It was during this voyage in 1623, to Delaware Bay, that Captain Mey gave to the Cape his name, and christened it Cape Mey, by which name it has ever since been known. He explored the bay, which was called "Zuydt" by the Dutch, while by the English "Delaware," and the Indians "Pontaxit," and river, and at length built a fort at Techaacho, upon a stream called by the natives Sassachon. This stream is now called Timber Creek and empties into the Delaware a few miles below Camden. He called it Fort Nassau, and this may really be called the first attempt of a settlement on the eastern shore of the Delaware river. Captain Mey announced to his home company the discovery of "certain new populous and fruitful lands, along Zuydt Riviere." He explored the Atlantic coast as far north as Cape Cod. He named the bay of New York "Port Mey;" the Delaware, "New Port Mey;" its north cape, "Cape Mey," and its south cape, "Cape Cornelius." Only one of his designations has been handed down to posterity, and that has undergone some change in its orthography; the "e" being changed to "a." The Delaware river was known at this time under various names, some of which were South, Nassau, Prince Kendrick's, and Charles'.

The West India Company, after the reports received from Mey, endeavored, by the offer of many advantages, to induce others to engage with them. They granted charters to individuals, subject only to Indian claims. Some purchased through agents lands on both sides of the river. When Captain Mey returned to Holland he left at Manhattan Island several families, sailors and men to explore and settle on the South river.

Upon the voyages and discoveries of Hudson and Mey the name of New Netherlands was applied to all the country lying on the coast between Cape Cod and Cape Henlopen, which claim was disputed by France and Great Britain. Of Cornelius Jacobsen Mey, who was formally installed during the summer of 1623, as first Director-General of New Netherlands, many good things are said. " 'Tis better to govern by love and friendship than by force," wrote his superiors in Holland; and he acted in the spirit of his instructions to "the great contentment of his people." Among the Indians at Fort Nassau, Mey's little colony of brides and grooms were unharmed, while at Fort Orange and Manhattan the Indians "were all as quiet as lambs, and came and traded with all the freedom imaginable." When at a time the residents of Manhattan were suffering from a want of clothes and stores, he supplied them from his ship.

Director William Verhulst, a successor of Mey, in presiding over New Netherlands, visited the Delaware in 1625, and extended his voyage up the river as far as the falls at Trenton.

In the meanwhile that the Dutch were attempting to discover and colonize along the shores of the Delaware Bay and river, King Gustavus Adolphus, of Sweden, at the suggestion of William Usselinx, of Holland, who in 1590 had proposed the Dutch West India Company, undertook to found a colony on its banks also, but none of them are known to have settled at Cape May.

In 1629 the West India Company endeavored to excite individual enterprise into colonizing the country which they now claimed. A number of the directors entered into a scheme, the outcome of which was they called themselves patroons for establishing colonies, in each of which were to be fifty settlers. Each patroon was granted a charter by the company, in which the patroon was given exclusive property in the large tracts of lands with extensive manorial and seignorial rights. Thus encouraged, several of the directors for whose use, probably, the charter was designed, among them Godyn, Bloemmart, Pauuw and Van Renselaer were most distinguished, resolved to make large territorial acquisitions. These directors sent out from Amsterdam three ships, and the whole management of the affair on this side of the Atlantic was entrusted to Wooter Van Twiller, a clerk of the Amsterdam department of the company. He was to select the lands for the individual directors. He entered the Delaware Bay with a ship and party about June 1st, 1629, a few days before the adoption of their charter by Holland, and landed on the south side of the bay, where he bought of three chiefs of an Indian tribe there a tract of land for Godyn about Cape "Henloop," or "Inloop," now known as Cape Henlopen.

As soon as the settlement on the south side of the bay had become fairly inhabited, Skipper Peter Heyssen, of the ship Walrus, visited the Cape May shore and as agents of Samuel Godyn and Samuel Bloemmaert, bought of ten Indian chiefs on, says an account, May 5, 1630, which sale was afterwards made a matter of record under date of June 3, 1631, a tract of land four miles along the bay from Cape May to the north, and extending four miles inland, containing an area of sixteen square miles. The deed for this land, which is still preserved among the old colonial records, reads as follows:

"We, Director and Council of New Netherland, residing on the Island of Manhattan at Fort Amsterdam, under the jurisdiction of Their Noble High Mightiness, the Lords-State's-General of the United Netherlands and the Incorporated West India Company, Department of Amsterdam, attest and declare herewith that to-day, date underwritten, appeared Peter Heyssen, skipper of the ship "Walvis," at present lying in the South river, and Gillis Hosset, commissary on the same, who declare that on the 5th day of May, last past, before them appeared personally, Sawowonwe, Wvoyt, Pemhake, Mekowetick, Techepepewoya, Mathemck, Sacoock, Anehoopeon, Janqueno and Pakahake, lawful owners, proprietors and inhabitants of the east side of Goddyn's East bay, called Cape de Maye, who for themselves in proportion of their own shares and for all the other owners in regard to their shares of the same land, declare of their own accord and deliberately in their said qualities, to have transported, ceded and conveyed as lawful, unalienable and free property by virtue and title of sale and in consideration of a certain quantity of goods, which they, the conveyors, acknowledge in their said quality to have received and accepted before the passing of this contract, and they herewith transport, cede and convey, to and in behoof of the Noble Honorable Samuel Godyn and Samuel Bloemmaert (who are absent and for whom they had accepted the hereafter described land subject to the usual reservation) to wit: the east side of Godyn's bay or Cape de Maye, reaching 4 miles from the said cape towards the bay and 4 miles along the coast southward, and another 4 miles inland, being 16 square miles, with all interests, rights and privileges which were vested in themselves in their aforesaid quality, constituting and delegating the aforesaid purchasers in their own stead as real and actual owners thereof and giving and surrendering at the same time to their Honors, full, absolute and irrevocable power, authority and special charge, that tamquam actores at procuratores in rem propriam the Noble Messrs. Godyn and Bloemmaert or those who might hereafter receive their property, enter upon, possess in peace, inhabit, cultivate, keep, use, do with, trade and dispose of the afore described land as they would do with their own inherited lands and fiefs, without that they, the conveyors, shall have, reserve or keep in the least degree any particle of claim, right or privilege thereon, be it of ownership, authority or jurisdiction, but for the behalf as aforesaid, they herewith entirely and absolutely desist from, give up, abandon and renounce it now and forever, promising further not only to keep, fulfil and execute firmly, inviolately and irrevocably in infinitum this, their contract and what might be done hereafter on the authority thereof, but also to deliver the said tract of land and keep it free against everybody, from any claim, challenge or incumbrance which any body might intend to create; as well as to have this sale and conveyance approved and confirmed by the remainder of the co-owners, for whom they are trustees; all this under the obligations required by law, in good faith, without evil intent or deceit. In testimony whereof this has been confirmed by our usual signature and our seal appended thereto. Done on the aforesaid Island of Manhattan, at Fort Amsterdam, the 3d of June, A. D. 1631."

The above patent and one for land on the south side of the bay were issued by Peter Minuit, while Director of New Netherland, and this is the only document found in Holland by Mr. Brodhead, as having come down to the present time from the West India Company, the rest having been sold as waste paper.

Gillis Hosset, or Osset, was a colonist, born in Holland. He was commander of the De Vries expedition, mentioned later. He sailed from the Texel on December 12, 1630, in the ship "Walrus.' He built a house on the Delaware side of the bay, and because of an attempt to play a trick on some Indians was killed by them in December, 1631. The sixteen square miles which was purchased was in the possession of the Lenni-Lenape Indians. This was the first recorded purchase of the natives within the limits of the State.

At the time of Godyn's and Bloemmaert's purchase the marshes of Cape May were very "extensive and the sounds and thoroughfares large. The inland waters were found to abound in oysters, clams, crabs, and other shell fish." Nothing is given in the old Dutch records, however, to prove that a colony was at this time established in Cape May.

The tract for Pauuw was purchased on Staten Island and about Hoboken, while a tract on the Hudson, near Fort Orange, was secured by Van Twiller for Van Renselaer. Godyn's territory was called "Swanwendael."

After Pieter Heyset concluded his purchase of the Cape May county land he entered into the whaling industry.

The impracticability of these great exclusive grants was subsequently discovered and condemned. Their ratification were never obtained by the States-General until they had admitted other directors to participate in the privileges.

In the course of time these directors formed an equal partnership with David Pieterson de Vries, a navigator of enterprise. They immediately planned to colonize the shores of the Delaware, to plant tobacco and grain, and to establish a whale and seal fishery. Of de Vries it is said that he was wise in counsel, that he conciliated the Indians of Swanwendael and Scheyichbi, and made the way smooth for the following settlers on both shores of the Delaware. In 1631 he entered the Delaware and left a colony at Hoornekill, near Boompjes Hoek (now Bombay Hook). He was the first resident patroon owner of Cape May, and was a religious and devout man. He went back to his Hoornekill colony the next year, but found that they had been massacred by the savages. "Finding the whale fishery unsuccessful, he hastened his departure, and, with the other colonists, proceeded to Holland by the way of Fort Amsterdam" (New York). "Thus," says Gordon, "at the expiration of twenty years from the discovery of the Delaware by Hudson, not a single European remained upon its shores."

De Vries, in his journal, says, "March 29th, 1633, found that our people have caught seven whales; we could have done more if we had good harpoons, for they had struck seventeen fish and only saved seven."

"An immense flight of pigeons is obscuring the sky. The 14th, sailed over to Cape May, where the coast trended E. N. E. and S. W. Came at evening to the mouth of Egg Harbor; found between Cape May and Egg Harbor a slight sand beach, full of small, low sand hills. Egg Harbor is a little river or kill, and inside the land is broken, and within the bay are several small islands. Somewhere further up in the same direction is a beautiful high wood." This was probably Somer's or Beesley's Point, clothed in its primitive growth of timber.

In 1638 a number of Swedes entered the bay and were ordered off by the officials of the Dutch West India Company. At the time all the Swedes were told to leave their possessions. The Swedes who entered the bay said that they were on their way to the West Indies and had put into "Zuydt" bay to rest after a stormy voyage.

Dr. Beesley says:

"About 1641 Cape May was again purchased by Swedish agents, a short time before the arrival of the Swedish Governor, Printz Tinicum. This conveyance included all land from Cape May to Narriticon, or Raccoon Creek."

Campanius, a Swedish minister, who resided in New Sweden, on the banks of the Delaware, from the year 1642 to 1648, says, "Cape May lies in latitude 38° 30'. To the south of it there are three sand banks, parallel to each other, and it is not safe to sail between them. The safest course is to steer between them and Cape May, between Cape May and Cape Henlopen."

CHAPTER II.
THE PIONEERS AND WHALING.

Whaling in the Delaware bay was noted as a considerable industry about this time. English colonists from New Haven and emigrants from Long Island, who made whaling their principal industry, must have come to Cape May as early as 1638. The New Havenites were led by George Lamberton. About this time Captain Nathaniel Turner bought of the Indians the land along shore from Cape May to Raccoon Creek, Varcken's kill, Hog creek or Salem river. The price paid was £30, and the deed is dated November 24th, 1638. At different subsequent times New Haven people bought more land and were aided in the purchase by refugee Pequod Indians, who had taken asylum with the Lenni-Lenapes. The New Haven people are said to have paid in the aggregate within five years about £600. Gordon, in his history of New Jersey, says: "Emigrants from New Haven settled on the left shores of the Delaware so early as 1640, some of whose descendants may probably be found in Salem, Cumberland and Cape May counties."

The first account of a visit to Cape May was published in a "Description of New Albion" (New England), written by Sir Edmund Plowden, under the nom de plume of "Beauchamp Plantagenet," which appeared in London in 1648. Plowden reproduced a letter from Lieutenant Robert Evelyn. "Master Evelyn," as Plantagenet calls him, left England with an expedition for the Delaware in 1634, and probably made his exploration of the cape soon after. Others had observed Cape May, he learned, as follows: Hudson in 1609; Argall, 1610; Cornelius Hendrickson, 1616; Dermer, 1619; Mey, 1620; Hossett and Heyssen, 1630, and de Vries, 1631, besides a party of eight sent to explore the bay in 1632, by Governor Harvey, of Virginia, who were killed by the Indians.

Evelyn's letter reads:

"I thought good to write unto you my knowledge, and first to describe to you the north side of Delaware unto Hudson's River, in Sir Edmund's patent called New Albion, which lieth between New England and Maryland, and that ocean sea. I take it to be about 160 miles. I find some broken land, isles and inlets, and many small isles at Eg Bay; but going to Delaware Bay by Cape May, which is twenty-four miles at most, and is, I understand, very well set out and printed in Captain Powell's map of New England, done as is told me by a draft I gave to Mr. Daniel, the plotmaster, which he Edmund saith you have at home: on that north side (of Cape May) about five miles within is a port or rode for any ships, called the Nook, and within liveth the king of Kechemeches, having, as I suppose, about fifty men. I do account all these Indians to be eight hundred, and are in several factions and war against the Sarquehannocks, and are all extreme fearful of a gun, naked and unarmed against our shot, swords and pikes. I had some bickering with some of them, and they are of so little esteem that I durst with fifteen men sit down or trade in despite of them. I saw there an infinite quantity of bustards, swans, geese and fowl, covering the shores, as within the like multitude of pigeons and store of turkeys, of which I tried one to weigh forty and six pounds. There is much variety and plenty of delicate fresh and sea fish and shellfish, and whales and grampus, elks, deere that bring three young at a time. * * * Twelve hundred Indians under the Raritan kings, on the south side next to Hudson's River, and those come down to the ocean about Little Eg Bay, and Sandy Barnegate, and about the South Cape two small Kings of forty men a piece called Tirans and Tiascons."

From this description there is no doubt that Evelyn visited and made a circuit of the country. The name Egg bay is still retained with little change in Egg Harbor Bay, and the many small islands, called beaches now, and on which are the seaside resorts, are the testimony that he actually saw them. Dr. Beesley says of the reference made to the Kechemeches:

"Now where it was the king of Kechemeches with his fifty men held forth, it would be difficult to ascertain: it might have been at Town Bank, or Fishing Creek, or further up the cove or 'nook,' as he was pleased to call it. Master Evelin must certainly have the credit of being the first white man that explored the interior, as far as the seaboard, and his name should be perpetuated as the king of pioneers. * * * His account of the great abundance and variety of fowl and fish seems within the range of probability, and the story of the turkey that weighed forty-six pounds, would have less of the 'couleur de rose' were it not qualified in the same paragraph, with 'deere that bring forth three young at a time.' And what a sight it must have been to see the woods and plains teeming with wild animals, the shores and waters with fowl in every variety, where they had existed unharmed and unmolested through an unknown period of years; and the magnificent forest, the stately, towering cedar swamp, untouched by the axe of the despoiler, all reveling in the beauties of Nature in her pristine state, the realities of which the imagination, only, can convey an impression, or give a foretaste of the charms and novelties of those primeval times."

At this time the county was the stamping ground of the bison, or buffalo, the black bear, the panther, the wolf, the catamount, the deer and other larger beasts. The smaller ones prevalent at the time were the opossum, raccoon, foxs, mink, otters and beaver.

Whether at this time, about 1640, the New Haven settlers, probably at Town Bank, and the Dutch or the Indians ever had any quarrels is not recorded, and they probably had not. Commissioner Huddle, of Fort Nassau, on the Delaware, in 1648, complained that the Cape May tribe of Indians made barter "rather too much against them," as "the Indians always take the largest and smallest among them to trade with us," by which the long-armed "tellers" compassed a "long price" for their clansmen's beaver skins. The money they used was called "sewan."

Concerning the Swedes who may have settled in Cape May county Dr. Beesley says:

"As history throws no light on the original occupiers of the soil, conjecture only can be consulted on the subject. It would seem probable, inasmuch as many of the old Swedish names, as recorded in Campanius, from Rudman, are still to be found in Cumberland and Cape May, that some of the veritable Swedes of Tinicum or Christiana might have strayed, or have been driven to our shores. When the Dutch governor, Stuyvesant, ascended the Delaware in 1654, with his seven ships and seven hundred men, and subjected the Swedes to his dominion, it would be easy to imagine, in their mortification and chagrin at a defeat so bloodless and unexpected, that many of them should fly from the arbitrary sway of their rulers, and seek an asylum where they could be free to act for themselves, without restraint or coercion from the stubbornness of mynheer, whose victory, though easily obtained, was permanent, as the provincial power of New Sweden had perished for ever."

On July 12, 1656, the Dutch West India Company ceded land from Boomtjes Hauken to Cape Helopen to Amsterdam for 700,000 guilders ($266,000), and the territory became under the control of that municipality in Holland. Whether the municipality secured any rights in the Cape May land is not known, but if they did the rights were never asserted.

The contest between the Dutch and the Swedes had been going on for some years, although the settlers in Cape May were seldom affected by it. The Dutch had made their principal settlement on Manhattan Island, while the main colonies of the Swedes were in Delaware and Southern Pennsylvania. The former was known as New Netherlands and the latter New Sweden. At last the Dutch secured the mastery of the whole territory. Their reign was short, however, because the constantly growing settlements made by the English in New York, Virginia and Maryland made the holding of the territory too much of a burden for the Dutch to carry.

Director Beekman, of New Netherlands, under date of June 10, 1661, writes to Governor Stuyvesant: "On the east side of this river are residing from English among the Manto savages; they arrived in a small boat in the neighborhood of Cape May about three months past; they apparently went home from Virginia, as they now seem induced to remain there, if their report of the savages is correct."

The English deposed the Dutch as easily as did the latter the Swedes, who really united their fortunes with those of the English.

In 1664 the English took absolute control of the territory, which they claimed by right of the discoveries made by the Cabots in 1498. New Jersey came into the possession of proprietary governors. On the 23d and 24th of June, 1664, the Duke of York, who had obtained a patent from King James, did "in consideration of a competent sum of money, grant and convey unto Lord John Berkeley, Baron of Stratton, and Sir George Carteret, of Sultrim, in the County of Devon, to their heirs and assigns forever, all that tract of land adjacent to New England, and lying and being to the westward of Long Island; bounded on the east part by the main sea and part by the Hudson River, and hath upon the west Delaware Bay or River, and extendeth southward to the main ocean as far as Cape May, at the mouth of Delaware Bay, and to the northward as far as the northernmost branch of said bay or river of Delaware, which is forty-one degrees and forty minutes of latitude, and worketh over thence in a straight line to Hudson river, which said tract of land is hereafter to be called by the name, or names, of NOVA CAESAREA, or NEW JERSEY." The name of New Jersey was given to the land because Carteret had been a governor of the Isle of Jersey, in the English Channel, and had defended it against the Long Parliament. In the same year Sir Robert Carr was sent into the Delaware with two frigates and the troops not required in New York to compel the submission of the Dutch, which he effected with "two barrels of powder and twenty shot."

Ten years after the granting of the possessions to Berkeley and Cartaret, the Dutch succeeded in retaking New York from the English. For a few months the old province of New Netherlands, including the country as far south as Cape May, was restored to Holland. But in the next year the whole territory was receded by the States-General to England.

The king gave his brother, the Duke of York, another patent for the land between the Connecticut and Delaware Rivers, and yet confirmed his patent to Berkeley and Cartaret. Notwithstanding both of these grants, he appointed that tyrant, Sir Edmund Andros, royal governor of all the English possessions in America. Berkeley, having become disgusted with the actions of King Charles and disappointed with the pecuniary prospects of the colony, offered his interests for sale. John Fenwick bought it as a trustee for Edward Byllynge. The latter afterwards became heavily involved with debts, and his share was consigned for the benefit of his creditors. William Penn, Gawen Lawrie and Nicholas Lucas were appointed the trustees. In 1676 Fenwick also assigned and his assignees were John Eldridge and Edmund Warner. On August 6, 1680, the Duke of York deeded to Penn, Lowrie, Lucas, Eldridge and Warner the territory of West Jersey in trust for Byllynge, to whom the government was conveyed. On the first of July, 1676, a division had been made of New Jersey, and Sir George Cartaret took all that part north of what is now the northern boundary line of Burlington county, which was named East Jersey, while Penn and the Quakers took all the portion south of that line and christened it West Jersey.

Within two years some four hundred families had arrived and settled, most of them near Salem, but none are known to have found their way to Cape May.

It was the next year that the "agreements" of the Quakers were made, in which they allowed freedom of conscience, the ballot box, equality before the law, the right of assembly, the freedom of election, of speech, of the press, popular sovereignty, trial by jury, open courts and free legislation.

The gradual growth of the number of settlers and the question of the division and barter of lands becoming an important one, the Assembly, in 1681, appointed a commission to prescribe rules for the land settlements. The surveyor was required to measure the Delaware front from Assunpink Creek to Cape May and to find a point of the compass for running partition lines between each tenth.

The question of the date of the first settlement of Cape May by English families has always been in doubt. Dr. Maurice Beesley says:

"After the most careful investigation and patient research in the State and county archives, and the early as well as the more recent chronicles of our past history, we find no data to prove that Cape May was positively inhabited until the year 1685, when Caleb Carman was appointed, by the Legislature, a justice of the peace, and Jonathan Pine, constable.

"These were independent appointments, as Cape May was not under the jurisdiction of the Salem Tenth. This simple fact, however, that the appointment of a justice and constable for the place was necessary, goes to prove that there were inhabitants here at this time; yet whence they came, in what number, or how long they sojourned, are inquiries that will most probably ever remain in mystery and doubt. Fenwick made his entry into 'New Salem' in 1675, and soon after extinguished the Indian title from the Delaware to Prince Maurice River. He made no claim and exercised no dominion over Cape May, and we have nothing to show at the time of his arrival that the country from Salem to the seashore was other than one primeval and unbroken forest, with ample natural productions by sea and land to make it the happy home of the red man, where he could roam free and unmolested, in the enjoyment of privileges and blessings which the strong arm of destiny soon usurped and converted to ulterior purposes."

Other authorities say that the Townsends and Spicers were the oldest white settlers and individual land owners of the county, and that John Townsend and Jacob Spicer came from Long Island in 1680, and that Richard, son of John Townsend, was the first white child born within the limits of the county. Bancroft's "History of the United States" gives the settlement of Cape May Town, or Town Bank, as forty years earlier than Dr. Beesley's positive knowledge. The records of the whalemen, which appear in New Haven, show that there was no permanent removal from that place to Cape May until 1685, and that about one-fifth of the old family names of Cape May and New Haven are similar. It is probable, however, that from 1640 there was a sheltering and resting place at Town Bank for these whalemen from Connecticut and Long Island. The names of residents of East Hampton, L. I., at that time are like those who are first mentioned as residents of Cape May county, also.

The whaling period extended from the middle of the seventeenth century to the early part of the eighteenth century. As early as 1658 there is said to have been fourteen skilled pilots who led the whalemen. The whalemen had troubles of their own, which at times got into the courts, and a search of the manuscript records of the earliest court at Burlington, where Cape May business was then (1685) transacted, bring to light the following cases, which are given condensed to show the grievances heard:

Burlington Court, 4th 7th month, 1685.
Caleb Carman & Jno Carman
vs.
Evan Davis.

Edward Pynde testified that he was at the plantation of Evan Davis, who told him that he had bought a fish of an "Indian called Nummy." Davis invited Pynde to go with him to see the fish, saying that the deponent should have a share therein if he did so. Pynde accordingly went, and "comeing to ye s'd ffish sayth it was a whale ffish and yt hee saw an Iron (with warp thereat) in ye said whale ffish, which Iron & Warp ye s'd depon't knowing them to belong to s'd Caleb Carman & Company," Pynde accordingly would have nothing to do with the matter. Whereupon "Davis seized upon ye s'd whale ffish and Tackling and hid ye same from s'd Carman and Company."

Then Caleb Carman, binding himself in the sum of 40s, presents the complainant.

A warrant was issued to Alexander Humfreyes, as deputy sheriff or under sheriff, to take Davis into custody for his appearance in Burlington. At the same time Abraham Wegton, wife and children, to answer, as well as Margrett, servant of Davis, as well as any others who "can give information," although it seems Wegton had had nothing to do with the whaling matter, but was summoned for abuse of the children.

At the court held the 12th of the 3d mo., 1686, "Evan Davis by his & Daniell England's Bond to appear at this Court" in the Carman matter fails to present himself, whereupon he forfeits his recognizance, disposing of the case.

At a court held 12-16, 3rd month, 1688, Jno. Skene, Deputy Governor, the Grand Jury present, "Caleb Carman and sonnes, John Peck & (others) concerned for taking, breaking up & disposing of Dubartus whales on this shore contrary to Lawe."

Divers persons by indictment were called to the bar. Among them was Caleb Carman, who "Pleads not guilty & referres himselfe to God and ye Countrey, whereupon ye Jury before are called and all accepted & attested, ye jury finde him not guilty in manner & forme as hee stands Indicted, and hee thereupon afterwards was cleared by P'clamation."

During the same court, Carman, his sons and Peck are presented by the Grand Jury. They claim they have sold no Dubartus whales, except they had permission from Tho: Mathews.

In the evidence Jno: Throp bought a supposed Dubartus whale, of which eleven barrels of oil were made. Rich'd Starr said Throp bought the whale of the Carmans, who claimed to own it. Henry Johnson said that Throp had agreed with the Carmans only for their labour. Sam'll' Mathews said that Ezekiell Eldridge, "(who had p'te of ye fish) said he had sold his p'te to Throp for 10s & ye rest had done ye same, and that they sold ye fish as theirs." Jno. Dennis said he "heard said Carmans say that all drift whales that came ashore there belonged to them by Thomas Mathews order." Jury find Carman and the rest concerned "not guilty."

In passing, it may be worthy of note to record that, at this court, among the "Constables p'sented & chosen" one was selected "about Cape May," in the person of Sam'l Mathews. He was duly attested. This is one of the earliest selections of officials for Cape May of which there is any record.

At a private session of the court held on the 16th of Feb'y, 1688, at the house of Richard Basnett in Burlington, at the request of Philip Richards, of Philadelphia.

Richards complained that having loaded the sloop "Susanna" (Peter Lawrison, Master) New York to Philadelphia —the said sloop "came on shore to the norward of Cape May." The master and men went ashore for relief and in the interim Caleb Carman and his sons went aboard, and vi et armis prevented the sailors from entering the sloop. The Carmans claimed half the goods for saving the wreck. Being overpowered, the sailors consented, whereupon the Carmans carried away the goods of the said Richards. At the request of Richards, Justices Edw: Hunlake, Jr: Marshall, Rich'd Basnett and Dan'll Wills order the appearance of the Carmans at next Quarterly Sessions. The sessions was held May 7, 1688, but no action was taken, nor at several subsequent sessions. It is to be presumed that the matter never came to trial.

Burlington Court June 3, 1690. Justices on the bench were John Skene, Edward Hunlak, Wm. Biddle, James Marshall, Daniel Wills, Sr., Richard Basnett and William Myers, with the following Traverse Jury: Symon Charles John Day, Eliakim Higgins, Peter Basse, William Budd, George Parker, Thos. Butcher, Christop: Weatherill, Bery: Wheate, Sam'll Ogbourne, Issac Horner, John Warwin, Joshua Humphries. Same Court June 4th.

John Dubrois, Plaint; Peter Perdrain, his wife Elizabeth; Elizabeth Meningault; Andrew Laurance, his wife Mary; Daniel Lucas, Augustus Lucas, Defendants. Action in slander and defamation. Jury as above.

Samson Gallois "ye Interpretter to ye ffrench people arrested."

In the testimony:—

James Monjoy said he heard Mrs. Rame and Mr. Perdrain say to Andrew Lawrence that Andrew should go to Burlington to "undoe John Dubois." Mrs. Rame further said that if Laurance did not do so "shee would never eat of s'd Andrew Laurance's bread more, and y't shee s'd this because they had no lodging at Cape May." Perdrain also said that Dubois would run away and that they would endeavor to have an English overseer.

Isiah Lebake said he heard Lawrence and Perdrain say in a boat coming from Cape May that Dubrois had an intention to run away.

James Peyrard said that Laurence remarked last December in the Burlington bake house that he (Laurence) would tell false things of the plaintiff Dubrois.

Benjamin Godfrey remarking to Laurence that his "testimonials such as hee declared against Dubrois was enough to hang him," s'd Lawrence answered "why then Mr. Dubrois wants only the Rope." Godfrey also repeated Monjoy's testimony against Mrs. Rame.

John Gilbert said all the defendants, except Augustus Lucas, had stated that Dubrois would run away and convert Dr. Coxe's goods to his own use.

Peter Rendard testified that Perdrain had told manager and plaintiff Dubrois that he (Dubrois) intended to run away. Rendard supposes to have been occasioned because Dubrois did not provide such a house as they expected. Perdrain also claimed rights as overseer and had several times threatened Dubrois by shaking his fist.

John Corson reiterated the testimony concerning Mrs. Brame and speakes of Andrew Laurence as "her sonne," presumably "in law."

Nicholas Malherbe attested that Peter Perdrain and Daniel Lucas, Sr., had said that Dubrois intended to take Dr. Coxe's property and escape.

Testimony for defense—

Heter Sespine testified that Dubrois had said "that he would get what he could out of Mr. Tatham's hand and then he would laugh at him." Lawrence told the testator the same. The son of Augustus Lucas had told Sespine that the manager wanted to go shares with the younger Lucas and made the proposition at John Teqts in Philadelphia. It was also proposed to send the sloop to Boston, Dubrois going therein with Captain Eberad.

Nicholas Martines testified that Dubrois said "that when he gott the Asse (Dr. Coxe) by the Tayle he knew how to lead him."

David Lillies testified that the whalery had ill success because Dubrois took the sloop up the River and the whale was consequently lost. The whalers said amongst themselves that Dubrois would "make the best of ye Doctor's Concernes for himself."

The Jury find for the plaintiff £5 damages, costs and charges.

Same Court and Jury, June 5th.

John Tatham on behalf of Dr. Dan'l Cox, plaintiff. John Dubrois defendant. Action upon the case. Entered June 3, two days allowed by court and plaintiff for defendant to consider the charge.

The Defendant pleads so that Tatham has no power to call him. The Court decided for the plaintiff. On request a letter of attorney from Dr. Coxe to Tatham was read. In the matter of fraud charged upon the defendant, a committee of Justices were to view the accounts and render decision on the 20th of the month.

Evidence for Plaintiff:

George Taylor testifies that manager Dubrois took the sloop from Cape May to New Castle when the whalery has occasione for her. In the meantime a whale was captured and held for six or eight days, but for want of a sloop the whale was lost.

For the defense:—

Isaac Matikett and others on depositions taken before Justices Salaway and Anthony Morris in Philadelphia show the reason why the manager went to New Castle, (reasons not amplified).

Isaiah Ebrad deposes before Justice Skene why Dubroise came to Burlington.

Benjamin Godfrey attested that Dubroise sold beef for the whalery's account and that the whalers needed provisions and salt. "Mr. Tatham makes it appear they had 26 bushels of salt down at Cape May."

Oliver Johnson thinks "ye whalery men below, on Doctor Coxe account had provision enough to serve ye winter." He stayed until the 25th of March and heard no complaint.

George Taylor said there was a vessel in the stocks at Cape May begun in the times of James Budd, but since Budd's death nothing has been done therewith. Manager Dubroise wanted whalemen to saw plank to complete her, but it was not done, although the whalemen had promised so to do.

Peter Perdrain says Dr. Coxe's boat was lost at Cape May for want of help from the shore.

The Jury find for the defendant and give him the costs of the suit.

CHAPTER III.

THE SETTLERS AND THEIR NEW HOMES.

On November 3-12, 1685, Cape May was first created a county, which included its present bounds, together with all that country embraced in a line drawn from a point about twenty miles up the Maurice River to the most northerly point of Great Egg Harbour. Justices of the peace and other officers for the county were appointed for keeping the peace and trying causes under forty shillings. The county was to so remain until a court was established, which was constituted in 1693. In civil or criminal actions, where declarations and indictments were to be traversed, were to be taken to the Salem Quarterly Sessions, but the Cape May justices could, if they wished, sit in hearing such cases with the Salem justices.

The first inventory on file in the Secretary's office at Trenton, from Cape May, is that of John Story, dated the 28th of ninth month, 1687. He was a Friend, who died in Lower township, and left his personal estate, amounting to £110, to his wife, he having no heirs. A copy of the inventory is here given to show the prices of various articles at that time. The original spelling is preserved:

	lbs.	s.	d.
A chest, and small things	0	16	0
A gon	0	10	0
2 bras citles an on frying-pan	0	10	0
2 axes an on shobel	0	5	6
On sadell	0	10	0
On blanket	0	2	6
On hous an improvments	10	0	0
On stier, 4 yer ould	5	0	0
2 stiers goin to yer ould	4	0	0
On bull	2	10	0

THE SETTLERS AND THEIR NEW HOMES. 37

	lbs.	s.	d.
On helfer whit calfe	3	10	0

Prased by us,
JOHN BRIGGS,
ALEXANDER HUMPHRIES.

The next inventories filed are those of Abraham Weston, November 24, 1687, and John Briggs in 1690.

John Townsend, ancestor of all in the county of that name, emigrated with three brothers to Long Island previous to 1680. They were members of the Society of Friends. One settled in New England, one in New York and John and the other came to Leed's Point, near Little Egg Harbor. The reason for John's coming to Leed's Point was that he had been banished from New York for harboring Friends or Quakers. For the first offense he was fined £8 and put in jail for a limited time, for the second £12 and imprisonment, and for the third offense £100 and imprisonment for a time. Yet, by his actions, he defied

TOWNSEND COAT OF ARMS.

the Governor, and when the Friends came around again he not only harbored them, but invited them to preach in his house and went around with his horse and cart giving notice of the meeting to the inhabitants. This made the Governor so wroth that he was brought before the court and banished from the State, and if he returned was to be tied and whipped in the streets. He first came over to Monmouth and from thence to Cape May county, where he resided until his death. His wife, Phebe, lies buried in the old burying ground near Thompson Vangilders, and was the first white woman ever buried in the upper township. About or previous to 1690 John (the other brother having gone to Philadelphia) traveled to Somers Point, crossed the Egg Harbor River, and followed the seaboard down about ten miles until he came to a stream of water that he thought would do for a mill. He returned to Egg Harbor, bought a yoke of oxen, got them across the river, took the yoke on his back, as there was not room for the timber to drive his oxen abreast, and drove them before him down an Indian path to the place of his future residence. They cleared land, built a cabin and a mill on the sight of the land of the late Thompson Van Gilders, near Ocean View. He died in 1722 and left three sons, Richard, Robert and Sylvanus. It is related of John Townsend that when he built his cabin, he traveled a great distance and found two other settlers to help him raise it. While they were doing this some Indians came around and also helped. The three white men, who wanted to impress the Indians of their superior strength, decided to demonstrate it upon the Indians. Among the three one was very strong and an excellent wrestler. The two weaker ones proposed a wrestling match, which had been previously planned. The wrestling began, and the strong man allowed himself to be easily thrown by the two ordinary men. Then the Indians decided they would like to wrestle with the supposed weak man. They began tugging at one another, when suddenly the first and only Indian that tried to wrestle was tossed into the crotch of a tree. The Indians then assumed if the weaker man could do such an act so easily they concluded that the others could not be moved. This little incident served to prevent any trouble between the whites and natives. John and Peter Corson were the first of the name that came to the county, and were here as early as 1692. The second generation was Peter, Jr., John, Jr., Christian and Jacob. This family became numerous. There were fifty-two families in 1840 of that name in Upper township.

Shamgar Hand settled at what is now Court House in 1690, on a farm of 1000 acres, which he purchased of Dr. Daniel Cox, agent of the West Jersey Society. Others settled there were the Stiteses, Crawfords, Ludlams, Hewitts and Holmeses.

All the Townsends in the county descended from John

Townsend, all the Corsons from Peter and John Corson, all the Leamings from Christopher Leaming, all the Ludlams from Joseph Ludlam, all the Schellingers from Cornelius Schellinks, all the Hughes from Humphrey Hughes, all the Whilldens from Joseph Whillden, all the Hewitts from Randall Hewitt, all the Stites from Henry Stites, all the Cresses from Arthur Cresse, all the Willets from John Willets, all the Goffs from John Goff, all the Youngs from Henry Young, all the Eldredges from Ezekiel Eldredge, all the Godfreys from Benjamin Godfrey, all the Matthews from Samuel Matthews.

John Reeves was one who rented land in the county. He leased 200 acres on the sound side on the 23d of May, 1690, from Jeremiah Basse, "now of burlingtown in ye province of West New Jersey, merchant," as agent of the West Jersey Society. The rental was a fee of £20 and yearly rental which was to consist of two fat hens on Christmas Day. The indenture was recorded on July 2, 1695, and bore the following memorandum: "That, whereas the rent of two fat hens or capons is menshoned in the with menshoned deed itt is a greede that the Rent for the futor shall be only on Eare of Indian Corne if Demanded." The memorandum is marked as being recorded December 20, 1699.

During the changes in proprietorship which had been going on in the province of New Jersey from 1675 to 1690 there were really so many rulers in the colony that it was a difficult matter to know whom to acknowledge as officers with authority. "The condition of New Jersey," says one authority, "was deplorable," and "for ten years thereafter the colony was vexed and distracted with the presence of more rulers than any one province could accommodate."

After a while Edward Byllinge, one of the Quaker purchasers of West Jersey, died in 1687, and the next year Dr. Daniel Coxe, of London, England, who had already become a large landholder in the province, purchased the interests of Byllinge's heirs in the soil and government. In the latter year, 1688, he also having become an acknowledged West Jersey proprietor, purchased 95,000 acres in Cape May county. The line commenced at the Hammocks below Goshen Creek, on the bay shore, and in its passage across the county came between Joseph Falkenburge's and John McCrea's, and thence on a direct line northeast by north over the head of Dennis Creek to Tuckahoe River, and included in the tract all the land southeast of this line. In April, May and June, 1691, John Worlidge and John Budd, from Burlington, came down the bay in a vessel and laid a number of proprietary rights, commencing at Cohansey, in Cumberland county, and so on to Cape May. They set off the 95,000 acres to Dr. Daniel Coxe, which was the first actual proprietary survey made in the county. In the copy of the original draft of these surveys and of the county of Cape May, made by David Jamieson in 1713, and from another deed made by Lewis Morris in 1706, Egg Island, near the mouth of Maurice River, is laid off to Thomas Budd for three hundred acres. "Since this survey was made," says Dr. Beesley, in 1857, "the attrition of the waters has destroyed almost every vestige of it—scarcely enough remaining to mark the spot of its former magnitude. Upon this map likewise is laid down Cape May Town, at Town Bank on the bay shore, the residence of the whalers, consisting of a number of dwellings, and a short distance above it we find Dr. Coxe's Hall, with a spire, on Coxehall Creek, a name yet retained by the inhabitants. As no other buildings or improvements are noted upon this map than those above mentioned, it is to be presumed there were but few, if any, existing except them at this day. The only attraction then was the whale fishery, and the small town of fifteen or twenty houses marked upon this map, upon the shore of Town Bank, in close contiguity, would lead us to infer that those adventurous spirits, who came for that purpose, preferred in the way of their profession to be near each other, and to make common stock in their operations of harpooning, in which, according to Thomas and others, they seemed to be eminently successful."

Dr. Daniel Coxe, son of Daniel Coxe, was born in 1640 or 1641, and died January 19, 1730, in his 90th year. He was a most eminent physician of his day, a prolific writer on chemistry and medicine and was physician to Charles II and afterwards to Queen Anne. Although he never came to America, he acquired large possessions, and was nomi-

THE SETTLERS AND THEIR NEW HOMES.

nally governor of the province from 1687 to 1691. He also acquired title to a tract imperial in its dimensions lying between latitude 31 degrees and latitude 36 degrees, and extending from the Atlantic to the Pacific, on which he spent a fortune in exploration, his vessels being the first to ascend the Mississippi from its mouth. This was called Carolina. He was a staunch Church of England man and interested himself in attempting the establishment of that church in West Jersey. He, like all other purchasers in New Jersey, did not take the land from the Indians without reimbursing them. While he had his titles from the English settlers, he, in 1688, made also a second purchase of the land from the Red Man. Three separate purchases were made and dated March 30, April 30 and May 16, 1688, respectively, and covered his proprietary purchases in Cape May and Cumberland counties. Dr. Coxe built Coxe's Hall, near Town Bank and Cold Spring, in 1691.

The late Judge John Clement says:

"Coxe Hall was sufficiently large for all the assemblages of the people, and with rooms for offices and other like purposes. It was two stories, and finished with a tower or observatory, intended for use more than ornament, as from it objects could be seen across the bay and far out on the ocean. Although built of wood, it remained for many years after its usefulness as a public resort had departed and was at last converted into dwellings for workmen, who neither knew nor cared anything for its uses in former days.

"As a public building Coxe Hall had various uses. Here it was that ministers of his own religious persuasion disseminated the doctrines belonging thereto, and where the Society of Friends were invited to assemble and proclaim their own tenets. The Baptists, a few of whom landed from Wales at an early date, were given the use of this building for regular service, and those of any other religious persuasion who were seeking proselytes in the wilderness country were welcome as well. The first court for the county (March 20, 1693) was convened here. John Worledge, Jeremiah Bass, John Jarvis, Joseph Houlden and Samuel Crowell were the judges. Timothy Brandreth was sheriff and George Taylor clerk.

"Where Coxe Hall stood, surrounded by a few dwellings, was given a name in the court records called Portsmouth."

Dr. Coxe soon became the largest holder of proprieties within the territory. He was a man of enlarged views and sought to develop the advantages of the new country as rapidly as possible. He encouraged emigration among the better classes of people, and was liberal in his inducements toward them. He was not slow to discover where his own interests lay, and ventured much to secure their greatest benefits, and although a strict adherent to the established Church of England, nothing appeared to show that any differences arose between himself and his Quaker associates touching their religious views.

While his proprietary interests were more than any one individual in the colony, yet he never fell into disputes with his associates as to the location of his surveys, for, in fact, the rules laid down in the "concessions and agreements" were suspended so that he could secure large tracts of land in one body and be safe in his title thereto. From the trustees of Byllinge and others holding under them, Dr. Coxe became the owner of nineteen whole shares of propriety in West Jersey, and began the development of his purchases. In 1691 he secured his title in severalty to portions of the land, and no doubt had already erected the hall, for Budd and Worledge marked the same on their maps, placing it some distance above Cape May Town and near the mouth of Wilson's Creek.

It is recorded that Dr. Coxe's servants sued him for wages on the 3d of June, 1690. The court sat at Burlington to hear the case. The servants had attached the tools of the plantation, which they wanted sold and proceeds applied to their accounts. The servants were brought, it seems, from Gravesend in 1688, and their contract was written in French, which the court at the time was compelled to have translated. George Taylor and John Dubrois, according to evidence recorded, were Coxe's overseers. The servants sailed vessels and were coopers. Later we find that Dubrois himself sued Coxe and was given judgment. Either disheartened by the difficulties he had experienced or tempted by an offer that would cover the disbursements he had made, Coxe

THE SETTLERS AND THEIR NEW HOMES. 43

resolved upon a sale of the whole of his interest in this province. He accordingly made an agreement, in the year 1691, with a body composed of forty-eight persons, designated by the name of the "West Jersey Society." To this company, on the 20th of January, 1692, the whole of the claim of Dr. Coxe, both as to government and to nearly all the property, was conveyed, he receiving therefor the sum of £9000. The remaining portions of the property passed under his will to his son, Colonel Daniel Coxe, who came to Burlington in 1709 and resided there. This sale opened a new era to the people of Cape May. As no land titles had been obtained under the old regime of the proprietors, except five conveyances from George Taylor, as agent for Dr. Coxe, the West Jersey Society became a medium through which they could select and locate the choice of the lands, at prices corresponding with the means and wishes of the purchaser.

The society, through their agents appointed in the county, continued to make sales of land during a period of sixty-four years of their having possession.

During the year 1691, the whaling interest having become large, and the purchase of land in Cape May having become a more easy matter, a large number of persons came from New Haven and Long Island to settle permanently. Cape May Town sprang up on the bay shore, for the accommodation of the whalers, where quite a business was done. This is considered to be the first town built in the county. Among the settlers were Christopher Leaming and his son, Thomas Caesar Hoskins, Samuel Matthews, Jonathan Osborne, Nathan Short, Cornelius Shellinks (now Schellinger), Henry Stites, Thomas Hand and his sons, John and George; Ebenezer Swain and Henry Young, John and Caleb Carman, John Shaw, Thomas Miller, William Stillwell, Humphrey Hewes, William Mason and John Richardson.

Christopher Leamyeng (now Leaming), and a brother who died on the passage, left England for America about 1670. In 1674 he married Esther Burnet, the daughter of Aaron Burnet, of Sag Harbor, East Hampton, L. I. He came to Cape May in 1691, took up 204 acres in 1694 and died at the house of Shamgar Hand, Cape May county, on May 3, 1695. His wife, Esther, died at East Hampton, L. I., November 5, 1714. Christopher, 1st, and Esther B. Leaming, had seven children, the most of whom were minors at the time of their father's death. Their names were: Thomas, 1st, Jane, Hannah, Christopher, 2d, Aaron, 1st, Jeremiah, 2d, and Elizabeth. Two of these daughters and the son, Jeremiah, 2d, settled in New England, as Thomas, 1st, the oldest son, says in his memoirs: "In August 22, 1715, I took my journey to Long Island and there I sold a piece of land for a hundred and twenty pounds. And from thence I went to New England to see my two sisters and brother." Thomas Leaming, 1st, the eldest son of Christopher, 1st, and Esther B. Leaming, was born in South Hampton, L. I., July 9, 1674. He came to Cape May in 1692, settled on his own farm in 1699, married June 18, 1701, when 25 years of age, Hannah Whilldin, the daughter of Joseph Whilldin, the elder, in her 18th year, and in October, 1706, Samuel Matthews took from him a horse worth £7 and sold it because he, as a zealous Quaker, refused to perform military duty. He died December 31, 1723, aged 49 years.

Jacob Spicer was another settler who came to Cape May about 1691, and became prominent. He was the second son of Samuel and Esther Spicer, of Gravesend, L. I., and the grandson of Thomas and Michael Spicer, who were New England Puritans. He was born January 20, 1668, removed from Long Island to Cape May, and died April 17, 1741, aged 73 years. His wife was, perhaps, Sarah Spicer. She was born in 1677 and died July 25, 1742, aged 65 years, and her tombstone is the oldest in the Cold Spring Church Cemetery. Spicer's remains lie on the Vincent Miller homestead, in Cold Spring. The inscription on his tombstone commemorates a father and son who occupied prominent stations in society in their day:

"In memory of Col. Jacob Spicer, who died April 17, 1741, aged 73 years—
"Death, thou hast conquered me,
I, by thy darts am slain,
But Christ shall conquer thee,
And I shall rise again."

THE SETTLERS AND THEIR NEW HOMES. 45

John Persons, 1st, was an Englishman. He came to America and settled at East Hampton, Long Island. He married Mrs. Elizabeth Garlick. Her maiden name was Hardie. As Mrs. Garlick, she was charged in 1657 with witchcraft, was tried at East Hampton, on Long Island, and acquitted. John and Elizabeth Persons had a daughter named Lydia, born at East Hampton, L. I., April 10, 1680. In July, 1691, they all came to Cape May county, and Mr. Persons bought a plantation about four miles below the present Court House, and settled on it in September, 1691. He died and was buried there in January, 1695.

John Persons, 2d, of Lower Cold Spring settlement, an Englishman, and probably a nephew of John Persons, 1st, came also from Long Island to Cape May about 1691. The earliest notice had of him is in reference to "ear marks" that he had publicly recorded, for the safety of his stock running at large, in 1693. He purchased 315 acres of land of Dr. Coxe, or of the West Jersey Society as early as 1696. Next we learn that he was one of the thirty-two persons to whom, as original trustees, Rev. John Bradner conveyed in perpetuity his estate in Cold Spring in 1718 for the use of the pastor of the Presbyterian church there. The last time we find him on his sick and dying bed, December 4, 1732, making his will, leaving his wife, Elizabeth, her proper share, and dividing the real estate between his two sons, John Parsons, 3d, and Robert Parsons, 1st, and appointing his wife and their eldest son, John, his executors, but died before he could have it properly executed.

The following is from the manuscript of Thomas Leaming, one of the early pioneers, who died in 1723, aged 49 years:

"In July, 1674, I was born in Southampton, on Long Island. When I was eighteen years of age (1692) I came to Cape May, and that winter had a sore of the fever and flux. The next summer I went to Philadelphia with my father, Christopher, who was lame with a withered hand, which held him till his death. The winter following I went a whaling, and we got eight whales, and five of them we drove to the Hoarkills, and we went there to cut them up, and stayed a month. The 1st day of May we came home to

Cape May, and my father was very sick, and the third day, 1695, departed this life at the house of Shamgar Hand. Then I went to Long Island, stayed that summer, and in the winter I went a whaling again, and got an old cow and a calf. In 1696 I went to whaling again and made a great voyage, and in 1697 I worked for John Reeves all summer, and in the winter went to whaling again. In 1698 worked for John Crawford and on my own land, and that winter had a sore fit of sickness at Henry Stites', and in the year 1700 I lived at my own plantation and worked for Peter Corson. I was married in 1701, and 1703 went to Cohansie and fetched brother Aaron. In 1706 I built my house. Samuel Matthews took a horse from me worth £7 because I could not train. In 1707 we made the county road."

Leaming was a strict Quaker at that time. The record of the Ludlams is contemporaneous with the growth of Cape May, the earliest records of the county showing this family to be among the first settlers.

The Ludlam name belongs to Yorkshire, England, where for many years the family had precedence. Anthony Ludlam, progenitor of the race in America, came from England in the earliest days, and by 1640 had become a member of the whaling colony in Southampton, Long Island.

Joseph, son of the New England settler, came to Cape May about 1692, attracted hither by the whaling, then being developed at Town Bank and Barnegat. Settling on the division line between Dennis and Upper, he purchased Ludlam's Beach, now Sea Isle City, and stocked it with cattle, the descendants of which survived until about 1875. He acquired 500 acres in Dennis Neck, paying £163 for his purchase.

Arthur Cresse came from Long Island about this time also. John Stillwell came about the same time from there.

By an act of the Assembly November 12, 1692, Cape May county was regularly instituted, as follows:

"Whereas, this province hath formerly been divided into three counties for the better regulation thereof; and whereas Cape May (being a place well situated for trade) begins to increase to a considerable number of families; and there being no greater encouragement to the settlement of a place than that there be established therein an order by government, and justice duly administered: Be it therefore enacted by the Governor, Council and Representatives in this present Assembly met and assembled, and by the authority of the same, that from henceforth Cape May shall be, and is hereby appointed a county, the bounds whereof to begin at the utmost flowing of the tide in Prince Maurice River, being about twenty miles from the mouth of said river, and then by a line running easterly to the most northerly point of Great Egg Harbor, and from thence southerly along by the sea to the point of Cape May; thence around Cape May, and up Maurice River to the first point mentioned; and that there be nominated and appointed such and so many justices and other officers as at present may be necessary for keeping the peace and trying of smaller causes under forty shillings. In which circumstances the same county shall remain until it shall appear that they are capable of being erected into a County Court; and in case of any action, whether civil or criminal, the same to be heard and determined at the quarterly sessions in Salem county, with liberty for the Justices of the County of Cape May, in conjunction with the Justices of Salem County, in every such action in judgment to sit, and with them to determine the same."

The time and place of holding the county elections were likewise directed, and the number of representatives that each was entitled to: Burlington to have 20; Gloucester, 20; Salem and Cape May, 5 members. Cape May continued to have five members until the time of the surrender in 1702, except in the year 1697, when she was reduced to one representative. No record, however, of the names of the members previous to 1702 has come to light.

The first town meeting for public business was held at the house of Benjamin Godfrey, on the 7th of February, 1692. "The commissions for Justices and Sheriff were proclaimed and George Taylor was appointed clerk." The first suit on record is for assault and battery—"Oliver Johnson against John Carman." The second, John Jarvis, is accused by George Taylor of helping the Indians to rum. A document is found reading in this wise:

"Wm. Johnson's testimony against John Jarvis for helping ye Indians to rum being accused thereof by George Taylor. Deponent attesteth that several days after the above sd laws were published at Cape May, he came into ye house of ye sd Jarvis and found Indians drinking rum and one of ye sd Indians gave of ye rum to ye sd Johnson and he drank of it with ym. The sd Jarvis refusing to clear himself by his oath according to law is convicted."

The explanation of this last phrase is that there was a law which cleared a man of an accusation against him if he took an oath that it was false. "Ye" should be read the; "sd," said, and "ym," him.

As early as 1693 a ferry was established at Beesley's Point, over Great Egg Harbor river; a proof there must have been inhabitants upon both sides of the river at that early period. The rates were one shilling for passengers, two penny a bushel for grain, four penny each for sheep or hogs, one shilling for cattle per head and one shilling for every single person.

The following is a specimen of the manner of tying the matrimonial knot in olden times:

"These may certify that on the fifteenth day of February, 1693, then and there came before me, Henry Stites and Hannah Garlick, and did each take the other to be man and wife, according to the law of this province, being lawfully published according to order, as witness their hands the day and year above said.

"HENRY STITES.
"HANNAH GARLICK.

"SAMUEL CROWELL, Justice.

"Witnesses—John Carman, Jonathan Pine, John Shaw, Jonathan Osborne, Caleb Carman, Shamgar Hand, Ruth Dayton, William Harwood, Jacob Spicer, Ezekiel Eldredge, Timothy Brandith."

At the court held at Portsmouth (Town Bank or Cape May Town) on the 20th of March, 1693, previously mentioned, which is the first of which we have any record, the following officers were present, viz.: Justices—John Wolredge, Jeremiah Bass, John Jarvis, Joseph Houlden and Samuel Crowel. Sheriff—Timothy Brandreth. Clerk—

George Taylor. Grand Jury—Shamgar Hand, Thomas Hand, William Goulden, Samuel Matthews, John Townsend, William Whitlock, Jacob Dayton, Oliver Johnson, Christopher Leayeman, Arthur Cresse, Ezekiel Eldredge, William Jacocks, John Carman, Jonathan Pine, Caleb Carman, John Reeves and Jonathan Foreman.

"A rule of Court passed, the grand jury shall have their dinner allowed them at the county charge."

"Their charge being given them, the grand jury find it necessary that a road be laid out, most convenient for the king and county, and so far as one county goeth, we are willing to clear a road for travelers to pass." "John Townsend and Arthur Cresse appointed Assessors; Timothy Brandreth, Collector; Shamgar Hand, Treasurer; Samuel Matthews and William Johnson, Supervisors of the Road; and John Somers for Egg Harbor. At same Court John Somers was appointed Constable for Great Egg Harbor." A record of the same court reads:

"The grand jury, upon complaint made by Elizabeth Crafford, and we have taken it into consideration, and we find that no fariner ought to rate ale or other strong drink to ye inhabitants of Cape May, except they have a lysence for so doing. So the court orders that no person shall sell liquor without a lysence, and that 40 Pounds be raised by tax to defray expenses, with a proviso that produce should be taken at 'money price' in payment." The above appointment by the Court of John Somers for Supervisor of the Roads and Constable for Great Egg Harbor, confirms the opinion advanced by Mickle that the county of Gloucester did not originally reach to the ocean, and that the inhabitants of the seaboard, or Great Egg Harbor, were under the jurisdiction of Cape May. The act of 1694, however, made them dependent upon Gloucester, and that of 1710 extended the county of Gloucester to the ocean.

Another act relating to the county courts in Cape May was that of October 3, 1693, which reads: "Whereas, it has been found expedient to erect Cape May into a county, the bounds whereof at the last session of this Assembly have been ascertained; and conceiving it also reasonable the inhabitants thereof shall partake of what privileges (under their circumstances) they are capable of, with the rest of the counties in this Province, and having (upon enquiry) received satisfaction that there is a sufficient number of inhabitants within the said county to keep and hold a County Court, in smaller matters relating to civil causes: Be it enacted by the Governor, Council, and Representatives in Assembly met and assembled, and by authority thereof, that the inhabitants of the county of Cape May shall and may keep and hold four county courts yearly, viz: on the third Tuesday of December, 3d March, 3d June, and 3d of September; all which courts the Justices commissioned, and to be commissioned in the said county, shall and may hear and try, according to law, all civil actions within the said county under the sum of £20." All above £20 were still to be tried at Salem.

The same Assembly passed the following, viz:

"Whereas the whaling in Delaware Bay has been in so great a measure invaded by strangers and foreigners, that the greatest part of oyl and bone received and got by that employ, hath been exported out of the Province to the great detriment thereof: Be it enacted, that any one killing a whale or whales in Delaware Bay, or on its shores, to pay the value of 1-10 of the oyl and bone to the Governor of the Province." Another act of the same Assembly empowered justices to issue warrants to constables for raising taxes specified in a concomitant law, albeit that there was yet no court in Cape May, the said court not being established for two months or until December.

The Assembly by act of May 12, 1694, made a new boundary line for the county, as "the bounds of the said county were not distinctly enough described." The starting place, twenty miles up Maurice river, remained the same, but its termination was at the "middlemost great river that runneth into the bay of Great Egg Harbour, so far as the tide flows up the same and thence down the said river into the said bay." This "middlemost great river" has been taken to be Tuckahoe, which is probably correct. The residents of Egg Harbour were by this act put into Gloucester county (now Atlantic). On the same date the Assembly passed the act requiring that the freeholders should meet yearly in "the town of Cape May," on the 6th of February, to choose five "good and sufficient men to serve in the General Assembly."

After the West Jersey Society was formed in 1692 the settlers were able to get titles to their lands. The earliest deeds on the books of the society are three granted in April, 1694, to William Dixon, William Whitlock and Christopher Leamyeng. In the next year thirty more deeds were recorded. In the latter year Jeremiah Basse was the agent of the West Jersey Society, and as a specimen of the indentures of those days and the bargains made between the agents and land owners, the following extract of an indenture of April 20th, 1695, is given:

"The said Arthur Cresse his Heirs and assigns shall yearly and every year pay or cause to be paid to the said Jeremiah Basse on account of the said Society the 24th day of December to fat Hens or capons at Coxe Hall as a Chief or quit Rent due and payable to the Society as Lords of Manor of Coxe Hall."

In this same year the Assembly, on May 12, appointed the following officials for Cape May: Joseph Houlding, Samuel Crowell, John Jervis and Shamger Hand, Justices; John Townsend, Sheriff; Timothy Brandereth, Clerk and Recorder, and Samuel Mathews, Coroner.

In 1696 Governor Andrew Hamilton appointed George Taylor his agent to collect the one-tenth of the "oyl" and whale bone due to Governor of the province, and also to look after wrecks which might come on the shore. Taylor's commission reads as follows:

"Andrew Hamilton, Esq., Governor of the Province of East and West Jersey to all whome these p'sents may come send Greeting Know ye that by virtue of the powers com'eted to Me I have Nominated Comishoned and appointed and Doe by these p'sents Comishonte and apponte George Taylor of Cape May, gent, My lawful Deputy and Attorney to take into his possession all wrecks or Drift whales or other Royall fish that shall be Driven on Shore any where upon the Coste of Cape May Egg harbour or within Dillawer River as far as Burlington or any wrecks floating near the Coaste and to Despose of the same according to his Deschreshon and to accounte to me for the Same as allso to make inquirey into any wreckes heare to fore Driven on shore or whales or whalebone or other Royall fish and make Demand of the Same into his Custody for my use paying Resonable salvage for the same and in Case of Refusall, to present for the same, acquittance and Descharges to give and Generally to Doo all and every other lawfull thing conserning the p'mises ass I might doo Myselfe before the making hereof.

"Witness: "AND. HAMILTON,
"Tho. Revelle.   "Oct. 3, 1696."
"John Taylor.

In May, 1696, the Assembly made a new set of Justices, appointing Samuel Crowell, John Jervis, Shamgar Hand and George Taylor. In the next year two additional Justices were appointed, they being Jacob Dayton and William Goulding. Ezekiel Eldridge was made Sheriff to succeed John Townsend.

The following named persons purchased of the agents of Dr. Coxe and the West Jersey Society, mostly previous to 1696, some few as early as 1689, the number of acres attached to their respective names, viz: Christopher Leamyeng 204, William Jacoks 340, Abigail Pine 200, Humphrey Hughes 206, Samuel Matthews 175, Jonathan Osborne 110, Nathaniel Short 200, Caesar Hoskins 250, Shamgar Hand 700, Joseph Weldon (Whilldin) 150, Joseph Houlding 200, Dorothy Hewitt 340, Thomas Hand 400, John Taylor 220, John Curwith 55, John Shaw, 2 surveys, 315, Timothy Brandreth 110, John Crawford 380, Ezekiel Eldridge 90, Oliver Russel 170, Samuel Crowell 226, John Carman 250, Thomas Gandy 50, Caleb Carman 250, William Mason 150, Henry Stites 200, Cornelius Skellinks 134, John Richardson 124, Arthur Cresse 350, Peter Corson 400, John Corson 300, John Townsend 640, William Golden and Rem. Garretson 1016, William Johnson 436, John Page 125, John Parsons 315, William Smith 130, George Taylor 175, Dennis Lynch 300, William Whitlock 500, Jacob Spicer, 2 surveys, 1000, Benjamin Godfrey 210, Randal Hewit 140, Elizabeth Carman 300, John Reeves 100, Benjamin Hand 373, James Stanfield 100.

THE SETTLERS AND THEIR NEW HOMES.

Some few of the above locations were made on the seashore; but the larger proportion of them in the lower part of the county. In addition to those who located land previous to 1700, the following-named persons had resided, and were then residing in the county, many of whom possessed land by secondary purchase:

Thomas Leamyeng, Alexander Humphries, John Briggs, Abraham Hand, Shamgar Hand, Jr., Benjamin Hand, Jr., Daniel Johnson, Oliver Johnson, William Harwood, Jacob Dayton, Richard Haroo, Jonathan Crossle, William Lake, Theirs Raynor, Thomas Matthews, William Stillwell, John Cresse, Morris Raynor, Joshua Howell, Arthur Cresse, Jr., William Blackburry, Daniel Carman, Joseph Knight, John Stillwell, John Else, John Steele, Thomas Hand, Joseph Ludlam, Sr., Anthony Ludlam, Jonathan Pine, John Wolredge, John Jervis, Jonathan Foreman, Thomas Goodwin, Jonathan High, Edward Howell, George Crawford, Joseph Badcock, William Dean, Richard Jones, John Howell, Thomas Stanford, George Noble, John Wolly, Peter Cartwright, Abraham Smith, John Hubard, Thomas Miller, Robert Crosby, John Fish, Lubbart Gilberson, Edward Marshall, James Cresse, William Simpkins, Thomas Goodwin, Thomas Clifton, Joshua Carman, William Duboldy, James Marshall, John Baily, William Richardson, Thomas Foster, Thomas Hewit, George Taylor, Jr., John Dennis, Isaac Hand, Daniel Hand, Jeremiah Hand, Joseph Hand, Thomas Bancroft, Edward Summis, Henry Gray, Abraham Weston, Thomas Going, Jonathan Edmunds, Nicholas Martineau, John Garlick, Samuel Matthews, Jr., William Shaw, Robert French, Jeremiah Miller, William Sharwood, Zebulon Sharp, John Story, Richard Townsend. Robert Townsend.

William Sharwood was a fore parent of the famous Chief Justice George Sharswood, of Pennsylvania.

Dr. Beesley (1857) says of the early pioneers of the county:

"Joseph Ludlam was here in 1692, and made purchases of land on the seaside, at Ludlam's Run, upon which he afterwards resided; and likewise purchased, in 1720, of Jacob Spicer, a large tract in Dennis' Neck. He left four sons:

Anthony (who settled upon the South Dennis property, which is yet owned in part by his descendants), Joseph, Isaac and Samuel, from whom all the Ludlams of the county have descended. He died in 1761, aged eighty-six years.

"Jonathan Swain and Richard Swain, of Long Island, were here in 1706, and soon after their father, Ebenezer Swain, came to Cape May, and followed whaling, Jonathan being a cooper for them. Their immediate descendants were Zebulon, 1721; Elemuel, 1724; Reuben, who died in the epidemic of 1713, and Silas, 1733. There was a Captain Silas Swain in 1778, from whom has descended Joshua Swain, recently deceased, who held many important trusts in the county, as sheriff, member of the Legislature nine years, and a member of the convention to draft the new Constitution in 1843.

"Henry Young came about the year 1713. He served the county as judge of the court for many years, and was a member of the Legislature ten years. Judge Young was an extensive landholder, deputy surveyor, and was judge of the court from 1722 till his death in 1768. He was surrogate from 1743 to 1768. He was a surveyor and a scrivener, and no one, of those times, was more highly respected, or acted a more prominent and useful part. All of the name now in the county have descended from him.

"In the Upper Township, William Goldens, Sen. and Sr., Rem Garretson, John and Peter Corson, John Willets, John Hubbard, and soon after Henry Young, were the pioneers, and at a later day John Mackey at Tuckahoe and Abraham and John Vangilder at Petersburgh. In Dennis, being a part of the old Upper precinct, we find on the seaboard Joseph Ludlam, John Townsend, Robert Richards and Sylvanus Townsend, sons of John, Benjamin Godfrey and John Reeves, who were amongst the earliest settlers.

"Dennisville was settled upon the south side of the creek, in or about 1726, by Anthony Ludlam, and some few years afterwards the north side by his brother, Joseph, both being sons of Joseph Ludlam, of Ludlam's Run, seaside. David Johnson was here in 1765, and owned at the time of his death, in 1805, a large scope of land on the north side of Dennis Creek. James Stephenson purchased of Jacob Spicer, in the year 1748, the property now owned and occupied by his grandson, Enoch, now aged over eighty-five years. East and West Creek were settled by Joseph Savage and John Goff, the last of whom was here as early as 1710. He had a son, John, and his numerous descendants now occupy that portion of the county.

"In the Middle Township, we may name on the seaboard, in the order in which they resided, Thomas Leaming, John Reeves, Henry Stites, Shamgar Hand, Samuel Matthews and John Parsons, William and Benjamin Johnson, Yelverson Crowell and Aaron Leaming, first, were first at Goshen, the latter with the ostensible object of raising stock.

"Cape May Court House has been the county seat since 1745. Daniel Hand presented the county with an acre of land as a site for the county buildings erected at that time. But litle improvement was made until within the present century, the last twenty-five years having concentrated a sufficiency of inhabitants to build up a village of its present extent and proportions, embellished by the county with a new and commodious court house, and by the people with two beautiful churches, one for the Baptist and another for the Methodist persuasion.

"Henry Stites, ancestor of all in the county of that name, came to the country about or in the year 1691. He located two hundred acres of land, including the place now belonging to the heirs of Eli Townsend. He made his mark, yet he afterwards acquired the art of writing, and was justice of the court for a long series of years, being noted such in 1746. He left a son, Richard, who resided at Cape Island, and he a son, John, from whom the Lower Township Stites have descended. His son, Isaiah, who died in 1767, and from whom the Stites of the Upper and part of the Middle Township have descended, lived on the places now occupied by his grandsons, John and Townsend Stites, at Beesley's Point. The Middle Township Stites, below the court house, are descendants of Benjamin Stites, who was probably a brother of Henry, and was in the county in 1705.

"John Willits was the son of Hope Willets, and was born here in 1688, married Martha Corson in 1716, left three sons, Isaac, James and Jacob. He was judge of the court many years, a member of the Legislature in 1743, and was living in 1763."

Henry Young was impressed in England, his native country, when very young, on board a man-of-war, from which he made his escape to a vessel bound to Philadelphia. Here, to elude pursuit, he was secreted in a hogshead in the hold of the vessel, and as soon as they put to sea he was relieved, but not until nearly exhausted for want of fresh air.

The members from Cape May objecting to the restriction placed on their court, by not allowing it to try cases over £20, and having to take them to Salem or Burlington, the Assembly passed an act on May 12, 1697, placing the court on the same equality with other county tribunals in the colony.

In the same year, May 12, 1697, "An Act for a road to and from Cape May" was passed.

"Whereas the inhabitants of Cape May county do represent themselves as under extreme hardship for want of a road from Cape May, through their county to Cohansey, in order to their repair to Burlington to attend the public services: Be it enacted by the Governor, &c., that George Taylor and John Crafford (Crawford), be commissioners appointed to lay out a road from Cape May the most convenient to lead to Burlington, between this and the 10th of September next."

It was ordered likewise that the expense be borne by the inhabitants of Cape May until such time as those lands through which the road goes are settled. This road, so important to the convenience and travel of the people of the county, was not finished till 1707. Prior to this the county was completely isolated from the upper districts of the State by the extensive bed of cedar swamps and marshes stretching from the headwaters of Cedar Swamp Creek to the headwaters of Dennis Creek, and no communication could have been held with Cohansey or Burlington except by the waters of the Delaware, or by horse-paths through the swamps that constitute the barrier.

A record of the grand jury and court of 1689 contains the following: "We the grand jury order that if any person will hang a gate anywhere between Joshua Carmans and old Elizabeth Carmans, and clear the old road to the gate, and from the gate to the mill, they may do it, and that shall be the road; and if that wont do, let them hang a gate in the old road." The same court presents John Coston for being drunk, and Henry Stites for breach of Sabbath in driving cattle and slaughtering a steer. Joseph Ludlam was admonished in court, "that for time to come he be careful in taking an oath, and to mind to what it doth relate to."

Gabriel Thomas, in his history of West Jersey in 1698, gives us the following particulars, viz: "Prince Maurice River is where the Swedes used to kill the geese in great numbers for their feathers (only), leaving their carcasses behind them. Cohansey River, by which they send great store of cedar to Philadelphia city. Great Egg Harbor (up which a ship of two or three hundred tons may sail), which runs by the back part of the country into the main sea; I call it back because the first improvements made by the Christians was Delaware river-side. This place is noted for good store of corn, horses, cows, sheep, hogs; the lands thereabouts being much improved and built upon. Little Egg Harbor Creek, which takes their names from the great abundance of Eggs which the swans, geese, ducks, and other wild fowls of those rivers lay thereabouts. The commodities of Cape May County are oyl and whalebone, of which they make prodigious quantities every year; having mightily advanced that great fishery, taking great numbers of whales yearly. This county, for the general part of it, is extraordinary good and proper for the raising of all sorts of cattell, very plentiful here, as cows, horses, sheep, and hogs, &c. Likewise, it is well stored with fruits which make very good and pleasant liquors, such as neighbouring country before mentioned affords."

Among those who purchased land of Dr. Coxe were William Jacoks and Humphrey Hughes, whose plots amounted to 340 and 206 acres respectively, mentioned in the foregoing list of purchasers of the West Jersey Society lands. Their lands were what is now a part of Cape May City, then called, 1700, Cape Island. The distance from the sea across the island to the creek was 265 perches. As the deed calls for a line of marked trees, it must have been on the upland, at which place the distance has been greatly reduced by the inroads of the sea since that time. They held this land individually until 1700 and "tilled the land to the water's edge." Jacoks afterward sold his interest to Thomas Hand, one of the original settlers of Cape Island. Randal Hewitt, another Cape May county settler, who first bought lands of the Society, purchased land within the limits of Cape Island. The first public improvement that is chronicled is the building of a causeway to the island in 1699 by George Eaglesfield, for the accommodation of the public.

John Crawford's purchase from the West Jersey Society, on April 1, 1699, was of 300 acres, which bounded on New England Creek, in Lower township, for more than a mile, and two-thirds a mile up the shore northerly. The land is said to lie for a quarter of a mile under water. George Crawford, a son of John, and George Eaglesfield, who built the causeway to Cape Island, in 1699, built a mill on this property, which was patronized by the residents of the county pretty liberally. We are told that a part of the strip of land washed away by the action of the waters of the Delaware Bay stood Town Bank, or the original Cape May Town, or New England Town, as it was severally known.

In December, 1699, owing to the increase in court business, three new "circular judges" were appointed by the Assembly of the colony of New Jersey, all of which were to hold court, with civil and criminal jurisdiction, on the 20th day of February and October of each year, at Cape May. On the 20th of December, the same year, 1699, we find the following as officials: Justices, Shamgar Hand, Jacob Dayton, William Golding, Samuel Mathews and John Townsend; Sheriff, Ezekiel Eldridge; Clerk and Recorder, Timothy Brandereth; Coroner, Joseph Whildin; and Provincial Judges for the Colony, with jurisdiction in Cape May, Francis Davenport, Edward Hemlock and Jonathan Beer.

The Assembly at the same time passed an act giving Cape May three representatives in the Assembly instead of five.

CHAPTER IV.
LIFE EARLY IN THE EIGHTEENTH CENTURY.

At the beginning of the eighteenth century we find Cape May county with probably between four and five hundred settlers, scattered along both the Delaware Bay and the Atlantic Ocean shores of the county, and find homes in an almost barren wilderness scattered along the uplands adjacent to sounds between Great Egg Harbor and Cape May. Those who did not go whaling began farming their recently purchased lands and spending their time in the sounds and thoroughfares fishing, claming, oystering and hunting for wild fowl, where such were then abundant.

The principal settlements in the lower part of the county at the time were about New England Creek, Town Bank and Cold Spring, and at Middletown (now Cape May Court House), in the middle part of the county.

It was during this time that the famous Captain Kidd was practicing his depredations along the coast by privateering and the like. He is reported to have buried his plunderings in the sands along the coast, and Cape May's sands has been said to contain some of them. Near Cape May Point a tree known as Kidd's tree was in existence near the light house until about 1893. In a report of the Lords of Trade to the Lord's Justices, under date of August 10, 1699, Captain Kidd and other privateersmen are spoken of, and their landing at Cape May with goods taken on the East Indian coast are mentioned.

The officers appointed for Cape May on May 12-25, 1700, were Shamgar Hand, John Townsend, Jacob Dayton, Samuel Mathews, Thomas Stanford, William Mason, Justices; Edmund Howel, Sheriff; Timothy Brandreth, Clerk and Recorder; Jonathan Osborne, Coroner, and John Crawford, King's Attorney.

The appointments for the following year are recorded as follows:

May 12-21: Justices, Shamgar Hand, George Taylor, William Mason. (These three a quorum) Jonathan Osbourn, Thomas Stanford and Arthur Cressis; Sheriff, Caesar Hoskins; Clerk, Timothy Brandereth; Coroner, Samuel Mathews; Provincial Judges, Edward Hunlock, George Deacon and Jonathan Beer; Assessors, John Creesey and Jacob Spicer; Collector, William Shaw.

At this same time Cape May's members of the Assembly were increased from three to five members, and the change in 1699 "hath occasioned an unexpected dissatisfaction."

A petition of the inhabitants of West Jersey, dated May 12, this year, asking that the colony be taken under the King's immediate control, was signed by Shamgar Hand, Joseph Shaw and George Taylor, of Cape May.

In the year 1702, when Queen Anne began her reign in England, many important changes were made in the colony of New Jersey, the colonies of East and West Jersey were united under one Royal Governor, Edward, Lord Cornbury, whose province also included the colony of New York. The government of New Jersey's colony was to be composed of the Royal Governor, twelve counsellors, nominated by the crown, and an Assembly of twenty-four representatives, who were to meet alternately at Perth Amboy and Burlington. The Assembly consisted of two members each from the towns of Amboy and Burlington, and two each from the counties of Bergen, Essex, Somerset, Middlesex, Monmouth, Burlington, Gloucester, Salem and Cape May, and the Assemblyman was compelled to be a land holder of at least one thousand acres before he was qualified to act. In the same year the West Jersey Society resigned all its governmental rights to the crown owing to the rapidly multiplying difficulties which were besetting the proprietors.

Peter Fretwell, the first member from the county after the surrender, and the first on record that ever represented her, belonged to Burlington. He was a Friend and a cotemporary of Samuel Jennings, as the record of the monthly meet there attests, and came over in the ship

LIFE EARLY IN THE EIGHTEENTH CENTURY.

Shield, in 1678, with his brother, John Fretwell, Mahlon Stacy, Thomas Revel and others. Revel was at one time a resident of Cape May. It is probable that no resident of Cape May at the time had 1000 acres of land, and that was why Fretwell, a non-resident, was selected to represent the county in the Assembly for a period of twelve years. It is not known that Jacob Huling, who was a member in 1716, or Jeremiah Bass, from 1719 to 1723, ever resided permanently in Cape May county. The balance of the list of representatives were all legitimately Cape May men, and taken in a body were the bone and sinew of the county.

Dr. Beesley says: "Of some of those ancient worthies in the list we know but little, except that they held important offices of trust and responsibility. Others among them seemed to live more for posterity than themselves, by inditing almost daily the passing events of the times, and they are consequently better known and appreciated. Their writings at that day might have seemed to possess but little attraction, yet they have become interesting through age, and valuable as links in the chain which connects our early history with the reminiscences and associations of times more recent, and to carry out this connection it will be the duty of some faithful chronicler to unite the history of those times and the present, which is so rapidly giving place to the succeeding generation, by a descriptive and truthful account, more full and complete, as the data and material incident to later times are more abundant and illustrative."

The first survey of Rumney Marsh, afterwards called Middletown, and then Cape May Court House, was made by Jeremiah Hand in 1703.

During this year Cape May's militia was put under the command of Captain Joshua Newbold, who was given by his commission of August 7, 1703, charge of the Salem and Gloucester militia. The second French and Indian war against the English colonists of New England and Nova Scotia had then commenced. We have no records to show, however, that any Cape May men went to battle in this conflict, which lasted until 1713. On the 16th of August, 1703, Daniel Coxe was made the colonel of a foot regiment belonging to the counties of Burlington, Gloucester,

Salem and Cape May. Daniel Coxe was the eldest son of Dr. Daniel Coxe, and was baptised in London, August 31, 1673. He probably accompanied Lord Combury to America in 1702, by whom he was appointed commander of forces in West Jersey. He was known as Colonel. He doubtless returned to England in 1704, for this year he was in London waging a vigorous defense against some of the attacks of some of the New Jersey proprietors. He came back to America in 1706, and was appointed by Cornbury one of the Associate Judges of the Supreme Court. He was a Quaker, but finally eloped with a maiden of that faith, and was married at three o'clock in the morning under the trees, by firelight, by Cornbury's chaplain. Lord Lovelace, in 1708, made him a member of council, but he was removed by Hunter in 1713. He died April 25, 1739. He was often in the Legislature from Burlington, Gloucester and Salem counties.

During this period the whaling industry had not abated, and the inhabitants sought the aid of the government, and the Lawrences, before mentioned, were granted the following commission, which is given in its original spelling:

"Edward Viscount Cornbury, Captaine Generall and Governor in Chiefe in and over her Majestes Provinces of New Jersey, New York and all the Territory and tracts of Land depending thereon in America and Vice Admirall of the Same &c. To Joseph Lawrence, James Lawrence Greeting You are hereby Lycenced and authorized to fit out two boates to fish for, kill Cut up, try for your proper use and advantage what whales or Other Royall fish you Can or may find on the Coust of this Province of New Jersey betwixt Sandy hook and barnegat Inlett as also to take and secure all boates, barques, ships and other vessels or things that may be cast away or Otherwise stranded on the Said Coust and within the said Destrict and when Secured you are forthwith to give me an acc't of the Same in order to receive further Direction from me the Said Lord Viscount Cornbury paying unto me or to such as I shall apoint to Receive, one twentyeth part of all the Oyle and bone of the Whales and Such Other fish as by Virtue of this Lycence they shall take and kill All the Charges of takeing,

Killing and trying the Same being first Deducted. Given under my hand and Seale this 11th day of December Anno Reg, Reg Anna Nunc Anglico 31 annoq Dom 1704.
Cornbury
By his Excellency's order J. BASS.

In another part of the record, under date of April 8, 1728, is found a document addressed to "(Jacob Spicer Gentleman," being signed by Basse and Cornbury, instructing Spicer to

"Take possession into Custody all boates, Sloopes, Parkes, Shipps or other Vessels or things that may be driven ashore, Ract or Otherwise strunded on any part of the Westerne Shore of the bay or River Delaware or on any of the Sholes being within the Same and a Long the Sea Coast of the Provinces of New Jersey to the high Sand of Never Sinkes and Sandy hooke and to Secure and save the Same until such time as you shall Give notice to me thereof and receive further Directions from me. As also all whales or other Royall fish that may be driven a shore within the sd. District to take into Custody, Cutt up and by such ways and means as is most proper to secure."

Peter Bard, Nathanael Jenkins and Aaron Leamyeng were at the same time each given a like commission.

The following newspaper extracts are interesting:

"Boston News-Letter," from March 17 to 24, 1718, says: "Philadelphia, March 13.—We are told that the whale men catch'd six whales at Cape May and twelve at Egg-Harbour."

"The Pennsylvania Gazette" of March 13-19, 1729-30, says:

"On the 5th of this Instant March, a Whale came ashore dead about 20 mile to the Eastward of Cape May. She is a Cow. about 50 Foot long, and appears to have been killed by Whalemen; but who they are is yet unknown. Those who think they have a Property in her, are advised to make their Claim in Time."

"The Pennsylvania Gazette," March 11-18, 1735-6, says: "Philadelphia, March 19. * * * On the 25th of Feb. last. there were two Whales killed at Cape May, the one is ashore on Cape-Island, and the other on the upper end of the Cape, on the East Side; 'tis suppos'd they will yield about 40 Barrels of Oil each; the one was 3 Years old, and the other a Yearling; the Whale-men are in hopes of killing more, for they have lately seen several on the Coast, near the Cape."

The "Pennsylvania Gazette" of 1742, reported two whales at Cape May early in April.

In 1704 the general sessions of the peace were ordered by Governor Cornbury to be held at the house of Shamgar Hand on the fourth Tuesdays of March, June and September, and on the first Tuesday in January. The Ancient Judge of the Supreme Court was to hold court there on the first Tuesday of June. At the same time John Townsend, Shamgar Hand and William Goulder were appointed a commission for laying out, regulating, clearing and preserving the common highways. Jeremiah Basse was authorized to administer the civil and military oaths authorized by Parliament.

In 1705 the grand jury decided to have a prison built "13 feet by 8, and 7 feet high in the first story, upon the Queen's Highway, eastwardly of Gravelly Run." Stocks and whipping posts were ordered at the same time.

A license was granted this year from Governor Cornbury to Captain Jacob Spicer, of the sloop Adventurer, owned by John and Richard Townsend; burden, 16 tons. She traded from Cape May to Philadelphia and Burlington, and no doubt was considered a vessel of some magnitude in those days. The next year the sloop Necessity was built and owned by Dennis Lynch. After this vessels were built and sailed in different directions.

During 1704 and 1705 the Assembly ordered that £2000 be raised every year for the support of the colony, the apportionment for Cape May county being, in 1704, £63: 11: 4, and for 1705, £65: 4: 6. The Receiver-General of the colony received in 1705, by John Hand, £61: 16: 4, and in 1706, by John Hand again, £54: 14: 1: 2.

The first doctor known in Cape May county was Richard Smith, of either Egg Harbor or Cape May, who was in 1705 given a license to practice "Cirurgery and Phisiq."

In 1705 Cape May was again reduced to one representative in the Assembly. This same year more military officers were appointed for Cape May, as follows: Samuel Mathews, captain of militia; Ezekiel Eldridge to be lieutenant of the same company; and William Mason to be an ensign of militia. In a civil capacity Shamgar Hand and Timothy Brandreth were appointed Assessors; John Hand, Collector, and Shamgar Hand, Samuel Mathews, William Golding, Thomas Hand, William Mason, Benjamin Godfrey, Peter Carson Le Bore and John Townsend, Justices of the Peace.

In 1706 Shamgar Hand and William Golden, commissioners for that purpose, laid out the road from Egg Harbor to Cold Spring, and thence to Town Bank, as follows: "Beginning at a bush near the water's edge on Great Egg Harbor River (Tuckahoe River), and from said bush along William Golden's fence to the gate post; from thence along the fence to the corner thereof; then by a line of marked trees to the first run; thence to the head of John Coston's branch; thence to the head of dry swamp; thence to the head of Joseph Ludlam's branch; thence around the head of John Townsend's branch to the going over the branch between Abraham Hand's and Thomas Leonard's; thence to the bridge over Leonard's branch; thence to the bridge over the branch towards the head of William Johnson's land, so on to the bridge over the Fork branch; thence to the bridge over John Cressee's Creek; thence to the bridge over Crooked Creek, so by a line of marked trees to the bridge over Gravelly Run; thence to the bridge over Cressee's Creek; thence to the old going over at John Shaw's; thence to the old going over at William Shaw's branch; thence to the head of John Taylor's branch; thence to the turning out of Cold Spring path, so on by a line of marked trees, partly along the old road down to the bayside, between George Crawford's and the hollow."

In 1707 John Townsend and Shamgar Hand, commissioners, laid out the road from the head of John Townsend's Creek to the cedar swamp and through it to a place called "Ludley's bridge, and toward Marice River as far as the county goeth." Thus, after fourteen years of hard talking, for it appears that nothing else had been done until now, the road through the cedar swamps, lying between the headwaters of Cedar Swamp Creek and Dennis Creek (then called Cedar Creek, Sluice Creek being named Dennis), was laid out, and according to records of the first Thomas Leaming, completed this year. It is a question by what route the inhabitants had communication with the other parts of the colony, as they appear to have been completely isolated until this road was made. This improvement was always a county road until 1790, when the road over Dennis was made, after which time the former seems to have been abandoned.

Oldmixon, 1708, says: "The tract of land between this (Cape May) and Little Egg Harbor, which divides East and West New Jersey, goes by the name of Cape May County. Here are several straggling houses on this neck of land, the chief of which is Cox's Hall; but there's yet no Town. Most of the inhabitants are fishermen, there being a whalery at the mouth of the Bay, on this as well as the opposite shore."

The name of Ezekiel Eldredge, Sr., is first mentioned March 12-16, 1688, as a witness before the Grand Jury at a court held in Burlington, on a whale case. He purchased in 1689, of Dr. Coxe, 80 acres of land; was Sheriff of Cape May county from 1697 to 1700, and his "ear marks" were recorded in 1706 for the preservation of his roaming stock. He was a member of the Legislature from 1708 to 1709.

At this time Richard, John and Robert Townsend owned a square-sterned sloop called the "Dolphin," which was built at Cape May, and whose master was George Crafford.

On June 23, 1709, more officers were appointed for the militia. Ezekiel Eldridge was made a captain in Colonel Coxe's regiment, William Shaw, lieutenant, and Humphrey Hews, ensign. Seven days later Major Jacob Spicer was commissioned to be "Captaine of a Company of fuzileers rased for the Expedition against Canada. You are therefore to take the said Company into Your charge," and Spicer was also to be whaler from Sandy Hook to Cape May, but one-half of the proceeds were to go to Governor Richard Ingoldsby. David Strongham and Lew Hooton were to be first and second lieutenants respectively of

Spicer's company. It was this year that Jacob Spicer first entered the Assembly, of which he was a member until 1723. A letter dated July 14, 1711, telling of the proceedings of the Council and Assembly of the province, says: "Major Spicer who went on the Expedition to Canada, is Superseded by Justice Tomlinson in Gloster County, and one Townsend a Quaker made Judge in Cape May County."

What Cape May county at this time paid in to the treasury of the Province for the support of the government can be proportioned when it was ordered to pay £99 tax out of a total of £3000 to be raised in the State. That year John Page and Barnebas Cromwell, or Crowell, were given the work of making the assessment on the land holders, and Joseph Weldon was made the collector.

Thomas Gordon, Receiver-General of the province, in his reports of cash received for His Majesty's Revenues of New Jersey from June 23d, 1710, to March 26th, 1719, credits as having received from Cape May for the support of government the following amounts: 1711 and 1712, £49: 11: 0; 1714 and 1715, £34: 7: 10; and 1716, 1717 and 1718, £105: 05: 04.

Owing to the uncertainties of many of the boundary lines in the province, several were changed on January 21, 1710, for the reason given in this preamble:

"Whereas by the uncertainty of the Boundaries of the Counties of this Province great Inconveniences have arisen, so that the respective Officers of most of these Counties cannot know the Limits of them," etc.

Cape May's boundary was changed to conform to the following bounds:

"Beginning at the mouth of a small creek on the west side of Stipson's Island, called Jecak's Creek; thence up the same as high as the tide floweth; thence along the bounds of Salem County to the southernmost main branch of Great Egg Harbor River; thence down the said river to the sea; thence along the sea-coast to Delaware Bay, and so up the said Bay to the place of beginning."

It seems the inhabitants on the western side of Maurice River, the Cape May boundary, were without any legal control until 1707, when an act was passed annexing the inhabitants between the river Tweed, now Back Creek (being the lower bounds of Salem county), and the bounds of Cape May county to Salem county, putting them under its jurisdiction. The act of 1710 extends Salem county, and curtails Cape May county, to Stipson's Island, or West Creek. Its greatest length, N. E. and S. W., was 30 miles; greatest breadth, E. and W., 15 miles; form, semi-oval; area, 252 square miles, or about 161,000 acres.

At the time the boundary was changed the requisites of an Assemblyman were raised to one thousand acres of land, or to be worth £500 current money, in either real or personal estate.

John and Peter Corson came to Cape May about 1685. The second generation was Peter, Jr., John, Jr., Christian and Jacob. Peter represented the county in the Assembly in 1707. This family, all of whom are descendants of Peter and John, numbered in the county, at the census of 1850, 295 souls; 253 of whom belong to the Upper Township, 6 to Dennis, 26 to the Middle, and 10 to the Lower Township.

The Hand family was well represented amongst the early settlers, there being eleven persons of that name previous to 1700.

Dr. Beesley says (1857):
"Another of the early settlers was William Golden. He emigrated to Cape May in or about 1691. He was an Irishman, and espoused the cause of James against William and Mary, and fought as an officer in the battle of the Boyne, in 1690. As he soon after came to America, he was most likely one of those stubborn Jacobite Catholics that William, in his clemency, gave permission to flee the country, or abide the just indignation of the Protestant authority for the part he took in said battle to promote its downfall. He, with Rem Garretson, located 1016 acres of land at Egg Harbor, now Beesley's Point. He was one of the justices of the court, and occupied other prominent stations. He died about 1715, leaving but few descendants, one of whom, his great grandson, Rem. G. Golding, now past eighty years old, lives near the first and original location,

and has in his possession at the present time the sword with which his ancestor fought, and the epaulette which he wore at the battle of the Boyne."

As early as 1710 Goshen was known as a village, its name being then applied to it. About this time Henry Stites purchased the land about the point of Cape May, which was known as Stites' Beach, until 1876, when it was called Sea Grove, and later Cape May Point. In 1610 Colonel Daniel Coxe was appointed judge, with jurisdiction in Cape May.

CHAPTER V.

DEVELOPMENT OF RELIGIOUS DENOMINATIONS.

The first Baptist church in Cape May was that established at Cape May Court House in 1712. Morgan Edwards, in his sketch of Baptists in New Jersey, published in 1792, says of the history of the Cape May church:

"For the origin of this church we must take a retrospect of affairs to the year 1675, in which year a vessel, with emigrants, arrived in Delaware from England, who settled, some at the Cape and some elsewhere; among the first were two Baptists, viz., George Taylor and Philip Hill. Taylor kept a meeting in his house, and with his exhortations, reading the Bible, expounding, etc., enlightened some in the article of believers' baptisms. After his death, in 1702, Mr. Hill continued the meeting to 1704, when he also died. Soon after Mr. George Eaglesfield visited the Cape and made more proselytes. These went to Philadelphia to receive holy baptism, as appears in the association book. In 1688 Rev. Elias Keach paid a visit to these parts and ordained one Aston (Ashton, I suppose) to be a deacon, who also exhorted. In the fall of 1711 Rev. Thomas Griffiths (of Welshtract) went to the Cape with a view to purchase land and settle among the people for life; but, failing of his design, he quitted them next spring, and recommended to them Rev. Nathaniel Jenkins, who had just arrived in the country. Mr. Jenkins came, and pleased the people, and June 24, 1712, he and they were constituted a church by Rev. Timothy Brooks, of Cohansey, and his elders, Dickison Sheppard and Jeremiah Bacon. The names of the constituents follow, viz.: Rev. Nathaniel Jenkins, Arthur Cresse, Seth Brooks, Abraham Smith, William Seagrave, Jonathan Swain, John Stillwell, Henry Stites, Benjamin Hand, Richard Bonns, Ebenezer Swain, William Smith, John Taylor, Abraham Hand, Christopher Church, Charles

Robison, Easter Jenkins, Ruth Dean, Lydia Shaw, Elizabeth Hand, Jeruthy Hand, Hannah Wildair, Sarah Hiscox, Elizabeth Stillwell, Elizabeth Taylor, Hannah Taylor, Hannah Stites, Margery Smith, Elothes Smith, Ruth Swain, Mary Swain, Mary Cresse, Mary Osborn, Abagail Buck, Elizabeth Robison and Mary Jennings. Two years after the constitution this church joined the association.

"Remarkables.

"Cape May church may be deemed an original church, having sprang from none other, but having originated in the place where it exists. (2) It has now existed for eighty-three years, and has increased from 37 to 63. (3) In 1714 many of them died of a grievous sickness, which had well nigh depopulated the settlement. (4) In 1715 they built their first meeting house, on land purchased from Isaac Stratten, but his title being naught, they lost both house and land."

"Rev. Nathaniel Jenkins * * * became their minister at the constitution in 1712, and continued in the ministry to 1730, when he resigned and went to Cohansey. He was a Welshman, born in Caerdicanshire March 25, 1678, arrived in America 1710, and in 1712 settled at the Cape. He was a man of good parts and tolerable education, and quitted himself with honor in the loan office (where he was a trustee), and also in the assembly (particularly in 1721), when a bill was brought in to punish such as denied the doctrine 'of the Trinity, the divinity of Christ, the inspiration of Holy Scriptures, etc.' In opposition to which Mr. Jenkins stood up, and, with the warmth and accent of a Welshman said: 'I believe the doctrines in question as firmly as the promoters of that ill-designed bill, but will never consent to oppose the opposers with law, or with any other weapon, save that of argument, etc.' Accordingly the bill was quashed, to the great mortification of them who wanted to raise in New Jersey the spirit which so raged in New England." He served in the Assembly from 1723 to 1733. Mr. Jenkins' wife was Esther Jones, who bore him nine children, one of which was Rev. Nathaniel Jenkins, 2d, his eldest son, who became his successor. The latter was born in Wales April 11, 1710, and brought as an infant to America. He was called to the ministry in 1744, ordained in 1747, when he took on him care of the church, but he continued not long therein, but fell into the power of hurtful spirits, which brought on fits and a premature dotage. He died in 1796. He was succeeded by Rev. Samuel Heaton, who was pastor from 1756 to 1760.

Rev. John Sutton was pastor from April 1, 1764, to May 6, 1766.

Rev. Peter Peterson Vanhorn was pastor from April 7, 1770, to 1775.

Rev. David Smith, the next pastor, was a native of the place; ordained pastor March, 1776; died Februray, 1784, aged 54.

Rev. Artis Seagrave was pastor from 1785 to 1788.

Rev. John Stancliff was pastor from October, 1789, to 1802, when he died.

James Carman, who was born at Cape May in 1677, was pastor of the Baptist church at Cranbury, N. J., and he was, no doubt, the son of Caleb Carman, who was justice of the peace in 1685.

The Assembly of 1713 voted to tax the province £1730 in two instalments. Cape May's apportions were £54 and £25. John Taylor and Major Jacob Spicer were the assessors and Ephraim Edwards collector. On the 16th of March, this year, Richard Downs was commissioned to be a captain of militia for the upper part of the county, and David Weles made his lieutenant and Arthur Cresse ensign, while Humphrey Hewes was commissioned six days earlier captain of the militia for the lower end of the county, with Ephraim Edwards as his lieutenant and Samuel Mathews ensign.

On March 17 John Townsend and Jacob Spicer were appointed judges, with Humphrey Hughes, Timothy Brandreth, Joseph Weldon and John Page commissioners of the pleas.

From old records at Trenton were gathered the following records of early marriages and their issues:

Justice John Townsend, June 6, 1715, married Cornelius Schillinger, Jr., and Mary Stiles. Witness: Cornelius Schillinger, Henry Stiles, Henry Stiles, Jr., Edmund Shaw, John

DEVELOPMENT OF RELIGIOUS DENOMINATIONS. 73

Taylor, Daniel Wiggins, John Willkiss, Richard Forteskue, Isaac Brooks, Jr., Benjamin Hand, Jr.

Isaac Strattron, Jr., married Mary Foster October 15, 1734.

Rev. Nathaniel Jenkins married George Taylor to Lydia Shaw May 8, 1720. Issue: William, b. June 7, 1722; "eldest daughter," b. Feb. 22, 1723-4; daughter, b. Jan. 24, 1726-7.

William Shaw married Lydia Parson April 8, 1695, by Jeremiah Crowell, in presence of Henry Stiles, Hannah Stiles, Abram Smith and others. Issue: William, b. Aug. 24, 1697, d. Dec. 13, 1714; Richard, b. Oct. 29, 1699; Lydia, b. Sept. 14, 1703; John, b. Feb. 4, 1705; Joshua, b. Mar. 26, 1707; Nathan, b. Dec. 23, 1710.

James Briggs and Margery Taylor, married by Justice Thomas Hand March 22, 1713. Issue: Mary, b. Aug. 19, 1715; Elizabeth, b. July 3, 1717; Keziah, b. Aug. 30, 1719; Martha, b. Aug. 10, 1721; Sarah, b. May 31, 1724.

Joseph Crowell married to Anne Eglesfield by Justice John Townsend March 2, 1709. Issue: Mary, b. March 14, 1711; Edward, b. June 7, 1713; Joseph, b. Sept. 6, 1716.

Justice John Townsend, 1706-7, married Benjamin Hand and Ann Chew. Issue: Isaac, b. Aug. 14, 1709; Pocianci, b. Aug. 9, 1711; Jacob, b. April 21, 1714.

Josiah Crowell married Mary Whelding, daughter of Joseph Whelding, December 17, 1708.

Richard Bass (?) married Elizabeth Duncan (?) May 11, 1709, before Captain Mathews and others.

Justices John Townsend, Humphrey Hughes, John Paige and Joseph Whillden married Thomas Bancrofts and Elizabeth Matthews April 6, 1715, in the presence of Richard Downes, John Taylor, John Buck, John Hughes, Mary Matthews, John Cresse, Zelophead Hand, William Seagrave.

John Taylor and Lydia Schillux were married October 14, 1722, by Rev. Nathaniel Jenkins. Issue: Mary, d. Aug. 5, 1723. Lydia, his wife, died November, 1725, and John marries "againe" to Deborah Gavinson, by Rev. N. Jenkins, May 8, 1726.

John Taylor, son of George Taylor, married Elizabeth Bolsher, of Boston, April 5, 1697, "after the maner of ye Church of England." Witnesses: George Taylor, justice;

Elizabeth Taylor, Jno. Worlidge, Tim Brandreth, clerk. Issue: Margery, b. Aug. 16, 1698; George, b. Dec. 11, 1699; John, b. June 14, 1704; Mary, b. April 25, 1707, d. Oct. 11, 1711; Samuel, b. March 27, 1710, d. Oct. 11, 1711; Jeremiah, b. Aug. 14, 1713, d. Dec. 22, 1713.

Children of John Osbornes: Abiah, b. Sept. 9, 1692; Ruth, b. Feb. 20, 1698; Bezabeel, b. Jan. 21, 1704; Nathan, b. Feb. 2, 1706; Ananias, b. Feb. 5, 1708.

Children of Joseph Hints: Thomas, b. Aug. 31, 1707; Mary, b. Dec. 18, 1708; Hester, b. Feb. 4, 1711; Anne, b. Oct. 10, 1712; Joseph, b. Jan. 26, 1715.

Robert Champion and Mary Mayps married at Cape May June 17, 1715, by "John Townsend, one of his Majesty's Justices of the Peace."

John Willits and Martha Corson married by Justice John Townsend October 5, 1716.

William, son of William Seagreaves, born October 14, 1716.

Thomas Leaming, in his manuscript, tells us of the severe epidemic which visited Cape May Court House in the winter of 1713-14. Some forty and more residents died. He says: "The disease came on with a pain in the side, breast, and sometimes in the back, navel, tooth, eye, hand, feet, legs or ear." Among the victims were Nicholas Stillwell, Arthur Cresse, Sr., and Jr., Reuben Swain, Richard Smith, Samuel Garretson, Cornelius Hand, Joseph Hewit, William Shaw, John Reeves, Richard Fortesque, John Stillwell, James Garretson, Return Hand, John Foreman, Jedediah Hughes, John Matthews, Daniel Wells and over twenty others. It can scarcely be conjectured from the above recital of symptoms what the true character of the disease could have been. It was a severe retribution in a population of some two or three hundred, and Providence alone, who saw proper to afflict, can solve the mystery.

The second oldest church established in this county was by the Presbyterians at Cold Spring in 1714.

The first Presbytery organized in this county was that of Philadelphia in 1705. The Cold Spring church was an outgrowth of this body. The first minister was the Rev. John Bradner, who was licensed by Messrs. Davis, Hampton and

DEVELOPMENT OF RELIGIOUS DENOMINATIONS. 75

Henry in 1714. Mr. Bradner, who lived on his own estate and gave his name to the little stream near the church, was a Scotchman, who remained as pastor until 1721.

The first church was a small log building, erected in 1718. A writer says of the meeting houses of those days:

"The plain meeting house was in harmony with the way of worship which they had chosen. If the pulpits were high, it was because the ministers were expected to stand far above the people, and to be shining examples of Protestant principles. They would have been afraid of low pulpits, lest they might tend toward popery and the service of the mass.

"Again, the meeting house was never lighted except by the sun, until singing schools made it necessary to introduce candles. Night meetings in the meeting house were considered quite improper, and the Presbyterian would have thought candles too suggestive of the superstitions of the Church of Rome. There were no fireplaces, or stoves, or other means of warming those old meeting houses for many years after the colony was planted. The people were exemplary in their attendance on worship, and they went regularly to the religious services. It was the spirit of that age. The Lord's day began at sunset on Saturday.

"The early ministers regarded the Sabbath as a time for the public worship of God and for religious instruction. The people came together at 9 o'clock for the morning service. In early times they were summoned by the beat of the drum. Sometimes the voice of the town crier, or the blowing of a conch shell, or of a horn, served instead of the drum. The old meeting houses were crowded, for the people were anxious to attend the services on the Sabbath. Inside the doors the most conspicuous object was the pulpit, with the things that belonged to it. In front of the pulpit, on a low platform, sat the deacons, facing the congregation. On a platform a little higher than the deacons sat the ruling elders. Above them in the pulpit itself sat the two ministers. This array of dignitaries, some of them, at least, in robes of office, looked down upon the congregation, and was looked up to by the people. The pastor began with a solemn prayer, continuing about a quarter of an hour. After this the teacher read and expounded a chapter in the Bible. This exposition of the chapter was one of the leading parts of the service. Then a Psalm was sung by the congregation. No instrumental music was allowed in the Puritan churches, partly because such music was very prominent in the services of the prelatical churches, and partly because it was believed to be contrary to the word of God. After the Psalm came the sermon by the pastor, and this was the great feature of the service. Its length was measured by the hour glass, which commonly stood on the pulpit. The minister turned the glass when he began to preach, and he was expected, on ordinary occasions, to draw his discourse to a close when the last sands were running out from the glass. Yet there were intances when the glass was turned two or three times.

"Although they were carefully prepared, the sermons of the early ministers were not as in this day, written. The sermon being finished, the teacher made a short prayer, and another Psalm was sung. Then baptism was administered to children who were presented by their Christian parents. Once a month the Sacrament of the Lord's Supper was administered, in connection with the morning services. The people were then dismissed with the benediction."

Among the first settlers of Cape May were many Quakers, notably the Townsends, Corsons, Leamings and Spicers. In 1716 a meeting house was built by that denomination at Seaville. The principal contributors to the building fund were John Townsend and his son, Richard; Peter Corson and Aaron Leaming, of Cape May county, and John Somers and one Scull, of Gloucester (now Atlantic) county. Meetings are held quarterly in this ancient structure, Friends coming usually from Salem county to conduct the services. It is known among the Friends by the name of the "Old Cedar Meeting House."

The following extracts are taken from a Friend's history of the meeting houses of that time:

"Great Egg Harbor.

"———?—A monthly meeting hath been held there for some years, composed of the Friends who live there and those of Cape May; they belong to Salem and Gloucester Quarterly Meeting."

"On the divis of Haddonfield Quarter from that of Salem

Great Egg Harbor and Cape May monthly meetings was embraced in Haddonfield. The monthly meeting was discontinued in ———?

"Great Egg Harbor.

"1702—The first convincement of Friends about Great Egg Harbor was about the year 1702, since which meetings have been settled there and two meeting houses built."

It is probable that one of the houses referred to was that at Cape May. The meeting at Great Egg Harbor has been discontinued and the few remaining members attached to Greenwich.

"Cape May.

"The meeting at Cape May was established early, and then formed a part of Great Egg Harbor monthly meeting."

The introduction to the Great Egg Harbor and Cape May monthly meetings says: "Several Friends of Great Egg Harbor and Cape May having for some time been under considerable inconvenience for want of a monthly meeting of men and women being erected amongst them for the well managing of the affairs of the church in the good and wholesome Discipline, have endeavored in an expostulatory letter directed to the Quarterly Meeting of Gloucester and Salem to set forth the same to said meeting's consideration. (Which was done 16th of 7th month, 1726.) Granted that it should begin and be held on the first Second-day in each month, that is to say, to begin at Richard Somers', on Great Egg Harbour side, in the ninth month next, and in the tenth month at Elizabeth Garretson's, on Cape May side, and so on interchangeable until Friends there shall see cause to make any alteration for their own conveniency.

"Pursuant to which conclusion the Friends of Great Egg Harbor and Cape May met at Richard Somers' the 7th day of the ninth mo., 1726, and proceeded to the business of the meeting.

"At s'd meeting Richard Townsend was chosen clarke of s'd monthly meeting.

"At s'd meeting Peter White and Jonathan Adams was appointed overseers of the meeting held at Japhet Leeds's, Peter White's and John Scull's. And for the meeting held at Cape May Richard Townsend is appointed overseer.

"At our monthly meeting for Cape and Egg Harbour this 5th day of the 10th mo., 1726.

"At s'd meeting Richard Somers and Judeth Letart Published their intentions of marriage with each other, etc."

These minutes were kept up until 1843.

Samuel Smith says: "The first convincement of Friends about Great Egg Harbor was about 1702, since which meetings have been settled and meeting houses built."

"For many years there seemed to be a great openness on the part of the inhabitants to receive the doctrines of Friends, and a number of Friends settling along the shore at various places, several meetings were established, viz.: Egg Harbor, Galloway, Tuckahoe and Cape May. These formed Great Egg Harbor monthly meeting. Friends having died and others removed, none were left to sustain the meetings, and they have all been laid down or abandoned, and the properties sold or devoted to other uses, with a single exception, that of Cape May, near Seaville, in that county. The meeting was established soon after 1700, and the meeting house built in 1716, by the Townsends, Leamings and others. It was rebuilt some years ago on a much smaller scale than formerly, and is still kept in repair, but, like the others mentioned, it has no congregation. The old burial ground is still kept up."

CHAPTER VI.

MARITIME TENDENCIES AND CATTLE OWNING.

"On May 6, 1715," says Aaron Leaming, 2d, "the Cold Spring mill was first set to work." Here grist was ground.
The old county road from Long Bridge to the head of Tuckahoe, and from thence to Gloucester Point, was made in 1716.

The Assembly of this year, of which Colonel Daniel Coxe was Speaker, made Christopher Hughes a captain of militia under Lieutenant Jacob Spicer, with Ezekiel Eldrigg (probably Eldridge) and John Cresy ensigns, and Samuel Eldridg lientenant. An act was also passed during the session to prevent the firing the woods between February 14 and April 14, under a penalty of forty shillings.

Spicer was not, it is said, an habitual attendant upon the sessions of the Assembly, and there are records to prove that his attendance was often forced. In 1716 the officers of the colony were sent after him to compel his attendance, and Spicer, avoiding them, he was expelled and a new election ordered. This, however, did no good, because the people immediately returned Spicer as Assemblyman.

At the council of the president and councillors of the province, held on March 30 and 31, 1716, at which were present Colonel Daniel Coxe, president, and Messrs. George Deacon, John Humphries, John Wills and Richard Bull, the "following surveys, with others, were inspected and approved by the Council of Propri'es and ordered to be recorderd:" Daniel Cox and Jacob Spicer, 3933 acres; do., 100 acres; do., 500 acres; do., 50 acres.

In 1719 Jeremiah Bass began his services as a member of the Assembly for Cape May, and served until 1723. He figured as as attorney at Salem from 1710 to 1716, but whether he was the same Jeremiah Basse who was an Anabaptist minister, agent for the West Jersey Society for Cape

May in 1694 and 1695, when he resided at Cohansey, and at Burlington, deputy governor of West Jersey 1698, and departed for England in 1699 or 1702, is not known. The former may have been a son of the latter, and probably was.

Whitehead says: "Jeremiah Basse was appointed governor of New Jersey July 15, 1697, for one year, and assumed the office April 7, 1698, and retained it until superseded by Governor Andrew Hamilton (whom he had succeeded), in December, 1699, returning to England before that time. He returned in 1703 as secretary of the province, under Lord Cornbury, by whom he was given various offices. In 1716 he was elected to the Assembly from Cape May, where he then resided. In 1719 he was Attorney-General of the province. He died in 1725, his will being proved August 9, in that year."

In the session of 1718-19 of the Assembly Colonel Jacob Spicer was appointed to collect two instalments of colony tax, amounting to £42 8s. and £17 6s., and Spicer was also to administer oaths to Isaac Sharp, appointed colonel of the Salem and Cape May regiment, and to John Ralph, who was made major.

Early in the development of Cape May the attention of the inhabitants was turned to the cultivation of the oyster, and the attention of the early legislators was turned toward the preservation of this industry. The first protective measure on record is that of March 27, 1719, which sets out in its preamble that oyster beds are "wasted and destroyed by strangers and others at unseasonable times of the year, the preservation of which will tend to great benefit of the poor people and others inhabiting this province." It was enacted, therefore, that no person should rake or gather up the oyster or shells from May 10 to September 1, that non-residents could not gather them up at any time to take away with them, under a penalty of forfeiting their vessels and equipments. Appointments were made to execute the provisions of the law, to inspect oyster boats and seize any which might be under suspicion. Jacob Spicer and Aaron Leaming were appointed the commissioners for Cape May, while for Gloucester (Atlantic) county Richard Summers and James Steelman were named. The fees of the commissioners were half of the forfeitures, while the other half went to the colony. In 1723 Richard M. West, one of the councillors appointed by the Crown for the colony, reporting to the Lords of Trade in England, complained of this act, protesting that it acted against non-residents, claiming that the non-residents had as much right, inasmuch as the beds were not located, as the Jerseymen to take the oysters. The law, however, was not interfered with.

Old newspapers contain these accounts of wrecks on the coast:

"Boston News-Letter," September 17-24, 1724, says: "Boston, Sept. 23.—We have advice from Cape May, by way of Philadelphia, the 10th instant, that there was a sloop drove ashore as a wreck, her hands having left her at sea, and was got safe in at Lewis Town. She was commanded by Captain Thomas Moussel, from Boston, loaden with rhum and molasses. The sloop is since got off and is at Cape May."

"The New York Gazette," July 30, 1733, said: "Philadelphia, July 26.—We hear from Cape May that last week the Bodies of three Men drove ashore there, one of them had good Cloaths on, Gold Buttons in his Shirt sleeves, two Gold Rings on his Finger, a Watch and some pieces of Gold in his Pocket, and Silver Buckles on his Shoes, but was shot thro' the Head, the other two had their Heads cut off. About the same time a small sloop drove on shore about 15 Miles to the Northward of the Cape, but it is not known who she or the Men are. We also hear that a Brigantine sailed up our Bay as far as Bombay Hook, then tacked about and stood to Sea. Some think it was the Brigantine bound from Bristol with a number of Convicts, and that they have mutinied, and Murdered the Master and Men. We expect a more particular Account of this barbarous Murder in a few days."

"The Pennsylvania Gazette," July 28, 1743, says:

"Philadelphia.—We hear from Cape May that a ship bound into Virginia from Aberdeen,—Stuart, Master, came ashore there last Friday morning just before day. 'Tis uncertain whether she can be got off, or not."

"New York Weekly Post Boy," January 9, 1744: "Philadelphia, December 29.—We hear from Cape May that on Friday, the 16th Instant, in the Evening, the Seneca, Capt. Wasbrough, from Bristol, bound to this Port, was drove ashore to the Northward of the Cape, bilged and filled with Water, but the People were all saved. She had been out 14 Weeks."

The following reports of arrivals and clearances of Cape May vessels and vessels bound to and from Cape May are given from early newspapers:

"The New England Courant," of November 6-13, 1725, says:

"Custom House, Boston.—Cleared Out—Freeman, for Cape May."

"New England Weekly Journal," October 16, 1727, says: "Custom House, Philadelphia, Octob. 5. Cleared Out, Tarresan for Cape May."

"New England Weekly Journal," April 17, 1727, says: "Custom House, Philadelphia, April 6. Cleared out Henry Stiles for Cape May."

"Boston Gazette, April 24, mentions same clearance.

"American Weekly Mercury," of October 9 to 16, 1729, says:

"Perth Amboy, October the 14th, 1729. Cleared for Departure. * * * Sloop Jane and Mary, Samuel Sears, for Cape May."

"The New England Weekly Journal," November 22, 1731, says:

"Entries at the Port of Philadelphia, Nov. 11. Outward Bound, Butler for Cape May."

"The Boston News-Letter," July 1-8, 1731, says: "Boston, July 7. Outward Bound, John Townsend for Cape May."

"Boston News-Letter," June 8-15, 1732, says: "Cleared Out Jos. Worth, for Cape May," from "Boston Post," June 14.

"Boston News-Letter," September 7-14, 1732, says: "Philadelphia, Sept. 7. Intred Inwards, Clymer from Cape May."

"New England Weekly Journal," April 2, 1733, says:

"Custom House, Philadelphia, March 6 to 13. Entred In. White from Cape May."

"New England Weekly Journal," April 16, 1733, says:

"Custom House, Boston, April 14. Entred Inwards, Joseph Worth for Cape May."

"Weekly Rehearsal," August 11, 1735, says.

"Custom House, Boston, Aug. 9. Entred inwards, Whillder from Cape May."

"The New England Weekly Journal," August 19, 1735, says:

"Custom House Boston Aug. 18, cleared out, Wildow for Cape May."

"Boston Weekly Post Boy," July 30, 1744:

"Newport, Rhode Island, July 27. Cleared Out, Davis for Perth Amboy, Stephens for Cape May."

Before the eighteenth century began Cape May's early pioneers, who had come from Long Island, New Haven and other places, began to own cattle, which they pastured in almost every part of the county. From 1690 to 1730 a large number of the brands used on the cattle were known as "earemarks," because these red-hot brands were socked into the flesh near some part of the ear, and the marks were used as identifications to show ownership of the stock. Those who owned cattle were probably the well-to-do part of the community. These marks were not confined to cattle alone, but stamped upon horses, sheep, swine and lambs. In "Liber A, of Deeds and Miscellaneous Records," at the county clerk's office can be found a large number recorded. A sample of the records given shows the quaint manner of recording them:

"Joseph Ludlon his Eare Marke and El under the Left Eare. Recorded this 13 Day of March 1696-7. Now the mark of his Son Anthony Ludlam."

"John Townsend's Eare Marke a Smalle forke on ye Right Eare and a half penny under ye Lefte. Recorded ye 20 of February 1694-5. Now the mark of Richard Townsend, Jr."

The following are the years and the names of those who

had ear marks recorded during the period, whose names are given to show the families then living in the county:

1691-2.—Henry Stites, Esaroh Stites.

1693.—James Cressie, George Taylor, Joseph Hondoin, John Taylor, Shamgar Hand, Constant Hughes, Jr., Joseph Houldoin, Jr., Caleb Curwithy, Samuel Johnson, Joseph Whilden, Isaac Whilden, Oliver Johnson, William Seagrave, John Parsons, William Shaw, Jonathan Foreman, William Johnson, Jonathan Richardson, Benjamin Richardson.

1694.—Robert Cressey, Timothy Brandreth, Samuel Crowell, Barnabas Crowell, Benjamin Land, Isaac Hand, Lubbart Gisborsen, Samuel Richardson, Caesar Hoskins, John Cresse, Jr., John Stillwell, William Simpkins, Thomas Goodwin, Peter Coston, Jonathan Carman, Samuel Eldridge, Thomas Gandy, Jonathan Osborn, Jos. Badcock, Daniel Johnson, Nathaniel Hand, Ezekiel Hand, William Smith, Joshua Carman, Thomas Langley, Jacob Dayton, Capt. Downs.

1694-5.—Nathaniel Shute, Cornelius Skelinger, John Townsend, Richard Townsend, Jr., William Jacox, Randall Huit.

1696.—George Booth, Edward Lumus, Joseph Ludlam, Abraham Hand, John Hand, Thomas Leaming, John Jervis, Thomas Hand, Daniel Hand, George Hand, Jeremiah Hand, Edward Foster, Jacob Crowell, Samuel Croell, Jr., Humphrey Hughes, Jr., Thomas Mathews, Lewis Mulford, Elijah Hughes, Jacob Spicer, Joseph Hand, Eliu Swain.

1696-7.—Randall Huit, Col. Spicer, Joseph Ludlow.

1703.—Richard Townsend.

1704.—John Crofford, George Crofford.

1706.—Ezekiel Eldridge, Robert Pereman, John Buck, Aaron Leaming, Richard Stites, Abigail Stites, Samuel Johnson, "formerly George Booth, who left the county;" Ebenezer Johnson, Abraham Bauer, Richard Swaine, Jonathan Swaine, Thomas Hand, Jr., Cornelius Hand, Jeremiah Hughes, Jeremiah Leaming, John Taylor, Nathaniel Short, Joshua Shaw.

1707.—John Crandall, Shamgar Hand, Jr., Henry Young, Benjamin Stites, Jonathan Stites, Ebenezer Swaine, Silas Swaine, William Matthews, Constant Hughes.

1708.—Josiah Crowell, Samuel Crowell, Robert Townsend, Zelopead Hand and son, Nathaniel.

1709.—Benjamin Hand, John Garlick, John Cresse and his son, Robert; Aaron Leonard, Aaron Leaming, Jr.

1710.—Moses Cressy, Richard Fortescue, Henry Stevens, Isaac Shutton, John Goafe.

1711.—Charles Robinson, Joshua Garlick, Ebenezer Nuton, Joseph Whilden, Senr., James Whelden, Peter Hand, Christopher Church.

1712.—Benjamin Holden, Henry Stephens, Jonathan Foreman, David Cresse, Lewis Cresse.

1713.—Jeremiah Church, Samuel Eldridge.

1714.—Nathaniel Hand, James Brigs.

1715.—Thomas Bancroft, Benjamin Crofford, Ezekiel Mulford, Samuel Swaine, John Willis.

1716.—William Robinson, William Mulford, Nathaniel Norton, Daniel Norton.

1717.—John Hand, William Nickkolls.

1718.—Thomas Langley, Richard Shaw, John Taylor, Jr.

1720.—Nathaniel Foster, Nathaniel Rosco, Joshua Crofford, Andrew Godfrey.

1721.—Zebulon Swaine, Charles Barnes, Thomas Leaming, John Cresse, Jr., "formerly Caesar Hoskins, who deserted the county;" John Stillwell, Samuel Richardson, John Hand.

1722.—Benjamin Johnson, Samuel Bancroft, William Smith and son, Richard; David Hildreth, Josiah Hildreth, Thos. Leaming and his son, Christopher; Cornelius Schilliux, Jr., Nathaniel Rosco, James Hawthorne.

1723.—John Smith, Zebulon Swaine, James Swaine, Wm. Mathews.

1724.—John Tomson.

1725.—Wm. Doubleday, Ephraim Edwards, John Crandell.

1726.—Anthony Ludlam, Providence Ludlam, William Nickols, Samuel Foster, Peter Paige, William Eldridge.

1727.—Cornelius Hand.

1730.—John Garlock, Thomas Stonebank.

1731.—Isaac Ludlam, Hezekiah Schull, Samuel Mathews, Jas. Jacocks, "formerly Jon. Swain, he leaving the county;"

James Edwards, Dan'l Norton, Moses Cresse, Ebenezer Norton, Caleb Norton.
1732.—Joshua Shaw, John Shaw.
1734.—Nathan Osborn, Deborah Golden.

Among the commissions made out at Fort George, New York, in 1721, were one of August 3, 1721, to Aaron Leamying to be clerk of peace and of court, and those of October 2, to Jacob Spicer, Thomas Leming and Aaron Leming, to administer civil and military oaths, and to Richard Downs to be high sheriff. The next year the commission of the peace was composed of Jacob Spicer, Humphrey Hughs, Joseph Whilding, John Hand, Robert Townsend, William Smith, John Parsons, Christopher Church and Henry Young. On September 11, that year, John Ralfe was made deputy surrogate for the counties of Cape May and Salem. During the same year Cape May county was required to pay colony tax amounting to £76 19s. 8p., and Richard Downs was appointed to collect it.

At various times during the early part of the eighteenth century the Spanish were at variance with England, and Spain was trying to secure some trade from the American colonies, and preyed upon English merchantmen. Early Cape May men saw some of these privateers, and the following newspaper reports of those times are here given:

The "Boston News-Letter," of from Monday, January 7, to Monday, January 14, 1712, says in its "Boston Notes:"

"By a certain Person come hither from Cape May in the Province of Jersey, we are inform'd, that on the 16th of November Last about 3 leagues off that Cape he was taken in the Sloop Betty of St. Christophers Walter Scot, Commander, bound from Jamaica to New-York, by a Martinico Privateer Sloop of 8 Guns 130 men, Scot had on board when he was taken 38 Hogsheads of Rum, and 48 Negroes. The Privateer sent his Prize to Martinico, with Some of her men, enough to condemn her, the rest he put on shore the next day at Cape May."

The "New England Courant," of Boston, from July 30 to August 6, 1722, says:

"Philadelphia, July 26. On Sunday the 22d arrived a small Sloop, Jonathan Swain Master, from Cape May, by whom we have Advice, That a Pyrate Brigantine and Sloop have been cruising on and off both our Capes for above Three Weeks. They several Times sailed up the Bay Ten or Twelve Leagues; and on the 8th Instant brought a large Sloop down with them, which they took up high in the Bay. That Night they anchored in the Bay about a League and Half off the Shore, beat Drums all Night and seemed to be very full of Men. What Vessels they have took we do not yet understand, none of the Prisoners being set on Shore. Our Trade is entirely stopped by them, no Vessel daring to go out and all took that offer to come in. They were both seen on Thursday last cruising about their old Station, not fearing disturbance from the Men of War, who, by dear Experience we know, love Trading better than Fighting. No Vessel has arrived here for a Week; except Hargrave in the Sloop Little Joseph, who sailed from hence about two months ago for the Island of St. Christophers, but was taken by the Pyrates three Times and rifled of most of her Cargo, so that she was obliged to return back."

"The Boston Evening Post," of August 11, 1740, says:

"New-York, August 4. Captain Janney, off of Cape May, saw a black Sloop (supposed to be a Spanish Privateer, and the same as mentioned in our last) laying to under her Foresail, but on seeing Janncey, she up with her Mainsail and made up to him, but a ship appearing she left Janncey, who saw her come up to the Ship, but missing Stays, the Ship got away, when the Sloop went after her again, but missing Stays a second time, the Ship who was under double Reeft Sails, let them out and got clear of the Sloop."

"The Boston Gazette or Weekly Journal," of September 29, 1747, says:

"Philadelphia, September 17. Monday morning last arrived here an express Boat from Lewis, the Advice that they had been under Arms there for three Days, on account of two Spanish Privateer Sloops being at the Capes, one of ten the other of Eight Guns: That they had taken the Ship Delaware, Cap. Sake of this Place, outward bound, one (unknown) bound in, and were in Chase of a Third; they had also taken three of our Pilots. But a Pilot Boat has come up since from Cape-May, who saw nor heard nothing of them so that tis thought they are gone off with their Prizes."

"The New York Evening Post," July 20, 1747, says:

"Philadelphia ——. Yesterday came up to Town, one of our Pilot Boats with 4 men lately belonging to a Sloop bound from Virginia to New-York, Constantine Hughes, Master, which was drove on Shore on Monday last on Cape-May, by a Spanish Privateer Sloop, which Sloop had taken a few Days before, 2 of our Pilot-Boats, one of which they mann'd with 30 Hands & sent up our Bay, above Bomb-Bay-Hook, where they landed on Sunday last, and to the Plantation of Mr. Edmond Liston, and took away 4 Negroes, and every thing else that they tho't they wanted to the Value of about 200l. from whence they went to another Plantation and took a Negro, but the People shutting the Door upon them they fir'd at them and shot a Woman thro' the Thigh, and in the Evening they went down the Bay again, where meeting with another of our Pilot-Boats, they stripped her of the Sails &c. and on Tuesday Morning she was seen going out of the Capes to look for the Privateer Sloop, having one of our Pilots on board, and they told the last Pilot they took, that they had taken 13 Vessels on our Coast, four of which they sent home, and sunk and burnt the rest."

"Boston Gazette or Weekly Journal," of July 21, 1747, says, in speaking of a privateersman's acts:

"Soon after they fell in with a poor Cape-May man, laden with Shingles, which they took, and gave to 25 of the Prisoners, with scarce any Provisions on board."

The "New York Evening Post," of August 10, 1747, says:

"New-York, August 3. Last Saturday arrived here Capt. Hughes from Virginia: who informs: that on the 13th of July being off Cape-May, he was chased by a small French Privateer Schooner, so near the Land, that he was forced to run her ashore and quit her, the Privateer came along Side of the Sloop, broke open the Hatches, and began to throw some of her Cargo over board, and by that means got off, next morning Capt. Huges came down and saw her under sail, soon after another Vessel hove in sight, they all left the Sloop to go after the other, he seeing this got a small

Craft with some men besides his Compliment, went on board hoisted Sail, and is safe arrived."

The "Boston Weekly Post Boy," of July 4, 1748, says: "Philadelphia, June 23. On Friday night came to Town, Capt. Wm. Clymer. jun. bound in here from S. Carolina, but was chased in near Cape May by a Sloop on Wednesday last, upon which he quitted his Vessel, and went ashore with his Men in the Boat."

About the same time Don Joseph Hautenoan, a Spanish privateersman, took four vessels off Cape May.

CHAPTER VII.
ANCIENT LOANS AND TAXES.

The accounts of the treasurer of West Jersey from September, 1720, to September, 1725, exhibit that Richard Downs, as collector, paid all the moneys from Cape May county during these five years. During the years 1722 and '23, the treasurer received £39 9s. 0d., of which Humphrey Hughes received £16 15s. 0d. for his attendance as representative for the county in the Assembly. In 1723 the tax received was £33 0s. 10¾d., of which, on March 16, Humphrey Hughes was paid £22 10s. 0d. and Jacob Spicer £10 for their services as members. In 1724 two equal payments of £21 14s. 0d. were received, and in 1725 £31 4s. 6d. The latter year the treasurer paid "Mr." (probably Nathaniel) Jenkins and Humphrey Hughes each £23 14s. 0d. for their services as members of the Assembly.

On July 2, 1723, the first court, of which records were preserved, was held in the Presbyterian meeting house at Cold Spring.

In 1723 bills of credit were issued by the province of New Jersey to the amount of £40,000. Cape May's share in this loan was £1115, and commissioners for this part of the fund were Humphrey Hughes and the Rev. Nathanael Jenkins, who were given an annual salary of £11. (In 1728 their salaries were reduced to £4 10s.) Cape May was required to furnish for ten years an annual sum of £31 4s. 6d. to go toward a fund to sink the bills. From the manuscripts of Aaron Leaming, 1st, and Aaron Leaming, 2d, the following facts are found: About 1723 the State of New Jersey had her obligations indorsed by Great Britain and a large sum of money obtained to loan on mortgage security in the different counties of the State. Under this and subsequent acts three loans were made to Cape May county by the State, viz.: First, £1115; second, 1731, £634; third, 1734, £1248.

In 1753 these loans matured and the State ordered them paid. Messrs. Hughes and Jenkins served as commissioners of the loan office until 1737. In 1733 the Legislature vested the power of selection of the commissioners in the justice of the peace of the county, and Henry Young and Henry Stites were the first appointed by the freeholders and justices to manage this loan, and continued until May 12, 1742, when they resigned, and the same day Aaron Leaming, 1st, and Aaron Leaming, 2d, father and son, were appointed commissioners, and remained so until the death of Aaron Leaming, 1st, in 1746, when Henry Young was chosen in his place, and they remained commissioners until the loan became due in 1753. The books remained in the commissioners' hands until August 14, 1765. Jeremiah Leaming, who was a collector of taxes, assisted the other commissioners in the performance of their duties. In 1765 Aaron Leaming, 2d, says: "The loans are all paid except some trifling sums, and the mortgages canceled."

Mr. Leaming further states in his diary:

"June 20, 1765—the Gen'l Assembly of N. J. passed a law for removing the Books out of the hands of the respective commissioners of the Loan Office in the several counties of this province, into the hands of the Clarks of the Peace of the counties, and as I hapepned to be one of Loan officers for Cape May (Henry Young, Esq., being the other), I thought proper to take the following extracts from the said books before they passed out of my hands." These extracts have been woven into the preceding paragraphs of this book.

In the accounts of John Allen, treasurer of the province from 1733 to 1751, in the exhibits of the moneys received from 1733 to 1736 for the support of the government are the following entries of receipts from Cape May county:

"Cape May, £97:19:06.

"Interest money recd acct £40,000 loan, Cape May, £7:09:08.

"Interest money recd on acct £20,000, Cape May, £133:-00:06.

"Interest money rec'd on acct £40,000, Cape May, £53:-28:00."

1739. "To int. money from Cape May £24:16:— on acct. £20,000, £43:8."

1740. "Int. money Cape May £73:13:6. Cape May, £160:4:—."

1743 and 1744. "Int. money from Cape May on £40,000 & £20,000, £146:5:0."

1745, 1746 and 1747. "To int. money recd from Loan Off. Com, from Cape May, £182:6:6."

1748. "Int. on £20,000 & £40,000, Cape May £39:19:6," and also, the same year, £28:5:6.

1750. "Int. money from Cape May £22:4:0."

1751. "Int. money from £14:8:0."

In 1751 Treasurer Allen paid Aaron Leaming £34:2:0 and Jacob Spicer £7:4:0 for services, which are not stated.

The county of Cape May was divided into three townships, Upper, Middle and Lower, April 2, 1723, of which the official record says:

"At a court of the General Quarter Sessions of the Peace, holden at the house of Robert Townsend, on the 2d day of April, 1723:

"Justices Present.—Jacob Spicer, (first), Humphrey Hughes, Robert Townsend, John Hand, Henry Young, William Smith.

The county divided into precincts, excepting the Cedar Swamp; the lower precincts being from John Taylor's branch to the middle main branch of Fishing Creek, and so down ye said branch and creek to the mouth thereof."

"Middle precinct, to be from the aforesaid John Taylor's branch to Thomas Leaming's, and from thence to a creek called Dennis Creek, and so down the said creek to the bay shore, along the bay to Fishing Creek."

"The Upper precinct, to be the residue of the said county, excepting the Cedar Swamp, which is to be at the general charge of the county."

In 1723 Aaron Leaming, 1st, purchased of the English owners Seven-Mile Beach, which had been first surveyed in May, 1721, and what was after that time known as Leaming's Beach for about a century. He gave £606 for the same, amounting to about $2500 of present United States money.

His deed for the property is here given in its full text, as follows:

"This Indenture made the Twenty forth Day of December in the ninth year of the Reign of George over Great Britain France and Ireland King Defender of the Faith &c Between Charles Dockminique John Bennet Edward Richier Robert Mitchele Thomas Skinner and Joseph Brooksbank Gentlemen all of the City of London in the Kingdom of Great Britain and other Proprietors of the Western Devition of the Province of New Jarsey Commonly Called & known by the name of the New Jarsey Society of the one part and Aaron Leaming of the County of Capmay & Providence of New Jarsey yeoman of the other part witnesseth that for an in the Consideration of the sum of six hundred & Six pounds of the old Currency of the western Devition of the province of New Jarsey or Seventy nine pounds & ten Shillings in mony according to our Late Queens Proclamation in hand paid to Lewis Morris Esqr agent and Attorney for Charles Dockminique John Bennet Edward Rechter Robert Mitchele Thomas Skinner and Joseph Brooksbank the Precept whereof is hereby acknowledged and the said Aaron Leaming his heirs executors & Administrators of the same and of every part and parcell thereof is acquitted Released exonerated and Discharged forever have Granted Bargained Sold Released enfeoffed and Confeirmed and by these presents Do fully absolutely and Clearly Grant Bargain Sell Releas Enfeoff and Confeirm unto him the said Aaron Leaming his heirs and asigns all that Tract of Land Beach and Marsh Lying and being in the County of Capmay and province of New Jarsey called or known by the name of the Seven mile beach it being an inlire Island from three Quarters flood to one Quarter Ebb Bounded as followeth (viz) Bounded on the Southeast by the main ocean or Sea on the Southwest by the Inlet Called Little hereford Inlet, and on the Northwest by the Creeks and Sounds that are flowed with water from three Quarters flood to one Quarter Ebb, and on the northeast by the Inlet Called Townsends Inlet Together also with all and all manner of woods under woods Trees mines minerals Quarres Haukings Huntings Foulings

Fishings fences Buildings Improvements heireditaments and appurtenances whatsoever thereunto belonging or in any ways appurtaining and all the estate right title property possession Intrest Claim and Demand whatsoever either in law or Equity of them the said Charles Dockminique John Bennet Edward Ruchier Robert Mitchell Thomas Skinner and Joseph Brooksbank and the Rest of the proprietors of the Western Devision of the Province of New Jarsey known by the name of New Jarsey Society their or either of their heir heirs of in too unto or out of the above Bargained and Granted or the hereby intended to be Bargained and Granted premises and every part and parcell thereof TO HAVE AND TO HOLD all the above Bargained and Granted or the hereby intended to be granted Land Marsh or Beach and promises unto him the said Aaron Leaming his heirs and asigns forever To the Sole and only proper use Benefit and Behoof of him the said Aaron Leaming his heirs and asigns forever and the said Charles Dockminique John Bennet Edward Richier Robert Mitchell Thomas Skinner and Joseph Brooksbank for themselves and each of them severrally for their respective heirs Executors and administrators Do Covenant Grant Bargain promise and agree to and with the said Aaron Leaming his heirs and assignes that all the time of the ensealing and Delivering of these presents those called and known of the, New Jarsey Society above mentioned Stand Lawfully Seized of the above Granted or Intended to be Granted Land Marsh & Premises of a Good sure perfect & undefeizable Estate of inheiritance in the Law in fee simple and that they the Said Charles Dockminique John Bennet Edward Richier Robert Mitchell Thomas Skinner and Joseph Brookebank have in them Selves good Right full power and absolute authority (all the time of the ensealing & Delivering of these presents) to Grant Bargaine Sell Convey and Confeirm the above Granted or the hereby intended to be Granted Land marsh & premises unto him the said Aaron Leaming his heirs & asigns as is above mentioned to be Granted Bargained Sold &c and that the above Granted and Bargained primises in the Quiet and peaceable posession of him the said Aaron Leaming his heirs & asigns free & clear & frely & Clearly acquited &

Discharged from all former & other Grants Bargains Sales Leases Releases Mortgages & all other incumberences in the Law whatsoever shall forever remain and the said Charles Dockminique Edward Richier Robert Mitchill Thomas Skinner John Bennet & Joseph Brooksbank for themselves & each of them severally for their respective heirs Executors and administrators Do furder Covenant Bargain and promise and agree to & with him and said Aaron Leaming his heirs and asigns that all the above Granted or the hereby intended to be Granted Land marsh & premises with all the appurtainces thereunto belonging in the peacable & Quiet possession of him the Said Aaron Leaming his heirs & asigns. against any manner of person or persons that shall ever Lay any Just or Lawfull Claim unto the same or to any part or parcell thereof by vertue of any Right had in the same any time before the Day of Date of these presents they will & shall forever warrant and Defend and each of their Respective heirs as above said the same in Like manner Shall forever warrant & Defend in the peacable & Quiet Possession of him the said Aaron Leaming his heirs and asigns after the same manner as is above mentioned and that all any time within the term of tenn years Next ensuing the Date Hereof they every of them and their agent for the time being Shall make and execute at the proper Cost and Charge in the Law of him the said Aaron Leaming his heirs and assigns all such furder and other deed & conveyances for the better asureing and confeirming the above mentioned Land & premises unto him the said Aaron Leaming his heirs and asigns forever as shall be by him the said Aaron Leaming his heirs or asigns or by any of his or their councells Learned in the Law advises Devised or Required.

 In Witness whereof the Said Partyes to these presents have interchangeably put their hands & seals the Day and year first above mentioned

    Thomas Skinner   Robert Mitchell
    Joseph Brooksbank Charles Docminique
    John Bennet   Edward Richier
 Signed Sealed and Delivered in the presents of us
    Ir S Hooper   Richard Ashfield

September 19th 1723—Received of Aaron Leaming the Consideration money mentioned in the within deed by money formerly Paid and a bond now given for the Remainder I say received by me Lewis Morris Agent.

In 1726 the first census of Cape May county was given, and there were then but 668 persons residing within its territory.

The census is abstracted from a letter of May 9, that year, from Governor Burnett to the Lords of Trade in London, and shows the total number of white residents to have been 654, of which 209 were males above 16, 156 females above 16, 148 males under 16, 141 females under 16, and the total number of negroes to have been 14, of which 8 were males above 16, 5 females above 16, and one male under 16. The total population of the State was 32,442, of which 2581 were negroes.

But the residents must have been a thrifty and pious set, because they seemed to accomplish a great deal with the little which they had to do. In the matter of religion they were a devout people. There had, with that small population, been established three meeting houses in the county, all on the one long main road which by that time had extended from Town Bank to Cold Spring, on by the Baptist church at Court House, and the old Cedar Quaker meeting house at Seaville to Beesley's Point. From the journal of Thomas Chalkley, a traveling Friend from England, who visited Cape May this year, it appears to have been a wilderness between Cohansey and the main road, but Chalkley, under date of 2d month, 1726, of his journey here:

"From Cohansey I went through the wilderness over Maurice River, accompanied by James Daniel, through a miry, boggy way, in which we saw no house for about forty miles, except at the ferry; and that night we got to Richard Townsend's, at Cape May, where we were kindly received. Next day we had a meeting at Rebecca Garretson's, and the day after a pretty large one at Richard Townsend's, and then went down to the Cape, and had a meeting at John Page's, and next day another at Aaron Leaming's; and several expressed their satisfaction with those meetings. I lodged two nights at Jacob Spicer's, my wife's brother. From Cape May, we traveled along the sea-coast to Egg Harbor. We swam our horses over Egg Harbor River, and went over ourselves in canoes; and afterward had a meeting at Richard Sumers, which was a large one as could be expected, considering the people live at such distance from each other."

In this year the tax levied upon Cape May was £157 19s. 8p., and Richard Townsend was entrusted to collect it. This was an average of four shillings for each inhabitant, or about $1.25, so that the tax was not very heavy upon them. On April 9th this year Benjamin Hand was commissioned a lieutenant in Captain Downes' company. On August 30, 1733, the following were appointed a Commission of the Peace: Jacob Spicer, Humphrey Hughs, Robert Townsend, William Smith, Richard Townsend, Henry Young, John Hand, Samuel Eldridge, William Seagrave, Henry Stites, Richard Stites, William Eldridge and Anthony Ludlam, and the judges selected were Jacob Spicer, Humphrey Hughs, Robert Townsend and William Smith.

CHAPTER VIII.

THE RELIGIOUS CONTROVERSIES.

After Rev. John Bradner, the first pastor of the Cold Spring Presbyterian Church, ended his labors there in 1731, he removed to Goshen, Orange county, New York, where he died two years later. His estate was purchased for the church in 1721 by the following persons: Humphrey Hughes, Barnabas Crowell, Nathaniel Rex, George Hand, Jehu Richardson, Yelverson Crowell, John Parsons, George Crawford, Josiah Crowell, Colonel Jacob Spicer, Benjamin Stites, William Mulford, Shamgar Hand, Jeremiah Hand, William Matthews, Joshua Gulicksen, Samuel Eldredge, Samuel Bancroft, Samuel Johnston, Recompence Hand, Jonathan Furman, Eleazer Norcault, Constant Hughes, Ezekiel Eldredge, Cornelius Schellenger, Eleazer Newton, Joshua Crawford, Jehu Hand, Nathaniel Norton, John Matthews.

After the removal of Mr. Bradner the church was without a pastor till 1726, when the Rev. Hugston Hughes was settled and stayed one year only, as he was given "to too strong drink."

From Aaron Leaming's, 2d, manuscript we read:

"My father's father, Christopher Leaming, was an Englishman, and came to America in 1670, and landed near or at Boston; thence to East Hampton. There he lived till about the year 1691, and then leaving his family at Long Island, he came himself to Cape May, which, at that time, was a new county, and beginning to settle very fast, and seemed to promise good advantages to the adventurers. Here he went whaling in the proper season, and at other times worked at the cooper's trade, which was his occupation, and good at the time by reason of the great number of whales caught in those days, made the demand and pay for casks certain. He died of a pleurisie in 1696. His remains were interred at the place called Cape May Town, was situated next above now New England Town Creek, and contained about thirteen houses; but, on the failure of the whale fishery in Delaware Bay, it dwindled into common farms, and the graveyard is on the plantation now owned by Ebenezer Newton. At the first settlement of the county, the chief whaling was in Delaware Bay, and that occasioned the town to be built there; but there has not been one house in that town since my remembrance. In 1734 I saw the graves; Samuel Eldredge showed them to me. They were then about fifty rods from the bay, and the sand was blown to them. The town was between them and the water. There were then some signs of the ruin of the houses. I never saw any East India tea till 1735. It was the Presbyterian parsons, the followers of Whitefield, that brought it into use at Cape May, about the year 1744-5-6, and now it impoverisheth the country."

"Aaron Leaming (the first), of the County of Cape May, departed this life at Philadelphia, of a pleurisie, on the 20th of June, 1746, about five o'clock in the afternoon. He was born at Sag, near East Hampton, on Long Island, Oct. 12th, 1687, being the son of Christopher Leamyeng (as he spelt his name), an Englishman, and Hester, his wife, whose maiden name was Burnet, and was born in New England. Christopher Leamyeng owned a lot at Easthampton, but he came to Cape May, being a cooper, and stayed several years and worked at his trade; and about 1695-6 he died at Cape May, and his land fell to Thomas Leamyeng, his eldest son; the rest was left poor."

Dr. Beesley says:

"Aaron Leaming was bound to Collins, a shoemaker in Connecticut, but did not serve his time out, and came into the Jerseys at about sixteen years of age, very poor, helpless and friendless; embraced the Quaker religion, lived a time at Salem, came to Cape May while yet a boy (in 1693), settled at Goshen, raised cattle, bought a shallop and went by water, gathered a considerable estate, but more knowledge than money. The 12th day of October, 1714, married Lydia Shaw, widow of Wiliam Shaw, and daughter of John Parsons. By her he had four children, Aaron, Jeremian,

Matthias and Elizabeth. He was first a justice of the peace at Cape May. In 1723 he was made clerk of Cape May, and in October, 1727, he was chosen assemblyman, and served in that post till July, 1744. He died June 20, 1748, aged 58, and his remains lie in vault 50, in Christ Church yard, Philadelphia. He was universally confessed to have had a superior knowledge; he amassed large possessions, and did more for his children than any Cape May man has ever done. He left a clear estate, and was buried in the church-yard in Philadelphia. At Salem and Alloway's Creek he became acquainted with Sarah Hall, an aged Quaker lady, mother of Clement Hall. She herself was an eminent lawyer for those times, and had a large collection of books, and very rich, and took delight in my father on account of his sprightly wit and genius, and his uncommon fondness for the law, which he read in her library, though a boy, and very small of his age (for he was a little man), and could not write; for the Presbyterians of New England had taken no other care of his education than to send him to meeting."

Another old record says:

"There was an Indian killed on Foxborough Hill, at Beesley's Point, in 1736, by old Joseph Golden, who got into a quarrel and probably unintentionally killed his opponent. It is said the Indians were so enraged against Golden that he was for a long time obliged to secrete himself to avoid their vengeance. A suit was instituted against him in the county which was removed to Burlington, where he was tried and acquitted; but its great cost obliged him to dispose of that part of his place northwest of the main road to the Point, to Nicholas Stillwell."

Concerning this event "The Pennsylvania Gazette," of August 2-7, 1736, says:

"Cape-May, July 17. Yesterday the Coroner's Inquest view'd the Body of an Indian man, said to be kill'd by Joseph Golden, an English Inhabitant here. Isaiah Stites being present and seeing the whole Difference, gave his Evidence to the Inquest, the Substance whereof was, That Golden having hired the said Indian with another Indian Man and Woman to pull some Flax, was to give them three quarts of Rum for their Labour, with which they got Drunk and quarrel'd with Golden, who then bid them begone from his House, but they refus'd going and gave him ill Language, whereupon a Quarrel ensued, and many Blows passing on both sides. Golden got a small Stick of Cudgel to drive them away, but the two Indians fell upon him and got him down, beat him very much and twisted his Neck, so that he seemed in Danger of his Life; Stites endeavored to part them; at length Golden (with Stites' help) got on his Legs, and then took a larger stick in his Hand to defend himself, bidding the Indians to keep off, but one of them coming violently at him, he struck him on the Head, knock'd him down, and he died without speaking a Word more: It appearing that there was no Difference between Golden and the Indians, before that sudden Quarrel and that they had put him in fear of his Life, before he struck that blow, the Coroner's Inquest found it Manslaughter."

Cape May county grew in its number of inhabitants from 668 in 1726 to 1004 in 1737-8, or an increase of 336 in eleven years. The whites numbered:

Males above 16 years 261
Females above 16 years 219
Males under 16 years 271
Females under 16 years 211

Total whites 962
Negroes and other slaves:
Males above 16 years 12
Females above 16 years 10
Males under 16 years 9
Females under 16 years 11

Total slaves 42

Total in county 1004

The first cattle brought over Cedar Swamp bridge were, according to Aaron Leaming driven over it in the year 1729. The keeping up of the road was troublesome because of the disputes over it. The three precincts of the county were each to care for a third of the road. But the lower precinct never did anything towards its maintenance, while the middle precinct did a small portion of the work. The bulk of the care fell upon the upper precinct, upon which the inhabitants of the others claimed the charge evolved. The others did not hesitate to use it when they wanted to use the only thoroughfare out of the county up the bay side.

The "Pennsylvania Gazette," October 16-23, 1735, contains the following advertisement:

"To be Sold,

"A very good Fulling Mill at Fishing Creek, in the County of Cape May, with all the Materials, as Press, Sheers, Tenters, and Copper; With one hundred Acres of Land. Enquire of Richard Downs."

At this fulling mill homespun cloth was made, and the wool was gotten from the sheep raised on the place. Downs must have sold his place and retired. He had previously been a militiaman, sheriff, and was an industrious citizen. He died in 1747.

"The Pennsylvania Gazette," May 28, 1747, gives the following notice to his debtors and creditors:

"Philadelphia, May 12, 1747.

"All persons indebted to the estate of Captain Richard Downs, late of Cape May, deceas'd, are desired to make speedy payment: And those who have any demands against said estate, are desired to pay the same, within Six months from the date hereof, to

"ELISHA HAND, and
"NATHANIEL FOSTER,
"Executors."

At the Governor's Council, held on December 1, 1739, the following officers were appointed for Cape May county: Jacob Spicer, Humphrey Hughs, Henry Young, William Smith, Robert Townsend, judges of the pleas and justices of the quorum; Henry Stites, Richard Stites, Ebenezer Swain, justices of the quorum; Joseph Ludlam, Junr., William Smith, Junr, and Nathaniel Foster, justices; Elijah Hughs, clerk; Constant Hughes, sheriff, and John Stites, coroner.

The first recorded license, that of a house of entertainment on the seashore, was taken out by Jacob Ludlam, Jr., in the year 1740.

Dr. Beesley says of the cedar swamps in the interior of Cape May:

"Between the years of 1740 and '50 the cedar swamps of the county were mostly located; and the amount of lumber since taken from them is incalculable, not only as an article of trade, but to supply the home demand for fencing and building materials in the county. Large portions of these swamps have been worked a second, and some a third time since located. At the present time there is not an acre of original growth of swamp standing, having all passed away before the resistless sway of the speculator or the consumer. The annual growth is sufficient to fill our wharves yearly with many thousands of rails and sawed lumber."

In 1741 the Baptists at Cape May Court House erected their church, a brick structure, on the land of Jeremiah Hand, who the next year gave what is now the old cemetery to the amount of one acre and three rods, on which the church stood until burned in 1854—113 years. Morgan Edwards, in his sketch, says, 1792, of the church's history:

"This church receives its distinction from the promontory which forms the bay of Delaware on the northeast side; the meeting house measures 34 feet by 26; it was built in 1741; the lot on which it stands contains an acre and three perches, and was given by Jeremiah Hand, esq.; the house is finished as usual, and is distant from Philadelphia 82 miles towards the S. S. E.; there is a fine spring of water by it, which is a great rarity in this part of the country; it is situated in the middle precinct of Cape May county; the families, which usually make up the congregation, are about 90, whereof 63 persons are baptised and in the communion, which is here administered every other month; the church was raised to a body politic July 29, 1786; the minister is Rev. John Stancliff; the salary about 80 pounds.— The above is the present state of Cape May, Apr. 19, 1790."

"Temporalities.

"Plantation, 70 acres, purchased by congregation; land, good; dwelling in tolerable repair; living at 80 pounds."

During the years 1742 and '43 there was an extended religious revival throughout the county. The pastors of the Baptist church and of the Cold Spring Presbyterian church, who at that time was Rev. Samuel Finley, who acted as a supply from 1740 to 1743. Mr. Finley was a man of deep learning, having been educated at the famous "Log College" in Bucks county, Pennsylvania. He became in 1761 the fifth president of Princeton College, and remained at the head of that seat of learning until 1766. The Baptist pastor and exhorter of that season were Nathanael Jenkins, Senr., and his son, Nathanael, respectively. Morgan Edwards, the Baptist historian of the event, gives his version of the event this way:

"In 1742, in 1743, the spirit of religion was raised high at the Cape; owing partly to the preaching of Baptist ministers, and partly to the labours of Presbyterian ministers of the new light order; but many of the latter's disciples joining the Baptists caused much grumbling; and issued in a public dispute and polemical writings. The occasion was as follows: About 1742 there was, at the Cape, a remarkable stir of the religious kind; this stir was owing partly to the preaching of Baptist ministers, and partly to the labors of Presbyterian ministers of the new light order; but some of one party's converts joining the other party caused a howling among the losing shepherds, and issued in a public challenge; Mr. Morgan (Rev. Abel Morgan, A. M.) accepted the challenge. His antagonist was Rev. (afterwards Dr.) Samuel Finley; the contest ended as usual, viz., in double triumph."

The courts were usually held in private dwellings previous to 1745. But a new court house had now been built, and the first court held in it was on the third Tuesday of May, 1745, when the following officers and jurors were present: Justices—Henry Young, Henry Stites, Ebenezer Swain and Nathaniel Foster. Sheriff—Jacob Hughes. Clerk—Elijah Hughes, Sr. Grand Jurors—John Leonard, John Scull, Noah Garrison, Peter Corson, Joseph Corson, George Hollingshead, Clement Daniels, Benjamin Johnson, Jeremiah Hand, Thomas Buck, Joseph Badcock, Isaiah Stites, Joseph

Edwards, James Godfrey, Thomas Smith, Isaac Townsend, Ananias Osborne, Robert Cresse and Thomas Hewit.

The number of residents of the county this year was 1188, according to the census taken by order of the Governor of the province. The population was divided as follows: 306 males above 16 years, 284 males under 16 years, 272 females above 16 years, 274 females under 16 years, 54 Quakers or reputed Quakers, 30 male slaves, 22 female slaves; 1188 whole number of inhabitants; 184 increase since 1737-8.

The Third French and Indian War (known as King George's War) was in progress from 1744 to '48, and there were several Cape May men commissioned. While none of them are known to have gone to Louisburg or the Canadian provinces, they were to be ready to do duty at home should the French marine come upon the Jersey shore. The commissions granted were:

August 3, 1747. Ebenezer Swaine, Esq., to be captain of a company of militia.

August 3, 1747. Thomas Ross, Gent., to be lieutenant of a company for the lower precinct, of which Ebenezer Swaine is captain.

Ellis Hughes to be ensign in the same company.

Aug. 3, 1747. Jonathan Foreman, gent., captain of a company of foot militia for the middle precinct, of which Nicholas Gibbon is colonel.

John Leonard, gent, to be colonel.

George Hand to be ensign.

April 8, 1748. Henry Young to be colonel of militia.

The value which the West Jersey proprietors placed upon land in Cape May county at this time can be surmised in reading the instructions from a committee of the West Jersey Society to the agent of the Society, under date of London, August 16, 1749, a portion of which reads: "We desire you will endeavor to dispose of what quantity you can of our Lands at Cape May at Twenty Pounds or more p' hundred Acres New York Money but not under that price and not less than One thousand Acres to be located &c. all together and not in different parts and to be free of all charges of Conveyance &c."

CHAPTER IX.

WEST JERSEY SOCIETY RIGHTS.

In the middle of the eighteenth century the two most prominent men of Cape May county were Aaron Leaming, Jr., better known as the second, and Jacob Spicer, 2d, who were also possessed of a reputation all over the province of New Jersey as brilliant men, with practical and methodical ways. Their fathers, Aaron Leaming and Jacob Spicer, had held many prominent offices before them, been in the Assembly, and paved the way for their sons to easily succeed them. Aaron Leaming, 2d, first entered the Assembly in 1740, and remained a member for about thirty years, with but two or three short intercessions. He was born July 6, 1715, O. S., and was a general favorite of the people. He possessed a splendid education and was an expert and clear penman; being a voluminous writer, to whom posterity owes much for the records and diaries he kept. He was a man of considerable industry and acquired much land.

Dr. Beesley says he "was one of the most prominent and influential men the county ever produced. The family lost nothing in caste through him. He was a heavy land operator, and a member of the Legislature for thirty years. From the manuscript he left behind him, which is quite voluminous, it would appear he was a man of great industry and much natural good sense, well educated for the times, and withal a little tinged with aristocracy; a trait of character not unexceptionable under the royal prerogative. No man ever received greater honors from the county, and none, perhaps, better deserved them."

Young Spicer was born the year after Leaming, and was also possessed of a good, practical education, and had the faculty of acquiring wealth and of grasping every opportunity which presented itself. He first entered the Assembly in 1745 and remained in it with Leaming for about twenty years. The Assembly about this time wanted the grants and concessions made to the lords proprietors and the laws of both East and West Jersey compiled, and Leaming and Spicer were the two men who finally compiled them. The Assembly's first act in this matter is recorded in Aaron Leaming's own handwriting in the State Library, and reads:

"Upon Saturday, the second day of February, 1750, Robert Lawrence, of Monmouth; William Cooks, of Burlington; William Hancock, of Salem; Jacob Spicer, of Cape May; Hendrick Fisher, of Somerset; John Wetherill, of Middlesex, and Aaron Leaming, of Cape May, gentlemen, being of the House of Assembly," were selected a committee to inspect the "Laws, Records and other Fundamental Constitutions relating to the first Settlement of New Jersey in each Division." The "Pennsylvania Journal," of November 8, 1750, contained the advertisement that the laws of New Jersey from 1700 to 1750 would be published and that Leaming and Spicer would receive subscriptions for the same. This committee went immediately and diligently to work on its task. On the following Thursday Chairman Lawrence made a report, wherein were shown the grants of Charles II to James, Duke of Yorke, and from the Duke of Yorke to Lord John Berkeley and Sir George Cartaret, and that there were "Certain Concessions and Agreements, Which Concessions and Agreements were esteemed the fundamental Plan of Government." Lawrence also reported the scheme of the twenty-four proprietors of East Jersey and the plan of government for West Jersey, and showing that different laws were passed for the two divisions according to the concessions. The committee also said that as some of the laws, particularly those appertaining to the taxing of lands and "Securing of Men's Property in Lands," were "lodged in several difficult Hands and not come so fully to the Knowledge of the Publick as could be desired," and recommended that all these things be published. The Assembly thereupon ordered them to be printed with "convenient dispatch and collected in one Volume," and the law and matter were to be corrected by the originals. Another committee was subsequently appointed by the committee, who could, if they wished, supervise this work. Speaker Nevill and Samuel Smith, the historian, were to have charge of the printing, and 170 books were to be printed at two pence per sheet.

Leaming and Spicer were the two most active members of the committee, and they had a great deal of research to do. The old State papers were not kept in the order in those days and with the care that they are now, because their value was not then realized. Some of the most important instruments were the hardest to secure, and once the committee was ordered to search for the "Instrument or Record or the Surrender made by the Proprietors of this Colony at the Surrender of the Government to the Crown; and also for what Concessions were entered into by the Crown at the Time of the Acceptance of Such Surrender in behalf of the People." On October 16, 1751, the committee, or three of them, were given power to write to London, and ask the New Jersey agent to send attested copies of the surrender.

The work, which finally, by authority or not implicitly given, devolved upon the two Cape May members, progressed until 1755. Aaron Leaming, in his diary, writes under date of the latter year, "Feb'y 2d. Spicer & I began compiling the New Jersey constitution," and again, under date of 1756 says: Nov. 29 Spicer & I began the Table of the Jersey constitution." In the meantime, when these men were compiling these laws, on August 20, 1755, an act for the support of the government was passed, in which it was stated that Leaming and Spicer had been empowered to print the laws at two pence per sheet, and binding allowances. They were to be bound in calfskin, and the details of payment is here stated.

On March 27, 1758, 126 volumes had been printed, and on the following 15th of April the final settlement was made by ordering that Leaming and Spicer be paid "after Three months Trial of the Sale," at the rate of £1 18s. 6d. per volume.

In 1750 Nicholas Stillwell, of Egg Harbor, took out a license to keep a house of entertainment; in 1752 Jacob Spicer at Cold Spring; in 1761 Aaron Leaming on the seashore two miles above the court house; in 1763 Christopher Leaming; in 1764 Daniel Hand at the Court House, and in 1768 Memucan Hughes and James Whilldin at and near Cape Island.

The second church established within the county, or at least which had Cape May residents as communicants, by the Baptists was at Tuckahoe in 1751, of which Morgan Edwards says (1792):

"Tuckihoe.

"Church is distinguished from a river which runs near meeting house; the house measures 28 feet by 24; it was built 1751, in Egg Harbour township, and county of Gloucester, 60 miles S. E. Philadelphia, lot on which stands contains about one acre, and was gift James Hubbard, deed dated May 15, 1750; house is now in ruinous condition, but the people talking of building another, in a more convenient place; Alderman Benezet promises to give them land, timber, glass and nails; there is another house which the church occupies, but it is not their own; it stands on May's landing, about 12 miles off of this. The families which usually assemble at Tuckahoe are about 60, whereof 63 persons are baptised, and in the communion, here administered the first Sunday of every month. Salary about 20 pounds.—About present state of church Ap. 14, 1790.

"History.

"When the gospel began to be preached at Dividing creek, by Rev. Nathanael Jenkins, several from these parts repaired thither, and received serious impressions; the consequence was, that said Jenkins was invited to preach among them; he came, and notwithstanding his age, and Morris river, stood in the way; and baptised some, who joined Dividing-creek; Mr. Sheppard, of Salem, visited these parts and baptised others; and after their deaths, Mr. Kelsey preached here and baptised. In 1770 Rev. James Sutton came hither with a view to settle among them; this put them on thinking of becoming a distinct church; accordingly, they were, July 23, 1771, incorporated, by the assistance of Rev. Mess. Vanhorn and Heaton; the names were, Rev. James Sutton, Joseph Savage, Esq., Jonathan Smith, William Goldin, Jacob Garrison, Joseph Ingersol, Thomas Ireland, Elias Smith, John Ingles, Esq., Lemuel Sayres, Lemuel Edwards, John Scull, Isaac Scull, Katharine Garrison, Mary Goldin, Jaen Ingersol, Debora Lore, Tabitha Scull, Mary Ireland, Elizabeth Garrison, Jaen Camp, Mary Camp, Abigail Scull and Catharine Weaver."

Rev. James Sutton was pastor until 1772; Rev. William Lock, 1773 to 1779, and Rev. Isaac Bonnell from 1783 to date (1792).

There has been found in the old burying ground of the Baptist church at the head of the Tuckahoe River these corroborative fac-similes of biographies and epitaphs:

Robert Campbell son of Henry and Ellen Campbell. Died March 20-1754.

Rev. Isaac Bonnel Departed this life July 25-1794, His age 64 years.

Ann Groom the wife of Rev'd Peter Groom, Departed this life May 4-1796, 46 years old.

Millicent Price, Departed this life July 28-1826, Age 56 years and 4 months.

An extremely interesting tomb is that of the Reverend Peter Groom, pastor of the Baptist Church at West Creek. The following mortuary lines show his worth:

"The friend of man
The friend of truth
The friend of age
The guide of youth."

He departed this life January 16, 1807.

In the year 1752 an association of persons was formed for the purpose of purchasing of the West Jersey Society their interests in the county, in order to procure the natural privileges of fishing and fowling and all the articles of luxury and use to be obtained from the bays and sounds, which were held in high estimation. The agreement reads as follows:

"Whereas, The West New Jersey Society once Stood seized in their Demense as of Fee of a certain Ninety Thousand acres of Land Situate at, and containing the chiefest part of that Island or Tract of Land called Cape may between Delaware Bay and Great Egg harbour River, which said

Society having sold and Transferred the greatest and most valuable parts of the said Ninety thousand acres to divers persons; And Whereas there is yet remaining unsold a parcel of broken and sunken marshes, sounds, creeks, barren Lands &c as of very little value, which never the less if the Same Should be purchased by any particular person or persons in large Tracts it might be an inducement for such purchaser to endeavour to monopolize the Fishery, oystering &c which nature seems to have intended for a General blessing to the Poor, and others who have bought the Lands and settled contiguous thereto And many of us the Subscribers having already given advanced prices for our Lands by reason of the vicinity of the said priviledges, are now unwilling to be deprived thereof; Wherefore we the Subscribers each and every of us do each of us seperately for our selves and for each of our heirs, Executors Administrators & assigns associate covenant Grant Bargain and agree to and with all and every other of the said Subscribers their heirs and assigns in manner and form following—To Wit—That we will each and every of us associate and Join in the purchasing of the Said Society the aforesaid unsold parts of the said Land which when So purchased To be holden in equal Shares amongst all and every of us the Subscribers Our heir and Assigns in common and undivided forever, as Tenants in Common, Except such parts thereof as we Shall Sell and Separate off as hereafter is mentioned And that Due Justice may be rendered unto all persons we do hereby covenant and agree that if any particular person or persons whither Subscriber or not hath actually a Survey made by Henry Young, Esqr. upon any part which we Shall So purchase, or if any Tract that is unsurveyed Shall lie within the inclosures or at the head or foot of any particular persons Land or Plantation Situate within the Said County if Such person discovers the Same to be there and will first consent to give the price the Said Society now Sells at In that case we will Sell the Same to Such person at a price not higher than the said Society hath immediately before this time been used to Sell for; The purchase money whereof shall be put into the General Stock and applyed towards the payment of the consideration that we Shall be obliged to Give for the

Said Land So by us intended to be purchased. And Further if any particular person who is a Subscriber hereto hath by himself, or his Predecessor in Title hath, actually made a Purchase of any of the Said Societys Said Lands and Such person Shall Doubt the validity of his Title to the whole or any part thereof In that case a Deed of confirmation and Release Shall be Granted Gratis to Such Subscribers he being at all charges—And for the Raising a Fund for carrying the Said undertaking into execution we each and every of us for and on behalf of ourselves Our heirs Executors and administrators and Assigns Do Consent—associate covenant Grant Bargain & agree to and with all the rest of the Said Subscribers their heirs & Assigns that the said money requisite for Such consideration. Shall be raised levyed and Assessed upon us our heirs Executors and Administrators according to the Several Estates that we Severally hold in the manner that other Taxes are usually raised by Law in New Jersey And Further that we will at some General Conference or meeting on the Said Subject chuse Such officers & persons as are or Shall be necessary for laying and raising the Said Intended Tax. and also chuse (when necessary) Such and So many persons as we Shall think Suitable and convenient to go and agree for the Said unsold Lands from the agents of the said West Jersey Society Provided never the less that if thirty Persons Freeholders of the County of Cape May do not Sign this Association the whole and every part thereof, Shall be void and of no effect—And Further that the above said Commonages of Fishery oystering &c Shall be construed to remain and extend to all the Children of us the Subscribers & all their children & children's children and so forever—And in any marshes that we Shall Sell the aforesaid commonages Shall be reserved thereout and not transferred but remain and above. And in case of any Doubts in Titles, when we Grant Releases, they Shall be so worded as to confirm the Same Estate as if the original purchase had been good & value—And that no Resurveys on any Persons Land whatever Shall be claimed or allowed on any pretentions whatsoever. Provided always that if any consideration Money Shall be paid for any Lands to be Sold by virtue of the directions of this agreement, after the consideration for the aforesaid Land Shall be fully paid, then Such money to be equally Divided amongst the Subscribers hereto in proportion to the respective Shares the Said Subscribers hereto Shall Severally pay towards Such consideration.

The instrument was dated November 20, 1752, and was signed by the following persons: James Edwards, James Hedges, Samuel Bancroft, Jonathan Fourman, Recompence Hand, William Matthews, Jacob Spicer, Ebenezer Swain, Nathaniel Foster, Richard Stillwell, Ephraim Edwards, Isaac Whilldin, Jacob Hughes, John Hase, Daniel Cresse, Benjamin Laughton, James Whilldin, Thomas Bancroft, Jacob Hand, Jere Leaming, Jacob Richardson, Joshua Shaw, Samuel Crowell, Cornelius Schelinks, Barnabas Crowell, Eleazer Crawford, Isaac Newton, George Stites, William Stites, Richard Shaw, Downes Edmonds, John Bancroft, Ebenezer Johnson, Uriah Smith, Aaron Leaming, Thomas Hand, Jonadab Jenkins, Carman Smith, Daniel Swaine, Jeremiah Hand, John Chester, John Smith, Elihu Smith, Marcy Ross, Thomas Leaming, Joseph Hewit, William Robenson, Joseph Hewit, Elisha Crowell, John Eldredge, Robert Parsons, William Simpkins Reuben Hewit, Amos Johnson, Timothy Hand, Ezekiel Hand, Daniel Hand, Silas Hand, Isaiah Hand, James Hand, Richard Stites, Caleb Newton, Caleb Newton on behalf of Thomas Page, Christopher Lupton, Ebenezer Newton, Henry Hand, William Flower, Eleazer Hand, Samuel Eldredge, Daniel Eldredge, Nezer Swain, George Taylor, Lewis Cresse, James Cresse, Shamgar Hand, Jonathan Smith, Daniel Hand, Robert Cresse, Benjamin Johnson aty of ye seaside, Henry Leonard, Annanias Osborne, John Leonard, Michael Iszard, Richard Smith, David Corson, Zebulon Swaine, Nathaniel Jenkins, Junr., Benjamin Johnson of Goshen, Richard Swain, Silas Goff, David Hildreth, Christopher Foster, Joshua Hildreth, Joseph Hildreth, Samuel Foster, John Hughes, Edward Church, Jeremiah Hand, John Willets, Joseph Corson, John Scull, John Van Gilder, Samuel Townsend, Daniel Townsend, Arthur Cresse, Esaiah Stites, Josiah Edwards, Jacob Corson, Andrew Corson, William Robinson, Isaac Luldam, Abraham Van Gilder, Isaac Willetts, John Goff, Isaac Bauer, David Corson, James Godfrey, Isaac Townsend, John Corson, John Machey, Stephen Young, Thomas Hewit, Wm. Smith, James Hildreth, Thomas Taylor, Seth Bowen, Franc's Crandol, John Hand, alias Willet, John Shaw, Jacob Smith, Henry Fisher, John Smith, Nathan Johnson, Thos. Johnson, Thomas Smith, James Miller, John Isard, Abraham Hand, James Townsend, Silvanus Townsend, Junr.

It was difficult to name a valuation upon a right so endeared to the people as this. This association being slow and cautious in its movements was no doubt astounded, in the year 1756, to find that Jacob Spicer, upon his own responsibility, had superseded them, and had purchased the right of the society, through their acknowledged agent, Dr. Johnson, of Perth Amboy, not only in natural privileges, but in the unlocated land in the whole county. Spicer, although he did not attempt or desire to prevent the people from using these privileges as they had heretofore done, received for his share in the transaction a large amount of obloquy and hostile feeling, which required all the energy and moral courage he possessed to encounter.

In 1756 the time had come when the remaining West Jersey proprietors were to at last dispose of their rights. As heretofore mentioned, an association had been formed in the lower precinct to purchase them. Dr. Coxe, who originally held most of the soil, made five sales altogether through his agent, George Taylor, to the West Jersey Society. The latter had by 1756 carried on the sale of its lands for about sixty-four years, and had nothing much left by this time excepting "vacant lands," and the natural privileges which they possessed of the sounds and bays. For the "vacant lands," Aaron Leaming, 2d, and Jacob Spicer, 2d, were competitors, but as the latter overreached his colleague he secured them. While they, two of the most popular men of that time, were opposed to each other at home in consequence of their land speculations, yet when at Trenton, as representatives of their county, they united their energies and were faithful and efficient public servants. In the sale of lands by the West Jersey Society they always included what was termed "vacant lands." Fifteen per centum over what was actually purchased was conveyed for the building of roads, and when these proposed roads were not constructed the land became vacant.

On August 2, 1756, Jacob Spicer, 2d, also purchased of the West Jersey Society (for £300) all the remain lands and privileges of that organization in Cape May county, consisting of uplands, beaches, swamps, savannahs, cripples, marshes, meadows, oyster beds, oyster grounds, clam flats, shores, bays, sounds, thoroughfares, creeks, guts, rivulets, brooks, runs, streams, pools and ponds of water, and finally all fast lands and waters, etc., woods, trees, mines, minerals, royalties, quarries, hawkings, huntings, fishing, fowling, etc." Dr. Maurice Beesley says:

"It has been handed down that Spicer obtained the grant for the proprietary right in Cape May, of Dr. Johnson, agent of the society at Perth Amboy, at a time when the influence of the wine bottle had usurped the place of reason, or he could not have obtained it for so inconsiderable a sum as three hundred pounds; and that the Doctor, sensible he had betrayed the trust reposed in him, left the society at his death a thousand pounds as a salvo."

Spicer, while a man who believed in thrift, had a sympathetic side to his nature, which is revealed by a record in his diary, under date of October 6, 1756, concerning the result of a missionary meeting. It reads: "We the subscribers do promise to pay the Rev. John Brainard, missionary among the Indians at Cranbery, or to his order, the sum affixed to our names for the purchase of lands for the uses of the missionary society: Charles Read, £2 14s.; Jacob Spicer, £2 0s.; Joseph Yard, £1 17s.; Robert Ogden, £3; Stephen Cresse, £1 10s."

CHAPTER X.

JACOB SPICER AND HIS SAYINGS.

The accounts of the treasurer of the division of West Jersey for the year 1754 show that Aaron Leaming on April 27 turned in a bundle of canceled money from Cape May to the amounts of £154:02:06, £1:0:0, and October 21, £1:17:6, and that Jeremiah Leaming paid for the support of the government, November 24, taxes amounting to £33:08:04, and on the same date other money, viz., £25:11:05¾. During the same year Leaming and Spicer, who were members then of the Legislature, received on April 15 these amounts: Leaming, £22:10:0; Spicer, £33:10:0.

In 1754 the French and Indian War broke out on the frontier of the English colonies and lasted until 1763. It was to decide the question whether France or England should rule over the American continent. The English outnumbered the French colonists ten to one, but the latter got possession of the two chief rivers of the country—the St. Lawrence and the Mississippi. To clinch their hold they built fort after fort, until by this date, 1754, they had a chain of them extending from Quebec, in Canada, to the Great Lakes, and thence down the Wabash, the Illinois and the Mississippi to the Gulf of Mexico. The principal scenes of the conflicts of this war, in which the English were finally successful, were upon the Ohio River and the Canadian borders.

Matters looked so serious just at this period that a convention of the northern colonies met at Albany to consider what mode of defense should be made. Most of the Indians were aiding the French, but the Iroquois Indians, who were staunch friends of the English, sent some of their tribe to the convention and warned them that if the colonists did not take up arms the French would drive every Englishman out of the country. This same year the Assembly of

New Jersey passed a bill making current £70,000 in bills of credit for a fund to assist in dispossessing the French on the frontier near the Ohio River, and Cape May's share in this expense was £1002, the raising of which was given in charge of the Loan Office Commissioners, who were to have an annual salary of £10. The bills, when paid by the colony, were to be cut and burned.

West Jersey was to furnish sixty men to go to the New York frontier, but whether Cape May sent any we do not have record to show. But we find that Aaron Leaming, with two other non-residents of the county, as a Colony Committee, was paid £171:10:0 to transport Captain Woodward's company and others, and for clothing for the same. This was New Jersey's first expedition. Aaron Leaming was during the period quartermaster-general of the province.

The next year England sent over General Braddock to operate on the Ohio, and the Jersey troops were sent north into New York and destined for Eastern Canada. At home in Cape May there were faithful Lenni-Lenapes, who were free from barbarities. Jacob Spicer, who was appointed by the colony commissioner for purchasing provisions for five hundred troops on the Canadian expedition, rallied the people of Cape May "to meet the great demand of the time," and demanded "a thousand pounds of stockings" " for our men in the field." Concerning the feeling in the county at the beginning of this last inter-colonial contest, Jacob Spicer, in his diary, under date of November 1, 1755, says:

"Attended the Baptist meeting house according to promise, to receive the advice of my constituents upon the subject of the Governor's calling the Assembly. It was expected he would insist on great matters to be done for the defense of the country, but so trivial was this affair that only Messrs. James Whilldin, Jeremiah Hand, Thomas Leaming, John Leonard, and some others, to the number of eight or ten, attended, whereas but a short time before I happened to be riding past by ye Court House on a court day and saw a great number of people, by estimation not less than 200, which to all appearances were drawn by idle curiosity, or trifling speculation. It is not astonishing that man dignified by nature should esteem himself so little as to pass his time in trifling speech, pitching of a bar, throwing of a stone, hopping, jumping, dancing, running, and at the same time not think himself obliged to attend to the defense of his country, or his exemption from debt bondage."

In March the following officers were appointed to command a regiment of foot: Henry Young, colonel; Ebenezer Swain, lieutenant-colonel; Jeremiah Leaming, major; John Shaw, adjutant; and the officers of the company for the "Lower Precinct" were Silaw Shaw, captain; Jeremiah Hand, lieutenant, and Daniel Swain, ensign; while those to command the officers of the "Upper Precinct" were Jacob Hand, captain; Lewis Cresse, lieutenant, and Jacob Richardson, ensign. On November 12 the order was given to Nicholas Gibbon to have the Cumberland and Cape May company ready.

For the clothing and feeding of the "Second Expedition" (probably to Canada), according to the accounts of the colony's treasurer, Jacob Spicer received these sums at the several times as recited:

1755.—Sept. 27.—"for cloathes," £768:12:00.
Oct. 6.—"for cloathes," £574:02:06.
Oct. 18.—"for cloathes," £55:07:00.
Nov. 5.—"for provisions," £753:15:00.
Dec. 5.—"for provisions," £573:15:00.
Dec. 17.—"for supplies," £544:00:6.
1756.—March 5.—"for tents, kettles, &c.," £526:10:00.
March 29.—"for ———," £25:00:0.
May 4.—"for lead, &c.," £100:00:00.

Samuel Smith, treasurer of West Jersey, reports of having received from Jeremiah Leaming, collector, by the hands of Josiah Hand, on November 22, 1755, the two separate sums of £25:11:05¾ and £50:02:06, as Cape May's share for the support of the government. This year Cape May lands, by law, were not to be valued above 20 nor below 5 acres to the £100. The share of the colony assessment was fixed at £25:11:05¾. This year Jacob Spicer received £27:18:00, and Aaron Leaming received £15:18:00 for their services in attendance as members of the General Assembly.

The agitation for a punishment of those who sold "strong

"drink" to the Indians culminated in the General Assembly's passage of an act in 1757, imposing a penalty upon such offenders. Spicer and Leaming were supporters of the measure. Spicer also had his opinions upon the too liberal use of liquor among the white people, too, and this is what he says about the habit in his diary, under date of July 16, 1756:

"I am informed that within two months past Henry Hand and Thomas Walker, James Reney and Marcy Ross, brought each of them into the Lower precinct a hogshead of rum. Hand's and Walker's is expended, and it is supposed that Reney and Ross have sold between them 1 hhd. in two months, consequently 18 in a year in the Lower precinct. But as it has been harvest time and the consumption something greater than common, the rate is, say, 12 hhds. in a year to the Lower precinct, or 1200 gallons, which at a moderate retail price of three shillings and six pence per gallon, is £210 per year in cash, a larger sum than ever I have received in money for goods both wet and dry, since I have traded in the said precinct, upwards of two years.

"So that it's not the dry goods, but the rum is our hurt, since it is frequently bartered for the industry of the populace, and sold for long credit."

While Spicer was a merchant he did much farming, and on July 5, 1757, he made the following note of the yield of corn on one of his fields: "I planted 1¾ acres of Indian corn in the orchard near my dwelling and it was esteemed good, especially near the house, and it yielded by measure but 27 bushels of good and 6¼ do. of offal corn, being 33¼ bushels in the whole, and at the rate of 17 bushels per acre, good and bad together. I am much at loss to reconcile what I have sometimes heard with respect to the greater yield of corn. I am sure 20 bushels per acre may be esteemed very good corn."

The knitting of mittens in those days occupied all the spare moments of the housewives and the ambitious maiden, but a great deal of the encouragement of the development of this industry is given to the wife of the eminent Benjamin Franklin.

Mrs. Franklin sent down to one of the fair daughters of the neighborhood of Cold Spring a cap of the fashion then in vogue. It was worn to meeting. The other maidens saw it and wanted caps like it. The people saw in it an opportunity to knit mittens and send them up to the "village on the Delaware," to exchange for caps and gaudy ribbons.

The effect of Mrs. Franklin's gift cannot be better explained than by the reading of a letter which Dr. Franklin sent to Benjamin Vaughan from Passy, France, on July 26, 1748, while discoursing "on the benefits and evils of luxury." The letter in part said:

"The skipper of the Shallop, employed between Cape May and Philadelphia, had done us some service for which he refused to be paid. My wife, understanding he had a daughter, sent her a present of a new-fashioned cap. Three years afterward this skipper, being at my house with an old farmer of Cape May, his passenger, he mentioned the cap and how much his daughter had been pleased with it. 'But,' said he, 'it proved a dear cap to our congregation.' How so? 'When my daughter appeared with it at meeting it was so much admired that all the girls resolved to get such caps from Philadelphia, and my wife and I computed that the whole would not have cost less than £100.' 'True,' said the farmer, 'but you do not tell all the story. I think the cap was, nevertheless, an advantage to us, for it was the first thing that put our girls upon knitting worsted mittens for sale at Philadelphia that they might have wherewithal to buy caps and ribbons there, and you know that that industry has continued and is likely to continue and increase to a much greater value and answer better purposes.' Upon the whole, I was more reconciled to this little piece of luxury, since not only the girls were made happier by having fine caps but Philadelphians by the supply of warm mittens."

In 1756 Jacob Spicer advertised to barter goods for all kinds of produce and commodities, and among the rest particularly designated wampum. He offered a reward of £5 to the person that should manufacture the most wampum, and advertised: "I design to give all due encouragement to the people's industry, not only by accepting cattle, sheep and staple commodities in a course of barter, but also a large quantity of mittens will be taken, and indeed a clam shell formed in wampum, a yarn thrum, a goose quill, a

JACOB SPICER AND HIS SAYINGS.

horse hair, a hog's bristle, or a grain of mustard seed, if tendered, shall not escape my reward, being greatly desirous to encourage industry, as it is one of the most principal expedients under the favor of Heaven, that can revive our drooping circumstances at this time of uncommon but great and general burden."

In his household, according to his records, he had a minutely systematic way of business. Under the superintendence of a tailor, tailoress and shoemaker the apparel of his family was made. The sons were taught to cobble shoes, the daughters to make clothing and knit. In 1757 Spicer speaks thusly in his diary of his household expenses:

"It is conceived that £14 13s. 4d., as above estimated, will be adequate to furnish all the boys with leather for breeches, a vest for Elisha, a coat and vest for Jack; calico for long and short gowns for all the girls, stripe linen and stripe linsey for short gowns and petticoats for the said girls, and a tammy quilt for Judith, for defraying of which £14 13s. 4d.—220 pairs of mittens at 16d. per pair, will be needed, which will require 44 pounds of wool, which will take 44 days' work of two girls to spin, and I'll pay for that or hire equivalent in the knitting if the girls will do the remainder of the service.

"I must pursue the following maxims invariably for the present year. I must fabricate 220 pairs of mittens, and for the present and future year, if I live, I must supply my boys with leather for winter breeches; about £3 8s. will be sufficient to furnish them all—24 pounds of grey skin at 2s. per pound, and 2s. 6d. for dressing and freight of each skin, supposed to consist of 8 skins, tho' I think summac red or short grey will be most profitable to buy as the hair is almost nothing, which is not so when the skin is fully coated.

"In the next place I must buy my leather and heels, and spin my shoe thread, and have all my shoes made up in the house, for I find if I even hire 'em made out, find my leather, the shoemaker gains, in all probability a profit of 3s. on the leather of a man's pair of shoes, waste in cutting excepted, for which I should think 4d. a large allowance, and the scraps of sole leather may be converted into lists; and an eye may be seen to the cutting, and the thread may be had from the family labour. And when I am shoeing my family it is requisite to supply each individual with two pairs, to prevent shoes being worn too green. And as a farther advantage in purchasing my leather, I can at all times take care that it be of good quality, and by having it made up together and in my house will avoid the loss of time in running after the same; and so I should get one of the boys instructed so as to mend shoes, to save money and prevent loss of time. The shoemaker should be obliged to do his day's work or pay for his board.

"In the next place I should hire by taylor and Tayloress in the house, and oblige my girls to assist in the service, for by this means my diet and female service will become a part of the Taylor's bill; besides, their day's wages, as far as I can discern, are not proportionate to the sum in gross they ask for their service, and having the clothes made at home and together there may be an oversight of the cloth and cut, and the loss of time in going to have clothes taken measure for and tried on.

"The best time of hiring I think is such seasons of the year when the weather is not so cold as to need a fire.

"In the next place it will be requisite to consult a blacksmith to know what allowance he will make for iron and steel.

"Daniel Harcourt informs me that mittens sell for 3s. and stockings at 7s. York money, at Albany, without any regard to the colour, and many of 'em ordinary too—but wampum will not sell since the reduction of Oswego, before that it was in great demand, equal if not superior to silver in value, and there were 60 or 70 wampum shops in Albany."

What he charged himself with under the head of "wets" would now be considered expensive. In a year he charged himself with using "fifty-two gallons rum, ten do wine, and two barrels cyder."

He gives us the following estimate of the resources and consumption of the county in the year 1758:

"And as my family consists of twelve in number, including myself, it amounts to each individual £7 3s. 8½d. annual consumption of foreign produce and manufacture. But perhaps the populace in general may not live at a propor-

JACOB SPICER AND HIS SAYINGS.

tionate expense with my family. I'll only suppose their foreign consumption may stand at £4 to an individual, as the county consisted of 1100 souls in the year 1746, since which time it has increased; then the consumption of this county of foreign manufacture and produce, will stand at £4400 annually, nearly one-half of which will be linens.

"The stock article of the county is about	£1200
There is at least ten boats belonging to the county which carry oysters; and admit they make three trips fall and three trips spring, each, and carry 100 bushels each trip, that makes 6000 bushels at what they neat 2s. per bushel	600
There is 14 pilots, which at £30 per annum	420
Mitten articles for the present year	500
Cedar posts	300
White Cedar lumber	500
Add for boards	200
Pork and gammons	200
Deer skins and venison hams	120
Furs and feathers	100
Hides and tallow	120
Flax seed, neats' tongues, bees' wax and myrtle	80
Tar	60
Coal	30
	£4430

Annual consumption of county	£4400	
Add public taxes	160	
For a Presbyterian minister	60	
For a Baptist minister	40	
Education of youth	90	
Doctor for man and beast	100	
	£4850	
		£420

In arrear £420, to be paid by some uncertain fund, or left as a debt."

It appears by the above statement, the mitten article of trade in 1758 amounted to the sum of £500, which was quite a reward to the female industry of the county.

On June 28, 1758, he says: "Mr. Caleb Newton and his wife propose to deal with me for a large number of mittens, 200 pairs and upwards. I told them if they were of extra quality I would give 18 pence in barter."

In another place he advertises for a thousand pounds of woolen stockings to supply the army, then in war with the French. Concerning stockings which sold the best, he wrote on July 5, 1757, that "Dark blue, light blue, and clear white, if large and fine, are the stockings that will sell best. Had mine been of that color they would have sold, the generality of people preferring a knit stocking to a wove one. They wash stockings in soap lather and draw them on a stocking board, which gives them that fine proportion and gloss they generally leave."

Spicer succeeded in procuring a quantity of the wampum, and before sending it off to Albany, and a market, weighed a shot-bag full of silver coin and the same shot-bag full of wampum, and found the latter most valuable by ten per cent. The black wampum was most esteemed by the Indians, the white being of little value.

He wrote, June 14, 1758:

"Told Enos Schillinks that while I trade I would venture to take 30£ value in wampum for such goods as I have wet and dry, and would endeavor to help him to provision if I conveniently could, and would suffer with him till his debt is paid to take out one-half of all such wampum as he should bring in supply of his wants." And on the same day he wrote: "I'll take in discount or barter a large quantity of wampum, both white and black, if offered and good in quality, such as the pattern left with Mr. Leek and here explained: It must be small, round and smooth, with square ends not broken. The black must be clear black without white spots or threads interspersed, which lessens the value and renders it unsalable, for it can't be too black, and it must be strung 100 on a string, with a little tuft of red at the ends when tied together."

Thompson, in his history of Long Island, page 60, says: "The immense quantity which was manufactured here may account for the fact that, in the most extensive shell banks left by the Indians, it is rare to find a whole shell; having all been broken in the process of making the wampum."

Commenting upon this Dr. Beesley says: "This curious fact applies especially to Cape May, where large deposits of shells are to be seen, mostly contiguous to the bays and sounds; yet it is rare to see a piece larger than a shilling, and these mostly the white part of the shell, the black having been selected for wampum."

Writing of spinning on February 22, 1757, he noted that "It seems to be an advantageous way of spinning our on linen wheel if it be patched over on the back of the hatchel. If spun this way it will answer for warp, and may be boiled as linen yarn, the twist being harder—but if spun on the great wheel will only answer for filling."

Concerning the sizes of dwellings, and their cost in those days, Spicer, on the same day, wrote: "John Mackey's house is 40x20, single story, with a hip, for which Joseph Edwards is to get the timber, frame cover, make the window frames, sashes, put the lights in, make the outside doors, and lay the floors, for 16£, and find himself and workmen, Mackey to find the lath sawed and shingle fit for covering."

In the last three years of the reign of King George II, which ended in 1760, the laws passed by the Colonial Assembly show that by act of 28 George II, Aaron Leaming was appointed one of the provision commissioners to equip five hundred men or "well affected Indians," to proceed to Crown Point, and that Cape May was to assist for three years in the expedition at £83:10:10½ per annum. By act of 29 George II, Jacob Spicer was made sole Commissioner for West Jersey to supply forces under Colonel Peter Schuyler. By an act of 31 George II, John Johnson was authorized to purchase stores in England for the protection of the colony. Cape May was to receive out of this purchase 33 guns, 33 pounds of powder, 132 pounds of lead and 132 flints.

By act of 32nd, George II, Jacob Spicer was named as one of the commission to settle Indian claims, which were to be regulated by lottery. On October 8, 1758, the conference began at Easton, Pa., at which were Governor Bernard and the five commissioners. Their object was that of extinguishing the Indian title in the State. The result was a formal release by the Indians of all the Jersey lands; claimed by them, excepting the natural right to hunt and fish in unsettled lands. The Minisink and Wapping Indians of all their lands for £1000. Among the lands claimed by the Indians were the following tracts in Cape May and Egg Harbor:

"One claimed by Isaac Still, from the mouth of the Great Egg Harbor River to the head branches thereof, on the east side, so to the road that leads to Great Egg Harbor; so along the road to the seashore, except Tuckahoe, and the Somers, Steelman and Scull places."

"Jacob Mullis claims the pine lands on Edge Pillock Branch and Goshen Neck Branch, where Benjamin Springer and George Marpole's mill stands, and all the land between the head branches of those creeks, to where the waters join or meet."

"Abraham Logues claims the cedar swamp on the east side of Tuckahoe Branch, which John Champion and Peter Campbell have or had in possession."

"Also, Stuypson's island, near Delaware River."

The troubles, perplexities and trials the members of Assembly endured previous to the Revolution, in visiting the seat of government at Amboy and Burlington, to attend the public service, cannot in this age of railroads and steam be appreciated or realized. A single illustration will suffice for all. Aaron Leaming gives an account of his journey to Amboy in 1759, on horseback, as follows:

"March 3d. Set out from home; lodged at Tarkil; arrived at Philadelphia on the 5th. On the 6th, rid to Burlington. 7th. Extremely cold; rid to Crosswicks, and joined company with Mr. Miller; rid to Cranberry, where we overtook Messrs. Hancock, Smith and Clement (of Salem), who had laid up all day by reason of the cold. 8th. Got to Amboy. 17th. Had the honor to dine with his excellency governor Bernard, with more members of the house. It was a plentiful table; but nothing extraordinary. The cheese he said was a Gloucestershire cheese; was a present to him, and said that it weighed 105 pounds when he first had it. He says it's the collected milk of a whole village that makes these cheeses, each one measuring in their milk, and taking its value in cheese.

"19th. Left Amboy for home. 20th. Rid to Cranberry, and lodged at Dr. Stites'. 25th. Arrived home."

In July, 1761, he attended the Assembly at Burlington on the 6th, and broke up on the 8th, and says: "July 9th. I set out homeward. 11th. Got home having been extremely unwell, occasioned by the excessive heat. Almost ever since I went away, the 5th, 6th, 7th, and 8th, were the hottest days by abundance that ever I was acquainted with."

"Sept. 3d. A rain fell five inches on a level. The lower end of Cape May has been so dry that there will not be but one-third of a crop of corn—here it is wet enough the whole season."

"14th. Went a fishing and caught thirty-nine sheepshead."

In the records of Pennsylvania Memuc au Hughes, of Cape May, is recorded as having been commissioned on May 2, 1759, a lieutenant, he having enlisted and become an ensign on the 20th of April. He served in Captain Johnson's company, belonging to Pennsylvania artillery, the regiment being Hon. William Denny's.

In the company of Pennsylvania militia which was mustered to serve for the campaign in the lower counties in that State, under Captain McClaughan, was Eleazer Golden, of Cape May, aged 34, who was a sailor by occupation, and enlisted April 25, 1758.

About the year 1760 there were numerous boats trading from the county to Oyster Bay, L. I., and Rhode Island and Connecticut, carrying cedar lumber mostly; and others to Philadelphia, with oysters and produce of various kinds. Spicer shipped considerable quantities of corn, which he purchased of the people in the way of trade and cash, and forwarded to a market. He owned a vessel which he occasionally sent to the West Indies.

On March 1, 1760, Spicer wrote in his diary that "This day agreed with James Mickel for a year's services, to commence when time expires with Reuben Ludlam, to be paid half in cash and the other half in goods at cash prices, and for the year, but if in any part employed by land and part by water along the coast, including North Carolina and up the Delaware, then to have eighteen pounds for the year's services, but if he proceeds from North Carolina and thence to the West Indies when at home, or can send his linen and other clothes then to leave his washing. He is to attend to such various business as I shall need to employ him by sea or land. If he is fully employed on land to have sixteen pounds, he is to have twenty pounds for the year's services." The cost of vessels in those days can be approximated by reading Spicer's experience recorded March 23, 1761: "Richard Willard, of Philadelphia, ship carpenter, told me he would build a vessel of 35 feet keel, 16½ feet beam, 6¼ feet hold, for £70, and find the material. Besides he would set the mast, make the bulk head, cabin floor and quarter rail in the bargain."

In his diary Spicer made the following references to Cape Island, now Cape May City:

Feb. 25, 1761:—"Agreed to let David Whilldin have pasturage on the Island for a horse from the middle of April to the 1st of November for 15 shillings."

May 13, 1761:—"Granted leave to Elizabeth Stevens to pasture a creature on the Island for a month, at the same rate David Whilldin gives." The time was afterwards enlarged.

Jan. 4, 1762:—"Agreed with Salanthiel Foster for the small house on the Island, the privilege of keeping two cows and calves, and have dry or decayed wood, to be taken from the Neck farm for one year, for the sum of four pounds."

Feb. 2, 1750:—"Applied to Mr. Thomas Hand, informing him that it did not suit me to sell the Island, but if he wanted the money upon six months' notice he should have it, which was according to his promise, there being those that are obliged to make it up when he needs it."

In 1761 the total number of persons in the county who voted were 225. Aaron Leaming in his diary says:

"March 13, 1761, the election of Representatives began, and on the 14th it was ended, when the poll was: Jacob Spicer, 72; Aaron Leaming, 112; Joseph Corson, 41. Whole amount of votes polled, 225. Spicer and Leaming elected."

Spicer's popularity was waning, and he, at this time, was

being severely condemned by the people for what they believed were a usurpation of their rights in purchasing the natural rights of the West Jersey Society. He was publicly arraigned by the people; the following account being from his own pen:

"Went to hear myself arraigned by Mr. Leaming and others before the publick, at the Presbyterian Meetinghouse, for buying the Society's Estate at Cape May, and at the same time desired to know whether I would sell or not. I said not. He then threatened me with a suit in chancery to compel me to abide by the first association, though the people had declined it, and many of the original subscribers had dashed out their names. I proposed to abide the suit and told him he might commence it. If I should see a bargain to my advantage, then I told the people I should be inclined to sell them the natural privileges, if I should advance myself equally otherwise; but upon no other footing whatever, of which I would be the judge."

The following is Aaron Leaming's version of the affair:
"March 26th, 1761.—About forty people met at the Presbyterian Meeting-house to ask Mr. Spicer if he purchased the Society's reversions at Cape May for himself or for the people. He answers he bought it for himself; and upon asking him whether he will release to the people, he refuses, and openly sets up his claim to the oysters, to Basses' titles, and other deficient titles, and to a resurvey, whereupon the people broke up in great confusion, as they have been for some considerable time past."

"Mr. Spicer says that his deed for the Society's reversions to Cape May bears date the 2d day of August, 1756."

But this affair did not seem to trouble Spicer so very much, because in his diary on April 4th following, he wrote:

"Told John Stevens, Esq., that I was willing to be concerned with him in purchasing the 70,000 acres of the Society's lands, provided on inquiry I can find it will answer, of which I am to acquaint him by way of Philadelphia, under the care of Richard Stevens, as also what price I think may be given of which Mr. Johnson may advise his constituents and know whether they will approve thereof. This tract lies under great advantage. Some doubts may arise whether the council of proprietors will admit of taking off the rights, nor can any person, I am well assured, afford to give for the land as located the price of rights, and were the rights even taken off it would be a great doubt whether such a quantity would ever sell, or if they would it can't be expected in any short time. I understand by Mr. Stevens that Doctor Johnson has asked £3000 for the lands that won't answer, I am well assured."

In June following he offered them his whole landed estate and the natural privileges in the county, excepting his farm in Cold Spring Neck, and a right for his family in the privileges, for £7000, which offer was declined.

His diary, June 4, says: "Told Mr. Joseph Corson I would sell the publick if they please all my estate in Cape May for £7000, taking some of their substantial men jointly and severally for my security in a bond drawing interest from date, reserving my Long Neck and March adjacent about 400 acres, a natural privilege for myself and posterity, in common with the rest of the community, and limiting the time of this offer to six months, if not overheard in that time I am to be at liberty." On December 22, that year, he made the same offer to Jeremiah Ludlam.

He further states: "Mr. James Godfrey, in behalf of the Upper Precinct, applied to me to purchase the natural privileges in that precinct. I told him I should be glad to gratify that precinct; and please myself also; and could I see a good foreign purchase, and thereby exchange a storm for a calm, to equal advantage to my posterity, I should think it advisable; and in that case, if I sold, I should by all means give the public a preference, but at present did not incline to sell. I remarked to him this was a delicate affair, that I did not know well how to conduct myself, for I was willing to please the people, and at the same time to do my posterity justice, and steer clear of reflection. Recollecting that old Mr. George Taylor, to the best of my memory, obtained a grant for the Five-Mile Beach and the Two-Mile Beach, and, if I mistake not, the cedar-swamps and pines for his own use and his son John Taylor reconveyed it for about £9, to buy his wife Margery a calico gown, for which he was derided for his simplicity."

He said, November 18, 1761: "Mr. Nathanel Foster desired to lease Jarvis sounds. I told him if he wouldn't stand between me and the people in point of blame I would, which he said he would do."

CHAPTER XI.

AARON LEAMING AND HIS TIMES.

Some extracts of the most interesting portions of Aaron Leaming's diary for the year, 1761, are here given:

"Burlington, January 1, 1761. The Assembly having provided for the pay of the New Jersey Regiment for November last and appointed me to make that month's pay (see Memoirs for December, 1760), we are now proceeding to make payment.

"January 1, 1761. Rid to Mount Holly, this being a pay day there.

"January 2. Last night we lodged at Mr. Read's, this morning I paid Mr. Read 30s. for N. P. John Bancroft. Rid to Burlington.

"Jan. 3 (page torn) returned to Burlington & lodged.

"January 4th 1761 rid to the ferry but it was after Sunset when we got over. Lodged at Mr. Cox at Moorestown.

"January 5. rid to Gloucester spent in making payment.

"6th Bought a p boots, they belonged to Mr. Jacob Clements I paid Mr Hugg 47s. for them. Rid to Capn Comrans & Jan 7th To Salem.

"Jany 8 Spent making payment.

"January 9th 1761 rid to Cohansie bridge.

"January 10th 1761 Spent at Cohansy Bridge making paymt. * * * *

"Jan 11 I rid to Tarkill.

"January 12th Got home. I have been gone ever since 28 of October about 76 days."

"Feb 17, 1761 Upon Viewing Mr Murr's account I find we gave him 6s 6 for binding each of the New Jersey Constitution books.

"March 26, 1761—I set out for Amboy yesterday.

"March 28—Rid to Burlington.

"29—Set out in company with several Lodged at Cranberry.

"30—got to Amboy and was qualified in ye house.
"Extract of Mr. Thomas Eatton's accts.

bro't forward 3927 10 0			
To my Commissions @ 5 p Cent..........	196	7	6
To my Commissions on 540£ paid by the Commissioners	27		
To further Commissions		2	2
	223	9	8
deduct for ye Comrs of 28 10 lost at ft. Wm Henry		1	8
	222	1	6

"April 8, 1761—Rid to Burlington.
"April 10th last night lodged at Mr Jno Coxe's, & to day rid to Philada.
"Apri 12—I came out of town. 14th was at Mr. Page's and 15th I got home.
"1761. New Jersey (to raise) 600 (troops which was 2-3 of 1760 quota.)
"May 31, 1761 I set out from home to go to Philada to buy a negro or two.
"June 2 got to Philada.
"Bought "Troy," of Willing Morris & Co., for £40.
"July 4, 1761, Set out to go to Burlington.
"6th Got to Burlington
"8 Broke up after passing a law to take 64 men & 2 officers into pay out of our Regiment, their service to commence the first of November 1761 & last a year; to have 3£ bounty & the officers 10s p of money this Levy money created a dispute. Wetherel & Spicer was uncommonly harsh against allowing levy money, and the reasons they assigned was the Poverty of Major McDonald who they suggested is to have the command of the 64 men—& they say is unworthy the reasons for it is that let who will enlist the men they must give a Dollar to drink the Kings health, that being so antient & established a custom that no soldier ever pertends to enlist without it they pushed this matter in a very uncommon manner—when we came to vote I proposed a Dollar being the exact Sum we all knew must be

given, but the leading voters placed it at 10s and I was forced to vote for the 10s or the voters for nothing would have carried it—and that would have defeated the Service & occasioned the Assembly to have been called again.

"9 of July 1761. I set out homeward.

"Got home.————"

Concerning the Baptist Church at Court House, Leaming said:

"Oct 24, 1761, met and made arrangements for parsonage, and pews always to be free. Wanted 62 acres Millicent Young's for parsonage—171£. 1741—undertook to build meeting house."

"Nov 6, 1761—Burned (branded) cattle on 5 mile beach, Nummy island & on 7 mile beach."

In the Assembly, on December 3, 1761, when a bill or proposition was being passed upon imposing a duty on the importation of slaves, which Leaming considered really prohibitive, Leaming voted against it, while his colleague, Spicer, voted for its passage.

In 1761, by act of the Provincial Assembly, Wills' Creek was ordered dammed to preserve the "marshes and cripple swamps." A bank was ordered erected from the upland of Thomas Smith to extend by the causeway then in existence, to the land of Nathan Hand. The managers were to be selected on the first Tuesday of each September, at the house of Thomas Smith. Smith and William Goff were appointed the first managers. Elihu Smith was appointed to make the county assessment for the year, and Joseph Hildreth was to collect the taxes. That same year Jacob Spicer was made one of the commissioners to provide aid for men wounded in the service of King Gorge III in fighting the French and Indians.

In 1762 Joseph Corson, Isaac Baner, John Mackey, James Willets and "sundry other persons," had petitioned for a toll bridge over Cedar Swamp Creek at Fast Landing. And the Assembly passed a law for its building and a causeway. The following were the

Rates of toll:

Waggon or ox-cart, with team and driver........6 pence.
Chaise or horse cart, passenger, horse, mare or gelding

thereunto belonging ....4 pence
Every passenger with horse, mare, gelding----2 pence.
Foot ....1 pence.
Cattle &c., led over. Each ....1 pence.
Sheep led over. Each ....1 farth.

This road opened by way of Petersburg a more direct communication with the upper part of the county.

March 22, 1762, Jacob Spicer and four others from other counties were appointed by the Assembly to "purchase convenient tract or tracts of lands" for the Indians who were satisfied with the New Jersey government to settle upon. These were purchased in Burlington county and measured 3000 acres, which extended to the seashore. The last Indian of the descendants of these settlers died in December, 1894. The same year Jacob Spicer was chairman of the Assembly's commission to settle claims for damages incurred by the French and Indian war.

On December 8, 1762, Henry Young, Nathaniel Foster, John Willetts, Nicholas Stillwell, Thomas Leaming, Joseph Corson, John Leonard, Jonathan Smith, Jacob Hand, Daniel Swane, Robert Parsons were commissioned to be Judges of the Common Pleas, while Henry Young was to be Judge of the Inferior Court of Common Pleas, holding office during pleasure. The same commission was granted to each Nathaniel Foster, Nicholas Stillwell, William Smith and John Willetts.

Clamming, as well as oystering, occupied the attention of the inhabitants when there was no farming or other work pressing them. The following petition was presented to the Royal Governor, which sets forth their grievances, as well as shows who at that time were interested in the matter:

To his Excellency William Franklin, Esq., Captain General
    and Governor-in-Chief in and over the province of New
    Jersey, Chancellor and Vice-Admiral in the same, and
To the Houses of Council and Assembly for the said province;
The petition of the inhabitants of the county of Cape May
    humbly sheweth—
    That the act for preserving oysters is of great advantage; but as it seems uncertain whether clams are included there-

in, strangers make so large a practice of gathering and carrying them away, that in some places where they are the best, there are not enough to be found for the use of the neighborhood, and as this evil is increasing, we beg leave to solicit a law to prevent persons, who are not inhabitants of this province, from gathering clams in or exporting them out of this county.

And your petitioners, as in duty bound, will pray.

Dated July 11th, 1763.

Thomas Stites,
Thomas Hewet,
Robert Cresse,
Jonathan Cresse,
Nathaniel Foster, E S Q
Jacob Hand, E S Q
Henry Young,
James Whilldin,
Jonathan Smith,
James Edwards,
Thomas Smith,
Daniel Smith,
Jeremiah Ludlam,
Recompense Hand,
Jacob Hughes,
Christopher Church,
William Matthew,
John Chester,
Elihu Hand,
Downs Edmunds,
Ezekiel Cresse,
Joseph Hildreth,

Ephraim Bancroft,
Charles Hand,
William Simkins,
William Goff,
James Hildreth,
Nathaniel Shaw,
Shamgar Hand,
Daniel Hildreth,
Jedekiah Hughes,
Jonathan Mills,
John Shaw,
Jonathan Stites,
Arthur Cresse,
James Cresse,
Silas Swain,
Henry Hand,
Henry Schellenger,
James Eldredge,
Jeremiah Mills,
Elijah Hughes,
Jeremiah Leaming,
George Stites.

By this year the French and Indian War was at an end, and the results of it were the retirement of French control from North America, the unification of the colonists, the training of thousands of men in the use of arms to face an enemy, and the preparation for the War for Independence, then not far from beginning, the removal of the need of the British protection because the frontier foe had vanished, and opened up the trend of thought toward a government of themselves and by themselves. The colonists were nearly all English speaking, and nearly all Protestant, and of the same social class from the mother country. They were humble, upright and persevering, and one might believe, almost ignorant of dangers. The foreign trade of the country was prosperous. The mass of the people lived simply, but comfortable. There were but two really rich men in the county—Spicer and Leaming, the latter, however, worth nearly four times the former.

The farm houses were generally built of huge timbers, covered with rough, unpainted clapboards, mostly one story. Usually the centre of the houses were taken up with an immense fireplace. On snapping cold winter nights there was no more cheerful sight, however, than such a fireplace, piled up full of blazing, burning wood, which had to be gathered in the day time by much hard work.

The farmer bought little at the store. He raised his own food; his sheep furnished wool, and his wife and daughters spun and wove it into stout "homespun" cloth. The old rags were saved, carefully washed, cut into strips and woven into "rag carpet." For recreation there were sleighing and skating parties in the winter and husking bees, wood-choppings and hog-killings at other proper seasons. The three-cornered cocked hats and knee breeches were worn. Travel was by sail vessel or slow-going stages and "carry-alls." Cape May had the stocks for punishment of criminals.

In 1763 a large number of the freeholders of the county petitioned the State Assembly for the privilege of erecting a court house and jail on the plantation of Daniel Hand, in Middletown, near his dwelling house. The petition was granted and the cost was limited to £300. The reason given by the petitioners was that the court house and jail were out of repair, much too small and incommodiously situated. In 1764 Hand, who was a grandson of Shamgar, deeded one acre for the purpose, free of cost, and the building was 24x30 feet, and lasted until 1840.

This Assembly decided to raise £25,000 tax in the colony in 1764, and Cape May's share was apportioned at £417 14s. 8½d.

On September 17, 1765, Jacob Spicer, 2d, died. With all the many records here presented of his life as a public and private citizen, we have nothing after his birth, May, 1716, to guide us in relation to his early days. His father died when he was a babe, and our first facts concerning this second Spicer was when he became a member of the Legislature, in 1744, which office he held until he died, excepting one year; the first in connection with Henry Young, Esq., and afterwards, until his demise, with Aaron Leaming (second), Esq.; being almost a moiety of the time he lived. He bore a prominent part in the proceedings and business of the House, as the journals of those days fully prove.

He was a man of exemplary habits, strong and vigorous imagination, and strictly faithful in his business relations with his fellow-men, being punctilious to the uttermost farthing, as his diary and accounts fully attest. He carried system into all the ramifications of business; nothing too small to escape the scrutiny of his active mind, nothing so large that it did not intuitively embrace. He married Judith Hughes, daughter of Humphrey Hughes, Esq., who died in 1747; and in 1751 he married Deborah Hand Leaming, widow of Christopher Leaming. The written marriage agreement which he entered into with the said Deborah Leaming, before consummating matrimony, is indicative of much sound sense and discriminating judgment.

He left four children, Sarah, Sylvia, Judith and Jacob; but there are now no male heirs of that name found living in the county.

In 1762 he made his will of thirty-nine pages, the most lengthy and elaborate testamentary document on record in this or perhaps any other State.

He was possessed of a very large amount of real estate that he held in his name and under his control, and which he left with much guarded care, first to the necessary payment of all his lawful debts, and secondly to his own family and their heirs, distributing to each a portion in due season, while he also made provision for annual gifts of five pounds each to the religious institutions of the Quakers in the upper precinct, Baptists in the middle precinct and the Presbyterians in the lower precinct. In this instrument he complained of the unjust treatment by the populace and claims that he was vilely defamed and grossly abused on account of the natural privileges, of which he claimed to be entirely ignorant. He gave his wife one hundred pounds and the buildings and real estate on his Cold Spring Neck farm and two negroes. Rev. Daniel Lawrence, pastor of the Presbyterian church, was made one of the guardians of his daughters until they became of age. At death he ordered his will read at the Baptist meeting house, and left directions that a sermon-like address to the good people of Cape May county on a text from Psalms ii, verses 1 and 2, in pamphlet form, to the amount of one hundred copies, be distributed.

This will was probated October 9, 1765. Ebenezer Johnston, Henry Hand, Christopher Church and Henry Stites were witnesses, and were sworn before Henry Young, surrogate of Cape May county. The five following persons, named in the will, were its executors: Deborah Spicer, Sylvia Jones, Samuel Jones, Sarah Leaming and Christopher Leaming, to whom probate and letters testamentary were granted by his Excellency William Franklin, Esq., Captain-General and Governor-in-Chief of the colony of New Jersey.

He was buried by the side of his father, in his family ground at Cold Spring, a spot now overgrown with large forest timber.

On his tombstone was this inscription:
"Jacob Spicer, Esq., departed this life, Sept. 17th, 1765, in the 49th year of his age—
"If aught that's good or great could save,
Spicer had never seen the grave."

His wife, who lies by his side, has upon her monument:
"Judith Spicer departed this life, Sept. 7th, 1747, in the 33d year of her age.
"Virtue and piety give way to death,
Or else the entombed had ne'er resigned her breath."

On May 6, 1762, Spicer, 2d, devised the natural privileges which seemed to be so exciting to the people, to his son, Jacob, who, November 9, 1795, conveyed by deed to a company or association of persons of the lower precinct and Cape Island, his entire right to the natural privileges, which were viewed and used as a bona fide estate, and the Legislature passed acts of incorporation, giving them plenary powers to defend themselves from foreign and domestic aggression, thus virtually acknowledging the validity of their title. Previous to the year 1840 a suit was instituted in East Jersey, the result of which was favorable to the proprietors; but on an appeal to the United States Supreme Court from the Circuit below, the decision was reversed, confirming the right of the State to all the immunities and privileges of the water thereof, barring out the proprietary claims altogether, and establishing the principle that the State possessed the right as the guardian and for the use of the whole people, in opposition to the claims of individuals or associations, however instituted or empowered.

Rev. Daniel Lawrence, who as pastor of the Cold Spring Church, became a popular and beloved man, died on April 13, 1766, and there. He had been pastor of the church since the spring of 1572, but was not installed until June 20, 1754. He was born on Long Island in 1718, and in his younger days was a blacksmith. He studied at the "Log College," in Pennsylvania, and was licensed to preach in Philadelphia in 1745. From May, 1746, he was pastor of the Presbyterian church at Forks of Delaware, and there shared in the labors of Rev. John Brainard, the Indian missionary. He was not robust in health and was directed to pass the winters and springs at Cape May. While there he received the call from the Cold Spring Church. The second church, which was built during his pastorate, in 1762, was a frame building. He was buried among his people in the Cold Spring Church graveyard. On his tombstone is the following appropriate verse:

> In yonder sacred house I spent my breath;
> Now silent, mouldering here I lie in death;
> Those silent lips shall wake and yet declare
> A dread amen to truths they published there.

After the decease of Mr. Lawrence, among other supplies, Rev. John Brainard supplied the pulpit during the winter of 1769-1770.

On August 22, 1767, William Smith, Nathaniel Foster, Nicholas Stillwell, Thomas Leaming, James Whilden, John

Townsend, John Leonard, Joseph Corson, Jacob Hand, Daniel Swain, Robert Parson, Henry Hand, Thomas Smith, Reuben Ludlam, James Godfrey, John Mackey were made justices of the peace. To these on June 7, 1770 Joseph Savage was added.

At the same time, in '67, Thomas Leaming, James Whilden, John Townsend, John Leonard were selected and commissioned judges of the Inferior Court of Common Pleas.

In April, the next year, Nicholas Stillwell was named to be a commissioner for taking recognizance of bail. He served the county in the Assembly from 1769 to 1771, and was a son of John Stillwell, of Town Bank. He purchased, in 1748, of Joseph Golden, the plantation at Beesley's Point. After his death, in 1772, the place fell to his son, Captain Nicholas Stillwell, who afterwards sold to Thomas Borden, who sold, in 1803, to Thomas Beesley, who resided on the premises until 1816, and on an adjoining property until his death in 1849.

In 1769 the people clamored for more law to protect the oyster industry, and the Assembly confirmed the law of 1719, and added new provisions, requiring that no beds should be raked from May 10 to September 1, under a penalty of forty shillings, two-thirds to go to the informer and one-third to the power of the township or city where the offense was committed; empowering the officers of the law to summon aid to the constables in making arrests; prohibiting oysters for lime under a forfeit of three pounds, onehalf of which went to the informer and the other half to the poor, and putting the burden of proof on the defendant and making the act valid for three years.

In 1770 the laws passed by the Assembly prescribed that there should continue to be two Loan Office Commissioners for Cape May county; that lands in the county should not be assessed at a rate higher than £30 per 100 acres nor less than £8 per 100 acres; and that Aaron Leaming was to be one of a committee to correspond with the colony's agent in reference to money matters. On May 12, this year, Rev. James Watt was installed as pastor of the Cold Spring Presbyterian Church, where he labored during the Revolutionary period, or for eighteen years, being the successor of

Rev. Daniel Lawrence. Mr. Watt was born March 12, 1743,. and died November 19, 1789, and was buried in the cemetery back of the church.

Jeremiah Eldredge was a prominent man at this time, and was frequently honored by his fellow-citizens in holding public trusts in Cape May county. When he was 23 years old he was elected clerk of court and held the office for nine years, from 1768 to 1777. When 35 years old he was elected to the Legislative Assembly one year, from 1780 to 1781, and then afterwards he was elected nine years to the Legislative Council, from 1784 to 1794. After that he was appointed a surrogate for two years, from 1793 until his death. He was a son of Samuel Eldredge, born August 3, 1745, and died April 28, 1795.

CHAPTER XII.
JOHN HATTON, THE TORY.

At the beginning of the Revolutionary period the various acts of the English Parliament which affected America, and in which the colonists had no voice by representation, began to meet with protests. The most impolitic measure of the government was the passage in 1765 by Parliament of the celebrated "Stamp Act," for the purpose of raising a revenue by taxing the colonies. The people resisted the measure, and so strong were the protests that Parliament repealed the act in 1766. The next year the English Ministry attempted to compel the colonists to assist in raising supplies for that government, imposing a tax upon tea, glass, paper and painters' colors. A storm of opposition, more strong, was again excited, and soon after all duties were withdrawn except that upon tea, which was taxed at three pence per pound. This was not satisfactory to the people of the colonies, not because of the amount of the duty, but because of the principle of taxing without consent or voice of the colonists. John Hatton, collector of the port of Salem and Cohansey, came to Cape May in November, 1770, to stop what he termed were illegal actions on the part of local and other skippers in landing goods at Cape May to avoid paying duty. The following is correspondence which grew out of the treatment of him by the common pleas justices, Thomas Leaming, John Leonard and James Whilden:

"Copy of a letter from John Hatton, Collector of Salem and Cohensy, to Gov. Franklin, dated Dec. 7th, 1770, complaining of the action of Mr. Jas. Whilden, Thomas Leaming and John Leonard, Justices at Cape May:"

"I humbly beg leave to inform your Excellency that I am again obliged to fly from and quit my Office, and distressed family by reason that his Majesty's laws and my actions in executing them as a faithful servant are misinterpreted by these Your Excelys Justices at Cape May viz James Whilden, Thomas Leaming, and John Leonard, Esqrs who I am informed could not get any others to join them,

"23 Novr—I arrived at Cape May from Burlington. My wounds being so bad prevented me getting there sooner.

"24.—I procured Joseph Corson, Esqr to go with me to J. Leonard & T. Leaming, Esqs, when I gave them your Excellencys Proclamation to which they paid no regard, and during my stay with them, being about two hours, they did not read it.

"I likewise delivered the Letter Mr. Pettit wrote by your Order on the 17th in regard to bailing my negroe, when they absolutely refused to admit him to bail.

"I then went to the Gaol from whence I found Hughes had been let out in order to go where he chose to procure himself bail, and without any guard he had ful liberty to go where he liked.

"My negro still close confined and very ill the Cutts in his skull being very bad from whence had been taken several pieces of bones.

"In the dead of night I returned home found my wife as I had been informed, just expiring thro' fright for me and her son, well knowing the danger we were in; and few of my neighbors, tho' I have several good ones durst venture to come to my house being threatened with destruction by Hughes or his friends, notwithstanding the distress of my family, I was obliged to leave home the next night in order to get some one to bail my man.

"This night was assaulted on the road by some man who with a stick struck me several blows in my arm; when a Blow with my Whip handle in his head, stunned him, I rode on.

28.—On my giving Nicholas Stillwell Esqr £200 security he was so kind as to bail my Negro, being well acquainted with my ill usage, & the distress of my family, a copy of the Bail piece now produced justly expresses it.

"29—Got my Negroe from Prison.

"Decr 5—Mills the Pilot who is advertised with your

Excellencys Proclamation was this day going about my neighborhood, armed with a Club and threatening me with destruction.

"6.—I met the said Mills on the Kings road who threatened me with his Club but on my putting my hand towards my pocket he went off. I immediately went to James Whilden, in order to request him to execute Justice against the said Mills, as I had some days before lodged a complaint before him, but I was told he was not at home, tho' he had been seen a few minutes before. About six hours after on the same day the said James Whilden, Thomas Leaming, & Jo Leonard Esqrs sent 5 men with their warrant now produced, who seized my man as he was going home with a loaded Team, he having been all the day with two of my neighbors getting some of my summers Crop which had been till then decayed on the ground. A few minutes after I was arrested on the same account as the warrant testifyeth. When I first entered the room Mills was sitting by the side of Jo Leonard Esqr with the same Club by his side he had in the morning—during my conversation with them in which I did not give any of them an uncivil word, the said Leonard expressed himself, in a very unbecoming manner.

"I then desired the said Mills might be secured and again repeated to them that he was the Pilot who on 8t November threatened me with death if I came near the Ship to execute my Office as his Majs Collr and likewise that he was one of the men who took away the Pilot boat I had seized her, and further that he was the man who laid hold of my son in the street at Philadelphia till a mob of Sailors came up when he and they most inhumanely treated him so that he was taken from them for dead.

"He acknowledged the threatening and obstructing me when I was going to the ship, and like wise taking away the Pilot boat I had seized, and said he would do it again when there was occasion—his conduct was not in the least disapproved by the Magistrates present.

"The Magistrates did not regard my Charges against him, but on my insisting on Mills, being some way secured they consented to bind him over to their own Court. An Uncle of Hughes, was ready for his Bondsman.

"They then bound me, and insisted on £200 security, but they refused any security I could give for my Negro which I offered them nor would they allow him to stay in the hands of the Constable till next morning: When I told them I would produce them any bail they should require as my friends were at some distance, but they ordered him immediately to prison.

"There were present Hughes and his brothers and other relatives who threatened destruction to any who gave me any assistance; during the whole time they could not produce any one to say that either I, or my Slave, ever was heard to use the least threatening word against the said Mills or any one else, since my first coming amongst them, the reason they give for binding me and sending my Slave again to prison, is, that Mills declared my son told him in Philadelphia, that his fathers Negro should do for him, but did not produce any proofs.

"Since my ill treatment on 8 Novr. His Majs Vessels having been very vigilant has greatly obstructed their smuggling by water therefore I being so distressed by these three Magistrates gives them full liberty to perform it on shore, for I am well assured, & have just reason to believe that there hath been & still is several thousand pounds worth of contraband Goods lodged on this shore since the 8th of November last, which Goods they are now conveying by Land to Philadelphia, and have been so during a few days since in the open day to go to my door with a loaded Waggon, and men armed with Pistols in their hands challenging me to appear if I durst, to seize them.

"Mills and the Boat now appear in public and he bids defiance to any.

"These my assertions I can prove if the Witnesses are impartially examined, therefore I hope your Excellency doth plainly perceive that it is for my Zealous attachment to his Majesty that I am thus injured abused, and interrupted by these three Magistrates—

"My Instructions are, in any difficulties to apply to Your Excellency for assistance and protection, therefore do most humbly pray from Your Excellency a speedy redress as His Majesty's Revenue suffers entirely by the Actions and Powers of these three Magistrates at Cape May.

"JOHN HATTON."

The following is a copy of the warrant for the apprehension of John Hatton, collector at Salem.

New Jersey, Cape May county, ss.

George the third by the Grace of God of Great Britain France and Ireland King Defender of the Faith &c To our Sheriff of the County of Cape May or the Constables of the said County or either of them Greeting Forasmuch as Jedediah Mills of the said County of Cape May Pilot hath personally come before Us James Whillden, Thos Leaming, and John Leonard, Esqrs three of his Majs Justices assigned to keep the Peace within the said County of Cape May & hath taken a Corporal Oath that he the said Jedediah Mills is afraid that John Hatton, Esqr. of the said County of Cape May will beat wound maim or kill him th said Jedediah Mills and hath therewithal prayed surety for the Peace and Good Behavior against him the said John Hatton Esqr. therefore We command and charge you jointly and severally or either of you that immediately upon the Receipt hereof you bring the said John Hatton Esqr Forthwith before us the said James Whilden Thos Larning & John Leonard, Esqrs or either of Us to find sufficient Surety and Mainprize as well for his personal appearance at the next General Quarter Sessions of Our Peace or Court of Oyer & Terminer of General Goal Delivery or which ever of said Courts should happen to be held first in & for our said County as also for our Peace and Good Behavior in the mean time to be kept toward us and all our Liege People and chiefly towards the said Jedediah Mills that is to say that he the said John Hatton, Esqr. shall not do nor by any means procure or cause to be done any of the said Evils to any of Our said People and especially to the said Jedediah Mills.

Given under Our Hands and Seals this 6th day of Decr in the 11th Year of the Reign of Our Sovereign Lord

George the third of Great Britain &c in the Year of Our Lord 1770.

(Signed)   J. WHILLDEN
T. LEAMING
J. LEONARD.

At the same time a warrant was issued for Hatton's slave, Ned, by the same justices, because Jedidiah Mills complained that he "is afraid that a Mulatto Slave called Ned by name belonging to John Hatton, Esqr. of the lower Precinct in said county of Cape May" might "beat maim or kill him."

The following is the correspondence, taken from official documents in the colonial office at London, England, concerning the Hatton matter:

"Copy of a Letter from Mr. Hatton, Collector of Salem, Etc., to the Commissioners of the Customs, dated Perth Amboy, Dec. 25, 1770, complaining of the ill treatment he had received.

"Perth Amboy, 25th Decemr 1770.

"Gentlemen

"On my way to the Governor with the inclosed Remonstrance I received Yours of the 10th Inst. on the Receipt of which I went to Mr. Skinner, Attorney General whose opinion I have now sent like wise the inclosed Remonstrance will give Your Honors a just Information of the further il treatment I have receiv'd Mr Read Collector of Burlington hath bailed out Hughes. Mr Read's actions are, as formerly; which is to distress me and the Service of the Revenue all He can. He is one of the 3 chief Judges of this Province & hath a Salary for it & is likewise one of the Governor's Council.

"I am credibly informed that a Set of Merchants at Philadelphia have remitted a Quantity of money to this Province in Order to gain any Point they want to likewise make this Cape their Stanch Store, as they say they cannot do without It for their Contraband Trade—for since the 8th of last November there have been 5 other Vessels unloaded with Illicit Goods.

"I have wrote three pressing letters to the Captain of His Majs Vessel in this River but no One hath yet appeared to give me any Relief. I hired a Sloop on purpose to go to them to get them to keep their Vessel or Tender in our Bay which would be the proper place, whereby they would perceive, with my assistance on Land, all the proceedings of the smuglers there; but they declined my Request saying they could not assist me on Shore, and Winter coming on they must lay up their Vessels, therefore I am obliged to keep concealed by day, & when I travel it is all by night, & expect no other than some Day to fall a Sacrifice to their Wicked Malice & Inventions. I left my Wife at the point of death thro' Fright for me and her Son. My Son being still Ill at the Tavern He was taken to first, & will lose either his Arm or the use of it, which cannot yet be determined & hath undergone a Severe Illness myself going Hundreds of Miles to endeavor to procure Justice & have almost expended my last Farthing and am in the greatest distress for more, who am

"Gentlemen &c

"JOHN HATTON."

"I am to call on the Governor on my way back for an answer to my Remonstrance of the 7th Inst. He having sent to the Attorney General for his advice & the Result thereof I will inform You Mr Skinner advises me to arrest the 3 Magistrates if I can get them before the Governor for their actions & false Imprisonment but I want money, having now expended in this affair upwards of 30£. Be pleased to excuse the Badness of this Letter as my Wounds in my Head & right Arm are still so bad that I can hardly think or hold my Pen."

Letter from Attorney-General Skinner to Mr. Hatton, giving his opinion on the proceedings of the magistrates at Cape May:

"Dec. 25, 1770.

"Mr. Hatton

"I have considered the Papers you have laid before me,

and those sent by Mr Petit and am of opinion that as the transaction was on the high Seas the Admiralty only hath Jurisdiction, & it is those you ought to apply.

"Upon the same principle the Magistrates at Cape May had no authority to issue their Warrant, or bind you over to Court the place where the Seizure & Rescue was made being without their jurisdiction or that of any Court but the Admiralty. CORTD SKINNER.

"to John Hatton Esqr."

Letter from Mr. Skinner, Attorney-General of East Jersey, to Charles Petit, Esq., secretary to Governor Franklin, giving his opinion on the conduct of the Magistrates at Cape May:

"Dec. 25, 1770.

"Sir

"I received Yours by Mr. Hatton with the Papers inclosed & have considered them as well as the Shortness of the time would permit, together with other Information given me by Mr. Hatton.

"I am of opinion that the place where the Seizure & Rescue were made is clearly out of the county of Cape May. That the Admiralty only has Jurisdiction and that the Justices of Cape May were forward in taking upon them any Enquiry; than issuing their Warrant & taking Mr. Hatton & his Slave after his Excellency's Proclamation is an insolent Contempt of his Proclamation and will, with other parts of their Behaviour, justify His Excellency in ordering their Attendance before him in Council, or upon very clear Affidavits of their Behaviour removing them from Office.

"It was their Duty to Support Mr Hatton the Collector & not suffer a Man Mills so principally concerned in the Matter to Sit with them when they illegally demanded Security of the Collector, then countenancing the outrage of the Pilots as well as the running of Goods are Sufficient to remove them—Be pleased to make my Compts to the Governor & am &c: CORTLAND SKINNER.

"To Chas Petit Esqr Govrs. Secretary."

Letter from Mr. Hatton, collector of Salem and Cohansey, to the commissioners of the customs, Boston, relative to his ill treatment by the magistrates at Cape May:

"Gentlemen

"I wrote to your Honours from Perth Amboy on the 25th instant, and inclosed you the Attorney General's opinion of the Actions of the Magistrates and likewise my last Remonstrance to Govr Franklin and also the Copies of two Warrants which has been served on me and my Negro. Two Days after I arrived at Burlington & waited on the Governor & delivered a letter from Mr. Skinner a Copy of which is inclosed, after much persuasion His Excellency granted according to Mr Skinner's Opinion an Non Ultimo Prosequi for me but as my Negro happened not to be mentioned in it, the Governor refused me one for him, therefore both he and me as one of his bonds men must appear at their next Court in February, what the issue may be I cannot pretent to say but no good. His Excellency has likewise wrote to the three Magistrates to appear before him and his Council sometime in the Spring the particular time not yet fixed, but if we may judge from former instances the result will be. I wrote this from opposite Philadelphia, the Tavern where my son is whose wounds are partly healed but has lost entirely the use of his Arm. I beg your Honours will consider the distress I am in for want of Money as I have now spent nearly forty pounds in traveling so many hundred miles & in fees for advice & other expences caused by this affair and I have still other Expences to pay by reason my man must attend their Court, therefore do most humbly beg your Honours will either grant me my Incidents now due or advance some of my salary or any other means you may think proper, which must be speedily & can be done by an Order on Mr Swift. I have taken out a Supreme Writt for Mills the Pilot by the Attorney Generaals advice as there is no Court of Admiralty in this Province.—I should be glad your Honours would interpose so as to get the Magistrates punished according to their deserts. I am &c   JOHN HATTON.

"Coopers Ferry opposite Philadelphia 30th Decr. 1770."

"N B The Letter referred to is not yet come to hand."

Copy of a letter from His Excellency, Governor Franklin, to the Commissioners of His Majesty's Customs at Boston:

"Burlington, April 10, 1771.

"Gentlemen,

"I yesterday received your Letter of the 26th of March, and am much surprized to find that Mr Hatton has not acquainted you with the Result of the Enquiry made by the Governor & Council into his Complaint against the Magistrates of Cape May, as on 26th of Febry he obtained a certified Copy of all the Minutes & Proceedings relative to that matter, which he said was to be immediately transmitted to you, agreeably to the Orders you had before given him. However as it appears by your Letter that you have not received them, I have directed the Secretary to make out another Copy, which I send enclosed; together with a Copy of sundry Notes & Observations made by him, explaining more particularly several matters relative to Mr. Hatton's Complaint, which are either omitted, or slightly mentioned, in the Opinion given by the Governor and Council. By comparing these with the several Paragraphs of the Complaint, as numbered you 'may be able to form a true Judgement of the Conduct of your Officer.'

"The Representation Mr. Hatton has made to you of the ill Treatment that he, his Son, and Negro, received from a number of Seamen belonging to the Ship Prince of Wales, in Delaware Bay, on account of his having seized a Pilot Boat, suspected to have some Contraband Goods on Board belonging to said Ship, and of the barbarous Usage which his Son afterwards received of them and a Number of others at Philadelphia may, for aught I know, be very just. They were Transactions entirely out of the Jurisdiction of this Government, and which I have had no Opportunity of enquiring particularly into. But as to his Complaints against the Conduct of the Magistrates, and of the Distress which they have occasioned him, I do take upon me to say they are entirely false and malicious.

"Altho' I have long had a very bad Opinion of Mr. Hatton's Principles and Disposition, yet as he appeared before me with several Wounds, which he said he had gotten on board a Pilot Boat, from some Irish Seamen, when doing his Duty, and told me a melancholy story of the ill Treatment he had received from three of the Justices, I was moved to give some Credit to his assertions. Accordingly, I issued a Proclamation for apprehending the Persons concerned in the Affray, in Case any of them should appear in this Province, and afterwards sent Orders to the Justices to appear before me in Council on the 21st of February, which (as they and most of the Gentlemen of the Council lived at a great Distance) was as soon as they could be well got together. I besides advised him to apply to the Governor of Pennsylvania for a like Proclamation, and to obtain the Chief Justice's Warrant for searching all suspected Houses & Places in Philadelphia, at which City the Seamen were at that Time. He was likewise advised by the Attorney Genl to apply to the Court of Admiralty, where only the offence was properly cognizable. Neither of which he did, as I have heard. On the contrary, he has done but little else but ride about the Country, taking a Number of unnecessary Journies to Philadelphia, Burlington and Amboy, with an Expectation, as I suppose, of receiving a handsome Allowance out of the Revenue for his Trouble and Expences, on pretence that he was engaged in what his Majesty's Service absolutely required.

"The Day fixed for the Hearing, and some Days both before and after, happened to be the severest Weather we had during the Winter, yet several of His Majesty's Council and the King's Attorney, tho' they had between 60 & 70 miles to Travel, gave their Attendance & spent with me near three Days in hearing the Parties, and enquiring into the affair, when they gave it as their unanimous Opinion, that there was no just Foundation for any of Mr Hatton's charges against the Justices.—The Particulars of his Complaint, and the Opinions of the Council and Attorney General, are set forth at large in the Minutes. I could not but concur with their Sentiments, as the Facts in favour of the Justices were, indeed, too evident to admit of any Hesitation in the Matter.

"Mr Hatton appears to be a Man of a very unhappy, violent Temper, sometimes bordering on Madness, so that it is impossible that he can live long in Quiet with his Neighbours. He has extravagant Notions of his Power and Importance as a Collector of the Customs—insists upon great Homage and Deference being paid him by the Country Magistrates—tells them he is exempted from paying Taxes out of England—& that he has it in his Power to get the Governor Council, Chief Justice, Attorney General, and every Officer of the Government removed, if they should at any Time refuse to do as he would have them. In short, there is nothing so absurd & outrageous, that he has not shown himself capable of saying or doing, on which Account I have had more Trouble with him than with all the other People in New Jersey. Besides, he has got a Notion in his Head, that by making great Clamour against the Inhabitants of this Province, representing them all as concerned in Smuggling, in Combination against him and his Authority, and that he is suffering from his active Zeal for his Majesty's Interest, he shall make himself a Man of Consequence with the Commissioners of Customs, & through them get preferred to a better Collectorship. In this I should most heartily wish him Success, so that it was any where out of this Colony, were I not well assured that he has been unfaithful to his Trust, and strongly connected with some of the most noted Smugglers in Philadelphia, and with the Only Person in all his District who is suspected to have any Concern in such illicit Practices. Nor indeed, have I the least Doubt, if the People on board the Ship and Pilot Boat had offered him Money instead of Blows, when he first came to them, but that he would readily have accepted it, and left them to pursue their Measures without any Disturbance from him whatever.

"I do not, however, expect that the Opinions of the Governor, Council, Attorney General & Secretary, now transmitted to you, will have much Weight with you, Gentlemen, or make you think the worse of the Conduct of your Officer. My Reasons for this I shall tell you candidly, that if I am in the Wrong in any of them you may set me right. They are

"1st Because you paid so little Regard to the Opinion of the Govr and Council, in the Year 1768, on a former Complaint of the same kind, that you thought it necessary to send to me for 'Copies of the several Affidavits and other Materials upon which it was grounded: thereby shewing that you either believed us to be incompetent Judges, or doubted the Justice of our Decision, and were therefore determined to make a fresh Enquiry into the Matter Yourselves.

"2d Because I am credibly informed, that so far from blaming or censuring Hatton for his extraordinary Conduct at that Time, you even gave him Marks of your Approbation, complimenting with a Place in the Customs, an infamous Fellow who he then sent to you with his groundless Complaints. I call this Fellow (whose Name is Clark) infamous, because he appeared evidently, both to the Council of me, to be determined to swear thro' thick & thin, in favour of Hatton, and contradicted himself so often in the Course of his Testimony, that several of the Council declared that they thought he ought to have been committed to the Goal for Perjury.

"3d Because your own Inspector General of the Customs (who was particularly directed by you to enquire what Foundation there was for Mr. Hatton's Complaint that Time) not only represented to you, in his Report or Letter of the 17th June 1769 that the Disputes Hatton had with the People were 'of a Private Nature, arose from trifling Matters, owing to an unwise Department in his private Station,' and not 'on Account of his Zeal for the Service,' or for 'exerting himself in his Duty,' as he had alledged, but at the same Time acquainted you with sundry Facts, and transmitted to you a Number of Proofs, fully evincing that he had been guilty of unwarrantable Practices in his Office, and had given Encouragement and Assistance to some of the most noted Smugglers, to the great Detriment of the King's Revenue: notwithstanding which you have suffered him to continue in Office, and have not, at least as I can learn, ever shewn any marks of your Disapprobation of his Conduct.—Had I not known that the Inspector General, after a strict Examination into the Matter, had made such a Report to you, I should myself have suspended Hatton from acting in his Office till further Orders from proper Authority. But as you were made fully acquainted with his conduct, and it was a Matter over which you had a particular Superintendency, I was unwilling to interfere; more especially as I had a Right to expect that you would have thought yourself in Duty bound, after receiving such Information, to remove him immediately from his Office in the Customs.

"There is one matter more, Gentlemen, which I think necessary to mention to you on this Occasion. It appears by Mr Hatton's Book of Letters (which has been seen by several Gentlemen in Salem) that he wrote you a Letter on the 23d of Jany 1769, containing some injurious Reflections on me & the Magistrates, accusing us of having treated him with Inhumanity, & intimating that we were Enemies to our King & Country. At the same Time he sent enclosed a Letter which he said he had received from an English Gentleman who arrived here the June preceding, and 'would give you an Insight of his disagreeable and precarious situation.' A Copy of this pretended Letter I have seen. It is signed with the name of John Murch, and is dated Novr 28, 1768. There never was, perhaps, considering the Time when it was wrote, a Letter penn'd with a more wicked Design: But as it seem'd to carry its own Antidote with it, being fill'd with an extravagantly ridiculous and improbable Account of the Disposition & Intentions of the People of this Province, I never took any notice of it, except writing to the Inspector General (when I heard he was at Philadelphia on his Way to Salem) acquainting him that I suspected it to be a Forgery of Hatton's, or at least that Murch was some low Fellow who had wrote it at his Instigation, and should therefore be much obliged to him if he would demand a Sight of the Original, and enquire Murch's Character and where he was to be found, that he might, should there be Occasion, be examined concerning it. Nor should I, Gentlemen, ever have thought it worth my while to have said anything to you on the Subject (having entertained too good an Opinion of your Understanding to suppose such an absurd Letter could possibly have any Regard paid it by you) had I not observed in your last Letter, that you 'thought it necessary to transmit to the Lord's Commissioners of His Majesty's Treasury, Copies of the several Letters laid before you' by Hatton, relative to his last Complaint, tho' no proper Enquiry had then been made into the Truth of his Representations, at least none which had come to your knowledge. This, I own, has alarm'd me. You may have likewise thought it necessary to transmit to their Lordships the two above mentioned false and scandalous Letters respecting me and the Inhabitants of this Colony, without so much as enquiring or thinking it your Duty to make any previous Enquiry into the Truth of the Allegations. And their Lordships, not being acquainted with the real Circumstances of the Case, and perhaps relying upon that you would not trouble them with any idle Informations, or such as you had not good reason to believe might be depended upon, may have conceived Prejudices greatly to my Disfavour. Had I received any such Letter concerning you, Gentlemen, and thought them worthy of the least attention, I am sure I should have deem'd myself bound in Honour to have informed you of it immediately, that you might have an Opportunity of clearing yourselves from any Imputations they contained, and of explaining your Conduct to His Majesty's Ministers: And I would willingly believe that you have not, as you never gave me any Notice thereof, transmitted those Letters to England respecting me; but if I am mistaken in this Point, and the Letters are actually transmitted, then I must desire that you will as soon as possible, send me Copies of them properly authenticated under the Great Seal of the Colony where you reside, that I may have it in my power to obtain that Justice from Mr. Hatton which I am entitled to. A Request so reasonable I hope you will not refuse, especially when I tell you that Hatton had the Assurance, when I lately tax'd him in private with having written & sent those Letters, to deny that he ever wrote a Syllable to you against me, or ever sent you any Letter from Murch, having, as he said, always entertained the highest opinion of me and my Conduct in this Government. But as I thought that he might afterwards deny he had ever made such a Declaration to me (no one besides being present at the Time) I took an opportunity of asking him about those Letters before the Council, when he again positively asserted, 'that he was very clear he never sent a Copy of a Letter from Murch to the Commissioners.' However, his Son (tho' he has as bad a Character as his Father) being soon after examined on Oath upon the same Subject, and not knowing what his Father had said, confess'd that Hatton did transmit to you a Copy of a Letter from Murch, and that it was relative to me and the People of this Province. A Copy of the Notes taken by the Secretary of their Examinations on this Point, and concerning the Place of the Collector's Residence (which is said to be without the District allotted him by his Commission) I send enclosed for your Perusal.

"That this Representation, Gentlemen, of Mr Hatton's Conduct does not proceed from any particular Enmity to the man,* or Inclination to do him a Disservice, you must do me the justice to allow when you consider, That it was not made 'till you call'd upon me for it (I having left him, after giving him a Copy of the Governor's and Council's Opinion for you, to tell his own Story in his own Way) and that I have not only shewn him no Resentment on Account of his Letters (tho' I have long known of them) but have never yet demanded of him my Share of the Seizure of the Sloop Speedwell (which he gave you such Pompous Accounts of it 1768,) notwithstanding I am well inform'd he has converted the whole of it to his own Use, not having even accounted for the Share due to His Majesty.

"I am with great Regard, Gentlemen,
"Yours, &c
"WM. FRANKLIN."

---

* Warrants were issued by the Supreme Executive Council of Pennsylvania in August, 1776, for the arrest of the Hattons, senior and junior, for "treasonable practices," in aiding in the escape from jail of Colonel Kirkland. The elder Hatton was arrested in New Jersey, taken to Philadelphia, and released on bail.

Copy of a letter from the Inspector-General to the Commissioners of the Customs:

"Gentlemen,

"By my Report of Delaware Bay & River, your Honours will see the Situation of the District of Salem; as to the Collector's Disputes with the People; they are in my Opinion of a private Nature, and arose from trifling matters. I can't find that Mr Hatton has ever disobliged any Person there as an officer and therefore has not given any Cause for Resentment against him on that Account, on the Contrary he indulged them in a very great Degree, even in giving them blank Certificates and blank Permits to be filled up by themselves.

"I send a number of those Permits and Certificates inclosed which Your Honors will see are filled up with as many different Hands, as they are for Persons. What Pretences Mr Hatton can form that he received ill Treatment from the People on Account of his Zeal for the Service, Your Honours will best judge. I am further to observe that every Vessell which entered with him from the West Indies was only in Ballast except 5, from April 1765 to May 1766, which was detected by the Man of War and Cutters, and what is still more remarkable he never entered any, but what belonged to noted Smugglers.—John Relfe is the Person who had the Permit from him for the 5 H'hds of foreign Sugar after they were seized by the Collector of this Port.

"Since September 1767, three Vessels entered with Mr. Hatton from Guadaloupe and one from Dom'nico, all in Ballast, and he has not received a Shilling Duties during that Time.—Every Smuggler speaks well of him as a Collector, but in his private conduct as a peevish, fretful, and not a very good natured Person.—Though I do not think myself concerned with the private Character of any Officer, yet I found myself under the necessity of mentioning this of Mr. Halton as he complained of receiving ill Usage from the People on Account of exerting himself in his Duty, that your Honours may the better see how far that was the case, and tho' it is probable that he might have been ill used yet there is little Doubt of its being owning to unwise Deportment in his private Station.

He has lived for twelve Month past at Raccoon Creek, and is now removed from thence to Cape May 90 miles below Salem, out of the way of all business, so that it is necessary he should fix his Residence in a proper Part of the District.

"By this Plain State of Facts I hope your Honours will see all Circumstances concerning Mr Hatton & his District in their Proper Light.—His situation having a Family to support with a narrow Income might account for some of the irregular Appearances in his Conduct as an Officer. That with his Time of Life in a distant Country renders him an Object of Compassion, and therefore I beg Leave to recommend him to your Admonishment as I presume it will come with more Propriety & Weight from Your Honours than me and wish it may have the Effect of his living upon a better understanding with the People, & being more Circumspect in the Duties of his Office.

"I am with great Respect, Your Honours
"Humble Servant
"J. WILLIAMS.

"Philadelphia 17 June 1769.
"To the Honble The Commissioners of His Majesty's Customs at Boston."

Governor Franklin to Earl of Hillsborough, concerning complaint of John Hatton, &c.:

"Burlington, May 19th 1771.
"The Right Honble the Earl of Hillsborough.

My Lord Inclosed I send your Lordship a Copy of the Minutes of the Privy Council of this Colony, from the 8th of January to the 26th of March, a great Part of which is taken up with an Enquiry into a Complaint made by John Hatton, Esqr Collector of His Majesty's Customs for the Port of Salem, against some Justices of the Peace living at Cape May. This Mr. Hatton is the same Person mentioned in my Letter to your Lordship of the 25th of Augst 1768, N. 11, and in the Minutes of the Privy Council sent with my Letter N. 6.—The Council, after a strict and impartial Examination of the Parties, were unanimously of Opinion that there was not the least Foundation for his Complaint against the Justices. I need not trouble your Lordship with any Recital of Particulars here, as they are so fully set forth in the Minutes, and in the Copies of Sundry Papers sent herewith.—I was in hopes that the Commissioners at Boston would before now have removed this man from his Office, as they have had the strongest Proofs of his Unfaithfulness in Execution of it, ever since June 1769, as your Lordship will see by the enclosed Copy of the Report of the Inspector General. What reasons they may have for continuing him in Office I know not, as they have not yet thought proper to return any Answer to my Letter of the 10th of April last, a Copy of which is among the enclosed Papers. ,

"I have the Honour to be, with the greatest Respect, My Lord, Your Lordship's most obedient & most humble Servant WM. FRANKLIN."

"Some Notes and Observations made by the Depu Secretary of New Jersey, on the Complaint of John Hatton Esqr. Collector of Salem, against three of the Magistrates of Cape May, after the Examination of the Parties before the Governor & Council, explaining more particularly several matters either omitted or but slightly ment'd in the Minutes of Council on that Subject."

"There is very little of Mr Hatton's Complaint, that, if true can affect the Magistrates of Cape May:—the Transactions which he and his Son received the Injury, being entirely without their Jurisdiction. It may be reduced to the following Heads.

"1. Their sending Their Warrant for him on the Oath of Hughes.

"2. Their sending their Warrant for his Negro on the same Foundation, and committing him after Examination.

"3. Refusing to admit the Negro to Bail.

"4. Demanding Surety of the Peace of Mr Hatton, on the

Affidavit of Mills,—on which they took his own **Recognizance.**

"5. Demanding the like Surety from the Negro, & committing him to Prison for want of Security.

"In all which Transactions it does not appear that he was under any Kind of Restraint more than for a few Hours, and that from absolute necessity, and not at a Time when the Duty of his Office required his Attendance. But even if it had interfered with the Revenue, the Cause of this Restraint was of a higher Nature;—for whenever the Kings Peace comes in Question all Civil Matters must give Way to the Enquiry. In the 4th Paragraph of his Complaint, Mr Hatton calls the Charge against his Negro a Pretense, and says 'the Oath of Hughes was only invented to distress him and his Family.' If the Oath was invented by the Magistrates for the Purpose, it was undoubtedly highly Criminal in them. But can it be supposed that they could induce Hughes to perjure himself to furnish such a Design? What motive could they have for wishing to distress him? They were not interested in the Goods seized, nor could he effect their Interest by any Seizures—They were not in Trade, nor had they any Property that could be affected by the Revenue Laws. On the other Hand they had lived on Terms of good Neighbourhood with the Collector; The Magistrate who administered the Oath to Hughes had, as he acknowledges shewn him particular Acts of Civility, But on Hughes's offering to make such an Oath, the Magistrates would have been Criminal in Omitting the Enquiry.

"The 5 Par. charges the Magistrates with 'sending five Men to his House and taking him out by Force thro' heavy Rain, tho' he was exceedingly ill and dangerously wounded.' The Magistrates, to make it as easy as possible to Mr Hatton, convened at the House of his nearest Neighbour, at a considerable Distance from their own Houses, and did not order Force to be used until they found other measures ineffectual; and it was proved to them by the Man at Whose House they were, that he had been riding about with him most of the Day in the same kind of Weather and the Constable (by whom they had received a Message from Mr

Hatton rather disrespectfull) reported to them that he was not so ill as to be in any Danger from coming out.

"The Arrogance and Rudeness with which he charges the Magistrates, was no more than the Language they thought it necessary to use to restrain him from insulting them in the Duty of their Office when he appeared before them, charged on Oath as a Criminal. The £500 Security he offered for his Negro was no other than his own Recognizance in that Sum, which they did not think a sufficient Security; nor did they think the Negro Bailable had the Security been ever so good. The Secretary's Letter contained no more than his Advice to admit the Negro to Bail if they should think it Legal so to do from the Circumstances of his Case, of which they were then the sole judges.

"The Justice's had seen the Governor's Proclamation before, and did not think it necessary to read it in the presence of Mr. Hatton, especially as it did not relate to what was then required of them.

"Par. 6. Hughes, in the mean Time, had procured a Writ of Habeas Corpus, and was admitted to Bail by the Honl Charles Read Esqr one of the Justices of the Supreme Court, and Collector of His Majesty's Customs for the Port of Burlington, by which he was entitled to his Liberty. But the Justices of Cape May did not think they had Power to admit him to Bail, tho' he was committed for a Crime of a less Nature than the Negro stood charged with.

"Par. 7. By the Complaint in this Paragraph, one would imagine Mills was one of the Persons pointed out in the Proclamation as being concerned in the Rescue of the Pilot Boat. But the fact is otherwise. Mills is not mentioned in the Proclamation in the Light of a Criminal; nor was he at all concerned in the Affray. Mr Hatton did influence the Printer to insert, under the Proclamation, an Advertisement, signed by himself, offering a reward for apprehending Mills; but he seems not to have been very desirous of having him taken up, as he declined making any Affidavit befor the Justices which they thought would be a proper Ground for issuing a Precept against him.

"Par. 8 & 9. These Warrants against Mr Hatton & his Negro, were grounded on Mills's Affidavit, and his demanding Surety of the Peace against them. From his going voluntarily before the Justices to make this Affidavit, it should seem that he did not fly from Justice, and that he had at least as much Reason to be affraid from the Threats of Mr Hatton, as the latter could have from his menaces. Mr Hatton insinuates that he wore Pistols in his Pocket, and he charges Mills with carrying a Club, they had quarrelled, and probably mutual Threats had passed. On Binding both Parties to their good Behaviour, the Judges Obliged Mills to find a Bondsman, but from Mr. Hatton they took no other Security than his own Recognizance, which, if it can be called Partiality at all, was in his Favour; tho' by the Words of his Complaint, a Stranger to the Fact would imagine they obliged him to procure a Bondsman.

"Par. 12 & 15. The Threats of Destruction to any who should give Mr Hatton any Assistance, appear nowhere but in the Complaint; the Magistrates deny any knowledge of it. And, indeed, all his Fears and Injury to his Person and Property appear to be chimerical and without Foundation. His Informations have chiefly come by his own Servants whom he sent out as Spies for that Purpose; and some of the People, knowing their Design, have dropped Expressions on purpose to furnish them with a Tale, that they might have an Opportunity to laugh at the Effects of his suspicious Disposition. Par. 13 & 14, are fully answered in the Minutes of Council.

"The Complaint of the 26th Jan. begins with an impudent Falsehood. No such Promise was ever made to him; on the Contrary the Governor repeatedly told him that he could not, consistent with the Royal Insctructions, deprive a Justice of his Office, but with the Advice of the Council, which could not be expected 'till after a Hearing. His complaint against the Magistrates, after his Answering a few Questions in Explanation of some Parts of it, afforded but a slender Foundation for calling upon them to answer it, much less to suspend them without a Hearing.

"He charges one of the Justices with pursuing the Constable, to know what Witnesses he had summoned, and tampering with such as he could influence—The Fact appears thus,

"Justice Whilden happened to meet the Constable at the House of one of the Witnesses sent for Mr Hatton, but did not know the Constable's Errand there, nor speak to the Witness on the Subject; nor did he ever, as he declared on Oath, signify the least Desire that any Person should decline testifying the whole Truth in Behalf of Mr Hatton. The Collector had sent his Negro to dog the Justice, who seeing him go into this House where the Constable was, and continue there for some Time, returned and told his Master of it—and his Imagination supplied the Rest.

"Mr Hatton says he was more likely to be insulted than to obtain Justice, when he had his Witnesses before the Justices to be sworn, and refers to a Certificate of the two Justices as a Proof of it.—This Certificate amounts to no more than this, That two Persons brought before the Justices refused to swear (which they had a Right to do) and that Mr Hatton's Son having written something for one of them to swear to, the man put the Paper in his Pocket and refused to return it.

"It must be observed that Mr Hatton procured the Depositions of twelve other Persons respecting the same Transactions; and it is remarkable that these Depositions are all drawn up in the Hand Writing of Mr Hatton & his Son, and in such Parts of them as relate to the Conduct of the Justices, particular Words and Expressions are selected, which, standing by themselves, may sometimes appear to have a meaning totally different from the real sense of them when connected with what was said before and after them.

"Mr Hatton concludes his Address in Language that would excite Compassion in the Breast of a Savage—if the Facts asserted in it were true.

"'I have left my Wife at the Point of Death thro' Fright, my only Child wounded and a cripple, And my Servants trembling thro' Fear; and I obliged to quit my Family and Office and to travel thro' snowy Desarts, all by reason of the Power and Actions of James Whilden, Thomas Leaming & John Leonard Esquires.'

"From all that has appeared concerning this matter, so far as I have been able to discover, he might with as much Truth, have inserted the Names of the Commissioners of the Customs, or the Directors of the East India Company, as the Justices of Cape May. For except that he was twice sent for by the Magistrates on Criminal Accusations, which took up but a very few Hours of his Time, he seems to have been as much at Liberty, and as free from Obstructions from the Magistrates and all other Persons within their Jurisdiction as any man in the Country.

"In his Remonstrance of the 20th of February he charges ' the greatest Part of the People of the County' with being 'Smugglers, boasting the Sweets of an illicit Trade, and depending on the Magistrates for Support in their Villany.'

"Mr. Hatton has resided among them for some years past and been particularly intimate with them, in all which Time he has made no Complaint of an illicit Trade being carried on amongst them, nor has he now pointed out any Instance of Smuggling, or shewed any Circumstances to induce a Belief that there has been any of that Business carried on by the People of Cape-May. The Bulk of the People and all the magistrates of whom he has complained, are Farmers, unacquainted with Trade and accustomed to a retired and peaceful Life. That there may have been Smuggling carried on from on board the Ship he mentions, is very probable; and it is beyond a Doubt that Mr. Hatton and his Son were much beat and wounded on board the Pilot Boat by Seamen belonging to the Ship—but it is not even alleged that the Magistrates of Cape May were privy to it, or gave any Contenance to the Perpetrators of it. Hughes, the only Person, except the Sailors, who was in the Affray, was taken up by the Magistrates and committed to Prison as soon as he came on Shore; and, notwithstanding the Violence of Mr. Hatton's Accusation, the Magistrate before whom he was examined, alleges that Hatton and his Son acknowledged, on their first coming on Shore, that they had intreated Hughes, during the Affray, to moderate the Fury of the Sailors & to save their Lives, and that Hughes had interposed in their Behalf. The Truth I believe is, that Mr. Hatton being disappointed of the Prize he had taken, was determined to turn his Wounds to some Account another Way. He seems to have had it in View, from the Beginning of his Quarrel, to provoke the Magistrates into Acts of Indiscretion, that might wear the appearance of Persecution; and stories to ground all their Transactions against him, on a Settled Dislike to his Office, as one that the People wish to be entirely rid of. He wants to induce a Belief in his Superiors that he is persecuted for a strict Adherence to his Duty, which he doubts not will procure him Preferment.

"It is not the Office but the Officer that is unpopular in the Province. He ascribes to himself the Attributes of Majesty, and considers himself as out of the Reach of the Laws—that his Person and his Servants are sacred, and not to be called to account for even the most attrocious crimes; —that his very Potatoes are to be treated with so much Respect, that a Servant employed in gathering them, must not be arrested tho' charged on Oath with a Design against the Life of a Subject! It is by no means strange that a Mind under the Influence of such Ideas should, on the other Hand consider the People of the Country as in a State of Rebellion, disregarding all Laws but such as they can exercise to the Oppression of his Majesty's Officers, and carrying on an illicit Trade in open Deflance of them, and that he should ascribe to the magistrates against whom he complains, an unbounded Influence over the Bulk of the People, and a more Arbitrary Exercise of Power than the Bashaws of Turkey could arrive at.

Some Notes taken by the Dept. Secretary on the Examination of John Hatton, Esqr before the Governor & Council, Febr. 23, 1771.

"John Hatton Esqr being examined by the Governor in Council says:

"That he resides in Cold Spring in the County of Cape May 50, or 60 miles or more from Salem,—that he does not know how far it is from Cohansie,—does not know where Cohansie is,—believes it is in Cumberland County—it is not in Cape May. Does not know any Place called Cohansie, but knows a Creek or River of that Name.

"Saw Inspector Williams, who was down at Cape May twice; saw him there but once being from Home the other

Time he came down. Mr. Williams borrowed Hatton's Book of Letters and returned it to him. Know a Person of the name of Murch who is a Gentleman,—believes he was a Merchant,—was acquainted with him,—received several Letters from him, but never sent any one of his Letters to the Commissioners. Does not recollect receiving any remarkable Letter from Murch characterizing the People of this Province. Does not know that he, Murch, was ever taken up by a Magistrate or committed to Prison. Since Murch went to England has recd a Letter from him (last Fall or Summer) requesting he would procure him a Certificate of the safe landing of some Tea he had to Philadelphia consigned to one Mr. Boyd to sell. Is very clear he never sent a Copy of a Letter from Murch, to the Commissioners."

Some Notes taken by the Depy. Secretary on the Examination of John Hatton junr Febr 23d 1771.

"John Hatton junr examined by the Governor & Council, on Oath says:

"His Father resides at Cold Spring in the County of Cape May,—knows Salem,—has been there, but does not know the Distance they are apart,—never travelled that Road,—it is above 5 miles,—not 100,—nor 80,—has heard it is about 60, or 70 Miles. Remembers Mr Murch, an Englishman, Christian Name John he thinks,—does not know his Occupation,—heard he intended to purchase Lands, but that he did not purchase any,—has seen him at his Father's House, —Mr. Murch wrote several Letters to his Father, one of which he remembers characterises the People, but does not remember what Character it gave,—believes he may have copied this Letter—(Objects to answering such questions as reveal his Father's Secrets) Afterwards says, his Father did transmit a Copy of the Letter to the Commissioners; this Letter declared Murch did not choose to purchase Lands in such a Country. Remembers there was something about the Governor in it,—is certain it was wrote by Murch,—does not know how the Letter came to the House, but saw it after it came.

"Never was at Cohansie,—does not know how far it is from his Father's House."

Copy of a Letter from the Commissioners of the Customs, to Governor Franklin.

"His Excellency Governor Franklin,
"Sir: Mr. Hatton Collector of Salem & Cohensy having represented to us that in the month of November last a large Ship called the Prince of Wales, Captain Crawford, arrived in Delaware Bay either from London or Liverpool which Ship was met by Several Pilot Boats (and as he had been informed) were employed to receive sundry Contraband Goods from on board said Vessel, that he attempted to go on board of her, but that they manned their Sides with Guns &c and threatened to Murder him, that he had made Seizures of one of the Pilot Boats, having some of those Goods on board, which was afterwards rescued out of his Hands by a number of Persons in a Barge belonging to the Ship, upon which occasion, he, his Son and a Negro Servant, were treated in a most barbarous manner, greatly wounded and with great difficulty got on Shore. That his Son was, afterwards met by a number of Sailors in Philadelphia, tarr'd and feathered, put in the Pillory, dragged by a Rope through the Water, and left in such a Condition that his life was despaired of—We thought it necessary to transmit Copies of the several Papers, laid before us, for the information of the Lords Commissioners of His Majesty's Treasury. We have since received further Accounts from Mr. Hatton complaining of the Conduct of the Magistrates, & of Distresses & Embarrassments which have appeared to us to be most extraordinary and in some Instances improbable, but as he informs us that your Excellency has issued your Proclamation and that the matter was to be heard before your Excellency and your Council on the 21st of February, We should be glad you would be pleased to acquaint us with the Result of this Enquiry, that we may be able to form a true Judgment of the Conduct of our Officer.—

"We are with great Regard Sir Your Excellency's Most Obedient Humble Servants,

     HEN. HULTON,
     WM. BURCH,
     BENJ. HATTOWELL.
Custom House Boston 26th March 1771.

Hatton, it will be noted by a careful perusal of the foregoing correspondence, was a man whose word seemed to be doubted. It is said of him that all through the Revolution he made himself particularly offensive, and was a Tory of the strictest kind. He was probably the only pronounced one in Cape May county. He lived on his plantation at Cold Spring, which was owned by the late Daniel B. Hughes, and this property was the only Tory's property confiscated in the county, of which notice is made further on in this history. Were it not for the leniency of the neighborhood, Hatton would have had more of a rough experience during the Revolution than he did.

CHAPTER XIII.
PREPARATIONS FOR WAR.

On April 29, 1771, the following military commissions were issued for Cape May county:

Thomas Hand, Colonel; John Mackey, Lieutenant-Colonel; Joseph Savage, Major; Downs Edmunds, Adjutant.

For the Lower Precinct: Silas Swain, Captain; Seth Whilden, Lieutenant; Levi Eldridge, Ensign.

For the Middle Precinct: Jacob Hand, Captain; Philip Cressey, Lieutenant; Jonathan Jenkins, Ensign.

For the Upper Precinct: Nicholas Stillwell, Captain; Enoch Stillwell, Lieutenant; Joseph Edwards, Ensign.

On November 7, 1770, Eli Eldredge was commissioned Sheriff of the county, and he served from 1771 to 1774. Eli Eldredge was born about 1730, and was the son of Samuel Eldredge. In the Revolutionary War he was First Major of Militia from August, 1775, to June, 1776. He was a member of the Legislature from 1773 to 1779, and was Clerk of Cape May county from 1779 to 1802.

On December 21, 1771, the following were chosen the "Commissioners of the Peace" for the county: William Smith, Thomas Leaming, James Whilden, Joseph Corson, Jacob Hand, Daniel Swain, Henry Hand, Reuben Ludlam, James Godfrey, John Mackey, Joseph Savage.

This letter of Aaron Leaming, who was about attending the Assembly at New Brunswick, which he had written to his constituents, is interesting, but when perusing it the reader should use his imagination in recalling expectant events at home:

"To the Freeholders of the County of Cape May:
 "Gentlemen:—
"Whereas there is a great Probability of a war, and the king having ordered an augmentation of his Forces; and

Inlisting Officers are soon expected to Raise recruits in this province as appears by the Governor's Proclamation I have lately received; and the ships of war having received orders to Rendevouze at Jamaica; and the militia of this Province are to be properly Regimented; and the Assembly being to meet the 17th Instant:

"From all these Indications I expect that an Expedition is to be carried on against some of the Spanish Settlements in the West Indies; and that the Governor will demand men and money from this Colony. As in such case I shall be greatly at a Loss to know what part to act; I desire my constituents, or so many of them as can spare the time to meet at the court house the 13th instant at 12 of the clock, prepared to give me their advice whether I am to vote for the raising either men or money.

"As from the present circumstances between Britain and America, this is a matter of very great importance, which I shall endeavor to explain at this time. I hope the Gentlemen of this county will not think the meeting improper.

"Their compliance will greatly oblige themselves and also their most obedient, Faithful Servant,

"April 4, 1771." AARON LEAMING."

In 1772 a change was made in the apportionment of Assemblymen, but Cape May's number of representatives was not changed from two, which it had had for about thirty years.

On July 1, 1772, a census was taken for the year ending at that date, in which the development of Cape May county was truthfully portrayed. The number of dwelling houses was 275, while there were 1648 people living in the county, divided into the following classes: Males under sixteen, 468; males between sixteen and fifty, 374; males from fifty to eighty, 42; males over eighty, 2; total males, 886. Females under sixteen, 384; females sixteen to fifty, 339; females fifty to eighty, 37; females eighty and over, 2; total females, 762. During the year there had been eleven marriages and eighteen deaths.

A majority of these dwellings were owned by their occupants, and were of that nature peculiar to those good, old times of which we delight to read. The farm house was a story and a half structure, with sealing boards on the sides of the rooms and on the ceilings, which served the purpose for which plaster is used to-day. The floor, if the owners were exceedingly wealthy, had rag carpet on the floor; and, if not, sand of the white, clean kind, which is found on Cape May's superb beach was the principal covering. Others had nothing on at all, and the tidy housewife kept her pine floor boards shining as the result of her daily diligent scrubbing. There were no stoves, and coal was not then known. The big open fireplace served the purpose, and the wood pile was made large in the fall, and during the cold weather, when little else could be done, the sturdy farmer chopped his wood and heightened his "pile" for spring and summer use. The old-fashioned tallow candles served the lighting for evening when necessary, but these were only used when extraordinary occasion required it. The glowing pine knots and big chunks of oak wood in the fireplace gave most of the light for the evening. Because the people at that day were "early to bed and early to rise." Candle light in the morning gave the illumination for breakfast, and before sunrise it was over, and the master with his slaves, for there were some in Cape May county, and the "hired man" were off to the fields to do their day's work. The people worked hard the six days of the week allotted for the purpose, but on the Sabbath they were devoted to their religion. The spirit which prevailed in New England prevailed to a great degree in Cape May. The sturdy Presbyterian, the hardy Baptist and the spirit-moving Quakers were the only denominations which had constituents here at the time.

Their principal holidays and sport days were court days, during which time the games of quoits, running, jumping, hurdling and of like nature were the leading diversions. There was always feasting on these occasions. At the same time public matters were discussed and all the prominent men of the county knew each other, by their regular attendance upon the court sessions.

The manner of conducting public meetings and elections of those days is interesting, from the fact that all who favored one candidate walked to one side of the room, while those opposed took the opposite side. Then the persons were counted for the result. In the same manner public questions were decided, and nearly every meeting and election were conducted on these lines. The ballot was seldom resorted to, and so fair were elections and the people trusted their neighbors so thoroughly that at times a very few voted. At one time only eight votes are recorded for members of the Legislature in the county, while it was known to contain nearly three hundred who had a right to the elective franchise.

Reading matter in Cape May was scarce at this time, and while but hardly a dozen, if that many, newspapers of Philadelphia came to Cape May, it was marvelous. There were some magazine readers in the county, but the number was confined to about a half dozen persons. Aaron Leaming was agent for a magazine at the time, and he had, as his accounts show, collected subscriptions from five persons. Most of the knowledge obtained, therefore, was from the word of the neighbor.

The sons usually followed in the footsteps of their fathers, adopting the same trade, while the daughters went out to service, and were not looked down upon as now for so doing.

There were no matches in those days, and the flint was struck to make the sparks from which the fire was started. The dishes were pewter, and glassware was indeed scarce. The men's clothing was a pair of leather breeches, a checked shirt, a flannel jacket, and a hat with its brim cocked up into three corners. The women spun their yarn, and wove their dress goods. Their life, while primitive, was as happy as the people of to-day, and while they had not the advantages, they knew not of them, and were not compelled to worry as to how thy might secure them.

On March 18, 1773, William Smith, Nathaniel Foster, Thomas Leaming, James Whilden, John Townsend, John Leonard, Joseph Corson, Jacob Hand, Daniel Swain, Henry Hand, Reuben Ludlam, Joseph Godfrey, John Mackey, Joseph Savage were made Justices of the Court of Oyer and Terminer for the county.

In 1774 the county jail, which had been built ten years

previous, was consumed by fire, and the Freeholders were authorized by the Assembly to rebuild the same, on or near the former site. The court house was also rebuilt at this time. An act was also passed to "suspend the prosecution of the County Collector of Cape May for a limited Time." What he had been doing is not known, but evidently the Legislature was not satisfied with him, and were trying to reprimand him, without convicting him of crime.

This year a new oyster law was passed to prohibit the taking of oysters from the beds from April 10 to September 1. Closely following this, on February 11, 1775, the last oyster act of the New Jersey Assembly, as the rulers over a colony of Great Britain, was passed. Under it no one was to take oysters from May 1 to September 1. Forty shillings was the forfeit, recoverable by action for debt, of which 26 shillings and 8 pence were to go to the informer. Burning the shells for lime was an offence, for which there was a penalty of three pounds. The last whaling record before the Revolution was the leasing by Aaron Leaming of Seven-Mile Beach on February 28, 1775, to whalemen for thirty days.

The British Government, being unable to obtain any revenue from duties on the tea shipped to America, in 1773 resolved to accomplish by policy what was found to be impracticable from restraint. It effected an arrangement with the East India Company, whose warehouses were overstocked with that article for want of a market, by which shipments of tea could be sold to the colonists at prices with the duties less than had been charged before duties were imposed. The colonists adhered to their principles, and would take the tea at no price. Ship loads were sent to Boston, New York, Philadelphia and Charleston. From New York and Philadelphia it was shipped back. In the port of Boston the tea was thrown overboard by the colonists disguised as Indians, and the news of this action spread through the colonies and caused a great deal of argument. As was natural, there were some Tories in every province, and there were some in Cape May as well as anywhere else. Parliament closed the port of Boston on June 1, 1774. On the same day people assembled in all the colonies to protest against the action of Parliament. On the approach of the tea ships to Philadelphia, the pilots who lived at Cape May, and operated on the Delaware, were warned not to conduct them into harbor. The Cape May pilots needed only a small excuse for refusing, and they let these merchantmen find their own way up the river. The Committee of Safety of Pennsylvania on October 16, 1775, paid Michael Dawson £9 for carrying like instructions to the Cape May pilots.

The necessity of a general Congress was now perceived throughout the colonies. On the 4th of September delegates from eleven colonies met in Philadelphia and organized into a Congress. They sent a petition of grievance to the colony agents in London to present to Parliament and the King. In the meantime British troops were arriving in America, mostly at Boston. Toward the close of the year news arrived of a proclamation of the King prohibiting the exportation of arms to America. Several of the colonies then began to prepare for their own defense by gathering up what cannon and ammunition they could get. Benjamin Franklin, who was Deputy Postmaster-General for America, was dismissed by Parliament for his sympathy with the colonists. His son, William Franklin, Governor of New Jersey, however, was a devout Royalist, and kept the New Jersey residents and Legislators in a quarrel with him the balance of his official life. In this State the Assembly appointed a committee of correspondence, which met in New Brunswick on May 2, 1775, and called a second provisional convention to meet at Trenton on the 23d of the same month. The British Government continued its coercive measures, and acts restricting trade with all the colonies were passed by Parliament.

On the 11th of January, 1775, the New Jersey General Assembly met at Perth Amboy, and was attended by Jonathan Hand and Eli Eldredge as the members from Cape May. They voted for the presentation to the King of a communication stating grievances in which New Jersey was particularly interested. The Assembly met at Burlington on May 15th, and both the Cape May members were present. They voted with a bare majority of the members to reduce the salaries of the State officers, who were adherents of the King. New Jersey became a foremost State in resisting the organization of British tyranny. The second Provisional Congress met at Trenton on May 23, according

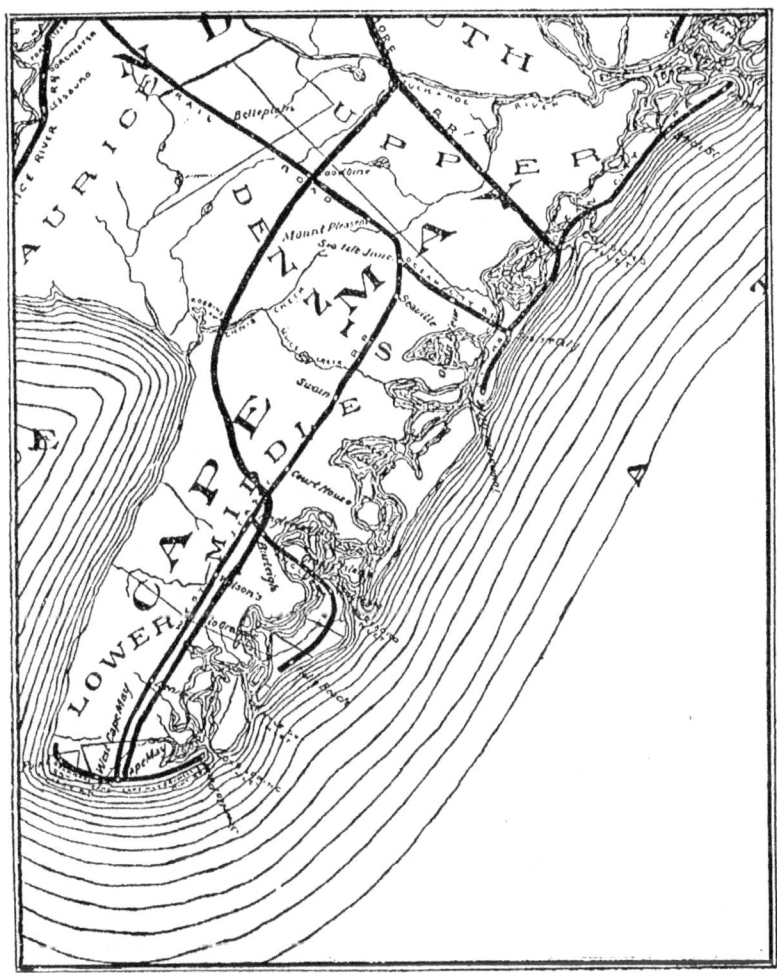

MAP OF CAPE MAY COUNTY.

to call. In the meantime important events had happened in Massachusetts and in New York. The battle of Lexington had been fought only a month before, and the news was just about getting to the distant parts of the colony. Thirteen days before Generals Ethan Allen and Benedict Arnold had captured Ticonderoga, and Crown Point was about being taken by the Americans. On the same day that Ticonderoga was taken the second Continental Congress met in Philadelphia, and the news from there that they had voted that 20,000 men should take the field and that George Washington should be commander, reached New Jersey before the knowledge of Arnold's and Allen's conquest. The second New Jersey Provisional Convention was attended by Jesse Hand as delegate from Cape May. The convention directed that one or more companies of eighty men should be formed in each township or corporation; and imposed a tax of £10,000 on the State to support these organizations. The Congress re-assembled on August 5, and directed that fifty-four companies of sixty-four minute men each should be organized. The counties of Cumberland and Cape May were to have independent light infantry and rangers. There were about 2000 inhabitants in the county at this time. On August 16 the county's quota was raised to one battalion and one company of minute men. The Jersey companies were appointed by recommendation of the Continental Congress. The Cape May county battalion, which was raised in accordance with this call, was not officered until September 21, when the county election took place at the court house. The following were selected by the people:

John Mackey, Esqr., Colonel; Henry Hand, Esqr., Lieutenant-Colonel; Eli Eldredge, Major; Thomas Leaming, Jr., Adjutant.

Aaron Leaming, in his diary, from which these facts are gathered, said that besides those elected, there were then the following officers:

"Nicholas Stillwell.
"Enoch Stillwell.
"Salanthiel Foster.
"Captains James Willits, Jr., Jonathan Jenkins.
"Frederic Otto, First Lieutenant; Joseph Edwards, Nathaniel Jenkins, John Newton, Second Lieutenants; Christopher Ludlam, Richard Matthews"—(here page is torn off).

It is unfortunate for history that the old diary containing

such valuable information should be torn at such a place. But putting these scraps with the roster of Adjutant-General Stryker, of New Jersey, there is some light given on the subject what offices these men filled and of those to which they were promoted. General Stryker's roster says:
"John Mackey, Colonel.
"Nicholas Stillwell, Captain, Lieutenant-Colonel, Colonel.
"Henry Hand, Lieutenant-Colonel.
"Enoch Stillwell, First Major, Lieutenant-Colonel.
"Eli Eldredge, First Major.
"John Hand, Second Major, First Major.
"Thomas Leaming, Adjutant.
"Nathan Hand, Quartermaster."

The uniform of the Cape May minute men were to be "hunting frocks to conform as near as may be to the uniform of riflemen in the Continental service."

The minute men entered into the following engagement: "We, the subscribers, do voluntarily enlist ourselves a minute man in the company of —————, in the county of Cape May, and do promise to hold ourselves in constant readiness, on the shortest notice, to march to any place where our assistance may be required for the defense of this and any neighbour colony; and also to pay due obedience to the commands of our officers agreeable to the rules and orders of the Continental Congress, or the Provincial Congress of New Jersey, or during its recess, of the Committee of Safety."

These men took precedence over other militia, and were entitled to be relieved at the end of four months, unless in actual service.

At this election at the court house, when the militiamen were chosen, Jesse Hand and Elijah Hughes were chosen as "delegates for the Congress," which was to assemble at Trenton. Leaming gives us the names of the "committee," chosen on that day also, which, no doubt, was the County Committee of Safety. The following were selected as members of it:

Joseph Corson,
John McKay,
Jose. Badcock,

John Baker,
Sylvanus Townsend, Jr.,
James Willits, Jr.,

Jos. Ludlam,
Hugh Hartshorn,
Elijah Townsend,
Joseph Edwards,
Christopher Leaming,
Zebulon Swain,
Jesse Hand,
Thos. Leaming, Jr.,
Aaron Leaming,
Jeremiah Ludlam,
Jonathan Jenkins,
Joseph Savage,
Joseph Hildreth,
Jonathan Leaming,
George Taylor,
Henry Hand, Esqr.,
Downs Edmunds,
Aaron Eldredge,
Abram Bennett,
John Hand, Jr.,
James Whilldin, Esq.,
Memucan Hughes,
John Newton,
Elijah Hughes.

One of the notes found in the papers of the Pennsylvania Committee of Safety, which was no doubt made the next year, shows that Aaron Leaming was the chairman of this Cape May Committee of Safety. It reads: "Memorandum. Hewes, a Committee man at the Cape, rows off pilots and others. Aaron Lemen presd't of Cape May Committee."

Mr. Leaming, in his diary, says, bearing on the loan question, which we here note before proceeding further on the acts of the county committee and delegates to Congress, that

"The Assembly having passed a Bill to strike £100,000 to let on Loan: and the same being returned with the King's approbation

"July 4, 1775—The Justices and Freeholders met to choose Two Loan Officers and unanimously chose Eli Eldredge & myself, the commissioners."

At the session of Provincial Congress held on Monday, October 9, Jesse Hand was appointed one of "a committee to prepare an estimate of the expenses necessary to put this colony into a posture of defence at this time."

On the following Saturday, the 14th, a motion was made and it was "Ordered, That commissions do issue to the several field-officers of the regiment of militia of Cape May, whose names are mentioned in the certificate of the county committee," which were those elected on September 21st.

On Saturday, October 28, it was ordered that all persons between fifteen and fifty were considered as able to bear arms in defense of the colony, and all "whose religious principles will not suffer them to bear arms" were ordered to pay four shillings per month "for such their exemption." This measure made the Quakers, of which there were several in Cape May, help to support those whose principles did not interfere with their taking up arms against the British. At the same session Jesse Hand's committee reported that it "appears generally necessary, at this time of increasing danger, that the inhabitants of this colony should be furnished with ammunition and other military stores, and that this colony should be put into some proper posture for defense." The Congress thereupon ordered bills of credit issued to the amount of £30,000 to provide necessary funds. To sink these bills it was ordered that £10,000 should be raised annually in the colony in the years 1784, 1785 and 1786. Cape May was to raise in each of these years £166 18d.

By the beginning of 1776 the British Government had sent over reinforcements to Boston, and their coming had continually excited the colonists. The spirit to obtain constitutional liberty had now begun to turn toward thoughts by the British, and were patriots of the first rank.
of complete independence. But this plan was only with the statesmen, and not with the common people, because there was still a disposition of the less stern to be neutral, and to jump to the victorious side.

The Committee of Safety had now been organized in the State, of which Elijah Hughes was a member from Cape May. It first met at Princeton, on January 9, 1776, and at New Brunswick on February 12. At that session the committee of Cape May are reported as having made returns of militia officers, and the committee. At the latter place, on the 6th of February, Mr. Hughes had been appointed to take a census of Cape May county, as directed by the Continental Congress, which varied little from that of 1772. On the 20th of February a tax to support the war was ordered raised in the colony amounting to £50,000 and 5 shillings, of which Cape May was to raise £156 18d. 2p., and the rates on which taxes were to be raised fixed as follows:

"All householders (exclusive of certain ties) at from 2 to 30s.

"Merchants—5 to 20s.

"Ferry—5s to 5£.

"Coasting sloop, schooner, shallow, flat, passage boat, pilot boat, wood boat, pettiauger, 3s to 30s.

"Single man, work for hire, keeps horse, mare or gelding, 2s. to 6s. Single man, works for hire only, 2s. to 6sh.

"Every bought serv. or slave, 2sh.

"Riding chair or kittereen, 1sh.

"2 horse chaise or curricle, 2sh.

"four wheel chaise or phaeton, 5sh.

"Coach or chariot, 9 shil.

"Every waggon, the body of which hangeth on springs, 2 sh. All cattle, etc., 8 sh."

On June 7th a motion had been passed by the Continental Congress in Philadelphia that the colonies ought to be free and independent, and their action and discussions soon spread across the river to New Jersey. On the 17th of March the evacuation of Boston by the British had occurred and Washington had entered the city. The news was generally spread by that time. The sister colonies had prepared for defense, and the British Parliament had declared the American colonies out of their protection. The British were sending soldiers to America, and 17,000 Hessians had been hired. This news precipitated matters in Congress and in the colonies.

CHAPTER XIV.

THE REVOLUTION BEGINS.

The Continental Congress at Philadelphia, on the 17th of April, passed these two resolutions:

"Resolved, That the secret committee be directed to supply Mr. Thomas Leaming with 200 lbs. of powder for militia at Cape May, he paying for the same.

"Resolved, That the commanding officer at New York be directed to order two companies of Col. Dayton's battalion to march to Cape May and there remain until further orders." And again Congress, on June 17th, voted "that two companies of the force now in the Delaware regiment be ordered to Cape May."

In the spring of this year, probably in March, the following Cape May men were elected as delegates to the New Jersey Council of Safety or Provincial Congress. Elijah Hughes, Jesse Hand, Thomas Leaming, Jr., Joseph Savage and Hugh Hathorn. Leaming was the man whom the Continental Congress voted 200 pounds of powder. They all attended the Congress for which they were elected, which met first at Burlington on the 10th of June, and continued its sessions at Trenton and New Brunswick. On the 18th of June the following military resignations were ordered accepted:

Henry Hand, Esq., Lieutenant-Colonel; Eli Eldredge, First Major; Thomas Leaming, Esq., Adjutant.

Three days later this Assembly decided to form a State government, and on the next day a committee of ten persons was appointed to prepare for the new government and present a Constitution. Elijah Hughes was one of the committee chosen. The Constitution was adopted on July 2, two days before the Declaration of Independence was proclaimed. This Constitution was drawn principally by Rev.

Jacob Green, and upon its adoption it received the assent of the five Cape May delegates.

Thomas Leaming, Jr., was a patriot, whose fame was wide in Philadelphia, as well as at home. He was a wealthy son of Thomas Leaming, who was a long time Judge of the Cape May courts. Leaming was born in Cape May, August 20, 1748, and died in Philadelphia October 29, 1797. He was educated at the University of Pennsylvania, studied law with John Dickinson in Philadelphia, and practiced his profession until 1776. He possessed large landed estates in New Jersey, and was, as before noted, a militia officer and member of the Provincial Congress. He declined to accept from Great Britain the protection offered to those who would not bear arms against the mother country. He, after the convention, went to Philadelphia. To him is given the credit of obtaining the signatures of the men who joined the Cape May battalion, of which he was drill master. In Philadelphia he joined the First City Troop, fought with it in the battle of Germantown, October 4, 1777, and remained a member of the organization until his death. At the close of the war he became a merchant. He was a member of the firm of A. Bunner and Company, which gave £6000, the second largest subscription toward upholding the Continental treasury. His firm was largely interested in privateering, and in 1785 he said their vessels had taken fifty prizes and 1000 prisoners.

The members of the colony Assembly at this time, which body appeared inactive, and was, no doubt, purposely so, were still Eli Eldredge and Jonathan Hand.

Closely following the act of the Continental Congress on July 4, when they declared that "these United Colonies are, and of right ought to be, free and independent States;" the New Jersey Provisional Congress thirteen days later passed a resolution that "Whereas, the honorable, the Continental Congress, have declared the United Colonies free and independent States, we, the deputies of New Jersey, etc., declared New Jersey a sovereign State." Dr. Beesley says of these trying times:

"In the contest of our forefathers for Independence, nothing praiseworthy can be said of the other counties of the

THE REVOLUTION BEGINS.

State, that would not apply to Cape May. She was ever ready to meet the demand made upon her by the Legislature and the necessities of the times, whether that demand was for money or men. Being exposed, in having a lengthened water frontier, to the attacks and incursions of the enemy, it was necessary to keep in readiness a flotilla of boats and privateers, which were owned, manned and armed by the people, and were successful in defending the coast against the British as well as refugees. Many prizes and prisoners were taken, which stand announced in the papers of the day as creditable to the parties concerned. Acts of valor and daring might be related of this band of boatmen, which would not discredit the name of a Somers, or brush a laurel from the brow of their compatriots in arms. The women were formed into committees, for the purpose of preparing clothing for the army; and acts of chivalry and fortitude were performed by them, which were equally worthy of their fame and the cause they served. To record a single deserving act, would do injustice to a part; and to give a place to all who signalized themselves, would swell this sketch beyond its prescribed limits."

Elijah Hughes was born on February 15, 1744. He was County Clerk from 1762 to 1768, and Surrogate from 1768 to 1787, as well as a member of the Provisional Congress. He was also a member of the Legislative Council (Senator) from 1781 to 1782, and from 1785 to 1786. He died November 23, 1797.

As soon as the Constitution for the New State went into effect Cape May was represented in the Legislature by Jonathan Hand in the Legislative Council, and by Eli Eldredge, Joseph Savage and Hugh Haythorn in the Assembly. Their experiences were trying in legislating for a new State, whose future at that time could hardly be predicted. They all served until 1778.

During the last half the year 1776 the British had taken possession of New York, driven Washington to New Jersey, and by the end of the year Washington and his men were struggling about Princeton and Trenton, and even Philadelphia was so threatened by the British that the Continental Congress had adjourned to Baltimore for safety.

On October 4, 1776, Joseph Ludlam and Abraham Bennett were appointed inspectors of gun powder. They were to qualify; to mark the powder—"S. N. J.," and were to be fined £5 for neglect of duty. Their pay was ⅛ of a dollar for every 100 wgt of powder; and should the inspectors ride over 10 miles to inspect over 1000 weight of powder the fees should be 3 pence a mile each way. The Court of General Quarter Sessions could supply a vacancy.

Early in 1777 General Washington's army had been successful in driving the British from New Jersey, and the latter then turned their attention to capturing Philadelphia, and in getting there by way of the Chesapeake Bay. The New Jersey men were called out in classes for thirty and sixty days' tours of duty in cases of general alarm, of which there were many during the next two years. Several of these militiamen did duty at various times in the "Jersey Line," Continental establishment.

About this time the new Legislature appointed Jesse Hand, of Cape May, a member of the Committee of Public Safety, on which he served from 1777 to 1781. The duties of this committee were the most arduous of any other body in the newly organized State. They were considered traitors by the British, and were patriots of the first rank.

From the isolated position of Cape May county, her distance from the theatre of war which extended but litttle below Salem county and her agricultural characteristics which would not be an inducement for British raids, the Peninsula was never the scene of an engagement. None the less however did the fire of patriotism burn brightly in the breast of Cape May folk of the time.

Colonel Richard Somers, of Atlantic county, having captured the brigantine "Defiance," and the inhabitants of Great Egg Harbor having aided him, it was ordered by law of February 28, 1777, that the Marshal of the Court of Admiralty should secure the cargo and sell the same and to distribute the money derived therefrom. On the fifteenth of March John Witherspoon, a signer of the Declaration of Independence and a delegate from New Jersey to the Continental Congress and President of Princeton College, and Abraham Clark, were appointed commissioners to supply

Cape May with 33 stands of arms, 187 pounds of gun powder, 347 pounds of lead, 334 flints, 7 quires of cartridge paper and one bullet mould.

It was also ordered that the Cape May militia should meet on the first Saturday of every month, and attend general review three times a year.

In the incidental bill of March 17th, are these items: To Eli Eldridge for Captain Henry Stevens in full for pay of militia £316.17.9. To Eldridge for Memucan Hughes as Commissary and Muster master, £213.9.9.

Aaron Leaming "held loan office," March 25th, says his diary.

On April 16th, 1777, the members of the second company of the Cape May battalion met to choose officers. Hugh Hathorn certified that he was present at the election. The certificate signed by members of the company reads as follows:

"These are to certifie that on the 16th day of April, 1777, the second company of ye Cape May Battalion of militia in the State of New Jersey being met, did nominate, choose and appoint James Willits Junr Captain; David Edwards first and Joseph Wheaton second lieutenants. Henry Young ensign, in witness whereof, the majority of the company of the company have hereunto set their hands,

"Moses Griffing,
Abel Lee,
Levi Corson,
John Goldin,
Darius Corson,
James Godfrey,
Abraham Van Gelder,
David Corson,
Rem Corson,
Jesse Corson,
Cornelius Corson,
Joseph Badcock,

Thomas Scott,
Uriah Young,
Japhet Hand,
Jeremiah Van Gelder,
Daniel Skull,
Parmenas Corson,
John Cone,
Samuel Insell,
Stephen Young,
Amos Willits,
Jacob Corson,
Isaac Van Gelder."

Commissions were issued to these four officers and dated April 16th. At the same time a commission was given to John Mackey, Esqr., to be colonel, which was dated May 7,

1777, and he was to rank from the date of his former commission as colonel.

An account of a training is given in the words of Aaron Leaming:

"The 3d of May, 1777, at a training Thomas Godfrey having his gun charged with small stones, by accident, shot James Parker in the Leg. The bone was much Splintered & Shattered and it was judged necessary to amputate it. For this purpose docr. Oto was Sent for from Gloucester County. The 12th of May afternoon, the Amputation was performed by Oto assisted by Dr McGinnis of Philadelphia, Docr Hunt & Dr. Benjn Stites. The 17th of May he died."

On the 19th of May, 1777, the Continental Congress at Philadelphia, received petition of Nathaniel Forster, of Cape May, in behalf of himself and divers other inhabitants of the said Cape, praying to be supplied with a few pieces of cannon, and a suitable quantity of ammunition for the defence of the inhabitants of the Cape, and protection of vessels that may be there driven ashore, whereupon it was "Ordered. That the marine committee supply the petitioners with six pieces of cannon, and that the board of war supply them with a suitable quantity of ammunition."

The following is the certificate of the officers of the third company.

"Cape May, May 23d, 1777.

"These are to certify that the under mentioned gentlemen were duly elected and chosen officers for the third company of the foot militia of the Cape May Battallion of which John Mackey, Esqr is Collonel, viz. Salathiel Foster Captain,. Robert Personsjun first Liutenant, John Newton 2d Liuet, and David Hand ensign.

"John Hand, major.

"Certifyed by me."

By this time vessels of the British fleet on their way from New York to the mouth of the Delaware and to the Chesapeake Bay made their appearance about the Cape, and the occasion caused considerable stir among the residents in preparing for defense. Aaron Leaming says, in his diary,

THE REVOLUTION BEGINS.

"On Guard, June 3, 1777.
"Benjn. Ruggins, officer of ye first guard, Samuel Erixon, George Lord, Samuel Wickwaus."

By act of June 4, 1777, the Cape May electors were exempted from voting by ballot. They only had to show their hands at the public meeting. When there were two candidates for an office, and but one to be elected, all who favored one man would go on one side of a room, while those who favored the opponent went to the opposite side, and the tellers counted.

STEAMBOAT LANDING, CAPE MAY POINT, IN 1859.

On June 5, 1777, Henry Hand and Jonathan Jenkins were appointed as commissioners to seize Tory property, sell it if the subject still held out against the new State government, and pay the same, less 3 per cent, to the State Treasurer.

On September 20, 1777, James Willets, Jr., and Thomas Ludlam for Cape May, were named as commissioners to purchase pitch, tar, turpentine, masts, yards, spars, and naval stores, for state uses. The exportation of these things were prohibited.

Later, November 25, 1777, Benjamin Stites and Jesse Hand were appointed commissioners to purchase army clothing. Cape May was required to furnish 50 blankets.

Major Stillwell's report of the officers of the Cape May regiment reads:

"To the Honorable the Legislature of New Jersey.

"Gentlemen—The Captains and Subalterns of the Battalion at Cape May are as follows, viz:

"First Company, Jonathan Jenkins, Capt.; John Cresse, 1st Lt.; Amos Cress, 2d Lt.; Richard Matthews, Ensign.

"2nd Company, James Willits, Capt.; David Edwards, 1st Lt.; Josept Wheaten, 2d Lt.; —————, ensign.

"3rd Co., Salanthiel Foster, Capt.; Robert Persons, first Lt.; John Newton, 2d Lt.; David Hand, ensign.

"4th Co., Henry Townsend, Capt.; Henry Ludlam, 1st Lt.; Christopher Ludlam, 2d Lt.; Jacob Cresse, Ensign.

"For all of which gentlemen, I pray commissions may be made out, as they have been chosen agreeable to the constitution.

"Enoch Stillwell, Major."

"dated
"June 7, 1777.

The commissions for the officers of the first and fourth companies were issued by the State on September 13, 1777, but dated June 7th. The commissions to the second and third companies had been previously issued.

On June 20th there appeared in Cape May Charles Cooke and Allen Cameron, two British agents, who were probably here to give aid to the troops who might land to march towards Philadelphia, then the British's next point of attack. They were apprehended, and Jonathan Leaming, the young son of Aaron Leaming, was sent on the following day with a letter to Robert Morris in Philadelphia, giving notice of the fact. The letter read in this way:

"Cape May, June 21, 1777.

"Dear Sir,
"Yesterday there came two Gentlemen here from Phila-

delphia, and there appearing some cause for suspicion, were taken care of by the Militia; and this day Examined by the Justices, when it appeared by the Oath of Mr. Thomas Hand, that they applied to him to assist them in getting on Board a Man of War. And Sundry papers being found upon them we apprehend they are prisoners of War, and have made their escape from Philadelphia—and say their names are Charles Cook and Allen Maddison; but by their Papers and Confession on a stricter examination, Confess their Names are Allen Cameron and Charles Cook—the former of which having made his escape out of your Prison by heaving himself out of the window. The Prisoners are in Custody, and we wait your Orders to know what further shall be done with them. The contents of which Letters and other particulars we refer you to the Bearer hereof, Mr. Jonathan Leaming.

"We are Sir, with great truth and regard, your most Obdt. Humble Servts.,

(Signed) "James Willdin,
"Henry Hand.
"Directed.
"To The Hon'ble Robert Morris, Esq., President of the Board of War, Philadelphia.
"Favor of Jonathan Leaming, Esq."

Cameron sent a letter to Dr. Thomas Bond, asking for relief from the Cape May committee, while Cooke appealed to his brother, an officer in the American army. They were subsequently released. Of Cameron his after life is not known to the author, but of Cooke we have it that he was afterwards, in 1780, driven from the country, and ever after resided in England. He had two brothers in the American army. Cooke was pensioned by King George III. for the loss of his property in America. The letters which these two prisoners sent on the day following, appealing for their release, are here quoted:
"Sir:

"No doubt you must before this reaches have heard of my escape from there, and I am very sorry to inform you that I am unfortunate enough to fall into the hands of the

Cape May Committee. However it's my fate, and altho' you and I differ widely in political sentiments, yet as there is a few British Ships in sight who have on board several persons of Consequence belonging to this place, whom the Committee seems anxious to have exchanged, I Beg leave to request that you will use your interest with your acquaintances in Congress, to allow those in authority here to Exchange me for one of those from the Ships of War. The Bearer goes purposely with letters concerning me and another Gentlemen who was taken with me. In complying with the above request you will unutterably oblige,

"Sir, Your very Humble Servant,

(Signed) "Alan Cameron.

"Cape May, 21st June, 1777.
"Directed,
"To Doctor Thoms. Bond, Philadelphia."

"Cape May, 21st June, 1777.

"Dr. Brother: In making my escape, I have fallen into the Hands of the Cape May Committee, who have treated me very politely. Several Ships of War lay off Here, in which there are many of your prisoners, & I'm very desirous of being exchanged, beg you'd use your utmost influence with the Congress to have it effected, by obtaining the liberty of Congress for this Committee to see it put in execution. You no doubt will do everything in your power to serve me on this occasion, as it would give me particular pleasure; the rest I must leave to your own good management.

"I am, D'r Brother, yours sincerely,

"Charles Cooke.

"P. S. If not exchanged, perhaps the Congress would allow my going to New York, either on Parole or Sending one in my Room.
"To Col. Jacob Cooke, Esq'r,
"Indian Queen, Philada."

The Continental Congress, in session on July 8th, found due and ordered paid a sum of money to Lieutenant David Edwards and Sergeant Amos Willets for their expenses and horse hire in bringing Elisha Hand, a suspected person,

THE REVOLUTION BEGINS.

prisoner from Cape May to Philadelphia, under orders of General Arnold.

On the 30th of this month a sufficient number of British Men of War had appeared within the bay to cause General Washington to give orders for the concentration of the Patriot forces in Philadelphia. The Cape May committee were then busy in reporting by pony express for a couple of months continually, the movements of the fleet, to the Board of War, the Continental Congress and the Council of Safety in Philadelphia.

The Supreme Executive Council of Pennsylvania on August 1st had in payment for such services, orders drawn in favor of Abraham Bennett for seven pounds and ten shillings for "riding express from Cape May to this city" (Philadelphia).

James Wilson (probably Whilldin) was paid the same amount. On the following day Matthew Whilldin was paid the same, while on the fourth David Hand was an equal recipient of money for his services.

When the officers for the Cape May foot militia were chosen there was no quarter-master selected. The other officers were given the power to select one, and on September 10, 1777, Nathan Hand was chosen by John Mackey, colonel; Nicholas Stillwell, lieutenant colonel; Enoch Stillwell, major, and John Hand, major.

Soon came the battle of Brandywine, and as the war was getting close to home, the New Jersey troops were hurried up to become a part of Gen. Philemon Dickinson's command. Aaron Leaming thus speaks of the activity:

"By a requisition issued from Governor Liviston all the Militia are called from this county & the neighbouring ones to rendevous at Woodberry without delay.

"The 11 of Sept, there was a Battle between General How & General Washington at Chad's ford & Jone's ford on Brandewine the american account is that Washington lost about 800 as some say.

"The english lost is computed by some to be 1300 kil'd by some 3000 & by some near 4000 all uncertain I believe & General Washington says our loss is much less than the

Enemy he is perswaded he says he lost 7 or 8 pices of cannon.

"All this acct I esteem vaug & uncertain. How remained Master of the field & wounded & that night Washington retreated to Chester & wrote the acct to Congress.

"the 19th Septr the militia march'd from Cape May said to be thus:

James Willet's company	50
Henry Townsend's company turned out about	30
Lieut John Cresse	23
Salanthial Foster	37
	140
Field officers	5
Sub. alterns about	11
	156

"A considerable number would not go

"The 22nd they rendevouzed at Woodberry and that day crossed Delaware to joyn Genl Armstrong who is under General Washington and by letters we hear that Genl How lies on the west side of Schuylkil at Sweeds fords and General Washington on the East side thereof 17 miles from Philada. The 22d some firing was heard there."

On the 26th of September the British Army and Hessian grenadiers, in command of Lord Cornwallis, entered Philadelphia, and the main body of the British Army encamped at Germantown.

To hold Philadelphia the British must control the Delaware River, and they finally captured the largest American boat in the bay, and thus secured what they wanted.

CHAPTER XV.

CAPE MAY PATRIOTS.

By the third of October General Washington had received all the reinforcements he expected, consisting then of 900 Continental troops, 600 New Jersey militia under General Forman and 1100 Maryland militia under General Smallwood, which made his force amount to 8000 troops and 3000 militia. Generals Sullivan and Wayne were ordered to enter Germantown by way of Chestnut Hill, while "General Armstrong, with the Pennsylvania militia," says Gordon, was to fall upon the British, gain their left and attack them in the rear. Generals Greene and Stephens were to attack the right, while the New Jersey and Maryland militia were to circuit the right and attack the enemy in the rear also. On the night of that day, the 3rd, the battle of Germantown was fought, the Patriots losing the battle. While Mr. Leaming said the Cape May men marched and joined General Armstrong, of the Pennsylvania militia, there is no doubt of the Cape May men being in the battle, and they fought under Armstrong, being detailed to his command.

On October 14, 1777, the second election for members of the Legislature took place and Elijah Hughes was chosen Councillor; Hugh Hathorn, Henry Y. Townsend and Jeremiah Eldredge, assemblymen. Only twelve persons voted. None of these, elected, however, served then, but did in a year or so later.

By act of April 14, 1778, the militia of the southern counties of the State was formed into a brigade.

From the compilation of Adjutant General Stryker and from local sources and genealogies of Cape May families we gather this list of officers and men who served in the Revolution from Cape May county:

John Mackey colonel, resigned March 27, 1778.

Nicholas Stillwell, Lieutenant Colonel, September 20, 1776, Colonel March 27, 1778, Colonel Regiment of State troops, October 9, 1779, resigned September 23, 1780.

Henry Hand, lieutenant colonel, resigned June 18, 1776.

Enoch Stillwell, 1st Major, September 20, 1776, Lieutenant Colonel October 7, 1778, resigned May 23.

Eli Eldridge, first major, resigned June 18, 1776.

John Hand, 2nd Major, September 20, 1776, first major March 27, 1778.

Thomas Leaming, adjutant, resigned June 18, 1776.

Nathan Hand, Quartermaster, September 10, 1777.

Eli Elmer, paymaster Cumberland and Cape May, 2nd lieutenant in Western Company of artillery.

Jesse Hand, paymaster.

Memucum Hughes, paymaster, July 6, 1776; commissary same date.

John Cresse, 1st lieutenant Captain Jenkins' company June 7, 1777, captain in the same.

David Edward, 1st lieutenant captain Willetts' company, April 16, 1777.

Salanthial Foster, Captain, May 23, 1777.

Jonathan Jenkins, Captain, June 7, 1777.

Seth Whilldin, captain First Battalion Cavalry; Captain in Col. Somers' Battalion, State troops, Dec. 25, 1776.

Henry Stevens, Captain.

Humphrey Stites, Captain, and Captain in Major Hayes' battalion state troops.

Henry Young Townsend, Captain June 7, 1777.

James Wilietts, Jr., Captain April 16, 1777.

Thomas Stites, Captain.

Henry Ludlam, 1st lieutenant June 7, 1777. Captain Henry Townsend's company, June, 1777.

Robert Parsons, Jr., 1st lieutenant June 7, 1777. Captain Forster's company May 23, 1777.

Amos Cresse, second lieutenant, Captain Jenkins' company June 7, 1777.

Christopher Ludlam, second lieutenant, Captain Townsend's company June 7, 1777.

John Newton, second lieutenant Captain Forster's company, May 23, 1777.

CAPE MAY PATRIOTS.

Joseph Wheaton, second lieutenant in Captain Willetts' company, April 16, 1777.

Jacob Cresse, ensign Captain Townsend's company, June, 1777.

David Hand, ensign, Captain Foster's company, May 23, 1777.

Richard Mathews, ensign, Captain Jenkins' Company, June 7, 1777.

Henry Young, ensign, Captain Willetts' company, April 16, 1777.

Joseph Edward, corporal, New Jersey line.

Of the privates the following were probably from this county:

Atkinson, Isaac.

Bran, Joseph, also 2nd Battalion, 2nd Est. Continental Line.

Brown, Thomas, also 2nd Battalion, 2nd Est. Continental Line, Captain Holmes' Co., also 2nd Regiment, third Regiment.

Campbell, Robert, 3rd Battalion, 1st Est., Captain Gifford's Company, 3rd Battalion, 2nd Est., Continental Line.

Chester, Hiram, 2nd Battalion, 2nd Est., Continental Line.

Corson, Cornelius, Captain Willetts' Company.

Corson, Darius, Captain Willetts' Company.

Corson, David, Captain Willetts' Company.

Corson, Jacob, Captain Willetts' Company.

Corson, Jesse, Captain Willetts' Company.

Corson, John, Captain Willetts' Company.

Corson, Levi, Captain Willetts' Company.

Corson, Nicholas, Captain Willetts' Company.

Corson, Parmenas, Captain Willetts' Company.

Corson, Rem, Captain Willetts' Company.

Crafton, John, also 2nd Battalion, 2nd Est., Continental Line.

Daniels, Jeremiah, also 2nd Battalion, 2nd Est., Continental Line.

Davis, William, also 2nd Battalion, 2nd Est. Continental Line.

Day, Thomas, also 2nd Battalion, 2nd Est. Continental Line.
Erickson, Moses, also 2nd Battalion, 2nd Est. Continental Line.
Gamble, Calvin, also State troops.
Godfrey, James, Captain Willetts' Company.
Golden, John, Captain Willetts' Co.
Goldin, Samuel, also 2nd Battalion, 2nd Est.
Griffings, Moses, Captain Willetts' Company.
Hand, Constantine, also 2nd Battalion, 2nd Est.
Hand, Cornelius, also 2nd Battalion, 2nd Est.
Hand, Eleazer, also 2nd Battalion, 2nd Est.
Hand, Jeremiah.
Hand, Japhet, Captain Willetts' Co.
Hand, Recompense.
Insell, Samuel, Captain Willetts' Co.
Kellony, John.
Kilsey, John, also 2nd Battalion, 2nd Est.
Lee, Abel, Captain Willetts' Co.
McQuay, John, New Jersey Line.
Plummer, James, 2nd Battalion, 2nd Est.
Schillenger, James.
Schull, Daniel.
Scott, Thomas, Captain Willetts' Co.
Shaw, John, also 2nd Battalion, 2nd Est.
Stevens, Stephen, also 2nd Battalion, 2nd Est.
Swan, Joseph, also 2nd Battalion, 2nd Est.
Vaneman, Richard, also 2nd Battalion, 2nd Est.
Van Gilder, Abraham, Captain Willetts' Company.
Van Gilder, Isaac, Captain Willetts' Company.
Van Gilder, Jeremiah, Captain Willetts' Company.
Van Hook, Lawrence.
Willett, Amos, Captain Willietts' Co.
Young, Stephen, Captain Willetts' Company.
Young, Uriah, Captain Willetts' Co.
Captain Nicholas Stillwell was an efficient officer.
Dr. Beesley says: "Capt. Moses Griffing, who married Sarah, a sister of Capt. Stillwell, was taken prisoner by the British towards the close of the war, and placed in the famous, or rather infamous, New Jersey prison ship; that un-

dying stigma upon the name and fame of Britain, where the dying, the dead, the famished and famishing, were promiscuously huddled together. A truthful, yet romantic story could be told of his young wife, who, upon hearing of his unfortunate imprisonment, true to her plighted vows, and actuated by a heroism which woman's love only can inspire, resolved to visit him and solicit his release, though one hundred miles distant through woods and wilds, marauders and tories, or die in the attempt. She made the camp of Washington in her route, who put under her charge a British officer of equal rank with her husband. She reached New York in safety, and after a long and painful suspense Sir Henry Clinton yielded to her importunities; her husband was exchanged, and both made happy."

Robert Parsons, Jr., was one of the prominent men of his day. He was born Sept. 17, 1748, was appointed first lieutenant in the army June 7, 1777.

He was chosen Captain of the Militia Company, Lower Precinct, and was commissioned as such by Governor William Livingston, at Trenton, March 21, 1778. He was also duly elected and commissioned by him Coroner of Cape May county, October 11, 1785, and October 10, 1786. He was again commissioned Coroner of the county by Governor Richard Howell, October 18, 1800, and was appointed by him a Justice of the Peace, November 13, 1800. He was frequently selected with others as an arbitrator to settle difficulties among neighbors, and was frequently given a power of attorney to attend important business for persons who were living at a distance from Cape May. And he was appointed by the Legislature, both Council and Assembly, to be one of the Judges of the Inferior Court of Common Pleas for Cape May county, and was commissioned as such by Governor Aaron Ogden, November 5, 1812. He died Nov. 7th, 1822, aged 74 years.

Abijah Reeves, one of three brothers who came to Cape May county from Cumberland, in 1772, was a Revolutionary soldier. He was born in 1750. He served also in the War of 1812. He died in 1822, and was buried at Cold Spring.

John Grace was another Revolutionary soldier not recorded in the list of General Stryker. He enlisted June 13, 1777, in Captain Samuel Flannagan's Company, Third New Jersey battalion, second establishment. He took part with the New Jersey Brigade in the campaign in Western Pennsylvania under General Sullivan against the Six Nations Indians. He also served in Captain Joseph I. Anderson's company, first regiment New Jersey Continental line, and was detailed to and served in the New Jersey Light Infantry battalion, Colonel Francis Barber commanding, and was with the New Jersey troops at the siege of Yorktown, Va., and at the battle of Yorktown and surrender of Cornwallis, on October 19, 1781. He was discharged June 5, 1783, by General Washington. He died April 10, 1835, and was buried in Union Cemetery, Dennisville.

The incomplete records show him acting in these capacities: 1777, fifer; 1778, March, fifer, and 1779, February, fifer.

The Pension office records say he was in the battles of Bennington, Brandywine, Monmouth and Yorktown. In March, May, June and July, 1779, he was a conductor of stores, and in each of these months Quartermaster General John Mitchell sent him in charge of stores to Colonel Hooper at Easton. He carried with him during the latter years of his service, a letter written by General Washington to General Gates, saying that John Grace was a scout and could be trusted with any important despatches which might pass between them relative to military affairs.

Henry Young Townsend, captain of the fourth company of Cape May, was born May 7th, 1744. He was a member of the Legislature from 1779 to 1780, and sheriff of the county from 1774 to 1777. He died May 13th, 1789.

The good services which the New Jersey militia performed in this state are recorded in history. Some of them participated in the fights and skirmishes at Quinton's Bridge, Hancock's Bridge, Three Rivers, Connecticut Farms, Van Nest's Mills, and in battles supporting the Continental army at Long Island, Trenton, Assunpink, Princeton, Germantown, Springfield and Monmouth.

Following is a statement of Revolutionary Pensioners on the rolls in 1818 and 1830. In 1833, Jeremiah Leaming, a member of the Legislative Council from this county, had other Cape May m n pensioned. The statement reads: "Statement showing the names, rank, of persons residing in Cape May county, who have been inscribed on the pension list, under the act of Congress passed on the 18th of March, 1818:

Joseph Edwards. corporal; annual allowance,$96.00; sum received, $1483.16; served in New Jersey line; placed on roll, August 1, 1821; age 77.

John Grace, private; annual allowance. $96 00: sum received,$1525 29; served in New Jersey line; placed on roll, June 30, 1818; age 78.

John Magway, or John McQuay, private; annual allowance, $96 00; sum received, $816 87; served in New Jersey Line; placed on roll, September 14, 1820; age 70; died, Februrry 13, 1829.

The following were pensioners under act of June 7, 1832:

John Dickinson, private; annual allowance, $40;00; sum received, $100.00; served in New Jersey militia; placed on roll, June 3, 1833; age, 75

Ebenezer Preston, private; annual allowance, $23.30; sum received, $69 99; served in New Jersey militia; placed on roll, June 3, 1833; age, 84

On October 17, 1777, the Council of Safety, then in session, passed a resolution, which in part was:

"In consequence of a resolution of Congress of the 31st July last, recommending the executive authority of each State to appoint proper persons to recruit men and apprehend deserters," each county was made a district, and persons were appointed to carry out the suggestion of Congress. In Cape May John Hand and James Willetts were appointed and the recruits were to rendezvous at Capt. James Willetts' house.

Before and during the Revolution there were many salt works along the shore of the Province, among them a very extensive one near Townsend Inlet, on the late James Townsend's place, the owner of which, Dr. Harris, incurred the special ill-will of the British because he furnished gun powder to the patriot army. While the British offered a reward for him and threatened, these works were not, however, in easy reach of the enemy, and as a consequence not disturbed.

Levi Huglingsworth had salt works at Turtle Gut Inlet, in 1777, and Aaron Leaming also had a salt works set up in May this year. John Holmes and Persons Leaming worked them. They made five tons of salt that year.

During the Revolution the Delaware was the object of British attack. At the virtual head of navigation lay Philadelphia with her opulent Quaker warehouses and stores and the fertile farm lands near by. To reach these the river must be ascended and to guard the town and the Delaware shore, New Jersey looked early to naval protection. Cape May and Cumberland being at the entrance to the Bay, they were considered of strategic importance. Armed boats and boatmen under various captains were gathered in the Delaware.

Charles Allen, of Cumberland, who was in charge of armed boat "Gilbert," as well as commanding boatmen on frontiers of Cumberland and Cape May. He was also a Captain of militia.

Nicholas Keen, of Salem, of the armed boat "Friendship" as well as commanding boatmen on frontiers of Cumberland and Cape May.

There are also mentioned in General Stryker's book the following captains, these names being prominent in Cape May:

Joseph Edwards in charge of Privateer "Luck and Fortune."

Francis Grice in charge of all the flatboats and artillery scows on Delaware.

——— Hand, in charge of armed boat "Enterprise."

Henry Stevens.

Enoch Stilwell.

Hope Willets in charge of Privateers "Black Jack" and "Luck and Fortune."

Among the list of seamen the following were from Cape May:

Corson, Jacob.

Crawford, Eleazer.

Goldin, John.

Steeelman, ———, drowned February 7, 1781, at Egg Harbor Inlet.

Abrams, Thomas.

Cox, Abram, sloop "Morning Star," taken prisoner January, 1778, confined to prison-ships "Judith" New York Harbour.

Edwards, John.

Corson, Darius.

Steelman, Richard.

Stevens, David.

The following is the list of "boatmen on frontier of Cumberland and Cape May:" Jeremiah Buck, Israel Davis, George Ewing, Ephraim Husted, Joseph Lummis, David Parvin, Jeffrey Parvin, Abraham Philpot, Abijah Preston, Isaac Preston, James Simpson. Buck, Husted, Lummis, Jeffrey Parvin, Philpot, both Prestons and Simpson, were also private militiamen. George Ewing was a quarter master sergeant of militia.

By the end of 1777, while the American arms had been somewhat successful in Northern New York and along the lakes between that State and New Hampshire in keeping the British from forming a chain of communication from Long Island to Canada, the hearts of the patriots in New Jersey had been made heavy because of the capture of Philadelphia by the British, and the retirement of the Continental army to Valley Forge. Here Washington and his men passed the terrible winter of 1777-8.

The success of the Army in the North had brought to the patriots the co-operation of France who early in the year made a treaty with the struggling Colonies and soon sent reinforcements to America. The British decided to evacuate Philadelphia and concentrate all its forces around and in New York City. The local government prepared to resist this, and on April 4, 1778, the Cape May men were placed in the Second Brigade of the Continental troops. On day previous an act was passed by the State Legislature for recruiting four regiments of Jerseymen for the United States Service.

Jonathan Jenkins, of Cape May, was appointed one of the paymasters to raise money for the purpose of the act, and Cape May's share was placed at £600.

As soon as the Winter 1777-8 began to break up and the

prospects of the British visiting Delaware Bay to attack Philadelphia, the people of Cape May desired to keep their malitiamen at home to protect them. Accordingly, the following petition, prepared by Aaron Leaming, no doubt was circulated and numerously signed, the signing beginning at Cape Island and being presented to each inhabitant along the seashore road until Beesley's Point was reached. The petition reads:

"To His Excellency William Livingston, Esqr. Governor, Captain General, and Commander in Chief, in and over the State of New Jersey, &c.:

"The Petition of Sundry of the Inhabitants of Cape May County.

"Humbly Showeth

"That your petitioners, from their Local situation, are greatly exposed to the incursions of their enemies, who from their ships and vessels of war have landed and often attempted to land; whereby the inhabitants more contigious to the shore might have been robbed of their property, had not the militia interposed for their relief.

"That your petitioners are very apprehensive, as the season is now advancing in which they can cruize along our coast without much danger from the inclemency of the weather; that they will again infest our shores and do all the mischief in their power, and the many threats repeatedly uttered by the enemy, that they will destroy our salt works, burn our houses, and plunder the country, all tend further to confirm us, in our apprehensions of danger.

"That the whole of the militia in a collective body are but few, and when one fourth part of those few is on duty abroad our condition is really weak and dangerous; especially as we cannot speedily obtain assistance from the adjacent counties.

"Your petitioners do therefore humbly request that it may please your Excellency to take the premises under your consideration and exempt the militia of Cape May from performing their tour of duty abroad, and to point out such methods as may enable the inhabitants to keep up a regular guard or any other measure your Excellency may think most conducive to safety.

"And your petitioners as in duty bound shall ever pray. 10th March, 1778.

"Aaron Eldredge, Isaac Newton, Ezekiel Eldredge, Thomas Hand, George Taylor, Daniel Crowell, Zebulon Swaine, Robert Parsons, James Cochran, Salanthiel Foster, Timothy Hand, Ezekiel Hand, Silas Swain, Henry Jones, George Campbell, James Whilldin, Henry Hand, Downs Edmunds, Daniel Smith, Jonan Jenkins, William Yates, Philip Godfrey, Enoch Willets, Isaiah Stites, Joseph Ludlam, Christopher Leamying, James Godfrey, Shamgar Hewit, Robt. Harris, Elijah Townsend, James Townsend, Benjamin Stites, Jacob Smith, Enoch Smith, Henry Stites, Richard Townsend, John Izard, Thomas Scott, Senr., Thomas Scott, Junr., John Young, John Hunt, Junr., David Hedges, Silvanus Townsend, Junr., Davis Corson, Sila Eldredge, Joseph Corson, James Godfrey, Junr., Jeremiah Vangilder, David Corson, Stephen Young, Jacob Corson, Peter Corson, Uriah Gandy, Rem Corson, Joseph Edwards, Daniel Edwards, Israel Stites, Jesse Corson, Henry Young, Thos. Stites, Jacob Willits, Joshua Garretson, John Baker, John Baker, Arch'd. Hughes, Stephen Young, John Goldin, John Stites, David Townsend, Jacochs Swain, Henry Young Townsend, Reuben Ludlam, John Townsend, Junr."

The following is a list, made on May 8, 1778, of recruits raised out of the Cape May battalion, of which Nicholas Stillwell was Colonel, and assigned to second battalion, second establishment, and enrolled for war, and called for by the Continental Congress:

Name.	Place of Abode.	Com.	Age.
Thomas Brown,	North Carolina,	—	27
Thomas Day,	Hattonfield,	1st	19
Joseph Brau,	Cape May	1st	17
Moses Erixson,	Cape May,	4th	19
John Crafton,	Cape May,	4th	20
John Kelsey,	Cumberland,	—	23
Richard Vaneman,	Cumberland	—	17
Joseph Swan,	Gloucester Co.,	—	27
Stephen Stevens,	Cape May,	—	25
Robert Camelle	Cumberland,	—	28
John Shaw,	Cumberland,	—	36

Name.	Place of Abode.	Com.	Age
Cornelius Hand,	Cape May,	1st	18
Jeremiah Daniels,	Cape May,	1st	18
Hiram Chester,	Cape May,	1st	18
Eleazer Hand,	Cape May,	2nd	25
Constantine Hand,	Cape May,	1st	19
Samuel Goldin,	Cumberland,	—	—
Daniel Scull,	Cumberland,	2nd	45
James Plummer,	Cape May,	2nd	21
William Davis,	Cumberland,	—	22

Jonathan Jenkins, paymaster and clothier, in his report made on May 25, 1778, to the State, shows that he paid for clothes for these recruits £600, and that he borrowed £500 of the sum from Joseph Eldridge and the remaining £100 from Jesse Hand. The money was about equally distributed and paid to the following men: Thomas Day, John Kelsey, Stephen Stevens, Moses Erixon, Jeremiah Daniels, Constant Hand, Cornelius Hand, Richard Venimon, Hiram Chester, Eleazer Hand, Joseph Brau, Joseph Swan, Thomas Brown, Robert Cambel, John Crafton, James Plumer, Samuel Goldin, Daniel Schull, William Davis and John Shaw.

The British, however, did not move from Philadelphia until June. Their presence there did not have a depressing effect upon the patriotism of the people of this county as might be expected, because on the 27th of May the following oath of allegiance was taken to the State government by the following persons:

Oath of Allegiance.—"I do sincerely profess and swear, I do not hold myself bound by allegiance to the King of Great Britain—so help me God. I do sincerely profess and swear, that I do and will bear true faith and allegiance to the government established in this State, under the authority of the people—so help me God. May 27th, 1778."

John Taylor,
Levi Hand,
Daniel Cresse,
Henry Stevens,
David Johnson,
Daniel Crowell,
Abner Perlman,
George Hollingshead,
John Stites,
William Schellenger,
Benjamin Ballenger,
Thomas Gandy,
John Nickleson,
Samuel Townsend,
John Baker,
Elijah Garretson,
Jonathan Townsend,
David Cressee,
Zebulon Cressee,
George Taylor,
George Campbell,
Daniel Ganetson,
James Hildreth, Jr.,
Jacob Crowell,
Henry Schellenger,
Daniel Johnson,
Samuel Peterson,
John Foster,
Jacob Stites,
Ellis Hughes,
Aaron Swain,
Aaron Eldredge,
Matthew Whillden,

CAPE MAY PATRIOTS.

Christopher Leaming,
Ezekiel Eldredge,
Simeon Izard,
Humphrey Stites,
Constantine Foster,
Memucan Hughes,
Richard Stevenson,
Thomas Hand,
David Townsend,
John Goldin,
Jacob Smith,
Rem. Corson,
Ezra Hand,
Jesse Corson,
Nezer Swain,
Philip Godfrey,
William Yates,
Jeremiah Richardson,
John Holmes,
Abner Corson,
Nathan Hand,
Richard Matthews,
George Norton,
Richard Edmonds,
Jesse Hughes.
Elijah Shaw,
Reuben Swain,
Constant Hughes,
Levi Eldredge,
Jacob Richardson,
Jonathan Eldredge,
Gideon Kent,
Silas Swain,
Daniel Hewitt,
Ellis Hughes, Jr.,
Uriah Gandy,
Stephen Foster,
Joshua Garretson,
Peter Corson,
David Corosn,
Joseph Ludlam,
John Goof,
James Godfrey, Jr.,
Lewis Cressee,
Israel Stites,
John Izard,
Jonathan Hildreth,
David Hildreth,
William Shaw,
Josiah Crowell,
Isaac Matthews,
Arthur Cresse,
Absalom Hand,
Jonathan Leaming."

CHAPTER XVI.

THE ENDING AND INDEPENDENCE.

It is handed down to posterity that in the dark days of the Revolution, when the army was barefoot and provisions so exceedingly scarce that the people boiled out, dried and strung large quantities of clams, and transported them to the army. No doubt they were esteemed a luxury by the half-starved soldiery, and substituted in some measure beef and pork.

In the operations of the remainder of 1778 the scene of the conflict was transferred to Northern New Jersey and New York. The battle of Monmouth was fought, and the French fleet had arrived in Long Island Sound to aid the patriots. Jesse Hand began his services this year as a member of the Legislative Council, and served during the years 1780, 1782 and 1783.

On the 5th of December the New Jersey Legislature passed an act to raise £100,000 for discharging the just debts of the State in an assessment of lands, of which the lands of Cape May could not be valued under £5 per acre, nor over £60. In the levy made upon the counties Cape May's share was £2000.

On the seventh of December, the causeway over Great Cedar Swamp Bridge being out of repair, the Legislature directed repairs to be made in conformity with the act of March 11, 1774.

The campaign of the year 1779 was barren of important events. In the summer the British infested the coast of Connecticut and captured a few towns there, while about the same time the American army counterbalanced this Connecticut loss by gains of positions at Stony Point, on the Hudson, and the capturing of useful military stores. In the early part of this year the principal events of the war were the gathering of the two armies in the South. The attention of the residents of Cape May during this year were turned to the water front and coast and frontier defense. During the first half of the year there was not much activity. On June 2 the Legislature ordered that for frontier defense Cape May should furnish one ensign, one sergeant, one corporal and eighteen privates. They were to receive bounty, subsistence money and mileage, and Henry Young Townsend was appointed to pay these men, and received £600 for the carrying out of his duty. On June 8 Cape May was assessed £21,103. 3d. toward the whole amount of £1,000,000 which was ordered raised in the State. It was in this assessment stipulated that Cape May lands were not to be assessed over £60 per 100 acres.

On October 9, 1779, to fulfil the New Jersey establishment, a regiment was formed to include men from Gloucester, Salem, Cumberland and Cape May, containing eight companies of 102 men each. Of this Nicholas Stillwell, of Cape May, was Colonel; Robert Brown, of Gloucester, was Lieutenant-Colonel, and Anthony Sharp, of Salem, was Major.

On December 18th, an act was passed to raise £3,375,000; Cape May's lands were not to be assessed above £60 per 100 acres. The levy was £31,200.14.

On December 25 Parsons Leaming was appointed a contractor for supplying stores of war and settling State accounts.

The inhabitants of Cape May, to protect themselves from the incursions of the British and refugees, armed and manned a number of boats and privateers. They manifested great bravery, and address, and were successful in taking prizes. They had the most to fear from refugees— as their names were synonymous with burglary, arson, treachery and murder. Only two, as far as is known, were from this county. They were finally taken prisoners. About the middle of the year 1779 the incidents relating to these privateers are first recorded. A list of them follow:

"June 2d, 1779. The brigantine Delight, Capt. Dawson, on the 20th ultimo, from Tortula to New York, mounting 12 guns, with 29 hands, came ashore on Peck's beach, in a fog, at Cape May. Her cargo consisted of 80 Hhds. of rum, some sugar, &c. Soon after she came ashore, our militia took possession of both vessel and cargo, and sent off the crew under guard to Philadelphia."

"About 1820, the tide being very low, one of the cannon thrown overboard, in the attempt of the British to get her off, was found by Mr. Uriah Smith, and placed at the corner of his yard for a fender. There were three balls in it."

"June 23d, 1779. An open boat, called 'The Skunk,' mounting 2 guns and 12 men belonging to Egg Harbor, sent in there, on Wednesday last, a vessel with a valuable cargo,—which was her nineteenth prize since she was fitted out."

"Upon one occasion this boat had quite an adventure, when commanded by Capt. Snell and John Goldin. They thought they had discovered a fine prize, off Egg Harbor, in a large ship wearing the appearance of a Merchantman. The boat approached cautiously, and, after getting quite near, the little Skunk was put in a retreating position, stern to the enemy, and then gave him a gun. A momentary pause ensued. All at once, the merchantman was transformed into a British 74, and in another moment she gave the Skunk such a broadside that, as Goldin expressed it, 'the water flew around them like ten thousand whale spouts.' She was cut some in her sails and rigging, but by hard rowing made good her escape,—with Goldin to give the word, 'Lay low, boys; lay low for your lives.'"

"Oct. 6, 1779. On Friday last, Capt. Taylor, of Cape May, sent into Little Egg Harbor, a transport from New York to Halifax, with a quantity of dry goods, and 214 Hessians, including a Colonel, who are properly taken care of."

"Feb. 7th, 1781. The brig Fame, Capt. William Treen, of Egg Harbor, about ten days ago took the privateer schooner Cock, Capt. Brooks, bound from New York to Chesapeake bay, and sent her into a port in New Jersey."

"On the night of the 22d of the same month, the brig Fame, while at the anchoring point near Egg Harbor Inlet, in a heavy gale from the NW. with some snow squals, on the flood tide, was tripped and upset—by which sad mishap some 20 lives were lost."

"Capt. Treen, Wm. Lacke, and three others, were on shore. Thomas Adams, Eleazer Crawford, Jacob Corson, and Steelman, succeeded in landing on the point of the beach. The cold was intense. Steelman, who was most active in cheering his companions and freeing the boat, perished when near land. Four only of the crew left on board were rescued in the morning, the rest having perished by

CONGRESS HALL CAPE ISLAND IN 1859

the cold. These kept alive only by constant and unremitting exertion—that being the only method of shaking off the sleep of death.

"Capt. Wm. Treen was bold and fearless, and very successful in taking prizes. He was, however, run down on one occasion by two frigates, for not immediately answering their summons to surrender. Both frigates passed quite over his vessel. Treen and a boy, only, caught to the rigging of one of the frigates, and were saved. Others made the attempt, but had their fingers and arms cut off by cutlasses. Treen implored for the lives of his crew—among whom was a brother of Jesse Somers, now (1842) living at Somers' Point. This being refused, he boldly upbraided them for their cruelty. They could not but admire his heroic bearing, and, while with them, he was well treated; but on their arrival at New York he was placed in that den of horrors, the New Jersey Prison ship, and was one of the few that escaped with life. In 1806 he went to the West. Nathaniel Holmes, who lived at the Court House, was at one time confined on board this prison ship."

"Jan. 3, 1782. William Treen and Joseph Edwards, commanders of the whale-boat Unity, captured the Betsey, which lately sailed from Jones' creek, Delaware, loaded with wheat, Indian corn and flour,—which was taken in the Delaware by a British cruiser, and retaken by said Treen and Edwards."

"Aug. 7, 1782. John Badcock took the Hawk, when commanding the Rainbow; her cargo consisted of spirits, tar, flour, coal and iron,—which was solt at James Willit's, (who kept tavern where Capt. John S. Chattin now does), for the benefit of those concerned."

"Capt. Hand, of the Enterprise, and Capt. Willits, of another boat, on the 5th of May, 1782, chased ashore, near Egg Harbor, the refugee boat Old Ranger, mounting 7 swivels and one three pounder, commanded by one Fryan, with 25 men, bound to the capes of the Delaware, and up the same as far as Christiana, with orders to take prisoners whom they pleased. They afterwards fell in with a schooner laden with corn, and another with lumber, which they took."

The Supreme Executive Council of Pennsylvania, on April 21, 1780, "Ordered, That a special commission be granted to Mr. Abraham Bennett, pilot, to qualify him in ———— and making reprisals on the enemy with an armed pilot boat called the Randolph." The same authority about this time gave Enos Schellenger a like commission.

Scraf and Westcott, in their history of Philadelphia, say:

"In consequence of depredations committed in the Delaware Bay and River this year by picarooning boats belonging to Tories, Capt. Boys was sent down with one of the State galleys to chase off the marauders. The packet 'Mercury' was also ordered by Congress to assist in clearing the bay and river, and commissions were issued to the pilot boats 'Randolph,' Capt. Abraham Bennett; the 'George,' Capt. Daniel Hand; and the 'Hell Cat,' Capt. Joseph Jacques."

Turning back again to the year 1780 the operations of the war were confined to the territory of the Carolinas, and it was not until June of this year, after Sir Henry Clinton, the British commander, had captured Fort Moultrie and Charleston, and, after hearing of the return to France of the French fleet, that he returned to New York by water, to begin again operations there. In the meantime the Continental Congress called upon New Jersey for 1620 men to fill up the "Jersey Line," for the campaign of that year. On the 11th of March the Legislature, in accordance with this demand, ordered it filled, and offered a premium of $200 to each officer who would procure a recruit, and among those appointed "Muster Masters" was Captain John Cresse for Cape May. The bounty of State volunteers was fixed at $1000, exclusive of the Continental army bounty. On the 18th of March the various counties of the State were called upon for their quota of supplies for the United States troops. Cape May's share was 200 wght of beef or pork, proportionate to price. Beef at $240 per one hundred weight; pork 220 pounds net to the barrel $880; fresh pork $280 per hundred weight. 1389 bushels of salt, $120 per 80lb. wght. 692 bushels of corn, 30 cts. per bushel. Philip Godfrey was the contractor for the Cape May dealings.

This muster of March "not answering the ends desired," on June 14th the Legislature amended the act by calling for 624 more men to remain in service until the following January. Cape May's apportion of this number was thirteen men, and Lieutenant Amos Cresse was chosen to recruit the men. This was the third or last "establishment" for the "Jersey Line" of the Continental troops. These thirteen men, of which one was an ensign, were to defend the frontier, and ordered to march to Monmouth Court House to meet the recruits from the other counties. On the 9th of June Cape May was again called upon for money to help pay toward the United States sinking fund, which was declared then at £39,000, 17s. 6d. On the 17th of the month Cape May was ordered to furnish 25 draught horses for the use of the United States.

On August 28, this year, Aaron Leaming died, much lamented and full of honor. He was born July 6, 1715, and after reaching manhood had been constantly a public man, whom his neighbors loved to honor. He must have been a quiet sort of a man, and well deserved confidence and respect by his talents and many good qualities, and served them as their faithful representative for thirty years. He was a man of great industry, a large land holder, and a voluminous writer. He died the richest man in the county, leaving an estate valued at £181,000. He was a thorough patriot, although not serving in the Legislature after conflict with Great Britain had begun. As chairman of the County Committee he did valued service to the patriot cause. He was buried two miles above the Court House, in Middle Township, in the old Leaming burying ground, and upon his monument were the following:

"In memory of Aaron Leaming, Esq., who represented this county in assembly, 30 years. Died Aug. 28th, 1780, aged 65 years, 1 mo., 11 days.

"Beneath this stone, here lies a name
That once had titles, honor, wealth, and fame:
How loved, how honored, now avails thee not,
To whom related, or by whom begot;
A heap of dust remains alone of thee,
'Tis all thou art, and all the proud shall be."

He left a large posterity, one of whom, Dr. Coleman F. Leaming, in 1891, removed the twelve sets of head stones from the Leaming burying ground and placed them side by side in the Baptist Cemetery at Court House.

By the end of the year of 1780 Sir Henry Clinton captured Fort Moultrie, and returned to New York, the treason of Benedict Arnold had become history and beyond these no decisive events had happened. On the 26th of December 820 men were ordered raised in New Jersey, and their terms of service were limited to January 1, 1782, but there were none from Cape May. On that very day, however, Lieutenant-Colonel Enoch Stillwell was made muster-master, and Henry Young Townsend bounty and subsistance master for Cape May by the Legislature.

In the beginning of the year 1781 the British were in the South principally, while the Continental troops under Washington were in Northern New Jersey and around New York. On the 8th of January the militia of the four southern counties of Cape May, Cumberland, Salem and Gloucester were again formed in a brigade, known as the "lower brigade." Henry Young Townsend, on the same day, was appointed the Cape May agent for the loan fund, probably to succeed Aaron Leaming, who had died five months previous. He had to do with the management of the fund in discharging the bounty to be paid New Jersey's troops in the quota required by Congress. During the middle of the month there were some dissatisfied Jerseymen in the Continental ranks, and an open revolt was made by them at Pompton, which was quelled by force by General Washington. These men were not Jerseymen, but non-residents serving in the Jersey Line.

As soon as spring opened the army of Washington moved to the Southern States, where they were joined by the Frenchmen who had come to aid the patriots. It was the intention this year of the British to compel the submission of Virginia. Several battles occurred in the Carolinas, and while these events were happening the Jerseymen were still getting men to fight for the Independence soon to be a reality. In Cape May Lieutenant Amos Cresse, on the 25th of June, 1781, was appointed a recruiter of this county's share of the 450 troops, and for each man he obtained to serve throughout the war he was to receive 30 shillings.

The county tax was fixed then at £156 1½d. On the 21st of June an act was passed to raise in the State £150,000 for war and other purposes. Cape May's share on the first payment of £100,000 was £2080. 11 pence, on the last payment £1040. 5½ pence.

Six days later an act was passed authorizing the Governor

to grant commissions for guard boats and coasting vessels, the commander to give a $5000 bond, and it is believed that two Cape May men availed themselves of the act, but who they were is conjectural.

Owing to the isolated position of Cape May, on October 6th £3 was voted to pay for sending copies of the laws to Cape May with other adjoining counties.

The final struggles of the war in Virginia were being enacted, and on the 19th of October the British army under Cornwallis surrendered to General Washington as prisoners of war. This news was received throughout New Jersey during the next fortnight, and there was great enthusiasm among the patriots. On the 20th of December the Legislature appointed Jesse Hand, Eli Eldredge and Nicholas Stillwell to assess damages occasioned by damage and waste on the part of the enemy, the Continental army or the State militia, and on the same day Jesse Hand was appointed for Cape May to the end that the public accounts might the more speedily be settled.

On the 26th Cape May's levy of the State loan of £150,000 was changed to £1560. 5½ pence.

On the 29th of December another call was made for troops to the number of 422 for the State, to do service until December 15, 1782. Humphrey Stites was made captain for the Cape May county company, which was to be composed of twenty men, and those of Cape May, Salem and Cumberland were ordered to do "duty on land and water."

In March, 1782, they were allowed to cruise on the Delaware bay, if necessary, between Cape May and Reedy Island and as far eastward on the ocean as Little Egg Harbor.

Mr. Andrew Higgins, of Cape May, was paid by the Continental Congress on January 14, 1782, for "his services at Cape May in watching the British fleet out of New York."

"The Pennsylvania Journal" of 29 May, 1782, contains the following:

"Captain Richard Grinnell who came to town last Saturday, we are informed, that he sailed from Cadiz, the 27 of March last, in the ship Lady Jay, bound for this port (Philadelphia) and on the 16th instant came to anchor in Cape May road, and took a pilot on board; but there being there six sailed English ships of war in sight, the pilot could not proceed, and the day following he was attacked by seven boats from the enemy, who boarded the ship, cut her cable, and towed her off under cover of the men of war, and the next day he had the mortification to see his ship in flame. Before he was boarded he got the ship within musket shot of the shore with a warpe, in order to ground her, but a brisk gale springing up from the eastward, the rope broke and prevented the accomplishment of his design.

"Captain Grinnell returns his sincere thanks to the inhabitants of Cape May who came to his assistance with their arms, but in a particular manner to the gentlemen who had the field piece and fought till all the powder was gone."

Cape May required, in 1782, to furnish £156. 1½d. for frontier defense. On June 22nd Cape May was apportioned to pay £936 of a State levy of £90,000.

By the end of this year, and the defeats of the British arms becoming unpopular at home, negotiations for peace had been commenced between the two countries, which culminated in England the next year virtually acknowledging the independence of America.

On the 20th of January, 1783, the articles of agreement were signed, and on April 11th Congress declared a cessation of hostilities. On the 9th of June a tax levy of £90,930 was ordered, and Cape May was to pay £926 of this. In October Congress ordered the army disbanded on November 3rd, and about two weeks later the British army evacuated New York, and America was a free country. In December, 1794, the Legislature ordered a tax levy of £10,000, of which Cape May was required to pay £149 15s. 9d, and two days after the county was ordered to raise £468:4:6d toward a levy of £31,259 and 5 shillings.

The rise of Methodism did not begin in Cape May until 1781, under Rev. James Crowell. He was succeeded by Revs. John Fidler, John McClosky, Benjamin Abbott and others; and ever since this denomination has been rapidly growing in numbers in the county, now having the largest society membership in the county.

The estates of Tories all over New Jersey were confiscated by the patriots during the Revolution. There is one recorded confiscation from Cape May county. That was the property of John Hatton, who was an ardent Tory, and who was Collector of the Ports of Salem and Cohansy in 1770 and 1771, who had much trouble in trying to enforce the odious duties imposed by the British Parliament. The record of this event in the Adjutant-General's office shows that Jesse Hand, agent for forfeited estates, paid into the treasury of the State on May 9, 1785, the sum of £125, 13 shillings and 4d., which was the money derived from the sale of Hatton's property. The account was sworn to before James Mott, State Treasurer, and those who had a part in the sale and settlement of the affair were Daniel Marsh, Philip Godfrey, David Smith, Salanthiel Foster, James Robinson, Jesse Hand, Thomas Shaw and Memucan Huwes.

A letter of the Port Wardens of Philadelphia, of November 12, 1785, shows that a lot had been bought at Cape May, on which a Beacon or light house was to be erected.

On the 21st of August, probably this year, the Council of Safety in Philadelphia directed its treasurer "to pay Dr. Frederic Otto for attendance on a man wounded at Cape May in the service of the State, £6:11:13." This was probably for attending Thomas Godfrey, who was wounded at a training on the 3d of May, 1777.

Jonathan Hand, County Clerk of Cape May from 1840 to 1890, says that it was in the year 1785 that the regular recording of deeds were begun for Cape May county in the Clerk's office. Some were recorded from 1694 to 1726.

On November 26, 1785, Cape May county was taxed by law for State expenses £149:15:9. By act of May 26, 1786, Cape May was to have £1497 17s. 6d. of the £100,000 State bills of credit, which were to be "let out on loan" by the commissioners for that purpose. On November 21, this year, the Legislature levied a tax of £59:17 upon the county to pay State expenses. The next year, on June 7th, Cape May was taxed £187:5 for State expenses.

On the 30th of October an act was passed empowering James Godfrey, Thomas Leaming and Christopher Ludlam to bank, dam and erect other water works at Mill creek, a branch of Dennis creek, which was extended from the fast land of Thomas Leaming's across the meadow and

Mill creek to the fast land of Christopher Ludlam. In the fall of this year Jesse Hand, Jacob Eldredge and Matthew Whillden were elected delegates to the State Convention to act on the ratification of the Constitution of the United States, which had been unanimously agreed upon by the delegates to the Constitutional Convention on September 17th. The State Convention met at Trenton on the second Tuesday of December, and on the 19th unanimously adopted it, when the members went in solemn procession to the Court House, where the ratification was publicly read to the people, New Jersey being the third State to ratify. Attending this convention was the last public act of Jesse Hand.

"He created," says Dr. Beesley, "great astonishment with the people, when he presented to their wondering eyes the first top-carriage (an old-fashioned chair) that was ever brought into the county. The horse cart was the favorite vehicle in those times, whether for family visiting, or going to meeting purposes, and any innovation upon these usages, or those of their ancestors, was looked upon with jealousy and distrust."

"Pennsylvania Gazette," of February 6, 1788, contains the following account of how Matthew Hand saved "the life of Capt. Decatur": "Sunday last Capt. Decature, in the Sloop Nancy, got safe into Hereford Inlet, (about twelve miles N. E. of the Pitch of Cape May) after a passage of 72 days from Demarara. He has been on the coast since the 25th of December, and fifteen times blown off. His mate and one of his hands were washed overboard, but the mate was fortunately saved by catching hold of a rope; another of his men had an arm broke by the same sea. The vessel being leaky, and his provisions expended, Capt. Decature almost despaired of being able to make any port, when fortunately fell in with Mr. Matthew Hand of the Cape May Pilots, who made it a rule to go out in his boat every fair day. To this vigilant Pilot Capt. Decature feels himself greatly indebted for the present safety of himself and vessel. As soon as the sloop was got into a place of safety, Mr. Hand went out in quest of two sloops then in the offing."

On November 27, 1788, an act was passed by the Legislature for the appointment of managers to build a bridge over Cedar Swamp Creek from the lands of Job Young on the southeast to the lands of John Van Gilder on the northwest. The bridge was to be twelve feet wide. Cranberries are first mentioned in the official records as being an important article, which, if then encouraged, might be profitable for exportation.

By this time the habit of pasturing cattle on Peck's Beach generally prevailed, and the owners of the Beach objecting to fences marking the property of each owner, petitioned the Legislature for allowing its use in common. The Legislature, on November 10, 1789, passed an act authorizing the pasturing of ten head of horses or cattle on every 100 acres. For allowing horses over 18 months or any hogs, sheep or goats to graze on the beach fines were to be imposed, as well as for the violation of more than ten head for each 100 acres. On the following day the Legislature passed an act authorizing David Townsend, Thomas Shaw, Henry Ludlam, Christopher Smith and Jacocks Swain to build a bridge over the north and south branches of Dennis Creek, and to claw out a public road from Thomas Leaming's ship yard. The road was to extend from the ship yard to the main road leading from Great Cedar Swamp to David Johnson's saw mill. Vessels were not to moor to the bridge nor take the planks from it.

Pastor Watt, of the Cold Spring Presbyterian church, died this year. On his tombstone are these words:

"In Memory of
the Rev. James Watt,
who departed this life
19th Nov'br. 1789
Aged 46 years.
If disinterested Kindness, Integrity,
Justice and Truth
Deserve the Tributary Tear,
Here it is claimed."

By act of June 12, 1790, when £30,000 was raised in the State, Cape May was to pay toward it the three separate sums of £182:15:4, £146:4:3, and £109:13:3. On November 25 the county was again taxed £219:6:6 for a State levy.

THE ENDING AND INDEPENDENCE. 221

The first general census of the United States was taken this year, and there were in the county, according to it, free white males of sixteen years and upwards, 631; free white males under sixteen, 609; free white females, including heads of families, 1176; all other free persons, 14; slaves, 141; total number, 2571.

The first case of freedom of slavery from Cape May county was that adjudged in the Supreme Court of the State in 1790, which was the case of the State against John Ware on habeas corpus proceedings of Negro Jethro, whose history is given in the following abstract from the decision of the court:

"It appearing to the Court that the said Negro Jethro was born on the 8th day of September, 1768, in county of Cape May," and that his mother, Charity Briggs, a Mulatto woman, was free at the time of birth, and that Jethro was bound by the overseer of the poor to Nathaniel Foster. In 1768 the mother was purchased by John Connell, with the infant Jethro at the breast. Connell sold her time of service to Jonathan Jenkins, who brought up the child Jethro. Jenkins then sold Jethro to Christopher Leaming, who sold him in 1788 to John Ware, and on motion of Joseph Bloomfield, Attorney-General, Jethro was freed.

David Johnson, James Ludlam and others petitioned the Legislature in 1792 for the right to construct a grist mill at Dennis Creek, and that body passed an act on May 26, allowing the mill to be erected at Dennis Creek, provided it was finished in two years' time. The flood gate was to be fourteen feet wide, and always to be ready to open for navigation. The land owners above the mill were to build dams to protect their property.

On November 22, 1791, the State tax was again fixed for the county at £219:6:6, and a year later, November 22, 1792, at the same amount.

About this time Cape May was provided with a military organization, and on November 30, 1792, an act was passed for its organization, and Eli Townsend was made a commissioner to organize them. On the 5th of the following June an act was passed forming the Cumberland, Cape May and Salem companies into a brigade. The Cape May men were to drill on the first Monday of each October and the day following.

During the years 1794, '95, '96 and '97 the county's share of the State expense amounted to £202:17:10½ each year.

On November 23, 1795, Eli Townsend was appointed judge of the court, and Christopher Ludlam a justice. On February 23, 1796, the Legislature empowered the inhabitants of Cape May to stow and lay their boats on "Cape Island road," leaving two-thirds of the road clear and not distant over 12 roods from high water mark. On March 16 this year the Legislature decided that the horsemen of Cape May, Cumberland and Salem counties make one company.

On January 28, 1797, Henry Ludlam, Reuben Townsend and Parmenas Corson were appointed judges, and Henry Ludlam, Reuben Townsend, Parmenas Corson, Elijah Townsend, Elijah Godfrey and Robert Edmonds justices of the peace, and on March 3 Christopher Ludlam was added to the list of judges and Eleazer Hand to the list of justices.

Military commissions were issued on March 27, this year, to Spicer Leaming as captain and Joseph Ware as ensign.

In the annual election of this year there arose a dispute over the election of sheriff and coroners, the result being that two sheriffs and a double portion of coroners received certificates of election, none of which the court justices refused to recognize. As a consequence the Legislature on the 6th of March passed an act requiring the county clerk to call an election for the 21st of the same month to settle the question. On the 14th of October following a State commission was granted Jeremiah Hand, the successful candidate for sheriff, and to John Swain, Jonathan Townsend and Seth Hand as coroners. Sheriff Hand served from 1798 to 1800. During this year, 1797, Persons Leaming became a member of the Legislature. He was born July 25, 1756. He served in the Assembly from 1797 to 1798 and from 1801 to 1803. He died March 29, 1807.

By act of the Legislature of the 8th of March this year (1797) the county's representation in the Assembly was reduced from three members to one, and Persons Leaming was the first Assemblyman under the new order. From then to present time Cape May county has had only one member of the Legislative Council (now Senator) and one Assemblyman. The election day at the same time was changed to second Tuesday of October.

During the year 1798 the following military appointments were made: Jacob Hughes, lieutenant, June 23; Seth Hand, ensign, July 23; Jeremiah Hand, Jr., ensign, July 23; Robert Edmunds, ensign, July 10, and Ludlam Johnson, ensign, August 7. The Cape May "training days" were then the second Tuesday of March and second Tuesday of November, and the "battalion training" on the second Tuesday of April.

By act of the Legislature of February 13, 1798, the county Board of Chosen Freeholders was incorporated, and soon after organized. On the 21st of February the Upper, Middle and Lower precincts were incorporated into townships, with boundaries nearly as those which exist to-day, excepting that Upper township formerly comprised all of what is now (1896) Upper and Dennis townships. The Common Pleas and Quarter Sessions Courts then met in Middle township four times a year, namely, in February, May, August and October, while the circuit judge of the Supreme Court appeared in Cape May only in May.

Jonathan Leaming was granted two State commissions as sheriff in October of both 1798 and 1799, but Jeremiah Hand seems to have actually served from 1798 to 1801, as mentioned before.

In the incidental bill of the Legislature of February 21, 1799, Elijah Townsend received £3 15s. for taking to Trenton the papers of the late Elijah Hughes, when the latter was surrogate.

CHAPTER XVII.

THE COUNTY IN 1800.

In the beginning of the present century the foundations of nearly all the villages now in existence had been laid by the sparsely settled hamlets. They were located upon the two natural highways that ran through the county, either parallel with the seashore or with the bay side. The total number of residents of the county in 1800, according to the Federal census, was 3066, of which 98 were slaves. The proportion was as follows: White males under ten, 487; between ten and sixteen, 242; between sixteen and twenty-six, 334; between twenty-six and forty-five, 264; over forty-five, 197; females under ten, 449; between ten and sixteen, 227; between sixteen and twenty-six, 272; between twenty-six and forty-five, 279; above forty-five, 137; all other free persons, 80.

Among the villages which were centres of life at the time were Middletown (now Cape May Court House), Cold Spring, Cape Island (now Cape May City), Tuckahoe, East Creek (now Eldora), West Creek, Dennisville, Goshen, Fishing Creek, Green Creek and Seaville. The first post-office was established at Dennis Creek in 1802, when Jeremiah Johnson was appointed postmaster, October 9. In the following year Jeremiah Hand was appointed the first postmaster at Cape May Court House, on January 1. On January 30, 1804, the office at Cape Island was established, with Ellis Hughes as postmaster. Cold Spring was designated a postoffice in 1809, and Aaron Eldredge commissioned in charge on October 1. The mails were previous to this time carried by private parties. The stage routes had not yet been established, and the vessel was probably the principal means of transportation.

In the fall election of 1800 Jonathan Leaming had been chosen sheriff and was commissioned October 21, and Robert Parsons, James Ludlam and Humphrey Stites, coroners, who were commissioned October 18.

Dr. Beesley, speaking of the cordwood industry, begun about this time, says:

"It was not until recently, within the present century, that cord wood became a staple article of trade. Many thousand cords are annually shipped from the county, in return for goods and produce of various descriptions, of which flour and corn were formerly the most heavy articles.

"The failure in some measure of wood and lumber, and the improvements progressing in all parts of our State in agricultural pursuits, have prompted our farmers to keep pace with the era of progression, so much so that the corn and wheat now raised in the county fall but little short of a supply; and when the grand desideratum shall have been achieved, of supplying our own wants in the great staple of corn and flour, it will be a proud day for Cape May, and her people will be stimulated to greater exertions, from which corresponding rewards and benefits may arise."

Among the civil commissions granted in the State in 1801 were: Christopher Smith, justice, February 26; Stephen Hand, justice, February 26; Aaron Eldredge, surrogate, July 31; Thomas H. Hughes, sheriff, October 17; Enoch Townsend, coroner, October 17; James Ludlam, coroner, October 17; Elijah Townsend, justice, November 24. In 1802 State commissions were issued as follows: John Townsend, surrogate, June 15; Thomas H. Hughes, sheriff, October 16; James Ludlam, Seth Hand and Aaron Eldredge, coroners, October 16. Aaron Eldredge, a son of Jeremiah Eldredge, was born June 13, 1771, and died August 21, 1819, and is buried at Cold Spring.

At the opening of the century Cape May was already known as a summer resort, and probably the first advertisement of the fact was that of Postmaster Ellis Hughes, of Cape Island, which appeared in the "Daily Aurora," of Philadelphia, on June 30, 1801, which read as follows:

"The public are respectfully informed that the subscriber has prepared himself for entertaining company who use sea bathing, and he is accommodated with extensive house-room, with fish, oysters, crabs, and good liquors. Care will be taken of gentlemen's horses.

"The situation is beautiful, just at the confluence of the Delaware Bay with the Ocean, in sight of the Light House, and affords a view of the shipping which enters and leaves the Delaware; Carriages may be driven along the margin of the ocean for miles, and the wheels will scarcely make an impression upon the sand; the slope of the shore is so regular that persons may wade a great distance. It is the most delightful spot the citizens can retire to in the hot season.

"A Stage starts from Cooper's Ferry on Thursday in every week, and arrives at Cape Island on Friday; it starts from Cape Island on Friday and Tuesday in each week, and arrives in Philadelphia the following day.

"Gentlemen who travel in their own carriages will observe the following directions: Philadelphia to Woodbury is 9 miles, thence to Glass-house, 10, Malaga Hill, 10, Lehman's Mill, 12, Port Elizabeth, 7, Dennis Creek, 12, Cape May, 9, pitch of the Cape, 15. is 84; and the last 18 is open to the sea shore. Those who choose water conveyance can find vessels almost any time.   ELLIS HUGHES."

The hotel which Ellis Hughes kept was called the Atlantic, and was made away with to give place to the New Atlantic. It was located at what is now the foot of Jackson street.

The resort grew in favor to some extent, but not so steadily until after the second war with Great Britain. The old way of getting to Cape May after the war was by carriages and by stage. In 1815 a sloop began to carry passengers, often taking two days to come to Philadelphia. At that time the Old Atlantic was the only hotel, and was the resort of men of prominence and wealth for years. Commodore Decatur, the gallant naval officer, for years visited the island. Congress Hall was built in 1816 and was at first a large boarding house, but when destroyed in the fire of 1818 was 200 by 300 feet in size. It was owned by Thomas H. Hughes.

In 1802 Ephraim Hildreth, a son of Joshua Hildreth, was busily engaged in running a packet from Cape May to Philadelphia, and we find that he made quick trips, leaving here on one day and reaching Philadelphia the next and vice versa. He was connected with many enterprises and recorded his doings faithfully in the diary which he kept.

The first Methodist church's meeting house in Cape May county was finished in 1803, in Dennis township, and its trustees were: Constantine Smith, James Ludlam, Christopher Ludlam, Nathan Cresse and J. Tomlin. John Goff preached the first sermon. The members of the class were Nathan Cresse and wife, R. Woodruf, William and John Mitchell, John Townsend, Jr., and wife, Jeremiah Sayre and wife, Sarah Wintzell, Mrs. Enoch Smith and David Hildreth, who was a local preacher.

Commodore Decatur, spoken of before, in 1804 began to keep his record of the encroachment of the sea at Cape Island. It is indorsed "Statement of No. of feet gained by the Sea at Cape Island from 1804 to 1829, by Commodore Decatur." It reads: "A statement of the number of feet gained by the sea on the Beach at Cape Island measured by Com. Decatur."

1804 from Ellis Hughes' house to beach............ 334
1806 "   "   "   "   "   "   324
1807 "   "   "   "   "   "   294
1808 "   "   "   "   "   "   273
1809 "   "   "   "   "   "   267
1810 "   "   "   "   "   "   266
1812 "   "   "   "   "   "   256
1816 "   "   "   "   "   "   225
1817 "   "   "   "   "   "   210
1818 "   "   "   "   "   "   204
1819 "   "   "   "   "   "   188
1820 "   "   "   "   "   "   180
1821 "   "   "   "   "   "   174
Aug. 30th, 1829, from Beach 64
1824 from Capt. Hughes' gate to Beach 606

The statement shows that the sea in that space of time had eaten away 275 feet of land. The late Jeremiah Mecray once told the author that he remembered when fields of corn were grown where the pavilion of the iron pier now (1890) stands.

Persons Leaming, the sixth son of Aaron Leaming, 2d,

represented Cape May in the Assembly from 1797 to 1798 and from 1801 to 1803. He was born July 23, 1756, and died March 29, 1807.

William Eldredge, who was a member of State Legislative Council (Senate) from 1805 to 1806, was an Englishman, who came from Long Island to Cape May late in the eighteenth century. His wife was Judith Corson, a daughter of Nathan Corson, a man of wealth, who owned what is now the Mount Vernon neighborhood. He was one of the early settlers of Cape Island, buying his land of Thomas Hand, it being located west of Ellis Hughes'. He was born about 1754, and was a Presbyterian in faith. He died in 1809.

Matthew Whilldin, who about this time was very prominent in affairs of the county, was a son of Joseph Whilldin, the patriot. He was born in 1749, and died July 16, 1828, aged 79 years.

He was for nearly a half century a ruling elder of the Cold Spring Presbyterian Church, to which position he was elected probably in the year 1790. Because of his long service in that church he was appointed June 27, 1828, to write a history of the church, which he was never allowed to do, because of a severe kick he received from a vicious horse, which ended his life nineteen days after his appointment. In a civil capacity Mr. Whilldin was a valued citizen, and was in the State Legislature for nearly twenty years. He was first in the Assembly from 1791 to 1794, and then in the Legislative Council from 1794 to 1796. Again in 1804 he re-entered the Assembly, serving one year, and then re-entered the Legislative Council twice afterward, serving from 1806 to 1807, and from 1809 to 1811.

Jacob Hughes, who was sheriff of Cape May county from 1808 to 1809, was born about 1770 and died in 1830. He was commissioned a lieutenant of the Cape May militia June 23, 1798.

Cape May men were early in the habit of saving life from wrecks. In February, 1809, the British ship "Guatamoozin," with a cargo of teas and silks from the coast of China for New York, came ashore on Seven-Mile Beach, near Townsend's Inlet. She was a full-rigged ship. The beach, then a desolate waste of cedars and sand, was covered with two feet of snow. An old hut was the only semblance of life there, and that was only temporarily occupied by Humphrey Swain, Nathaniel Stites and Zebulon Stites, who were there gunning. These gunners went to the mainland, notified the farmer residents, and then all returned to aid the shipwrecked mariners. The crew was safely landed, but the cargo was lost. The rescuers and rescued experienced great hardships, and that was probably the most disastrous shipwreck that ever came upon Cape May's shores, save one ten or fifteen years later.

By the census of 1810 Cape May county had a population of 3632, of which 81 were slaves and 111 were free negroes; 1803 were males and 1637 females.

In 1810 the first Methodist preachers appeared in Cape Island. They were Rev. William Smith and Rev. Joseph Osborn. They preached at the house of Mennican Hughes, a well-known Delaware River pilot.

Of Nicholas Willets, who served in the New Jersey Assembly from Cape May county, from 1806 to 1807, from 1808 to 1809, from 1811 to 1812, from 1815 to 1819, and from 1821 to 1822, Dr Maurice Beesley says:

"Among those who deserve a passing notice as one of Cape May's favorite sons, was Nicholas Willets, a grandson of John. In 1802 he took up the profession of surveying, which he practiced with great success, and obtained the confidence and respect of all who knew him, by the sprightly and urbane deportment which he ever manifested, together with stern integrity and strict impartiality in his various business relations with his fellow-man. It will be seen he was a member of the Legislature nine years, and closed a life of general usefulness in the year 1825, aged about fifty-six years."

The centre-board which has given to America the victory in every international yacht race for forty years was invented by shipbuilders in this county in 1811, and the letters patent granted them by the United States are still preserved, so that the evidence is beyond dispute that the famous device was first made use of in Cape May county. The shipbuilders referred to did business near Seaville, and were Jacocks Swain and his two sons, Henry Swain and Joshua Swain.

The name given to the patent was "leeboard." The patentees, it is said, made very little money out of the invention, because the patent was evaded by building centre-boards to work between the main keel and a kelson instead of through the middle of the keel, as provided in the patent. A copy of the patent follows:

"The United States of America.
"To all to whom these Letters Patent shall come.

"Whereas, Jacocks Swain, Henry Swain and Joshua Swain, Citizens of the United States, have alleged that they have invented a new and useful improvement
in the Lee Board,
which improvement they state has not been known or used before their application and have affirmed that they do verily believe that they are the true inventors or discoverers of said improvement, have paid into the Treasury of the United States the sum of thirty dollars, delivered a receipt for the same and presented a petition to the Sec'y of State, signifying a desire of obtaining an exclusive property in the said improvement, and praying that a patent may be granted for that purpose; These are therefore to grant according to law, to the said Jacocks Swain, Henry Swain and Joshua Swain, their heirs, administrators or assigns for the term of fourteen years from the tenth day of April, 1811, the full and exclusive right and liberty of making, constructing, using and vending to others to be used, the said improvement; a description whereof is given in the words of the said Jacocks Swain, Henry Swain and Joshua Swain themselves, in the schedule hereto annexed and is made a part of these presents.

"In testimony whereof, I have caused these Letters to be made Patent and the Seal of the United States to be hereunto affixed.

"Given under my hand at the City of Washington this tenth day of April, in the year of our Lord one thousand eight hundred and eleven, and of the Independence of the United States of America the thirty-fifth.

"JAMES MADISON.

"By the President.

"JAS. MONROE,
"Secretary of State."

"City of Washington, to wit:

"I do hereby certify That the foregoing Letters Patent were delivered to me on the Tenth Day of April, in the year of our Lord one thousand eight hundred and eleven to be examined; that I have examined the same and find them conformable to law; and I do hereby return the same to the Secretary of State, within fifteen days from the date aforesaid, to wit: on this tenth day of April, in the year aforesaid.

"C. A. RODNEY,
"Attorney General of the United States."

The "schedule" referred to reads as follows:

"The schedule referred to in these Letters Patent and making part of the same, containing a description in the words of the said Jacocks Swain, Henry Swain and Joshua Swain themselves, of their new invented Lee Board.

"The vessel that is intended to be built with a Lee Board through the bottom, the keel must be worked wide in the middle so as to give sufficient strength after the mortice is worked through for the Lee Board to pass; then there must be two pieces of timber worked the same thickness that the mortice is through the keel, and wide enough to be sufficiently strong, and one set at the forward end and the other at the after end of said mortice, and let down into the keel two-thirds of the depth through, so as to stand on a square from the keel and bolted into the keel; then a rabbet is to be cut on each side of said mortice in the keel, of the same width of the thickness of the plank that is intended to plank up the sides of the sheath for said Lee Board, and deep enough into the keel to spike into the same; then fit down a plank on each side into each rabbet and spike them in the first mentioned timbers, then the lower part of the sheath is formed; then after floor ribbands of the vessel is run, then fit knees enough on each side of said sheath to make it sufficiently strong, running from the floor heads to the aforesaid plank, from thence by plumb line high enough to tennant into the combing fitted into the beams, then when the deck frame is in fit up plank on each side to the deck, fitting the same tight to beams, then in planking up the intermediate space may be trunneled on every other one, first and leaving one end of the opening an inch or two wider than the other, and then when the shutters are put in by working them large and driving them in end foremost it may be made sufficiently tight without any caulking.

"The Lee Board is made as follows: It is to be made of two thicknesses of plank laid together crossing each other enough to make it sufficiently strong and thick enough to play through the aforesaid mortice and haul up into the said sheath when ever necessary, and wide enough to fill up said sheath from near the bottom of the keel to the beams that passes across the top of said sheath and the length agreeable to the length of said sheath with the after end sweep off on a true sweep from the bolt hole that it hangs on; said bolt hole to hang it by is to be about four fifths from the after end and near enough to the bottom for a true sweep that strikes the forward end to strike the bottom, and worked off to the same; it is to be hung on a bolt sufficiently strong passing through one pair of the aforesaid knees with a head on one side and a forelock on the other, high enough to fetch the bottom within the knee; with a clasp and thimble ribbeted on the upper side of the after end for the purpose of a lanyard or a tackle to be made fast to hoist it into the sheath when necessary, the top of the sheath the after part to pass through the deck, with a chock fitted at the after end of the same with a shreve in it for a lanyard to pass through for the purpose of hoisting it up; and to make the said sheath sufficiently strong there must be a keelson run on each side of the same and bolt through the aforesaid knees into the keel.

"Witnesses,
    "Elijah Townsend,
    "John Townsend."

CHAPTER XVIII.
THE WAR OF 1812.

Previous to the second war with Great Britain regular "trainings" were kept up by the Cape May militia, and the residents were ready for any emergency which might arise. They were trained in both land and sea service. The military commissions issued from 1800 to the opening of the war follow:

Uriah Smith, captain, March 11, 1800.
Jeremiah Daniels, ensign, April 8, 1800.
James Ewing, captain, March 15, 1802.
Jeremiah Daniels, lieutenant, March 15, 1802.
Daniel Garretson, ensign, March 15, 1802.
Nicholas Willets, captain, March 27, 1802.
Enoch Young, lieutenant, March 27, 1802.
Joseph Hughes, adjutant, June 1, 1802.
Abijah Smith, paymaster, June 1, 1802.
Jonathan Hand, Jr., captain, May 28, 1802.
George Cresse, lieutenant, May 28, 1802.
Cornelius Bennett, ensign, May 28, 1802.
John Dickinson, colonel, November 25, 1806.

Commissions were issued November 23, 1808, to Cresse Townsend, Jeremiah Johnson, James Ludlam, Joseph Corson, Isaac Smith, Jacob Foster and Levi Foster for various officers from captain and under. On November 25, 1809, a commission was issued to Eli Stephenson, and November 1, 1810, commissions were given Shamgar Hewitt and Levi Smith. What offices these commissions were for we have not discovered. When the War of 1812 broke out Cape May county had its "Independent Regiment," and the commissions issued to its officers were as follows:

First Battalion.

Jacob Foster, lieutenant, first company; appointed August 9, 1806; commissioned December 26, 1806.

Jonathan Nottingham, ensign, first company; appointed August 9, 1806; commissioned December 26, 1806.

Jacob G. Smith, captain, second company; appointed March 12, 1814; commissioned May 6, 1814.

Elisha Collins, lieutenant, second company; appointed March 12, 1814; commissioned May 6, 1814.

Richard S. Ludlam, ensign, second company; appointed March 12, 1814; commissioned May 6, 1814.

John Goff, lieutenant, third company; commissioned February 12, 1814.

Jacob Eldridge, ensign, third company; appointed August 9, 1806; commissioned December 26, 1806.

Second Battalion.

Amos C. Moore, major; appointed November 3, 1813; commissioned same day.

John Douglass, captain, second company; appointed March 17, 1814; commissioned May 6, 1814.

Christopher Hand, lieutenant, second company; appointed March 17, 1814; commissioned May 6, 1814.

Swaine Townsend, ensign, second company; appointed March 17, 1814; commissioned May 6, 1814.

Aaron Hughes, captain, third company; appointed March 27, 1813; commissioned April 15, 1813.

Jacob Hughes, captain, third company; appointed March 12, 1814; commissioned May 6, 1814.

Jonathan Crawford, lieutenant, third company; appointed March 27, 1813; commissioned April 15, 1813.

Aaron Eldredge, lieutenant, third company; appointed March 12, 1814; commissioned May 6, 1814.

John Schellenger, ensign, third company; appointed March 12, 1814; commissioned May 6, 1814.

Jesse Springer, captain, fourth company; appointed July 7, 1813; commissioned July 21, 1813.

William Hildreth, ensign, fourth company; appointed July 7, 1813; commissioned July 21, 1813.

Furman Leaming, captain, artillery; appointed October 2, 1813; commissioned October 27, 1813.

Joseph Ludlam, first lieutenant, artillery; appointed October 2, 1813; commissioned October 27, 1813.

John Haines, second lieutenant, artillery; appointed October 2, 1813; commissioned October 27, 1813.

Isaac Smith, captain, artillery; appointed June 30, 1814; commissioned August 4, 1814.

Stephen Stimson, first lieutenant, artillery; appointed June 30, 1814; commissioned August 4, 1814.

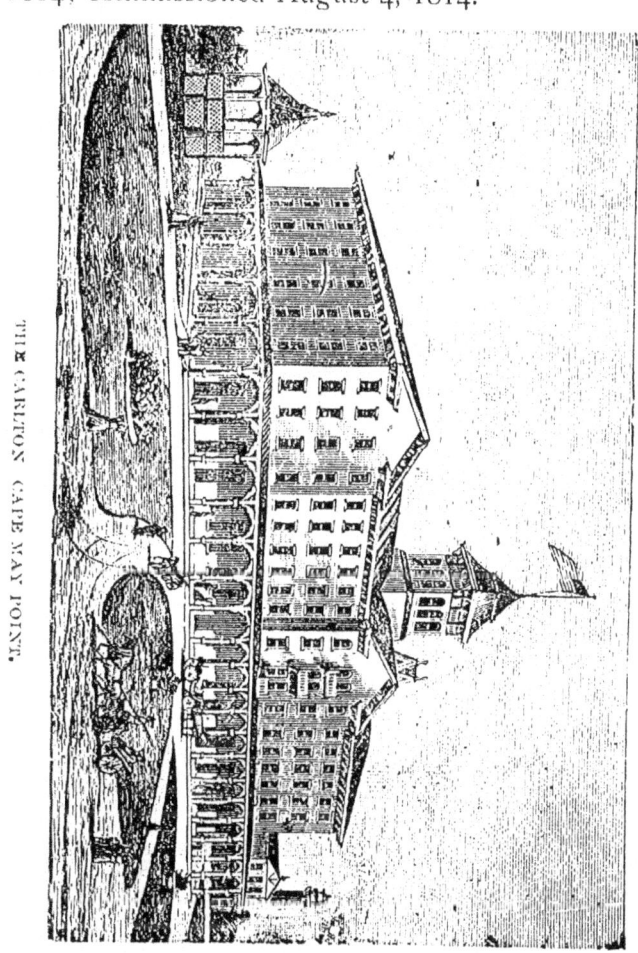

THE CARLTON CAPE MAY POINT.

Ezekiel Stevens, second lieutenant, artillery; appointed June 30, 1814; commissioned August 4, 1814.

Richard Thompson, captain, Fishing Creek artillery; appointed July 16, 1814; commissioned August 4, 1814.

Aaron Woolson, first lieutenant, Fishing Creek artillery; appointed July 16, 1814; commissioned August 4, 1814.

Recompence Hand, second lieutenant, Fishing Creek artillery; appointed July 16, 1814; commissioned August 4, 1814.

Amos C. Moore, the major of the second battalion, was born at Lamberton, near Wenton, March 19, 1776, and was a son of Nathaniel Moore, the ferryman there. He served in troops which went to put down the Whisky Insurrection in Pennsylvania in 1794.' He died at Dennisville June 25, 1857, aged 82 years. He was fifty years a member of the Methodist Episcopal church, and for thirty-seven years was a teacher and Sunday school superintendent. He "rendered efficient service in the late war (1812) in defense of the coast of Cape May."

Captain George Norton's company, an organization of volunteers, which was composed of four officers and ninety-one men, did service at Town Bank principally and at other places along the Delaware Bay shore. It belonged to the "Cape May Independent Regiment" and was ordered into service by Governor William Pennington for the defense of the sea coast of Cape May county. They were first called out in May, 1814, and from that time until the close of the war they were often under arms and performed several tours of duty away from home during their service. They were all enrolled into the service on May 15, 1814, and continued in active service or in readiness therefor until February 17, 1815, when they were finally discharged. The following were the members of the company:

Captain, George Norton.
Lieutenant, Joshua Townsend.
Ensigns, Jesse Springer, James T. Scott.
First sergeant, Ezekiel Van Gilder.
Sergeants, Samuel R. Springer, George Rutter, Jedediah Tomlin, Joshua Crawford.
Corporals, Webster Souder, McBride Corson, Gideon Palmer, Jacob Nottingham.
Fifer, Jonathan Hewitt.
Privates, Jacob Baner, Constantine Blackman, Joseph Bowker, John Braddock, David Camp, Eli Camp, Daniel Church, Zebulon Collings, John Conover, Aaron Corson, Amos Corson, Cornelius Corson, Jr., Elijah Corson,

Jacob Corson, John Corson, Nathaniel Corson, Ezekiel Creamer, Anthony Cresse, Jeremiah Dagg, John Daniels, Thomas Douglass, Mauldare Earnest, Amos Edwards, Jacob Eldredge, Jeremiah Ewing, Jr., Stephen Foster, Thomas French, David Gandy, Joshua Garretson, John Gaskill, Elijah Godfrey, Jr., John Godfrey, Daniel Goff, William Hacket, Aaron Hand, Miller Hand, Elijah Hays, Job Hickey, James Hildreth, William Hogburn, Jacob Hughes, Moses Hughes, William Hughes, Edward James, Jacob Johnson, Daniel King, Spicer Leaming, Jr., Abel Lee, Anthony Ludlam, Norton Ludlam, Thomas Ludlam, Jr., Elijah Mathews, Enos Mulford, James Nickerson, Jeremiah Norton, Samuel Oram, Jr., Amos Pepper, William Peterson, John Pierson, Thomas Pierson, Joseph Ridman, Abel Scull, Jeremiah Shaw, Smith Sloan, John Smith, Uriah Smith, George Stites, Israel Stites, Charles Strong, Daniel Swain, Samuel Taylor, Wallace Taylor, James Thomas, Zebulon Townsend, Daniel Vaneman, Joseph Ware, Samuel Warwick, Jonathan Wheaton, Joseph Wheaton, John Yates.

During the years 1813 and 1814 the Delaware was blockaded a part of the time, and there was almost continually some British man-of-war upon its waters.

It is related that on one occasion while the British fleet were blockading Delaware Bay, a boat was sent ashore from the 74-gun-ship Poictiers, with a flag of truce to Cape Island, with the request to Captain Humphrey Hughes, commander of a small body of men stationed there, to allow them to obtain a supply of water. On his refusal the boat returned, and shortly after another was sent ashore with the threat that unless allowed peaceably to get water they would bombard the place. Captain Hughes, with the advice of his officers, discreetly acceded to their demand. He was, however, arrested on a charge of treason, for giving supplies to the enemy, and narrowly escaped severe punishment.

Another story, which probably refers to the same incident, reads in this way:

One day, while the British ships were lying off the Capes, it was observed that several barges from the ships were being rowed ashore, containing numerous Redcoats. "Long

Tom," a long gun, twelve feet in length, belonging to the county, was run down to the beach and planted behind the breastwork of a sand dune. As the barges approached our men wanted to fire on them, but among the crowd gathered was Abigail Hughes, grandmother to Pilot Albert Hughes, who in her excellent judgment quickly decided in her mind that to fire on the British boats meant but to invite their wrath and bring destruction on our own heads. So, placing herself in front of the gun, she said sternly: "You shall not fire. We may not be disturbed if we don't, but we will surely suffer their vengeance if we do." The men obeyed her mandate. The British, instead of landing on our beach, rowed into the bay and landed at Town Bank, where they raided cattle and appropriated whatever was useful to them that could be carried away. This wise and brave woman's first husband had been a Revolutionary soldier, a lieutenant col. in Washington's army, belonging to the Fifth Pennsylvania Brigade. His name was William Williams, and he fought on Long Island and in the various battles in New Jersey and at Trenton.

Captain Humphrey Hughes was a privateer and used to relate how, when they had run into Egg Harbor, they would disguise their vessel's masts, in order to escape detection by the British, by cutting off pine trees, which they would stand upon shipboard beside the masts, the thick browse hiding the vessel's rigging, so that from sea they could not be observed. He was the fifth Humphrey Hughes, and was born November 10, 1775, and died August 21, 1858. It was he who, when in Rome, met his Holiness, the Pope, and his reckless, never-caring way, refusing to "do as Rome did," got him in prison there, the custom being then for all to bow on their knees as the Pope passed. He did not, calling out that he was an American, and recognized no one to be his better. He was, for this decorous act, seized and hurried to prison. His sailors, who were as bold as their captain, broke into the jail and released him. They quickly sailed away.

On the bay shore the people fared badly in the loss of cattle and other possessions which could be carried away. Vessels owned by Reuben Foster and Aaron Crowell, of

Fishing Creek, were destroyed by fire by the English. Two sisters, Mrs. Anne Edwards and Mrs. Webster Church, while coming home from Philadelphia in a sloop, were taken prisoners from it and the craft burned. Elijah and Jacob Hand had salt works there, which were molested at times.

Abijah Reeves was a soldier in the Revolution and in the War of 1812, it is said. He was born in Cumberland county in 1750 and came to Cape May with his two brothers, Adonijah and Abraham, in about 1772. He died in 1822.

Richard Thompson (the first), who was captain of the Fishing Creek artillery, was born February 12, 1768, at Fishing Creek. He died at Goshen December 21, 1824.

In the latter part of 1813, as several small coasters were sailing around Cape May from the Delaware River, bound for Egg Harbor, they came in contact with a British armed schooner, lying at anchor off the Cape. She put to chase, fired upon and overtook the schooner "New Jersey." from May's Landing, which was manned by the master, Captain Burton, and two sailors. Having placed on board as prize-master a young midshipman, with three men (two Englishmen and an Irishman), she ordered the sloop to follow her, and continue the pursuit of the other vessels. As they neared Egg Harbor, the approach of night compelled her to cease the chase, and she then put about for the Cape. The sloop followed, but made little headway, the young midshipman being an indifferent seaman. He at length placed the sailing of the vessel under the direction of Captain Burton, directing him to steer for the Cape. He designedly steered the vessel so that no headway was made. Morning dawned and found them off the mouth of Great Egg Harbor. Burton feigned ignorance of the place. Shortly after a man was sent aloft to look out, the prize-master and one of his men went below to examine the charts, leaving the three Americans and one of the enemy on deck. Burton availed himself of the opportunity. He and his two men secured the one on deck and fastened the others in the cabin, having made all prisoners within an hour. With a fair wind he brought his vessel to anchor off Somers' Point. The prize-master was imprisoned for a short time, the two Englishmen found work in the neighborhood, and the Irishman afterwards fought under the Stars and Stripes.

The Philadelphia "Daily Aurora and Advertiser," of December 11, 1815, says that a London paper of a few weeks previous said that a court-martial had been held on the ship Queen Charlotte for the trial of Midshipman Richard Willinin, of the Royal Navy, on the charge of desertion. He was an officer on the Jasseur, which had captured many prizes in the Delaware Bay. He was recommended to mercy, although condemned to die. When this young officer had charge of one of the Jasseur's boats, the sailors ran it on shore near Cape Island and deserted. He could not return to the ship alone, and was surrounded and made prisoner by the inhabitants. He was delivered by them to authorities in Philadelphia, but through some misunderstanding he got away, but had on his person a letter requiring him to keep within certain bounds, of which his English superiors got possession, and used as evidence against him.

From the beginning of the war with Great Britain the people of New England had been opposed to the conflict, and that spirit prevailed to some extent in New Jersey. The leaders in this opinion in Cape May county were Joseph Falkenburge, who was then a member of the Legislative Council (Senate), and Robert H. Holmes. They were the two delegates from Cape May county who met in the State convention at Trenton on July 4, 1814, to name candidates for Congress who would vote to discontinue the war. Holmes was elected to the Assembly that autumn on this platform. Falkenburge had previously served in the Assembly from 1803 to 1804 and from 1810 to 1811. He was a member of the Legislative Council from 1808 to 1809 and from 1812 to 1814. He was born in Gloucester (Atlantic) county April 24, 1769. He came to Cape May in 1790, a poor boy, but when he died, April 30, 1846, he was the wealthiest man in the county. He was a tailor and merchant. After the close of the war the military organization, "First Regiment—Cape May," was kept up until 1835. The officers of the regiment up to the disbandment of the same were:

First Battalion.

Somers Corson, lieutenant, first infantry; appointed April 6, 1816; commissioned May 20, 1816.

Edward Cole, ensign, first infantry; appointed April 6, 1816; commissioned May 20, 1816.

Somers Falkenburg, captain, light infantry; appointed April 9, 1816; commissioned May 20, 1816.

Jacob Souder, lieutenant, light infantry; appointed April 9, 1816; commissioned May 20, 1816.

Jonathan Crandol, ensign, light infantry; appointed April 9, 1816; commissioned May 20, 1816.

Jacob G. Smith, captain, second company; appointed April 9, 1816; commissioned May 20, 1816.

Richard Smith Ludlam, lieutenant, second company; appointed April 9, 1816; commissioned May 20, 1816.

John Iszard, Jr., ensign, second company; appointed April 9, 1816; commissioned May 20, 1816.

Joshua Townsend, captain, fourth company; appointed April 10, 1816; commissioned May 20, 1816.

Hugh H. Young, lieutenant, fourth company; appointed April 10, 1816; commissioned May 20, 1816.

Christopher Ludlam, ensign, light infantry; appointed April 20, 1818; commissioned May 15, 1818.

Cornelius Corson, captain, first company; appointed March 19, 1818; commissioned May 15, 1818.

Allen Corson, lieutenant, first company; appointed March 19, 1818; commissioned May 15, 1818.

Enos Corson, lieutenant, fourth company; appointed March 20, 1818; commissioned May 15, 1818.

David Corson, ensign, fourth company; appointed March 20, 1818; commissioned May 15, 1818.

Moses Willet, ensign, first company; appointed April 8, 1820; commissioned May 20, 1820.

May Lawrence, ensign, third company; appointed May 9, 1820; commissioned May 20, 1820.

Joseph Goff, lieutenant, third company; appointed May 9, 1820; commissioned May 20, 1820.

John Goff, captain, third company; appointed May 9, 1820; commissioned May 20, 1820.

Christopher Ludlam, lieutenant, second company; appointed April 7, 1820; commissioned May 20, 1820.

Jacob Smith, ensign, second company; appointed April 29, 1820; commissioned May 20, 1820.

John L. Smith, surgeon, second company; appointed March 6, 1820; commissioned May 20, 1820.

Joseph Fifield, surgeon's mate, second company; appointed June 14, 1821; commissioned August 28, 1821.

Allen Corson, captain, first company; appointed April 15, 1822; commissioned May 21, 1822.

Seth Corson, lieutenant, first company; appointed April 15, 1822; commissioned May 21, 1822.

Smith Van Gilder, ensign, first company; appointed April 15, 1822; commissioned May 21, 1822.

Joshua Swain, Jr., captain, fourth company; appointed May 3, 1823; commissioned May 22, 1823.

German Smith, ensign, fourth company; appointed May 3, 1823; commissioned May 22, 1823.

Aaron Corson, lieutenant, first company; appointed May 5, 1823; commissioned May 22, 1823.

James L. Smith, ensign, third company; appointed May 10, 1823; commissioned May 23, 1823.

Jacob Souder, captain, light infantry; appointed May 10, 1823; commissioned May 23, 1823.

Edward Rice, lieutenant, light infantry; appointed May 10, 1823; commissioned May 23, 1823.

Christopher Leaming, ensign, light infantry; appointed May 10, 1823; commissioned May 23, 1823.

Christopher Ludlam, captain, second company; appointed June 12, 1824; commissioned July 27, 1824.

Samuel Matthews, lieutenant, second company; appointed June 12, 1824; commissioned July 27, 1824.

Nathaniel Dickinson, adjutant; appointed February 1, 1825; commissioned March 4, 1825.

Joseph Fifield, surgeon; appointed February 1, 1825; commissioned March 4, 1825.

Samuel S. Marcy, surgeon's mate; appointed February 1, 1825; commissioned March 4, 1825.

Jeremiah Hand, captain, fourth company; appointed February 1, 1825; commissioned March 4, 1825.

Joshua Crawford, lieutenant, fourth company; appointed February 1, 1825; commissioned March 4, 1825.

Philip Stites, ensign, fourth company; appointed February 1, 1825; commissioned March 4, 1825.

Seth Miller, captain, first company; appointed February 11, 1825; commissioned March 4, 1825.

Ephraim Hildreth, lieutenant, first company; appointed February 11, 1825; commissioned March 4, 1825.

David Hildreth, Jr., ensign, first company; appointed February 11, 1825; commissioned March 4, 1825.

Samuel Springer, captain, first artillery; appointed February 12, 1825; commissioned March 4, 1825.

Absolom Hand, Jr., first lieutenant, first artillery; appointed February 12, 1825; commissioned March 4, 1825.

Miller Hand, second lieutenant, first artillery; appointed February 12, 1825; commissioned March 4, 1825.

Robert Edmunds, captain, second artillery; appointed February 18, 1825; commissioned March 4, 1825.

Artis Hewitt, second lieutenant, second artillery; appointed February 18, 1825; commissioned March 4, 1825.

Aaron Schellenger, captain, third company; appointed February 18, 1825; commissioned March 4, 1825.

Samuel F. Ware, lieutenant, third company; appointed February 18, 1825; commissioned March 4, 1825.

Thomas Eldredge, ensign, third company; appointed February 18, 1825; commissioned March 4, 1825.

Enos Corson, captain, fourth company; appointed March 27, 1826; commissioned April 11, 1826.

Ezra Corson, lieutenant, fourth company; appointed March 27, 1826; commissioned April 11, 1826.

James Van Gilder, lieutenant, first company; appointed March 27, 1826; commissioned April 11, 1826.

Joseph Goff, captain, third company; appointed March 28, 1826; commissioned April 11, 1826.

James L. Smith, lieutenant, third company; appointed March 28, 1826; commissioned April 11, 1826.

Jeremiah Foster, ensign, third company; appointed March 28, 1826; commissioned April 11, 1826.

David Cresse, captain, second artillery; appointed April 20, 1826; commissioned February 15, 1827.

Robert E. Foster, first lieutenant, second artillery; appointed April 20, 1826; commissioned February 15, 1827.

Joseph B. Hughes, lieutenant, third company; appointed April 20, 1826; commissioned February 15, 1827.

James J. Ludlam, ensign, second company; appointed April 19, 1828; commissioned April 28, 1828.

John Little, ensign, light infantry; appointed April 19, 1828; commissioned April 28, 1828.

Christopher Cole, ensign, first company; appointed April 21, 1828; commissioned April 28, 1828.

Richard F. Cresse, captain, fourth company; appointed April 21, 1828; commissioned April 28, 1828.

George Ludlam, lieutenant, fourth company; appointed April 21, 1828; commissioned April 28, 1828.

Second Battalion.

Joshua Hildreth, captain, fourth company; appointed June 7, 1815; commissioned July 15, 1815.

William Hildreth, lieutenant, fourth company; appointed June 7, 1815; commissioned July 15, 1815.

Henry Hand, ensign, fourth company; appointed June 7, 1815; commissioned July 15, 1815.

Aaron Woolson, captain, second company; appointed July 4, 1815; commissioned July 15, 1815.

Richard Thompson, first lieutenant, second company; appointed July 4, 1815; commissioned July 15, 1815.

James Hoffman, second lieutenant, second company; appointed July 4, 1815; commissioned July 15, 1815.

Jonathan Nottingham, captain, first company; appointed December 8, 1815; commissioned February 4, 1816.

Nathaniel Tomsen, lieutenant, first company; appointed December 8, 1815; commissioned February 4, 1816.

Joseph Norbury, ensign, first company; appointed December 8, 1815; commissioned February 4, 1816.

Daniel Cresse, Jr., captain, fourth company; appointed January 13, 1816; commissioned February 4, 1816.

Jeremiah Hand, lieutenant, fourth company; appointed January 13, 1816; commissioned February 4, 1816.

Joshua Crawford, ensign, fourth company; appointed January 13, 1816; commissioned February 4, 1816.

THE WAR OF 1812.

Joseph Ludlam, captain, artillery; appointed May 20, 1816; commissioned June 22, 1816.

John Haines, first lieutenant, artillery; appointed May 20, 1816; commissioned June 22, 1816.

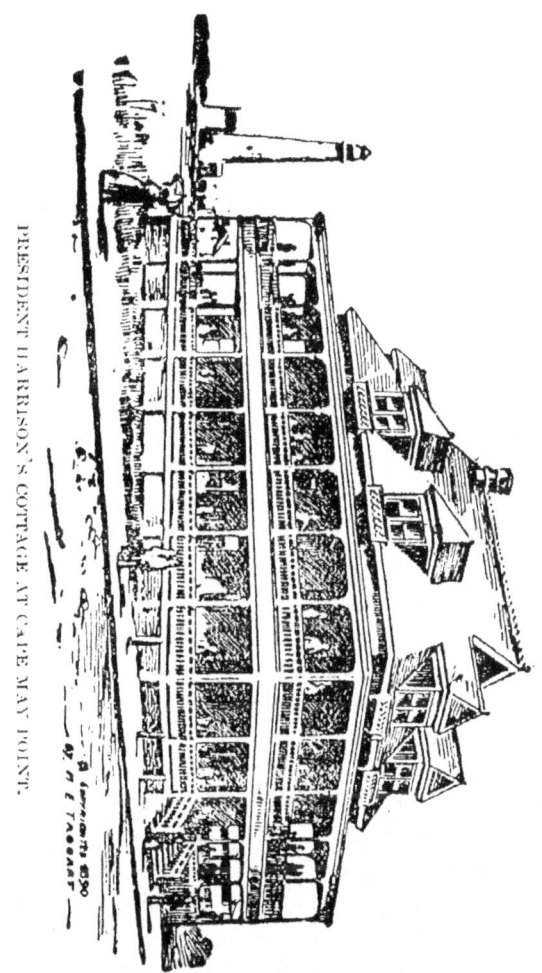

PRESIDENT HARRISON'S COTTAGE AT CAPE MAY POINT.

Harvey Shaw, second lieutenant, artillery; appointed May 20, 1816; commissioned June 22, 1816.

John Dickinson, Jr., lieutenant, second company; appointed June 12, 1816; commissioned June 22, 1816.

Joseph Baymore, ensign, second company; appointed June 12, 1816; commissioned June 22, 1816.

William Thompson, captain, first company; appointed April 11, 1817; commissioned June 10, 1817.

John Price, lieutenant, first company; appointed April 11, 1817; commissioned June 10, 1817.

Elijah Corson, ensign, first company; appointed April 11, 1817; commissioned June 10, 1817.

John Haines, captain, first artillery; appointed May 12, 1818; commissioned July 7, 1818.

Harvey Shaw, first lieutenant, first artillery; appointed May 12, 1818; commissioned July 7, 1818.

Samuel Eldredge, second lieutenant, first artillery; appointed May 12, 1818; commissioned July 7, 1818.

Aaron Hughes, captain, third company; appointed May 9, 1818; commissioned July 7, 1818.

Jeremiah Eldredge, lieutenant, third company; appointed May 9, 1818; commissioned July 7, 1818.

James McCane, ensign, third company; appointed May 9, 1818; commissioned July 7, 1818.

Jeremiah Eldredge, captain, third company; appointed September 25, 1819; commissioned January 17, 1820.

Aaron Schellenger, lieutenant, third company; appointed September 25, 1819; commissioned January 17, 1820.

Jeremiah Ewing, ensign, third company; appointed September 25, 1819; commissioned January 17, 1820.

John Price, captain, first company; appointed April 17, 1820; commissioned July 10, 1820.

Seth Miller, lieutenant, first company; appointed April 17, 1820; commissioned July 10, 1820.

Ephraim Hildreth, ensign, first company; appointed April 17, 1820; commissioned July 10, 1820.

Wade Dickinson, ensign, second company; appointed June 14, 1820; commissioned July 10, 1820.

Almain Tomlin, captain, second company; appointed April 16, 1821; commissioned June 28, 1821.

Wade Dickinson, lieutenant, second company; appointed March 15, 1823; commissioned April 1, 1823.

Thomas Hewitt, Jr., ensign, second company; appointed March 15, 1823; commissioned April 1, 1823.

David Reeves, lieutenant, third company; appointed December 8, 1827; commissioned February 11, 1828.

George Bennett, second lieutenant, artillery; appointed December 8, 1827; commissioned February 11, 1828.

Philip Stites, lieutenant, fourth company; appointed June 13, 1827; commissioned February 11, 1828.

Joshua Hildreth, ensign, fourth company; appointed June 13, 1827; commissioned February 11, 1828.

Wade Dickinson, captain, second company; appointed May 13, 1828; commissioned February 1, 1829.

Thomas Eldredge, lieutenant, third company; appointed March 27, 1830; commissioned May 26, 1830.

Nathaniel Holmes, captain, artillery; appointed June 12, 1833; commissioned October 25, 1833.

Benjamin Springer, first lieutenant, artillery; appointed June 12, 1833; commissioned October 25, 1833.

William Hewitt, second lieutenant, artillery; appointed June 12, 1833; commissioned October 25, 1833.

CHAPTER XIX.
PROGRESS AFTER THE WAR.

During the latter half of the eighteenth century once in a very great while an itinerant school teacher would appear. As early as 1765 we find the children of Aaron Leaming, 2d, attending school for about a month, but in the beginning of the present century we find three school teachers of prominence going about the county, boarding out their claims for teaching at the homes of the parents. From 1810 to 1820, Jacob Spicer, 3d, Constantine and Joseph Foster were the teachers of prominence. From 1830 the presence of teachers became general. The old school places had no desks, and hard wooden benches with straight backs, and sometimes no backs at all were afforded. The books were such as could be gathered for the scholars by the parents themselves, and sometimes there were no books at all. The "rule of three," or reading, arithmetic and writing, were all the studies that were then considered necessary.

In the latter part of December, 1815, the brig Perseverance, Capt. Snow, bound from Havre to New York, with ten passengers and a crew of seven men, was wrecked on Peck's beach, opposite the residence of Thomas Beesley.

The Perseverance had a very valuable cargo on board, of rich goods, china, glass, silks, &c., which were strewn for miles along the beach.

On Friday, the day before she was cast away, a ship from New York was spoken, which deceived them by stating that they were 200 miles east of Sandy Hook. It was with great gratification that the passengers received this joyous news; and, elated with the hope of soon resting on "terra firma," gave themselves up to hilarity and merriment—whilst the captain, under the same impulse, spread all sails to a heavy northeaster, with high expectations of a safe arrival on the morrow.

Thus she continued on her course until three o'clock Saturday morning; when the mate, whose watch it was on deck, was heard to give the dreadful cry: "Breakers ahead!" The brig, by the instant efforts of her steersman, obeyed her helm; but as she came around, head off shore, her stern striking knocked off her false keel, deadened her headway, and she backed on the beach stern foremost. In less than fifteen minutes the sea made a clean breast over her. The scene, in the meantime, beggars description; the passengers rushed out of the cabin, some of them in their night clothes; six of whom, and two of the crew, got in a long boat. One of these was a young French lady, of great beauty. The remainder of the crew and passengers succeeded in reaching the round-top, excepting a Mr. Cologne, whose great weight and corpulency of person compelled him to remain in the shrouds. Soon the sea carried the long boat and its passengers clear of the wreck, when it was too late discovered she was firmly attached to it by a hawser, which it was impossible to separate. Had it not been for this unfortunate circumstance, they might possibly have reached the shore. Their cries were heartrending, but were soon silenced in the sleep of death; the boat swamped, and they were all consigned to one common grave. The body of the lady floated on shore.

The sea ran so high that it wet those in the round-top; and although many efforts were made, on Saturday, to rescue them, it was found impossible, as the boats would upset by turning head over stern, subjecting those in them to great danger. Capt. Snow lost his life in attempting to swim ashore. On Sunday the sea fell a little, and those on the wreck were made to understand they would have to build a raft of the spars, and get on it, or they could not be saved. The mate had fortunately secured a hatchet, with which one was constructed; by which the survivors (except a negro who was washed overboard, and reached the shore in safety, whilst making the raft), were rescued by the boats. There were four saved out of the seventeen souls on board, viz: one passenger, who was badly frozen, the mate and two of the crew, including the negro. Three perished in the round-top, and were thrown over.

Mr. Cologne, who was in the rigging, and unable to descend from the shrouds, let go and fell into the water, and was caught as he came up by his hair, and thus towed ashore. He lived only three days after, though every possible attention was paid him. He and his niece, the young French lady, were buried side by side in the Goldin buryingground, at Beesley's Point. An eye witness, Dr. Maurice Beesley, from whom the above account is derived, says: "I saw this young and beautiful female after she had been transferred from the beach to the main. Her features were perfectly natural; her cheeks bore the crimson tinge of life; and it was scarcely possible to realize that, instead of a concentration of all the graces of the female form, animated by the fervor of life, I was gazing upon a cold and lifeless corpse."

In 1815, during the summer season, a sloop was run regularly from Philadelphia to Cape May for the conveyance of passengers. In 1816 Thomas H. Hughes, whom we will mention later, built the first Congress Hall.

In 1818 postoffices were established in the villages of Goshen and Fishing Creek, at the former place on June 5, and at the latter place fifteen days later. Richard Thompson, Jr., was the first postmaster at Goshen and Robert Edmunds at Fishing Creek.

The Sheriff of Cape May county during the War of 1812, or from 1812 to 1815, was Aaron Leaming, 3d. He was really the sixth Aaron Leaming, and was a son of Persons Leaming, and grandson of the famous Aaron Leaming, 2d. Sheriff Leaming was born May 15, 1784, and died January 7, 1836. He, like his grandfather, had large landed possessions.

Spicer Hughes, in 1815, succeeded Aaron Leaming, 3d, as Sheriff. He served until 1818, and was a second time in that office, from 1821 to 1824. He was born in 1777 and died in 1849.

Nathaniel Holmes, who served in the Assembly from 1811 to 1812, was born March 17, 1757, in Ireland. He landed in Philadelphia on August 8, 1773, and during the month came to Court House, where he settled. He died there January 28, 1834.

By the census of 1820 Cape May county's population had

grown to a total of 4265, of which 28 were slaves and 205 were free negroes. The inhabitants were then mostly engaged in agriculture; wheat, rye, oats and Indian corn being the principal crops. Large quantities of timber were then annually exported to market, and the traffic in salt hay gathered from the meadows was of considerable extent. A great

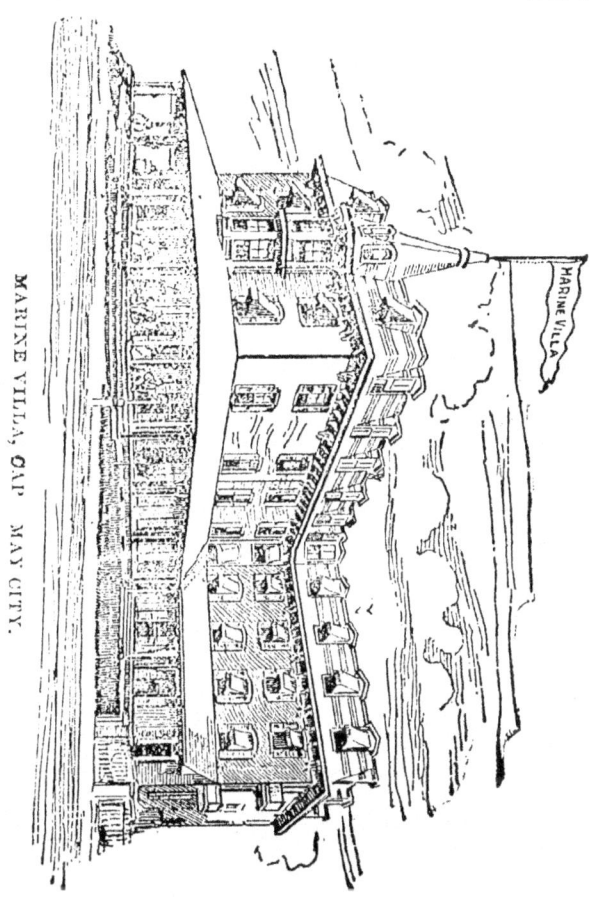

deal of lumber was "mined" from the sunken cedar swamp about Dennis creek.

Beginning about the middle of the seventeenth century negro slavery began to grow, and it flourished until it became a part of the New Jersey social system. All the people in the State were not, however, satisfied with this condition of servitude which had grown up in their midst by degrees, almost imperceptibly. At first everybody who could afford it owned slaves, and the Quakers, of which there were some in Cape May county, bought the negroes as did the other colonists; but about the end of the century some of the Quakers began to think that property in human being was not a righteous thing, and the Jersey Quakers united with those of Pennsylvania in an agreement recommending that they should no longer employ negro slaves, or else, at least not to import them thereafter.

A strong party among the Quakers of New Jersey opposed slavery for many years following, and the system began to be denounced regularly by them at their yearly meetings. By the middle of the eighteenth century the practice had been discouraged among the Society of Friends, and a rule made against it. As years passed on the other residents of the State began to think as did the Quakers, and the feeling became very strong against the custom at the beginning of the present century. Finally, in 1820, an act was passed by the Legislature for the emancipation of the slaves. They were not set free all at once and turned into the world to make livings for themselves, but the emancipation was to be gradual, by which young people obtained their freedom when they became of age, while the old negroes were taken care of by the masters as long as they lived. By this method slavery was abolished in Cape May county, and in 1830 there were but three slaves within its territory, that being the last date that any are reported in the census.

About 1820 Cape May Court House village is recorded as having eight houses, while Watson, two years later, in his "Annals," says that Cape Island "is a village of twenty houses, and the streets are very clean and grassy." Many of these houses, he says, were for the accommodation of summer guests.

On November 28, 1822, the line of partition between Cape May and Cumberland and Gloucester (now Atlantic) counties was changed "to begin at the place where the waters of Mill or Hickman's creek fall into the channel of Tuckahoe river, at the boundary line of Gloucester county, and running thence directly into the mouth of said creek, continuing the same course by a line of marked trees (which by present position of the compass is south, fifty-seven degrees and about thirty minutes west) until it strikes Hughes' or the lower mill pond, on West or Jecak's creek, thence down the middle of the ancient water courses thereof, until it falls into Delaware bay, and thence continuing a due northwest course until it strikes the line of said counties, at the ship channel of the said bay."

The first light house in the county, built by the government, was Cape May light. This light is situated on the northeastern side of the entrance to Delaware Bay. It stands in latitude 38° 55' 59", longitude 74° 57' 39". Cape May light was originally built in 1823, and rebuilt in 1859. Its height of tower is 145 feet, and the elevation of its light is 152 feet above sea level. Its lens is of the first order, with white flash-light at intervals of 30 seconds, visible at a distance of 18 nautical miles. Arc illumination N. E. by southward to N. W. Its tower is painted gray. It is distant 12½ nautical miles from Cape Henlopen main light, and 17¾ miles from Five Fathom Bank lightship.

The third and present (1897) edifice of the Cold Spring Presbyterian Church was built in 1823, and was the first brick church in the county.

At this time Joshua Townsend was a prominent citizen of the county, and a member of the Legislature. He was a merchant at Seaville, and a son of Henry Young Townsend, captain in the Revolution. Joshua Townsend was born July 9, 1786, and when a young man was at first a lieutenant in Cape May company in the War of 1812, and later a captain in the Cape May regiment of militia. In 1819 he was first elected to the Assembly and served until 1821. He served in that body also from 1822 to 1823, and from 1827 to 1830. From 1831 to 1834 he was an active member of the Legislative Council. In 1840 he was a Presidential elector on the Harrison and Tyler Whig ticket, and was elected, casting his ballot for them. He died November 29, 1868. He built the schooner "Vitruvius."

In 1823 Israel Townsend, of Lower Township, was first elected to the Assembly, serving four years. And in 1827 he was chosen a member of the Legislative Council and served in that body until 1831. For several years thereafter he served in the Board of Chosen Freeholders from Lower Township. He was a son of John Townsend, and was born May 12, 1782, and died November 3, 1862.

In 1825 a new County Clerk's office was built by contract with Ellis Hughes, of Cape Island. This structure was used until the present brick building was erected.

The steamboat "Pennsylvania" was in July this year placed on the line from Philadelphia to Cape May, carrying passengers distinctly for the Cape Island House. The

JOSHUA TOWNSEND.

"Delaware" was also put on the line a few years later, and since that time steamboats have never ceased to run to Cape May during the summer season.

Dennis Township was formed in 1826, out of Upper. It was thirteen miles long, with an average width of about six. It is bounded N. by Upper Township, E. by the ocean, S. by Middle Township, and W. by Maurice River swamp.

The cost of running the county during this decade was an average of about $3000 per annum, according to the annual appropriations of the Board of Freeholders.

In 1827 Thomas P. Hughes, of Lower township, was

elected Sheriff, and he served three years. He was a son of Congressman Thomas H. Hughes, and was born January 19, 1790; died September 9, 1863. He was a member of Assembly from 1838 to 1840, and of the Legislative Council from 1840 to 1842.

In 1827 preachers of the Methodist denomination first began to travel in Cape May county regularly and preach. The county was then in the Cumberland circuit. Rev. Charles Pitman traveled over the district as presiding elder, preaching in private houses principally. The three preachers in the circuit were Reverends John Woolson, Sedgewick Rusling and Robert Gerry, and they each received about $700.00 per year for their services.

The steamboat traffic on the Delaware now became a thriving industry. The boats for Cape May stopped at New Castle to take up the Baltimoreans and Southerners who would come down on the old Frenchtown and New Castle Railroad—the first railroad ever run in this country. They would come over in carriages from Baltimore to Frenchtown, in Maryland, on the Susquehanna, near Havre de Grace.

Tuckahoe was provided with a postoffice on January 14, 1828, and John Williams was the first postmaster, and on August 27 the following year an office was established at Green Creek, and Matthew Marcy was first chosen to keep the office.

In 1837 a new gaol, or jail, was built, and Richard Thompson, of Middle township, was appointed to superintend its construction. In the same year the bridge at West Creek was ordered built, and Nathaniel Holmes, of Dennis township, ordered to superintend the work.

May 26, 1829, the new jail was completed and accepted by the Board of Freeholders. It was after the architecture of Strasburg Cathedral. Its floor was of wood, but owing to the escape of prisoners later, an iron floor replaced the wooden one. It was used until 1894.

Probably the most popular man in Cape May at this time was Thomas H. Hughes. As a citizen he had been prominent for his thrift and enterprise, and was a man of large experience. He was the son of Ellis Hughes, the first postmaster at Cape Island, and was born at Cape May on January 10, 1769. His first office was that of Sheriff, which he held from 1801 to 1804. Following this, in 1807, he was elected to the Assembly, and served one year. He served there also from 1809 to 1810, and from 1812 to 1813. In 1816 he built the first Congress Hall at Cape Island. The people laughed at him for his folly in erecting so large a building in those times. He predicted that the time would come when a purchaser would have to cover every inch of land with a dollar to obtain sufficient space on which to erect a dwelling. His predictions have almost been verified. In 1819 he was again chosen by the people to the Legislature, but this time to the Council, and served there until 1823, and again from 1824 to 1825. He was also prominent as a trustee of the Cold Spring Presbyterian Church, and in the temperance cause. A man of commanding presence and large frame, he was noticed. He was blind in one eye, but this did not detract from his popularity. His fame had gone abroad over the State.

In the debates in Congress in 1828 the tariff question turned up—the question of levying duties on imported goods to produce a revenue for the government and to raise the price of articles from foreign countries in order to stimulate home industries was taken up. This was the beginning of the protective tariff. President John Quincy Adams favored this tariff, and in that year the duties on foreign made goods were greatly increased. This was the beginning of a new political epoch in the United States. The political partisan elements of the country had been whiling about in a choatic condition, but it now resolved itself down to the two quickly forming parties—the Whig and the Democratic. The people of the Eastern and Middle States favored the tariff, and were allied to the new Whig doctrine, while the agricultural States of the West and South were opposed to the tariff. John Quincy Adams was a candidate for re-election as President on the new Whig platform, and his opponent was Andrew Jackson, the Democratic nominee.

In New Jersey the Whigs named as their candidates for Congress Thomas H. Hughes, of Cape May; Richard M.

Cooper, of Gloucester; Lewis Condict, of Morris; Isaac Pierson, of Essex; James Fitz Randolph, of Middlesex, and Samuel Swan, of Somerset. When the election took place they were chosen, and New Jersey's electoral vote was cast for Adams for President and Richard Rush, of Pennsylvania, for Vice-President, but Jackson was elected. Mr. Hughes served in the 21st and 22nd Congresses, or from 1829 to 1833. One of his colleagues in the two sessions was Henry Clay. The tariff question was reopened and occasioned great excitement in Congress and throughout the country. Daniel Webster and Senator Hayne, of South

COUNTY JAIL, USED FROM 1839 TO 1894.

Carolina, had their great debate during Hughes' second term. In the stirring scenes of 1831-2, when South Carolina declared her right to nullify the laws and Constitution, he was present. In Mr. Hughes' second term ex-President John Quincy Adams became one of his colleagues as a representative from Massachusetts. After he retired from Congress he remained in private life until he died on November 10, 1839, aged 70 years. His remains lie in Cold Spring Cemetery.

By 1830 the population of Cape May had increased to 4936 souls, of which there were but three slaves, and 225 free colored persons. The census of that year exhibited the following facts concerning the county:

Number of acres, 161,500; acres of improved land, 59,528; lots of and under ten acres, 188; householders, 669; single men, 188; taxables, 1000; merchants and traders, 29; grist mills, run of stone, 8; saw mills, 16; carding machines, 2; male slaves, 2; chairs, sulkies and Dearborns, 72; covered wagons, 148; two-horse stage, 1; poor tax, $1,125; road tax, $1,650.

At this time large quantities of cord wood was being shipped to Philadelphia and New York. Rye and corn were the most abundant crops.

From a writer of 1830 we gather the following concerning the county then:

"That portion of the State (Cape May county) has not generally been holden in due estimation. If its inhabitants be not numerous, they are generally as independent as any others in the State, and enjoy as abundantly the comforts of life. They are hospitable, and respectable for the propriety of their manners, and are blessed, usually, with excellent health. Until lately they have known little, practically, of those necessary evils of social life, the physician and the lawyer. Morse assures us that their women possessed the power not only of sweetening life, but of defending and prolonging it, being competent to cure most of the diseases which attack it."

Of the villages the writer notes:

"Cape May Court House contains a court house of wood, a jail of stone, fire-proof offices of brick, 2 taverns, 8 or 10 dwellings, and a Baptist church of brick. It is called Middletown in the post office list."

"Cape May Island—It is a noted and much frequented watering place, the season at which commences about the first of July and continues until middle of August or first of September. There are here six boarding houses, three of which are very large; the sea bathing is convenient and excellent, the beach affords pleasant drives, and there is excellent fishing in adjacent waters."

"Marshallville—several mills there."

"Tuckahoe contains some 20 dwellings, 3 taverns, several

stores. It is a place of considerable trade in wood, lumber and ship building."

"Cold Spring contains 1 tavern, 2 stores, 15 to 20 dwellings, an Episcopal church (Presbyterian). It derives its name from remarkable spring near it, which rises in the marsh, and is overflowed at every tide."

"Dennis's Creek—contains 30 to 40 dwellings, 2 taverns, 5 stores, a tide grist mill. Town built on both sides of creek, about a half mile. Ship building and trade in lumber are carried on extensively here."

"Etna, furnace & forge & grist mill. On Tuckahoe river, 15 m. from sea."

"Goshen contains tavern, 2 stores, a steam saw mill, 12 or 15 dwellings, a school house, in which religious meetings are held."

"Beasley's Point, Upper township, on Great Egg Harbor Bay. There are here, upon a neck of land, between the salt marshes of about one mile wide, 2 taverns and several farm houses, where visitors to the shore may find agreeable accommodations."

The bridge over West Creek, on the road between Leesburg and Dennisville, was built about 1830. On September 25th the Chosen Freeholders of both counties met at West Creek to inspect the structure.

It was during this decade that the first spring carriage was built in Cape May county. John Farrow, who was a carriage wright and keeper of a public house, at Court House, was its builder. He was the father of William Farrow, who is now chief of police of Cape May City.

Jeremiah Leaming was elected to the Assembly in 1830, and was prominent in the affairs of the county. He was a son of Persons Leaming, and a grandson of the second Aaron Leaming, having been born May 26, 1792. He served in the Assembly from 1830 to 1834, and then in the upper branch of the Legislature, the Council, from 1834 to 1836. He interested himself in securing pensions for the survivors of the Revolutionary War, and for the widows of these patriots. In 1836 he was candidate on the "Democratic Whig Ticket" for Presidential elector, and was elected, casting his vote for Harrison and Granger. On the

Democratic-Republican ticket the same year James Maguire, of Goshen, was a candidate for Presidential elector against him. Mr. Leaming died April 26, 1839, from being overheated by fighting a fire on his plantation.

Richard Thompson, who in 1830 was elected Sheriff, and served three years, was the son of Richard Thompson, captain of Fishing Creek artillery in 1814, and was born in this county December 3, 1795. The first position he held was that of County Clerk from 1824 to 1829. When he was chosen Sheriff he was a member of the Board of Chosen Freeholders, and the Director (President) of that body. From 1834 to 1836 he was a member of the General Assembly, and during the two years following sat in the Legislative Council. From 1847 to 1851 he served as a Middle township member in the Freeholders again. He was Loan Commissioner of the county from 1840 to 1844, and again in 1856. He died at Cape May Court House, September 27, 1857.

The Reverend Moses Williamson became the pastor of the Cold Spring Presbyterian Church on July 6, 1831, and for forty years thereafter was a prominent citizen of the county. He was born at Newville, Pa., May 7, 1802, and obtained his education, a liberal one, at Hopewell Academy, Carlisle, Pa., Jefferson College, Conansburg, Pa., and at Dickinson College, in Carlisle, from the latter graduating with honors in 1824. He then took a full course of three years in the Theological Seminary, at Princeton, N. J., graduating September 22, 1828. He was licensed to preach by the Presbytery of Carlisle six days later, and entered upon labors in Delaware and Maryland. When his health failed him a short time after he was advised to come to Cape May for his health, and did so, coming down the Delaware by steamer. On the Sabbath after his arrival at Cape May, August 16, 1829, he was invited to preach in Cold Spring Church, and did so. That day the pastor, Rev. Alvin H. Parker, resigned, Mr. Williamson was called upon as a supply, and acted as such for two years, excepting for six months when he was studying Hebrew scriptures at Andover Theological Seminary. He then became the regular pastor of the church, and remained with it until he was released at his own request, from the charge by the Presbytery of West Jersey, April 18, 1873. In his civil capacity he was one of the best of men. He was a thorough scholar, and had as his pupils those who afterwards became the foremost men of the county. He was a county examiner of teachers, with Dr. Jonathan F. Leaming, for many years, from about 1845. He erected and conducted at much expense and effort the Cold Spring Academy. During his pastorate 490 persons were added to his church, he married 250 couples and officiated at over 500 funerals. Besides

REV. MOSES WILLIAMSON

preaching at Cold Spring he conducted meetings at Cape Island and Green Creek. He died at Cape May City on October 30, 1880, aged 78 years.

On June 12, 1833, the Board of Freeholders ordered an almshouse built, 18 by 30 feet, and two stories in height. The committee who had charge of its construction were Jeremiah Hand, Samuel Springer and Samuel Matthews.

About 1834 the steamer "Portsmouth" began to make weekly trips to Cape May, Lewestown, from Philadelphia.

In 1837 the Board of Freeholders accepted Cape May's share of the "Surplus Fund," which was to loan out on security. Robert M. Holmes was made Loan Commissioner, which position he held until he died..

The "Surplus Fund" was composed of money which had accumulated to the government of the United States mainly from sales of government lands, and was not needed for its expenses. By an act of Congress it was divided among the several States and each State then divided its quota among its several counties. In 1829 President Jackson suggested the distribution and the House of Representatives' resolution was passed next session, for distribution of proceeds of land sales among the States. Henry Clay advocated the measure in 1832, but it failed in the House. After much legislation, during which time (until 1836) the land sales reached a point giving $66,000,000 in the U. S. Treasury as surplus. Consequently Congress enacted a law in June, 1832, providing for the apportionment of the surplus yearly among the several States, reserving $5,000,000. This act was repealed in October, 1839, after $37,000,000 had been apportioned. By act of the State Legislature of November 4, 1836, the Governor, Speaker and Treasurer were appointed to receive this State's share, and by an act of March 10, 1839, the method of its apportionment among the various counties was defined.

During Andrew Jackson's administration the United States Government paid to the several States their share of the Surplus Fund. The amount paid to Cape May county was from $18,000 to $20,000. The Freeholders of the county received it and placed it in the hands of a Loan Commission, who loaned it out on promissory notes. Several of these note givers became bankrupt, causing a loss to the fund of several thousand dollars. The Freeholders then ordered the Surplus Fund loaned only on bond and mortgage. Still, interest was irregularly paid and some losses on principal occurred. Several years ago the Freeholders abolished the office of Loan Commissioners, ordered the County Collector to take charge of the Loan Fund, then amounting to $12,349.14, and to pay to the several public schools inhabitants are mostly engaged in agriculture or maritime pursuits. There are in the township six stores, three saw mills, six schools, 240 scholars. Population, 1133.

"Fishing Creek, on the bay shore, six miles southwest of Court House, is an agricultural village similar to Cold Spring. A survey has been made for a breakwater, at Crow's Shoal, in this township, near the mouth of the bay. When the wind is northeast a good harbor is afforded at that place, as sometimes as many as one hundred vessels are anchored off here. On a sudden change of the northwest vessels are frequently driven ashore. The breakwater, if built, would have been an effectual protection against winds from this direction.

"Cold Spring, ten miles south of Court House, is a thickly settled agricultural neighborhood, containing about forty houses within the circle of a mile. It derives its name from an excellent spring of cold water flowing up from the salt marsh, which is much frequented by sojourners at Cape Island. It contains an academy, a Methodist and a Presbyterian church.

"The village of Cape Island is a favorite watering-place in the southern part of this township, thirteen miles south of Court House. It began to grow into notice as a watering place in 1812, at which time there were but a few houses there. It now contains two large hotels, three stories high and 150 feet long, and a third one, lately erected, four stories high and 100 feet long, besides numerous other houses for the entertainment of visitors. The whole number of dwellings is about fifty. In the summer months the Island is thronged with visitors, principally from Philadelphia, with which there is then a daily steamboat communication. It is estimated that about 3000 strangers annually visit the place. The village is separated by a small creek from the main land; but its area is fast wearing away by the encroachments of the sea. Watson, the antiquarian, in a MSS. journal of a trip to Cape Island in 1835, on this point says: 'Since my former visit to Cape Island in 1822, the house in which I then stopped (Captain Aaron Bennett's), then nearest the surf, has been actually reached by the invading waters. * * * The distance from Bennett's house to the sea bank in 1822 was 165 feet; and in 1804, as it was then measured and cut upon the house by Commodore Decatur, it was 334 feet. It had been as much as 300 feet further off, as remembered by some old men who told me so in 1822.' A large portion of the inhabitants of the village are Delaware pilots, a hardy and industrious race. About two miles west of the boarding houses is the Cape May lighthouse."

of Cape May county six per cent. annually on this sum, or $740.96 a year.

About 1840 there were fears that Cape May citizens might lose through the multiplicity of State laws their rights to the natural privileges in the sounds, and on the 5th of February, 1839, the Board of Freeholders authorized Jeremiah Leaming to go to Trenton to work for the passage of an act to preserve these privileges.

During the year 1839 there were within the bounds of Cape May county ten licensed inns or hotels, kept by the following persons: Richard S. Ludlam, James J. Ludlam, Clark Henderson, Humphrey Hewitt, David Saint (?), Mackey Williams, Benjamin Owen, Mark A. Carroll, John Smith and Stephen Young.

The first signal of danger erected by the government off the Cape May coast was the Five-Fathom Bank lightship. This vessel is located near the shoal called the Five-Fathom Bank, off the entrance of Delaware Bay. She was established in 1839, and last refitted in 1855. She is now moored in twelve fathoms of water. She is supplied with a twelve-inch steam fog whistle, giving a blast of four seconds during each half minute. "Five-Fathom Bank" is painted in bold letters on each side. She has two lights, with reflectors, and two hoop-iron day marks, one on each mast. Her lights are a fixed white, forty and forty-five feet above sea level, and visible a distance of eleven nautical miles. Arc illumination, the entire horizon. She is painted a straw-color, and is distant $17\frac{3}{4}$ miles from Cape May light and $23\frac{1}{2}$ from Cape Henlopen main light. Shoal part of bank bears, per compass, N. W. $\frac{1}{2}$ N., distant $2\frac{1}{2}$ miles. She is in latitude 38° 51′ 20″, longitude 74° 36′ 10″.

The sheriff of the county from 1838 to 1841 was Samuel Springer, who was born September 5, 1800, and died March 7, 1877. He was a prominent resident of Middle township.

The population of Cape May county in 1840 was 5324, of which 218 were colored persons, all free. The conditions of the townships by that census are exhibited by the following:

"Upper—Population, 1217. Its surface is level; soil, sand and loam, and well timbered with cedar, oak and pine. It contains four stores, one grist mill, four saw mills, five schools, 219 scholars.

"The village of Tuckahoe is situated on both sides of Tuckahoe River, on the county line, 18 miles from court house, 11 from the sea, 28 from Bridgeton and 13 from May's Landing. It contains three taverns, several stores, about sixty dwellings and a Methodist church. There are besides in the township one Baptist, one Methodist church and a Friends' meeting house. Wood, lumber and ship building constitute the business of the village.

"Dennis—This township, except that part cultivated, or meadow, is covered with oaks, pines and cedars. There are in the township seven stores, two grist mills, six saw mills, four schools, 205 scholars. Population, 1350.

"Dennisville is a post village, extending on both sides of the creek for a mile. It is eight miles north of Court House, eight south of Tuckahoe, and twenty-eight from Bridgeton. It contains five stores, about seventy dwellings, a neat academy, the upper story of which is used for a lyceum and for religious meetings. Ship building and the lumber trade are carried on here. The Methodist church at this place was the first erected in the county. There is a Baptist church in the eastern part of the township. West Creek, four miles northwest of Dennisville, is a thickly settled agricultural neighborhood.

"Middle—About half the township is salt marsh or sea beach; the remaining portion is mostly sandy loam. The township contains twelve stores, two grist mills, two saw mills, five schools, 328 scholars. Population, 1624. Goshen, five miles northwest of Court House, has a Methodist church and about twenty dwellings. The village of Cape May Court House is in the central part of the township, 110 miles from Trenton, and 36 southeast of Bridgeton, and contains a court house, a jail and the county offices, a Methodist and a Baptist church, and thirty or forty dwellings in the vicinity.

"Lower—A great portion of its surface is covered with a salt marsh and sea beach. On the ocean shore the soil is loamy, the bay shore is sandy, and the central part sandy loam. There is much young timber in the township. The

CHAPTER XX.

NOTED MEN OF A GENERATION.

In 1840 Jonathan Hand, Jr., was appointed county clerk of Cape May by the Legislature, which position he held continuously thereafter until 1890. He was a descendant of Shamgar Hand, one of two brothers who bought proprietary interests in Cape May county and settled here in 1685. He descended from Shamgar, down through Thomas, Recompence, Jonathan, his grandfather, and Jonathan, his father. His grandfather served in the Colonial Legislature from 1771 to 1776, and when the State's new Constitution was adopted was a member of the first Legislative Council, serving from 1776 to 1778. His father was commissioned a captain of the Cape May regiment in 1802, and is said to have served in the War of 1812 in the coast defense of Cape May county. His mother was Sarah Moore, a daughter of the Trenton ferryman. She, when a girl of twelve years, was selected and was one of the twenty-four girls who, in 1789, when George Washington was on his way to New York to become the first President of the nation, strewed flowers upon his path. When she was married to Jonathan, the second, she was a widow, Wilson by name. She lived at Cape May Court House until she died, in 1871, aged 93 years. She was a devout Christian woman, and a member of the Baptist denomination.

Jonathan, the father, had served as county clerk from 1831 to 1834, and Jonathan, Jr., had assisted his father, who died the latter year. From 1834 to 1835 he assisted Jacob G. Smith, the clerk, and was deputy clerk the five following years under Swain Townsend. In 1840 he was appointed by the Legislature, and was chosen by the people nine times, often receiving every vote in the county.

Jonathan, the third, as he will be known in history, was born at Cape May Court House December 22, 1818. In early life he was a Whig, and later a member of the Republican party. In 1862 Governor Olden appointed him a draft commissioner of the county to draw men for the service of their country in the Civil War, then in progress. In 1852 he was appointed a master in chancery of New Jersey. He died at his home at Cape May Court House on the morning of March 2, 1897, aged 79 years. Of him it is said that he was a painstaking, systematic official, and was considered by lawyers to have the best-kept office in New Jersey.

JONATHAN HAND.

The amount of the school-fund of Cape May county in 1841 was $484.48, which was divided according to the number of scholars, pro rata, to the various townships: Upper, $111.93; Dennis, $120.20; Middle, $160.76, and Lower, $91.59.

The next post office to be established in the county was that at East Creek in 1842, when John Wilson was appointed postmaster on April 22.

By an act of the Legislature of March 13, 1844, a strip of Cumberland was thrown into Cape May. The bounds were: Beginning at the Cumberland and Cape May line, where the old Cape May road intersects the same; and running thence in a northward course along said road to a station formerly called Souder Place; thence northwardly the most direct course to the Cumberland and Atlantic line; thence by the Atlantic line and the Cape May line to the beginning. The commissioners appointed to run the line were Francis Lee, James Ward and James L. Smith. Arrangements were made that the township committees should make division of the property, that Cumberland officers should hold power to second Monday of April, 1844, and after that time shall act as if appointed or elected from Cape May, provided judges and justices take the official oaths before May 1. Judgments and legal actions were to be in no wise affected. On the 26th of February, 1845, the act was repealed and the bounds were once more made in conformity with "the ancient boundary line."

In 1844 the State of New Jersey was given a new Constitution. The people of Cape May sent as their delegate Joshua Swain, aged sixty-six, a farmer. This convention met at Trenton on May 14 and continued its sessions until June 29, when it was voted for by the convention with but one dissenting voice. Mr. Swain voted in the affirmative. This Constitution was ratified by the people by a large majority on the 13th of August following.

Joshua Swain was born February 2, 1778. From 1813 to 1814 he was a member of the State Assembly, and a member of the Legislative Council at three different times, from 1815 to 1819, from 1823 to 1824, and from 1825 to 1827. He was sheriff from 1809 to 1812. With his father, Jacocks, and brother, Henry, he patented the centre board in 1811. He died August 24, 1855.

On March 4, 1847, Harvey Shaw, Benjamin Tomlin, Jr., Robert Baymore, Jr., and Ezra Norton, of Middle township, were authorized by the Legislature to build a bridge over Cedar Creek at Goshen.

The Legislature in 1848 passed an act to better protect the propagation of oysters by prohibiting the vending of them in Cape May county from May 1 to October 1. This law remained in force until 1853.

In 1846 the people elected James L. Smith a member of the State Senate, in which he served the county three years. He was a resident of West Creek when elected. He was born at Goshen January 28, 1795, and was educated for a surveyor at Bridgeton, in Cumberland county. He was the son of Abijah Smith, who was county clerk from 1804 to 1824. In 1819 he married Deborah Tomlin, and settled at West Creek. In 1866 he was appointed by Governor Ward one of the judges of the Court of Common Pleas of

JAMES L. SMITH.

the county, holding the position until he died, in 1871. He was for years a member of the Board of Freeholders from Dennis township, as follows: 1833, 1835, 1839, and from 1841 to 1854. In private life he was a farmer, a director of the Cumberland Bank, and was a Methodist of the foremost type. He was one of the pillars of that denomination in this county.

From 1846 to 1847 Richard Smith Ludlam was the Assemblyman. He was a hotel keeper of Cape Island, who, in 1847, entertained Henry Clay at the Mansion House. He was born at Dennisville in 1792, and conducted a general store there, as well as a cord wood business. While in the Legislature he secured the incorporation of Cape Island as a borough. He served in the Board of Freeholders from Cape Island in 1853, 1855 and 1862. He died at Cape May City on June 15, 1881.

He built the Mansion House in 1832, being the second large hotel erected. It stood on four acres of ground. He opened the first part of Washington street, which he then laid out only between Jackson and Perry streets. The Mansion House was the first lathed and plastered hotel here, old Congress Hall being only weather-boarded and sheathed.

It was in 1847 that Henry Clay, the great Kentuckian, came to Cape May, and Mr. Ludlam years afterward said: "The big time was when Harry Clay came. He had been at the White Sulphurs, and said he had a notion to go to some of the Northern watering places; that was in 1857. So I sent him an invitation and he accepted, and stopped at the Mansion House for a week. It was in the latter part of August, and the people had before that thinned out. When, however, it was announced that Harry Clay was to be here, the place filled up to overflowing. Two steamboat loads came on from New York. They wanted him there. Horace Greeley came down to see him, and the people from Salem and Bridgeton and all the country around flocked in their carry-alls to Cape May to see Harry of the West."

As soon as it was known that Clay was to become a visitor the people began to arrive from all over the Middle and Southern States. United States Senator James A. Bayard, of Wilmington, accompanied by Charles C. Gordon, of Georgia, was among the first to arrive. On the Saturday previous there came a large party from Philadelphia. Clay had come by stage and rail, so far as there was any, to Philadelphia, being greeted on his route by hosts of friends who had, and by others who had not, cast their ballots for him three years previous, when he ran for the Presidency against Polk. Clay came for rest, and to wear away sorrow which had come upon him by the killing of his son, who had just previously fallen in the Mexican War.

On the morning of Monday, August 16, 1847, the great

statesman, with his party, left Philadelphia on the steamboat then plying between that place and Cape Island, and arrived at the landing about one o'clock in the afternoon. The party was driven over the turnpike to the Mansion House, where a big dinner was in waiting for the distinguished guests. The band engagement having expired before this event, Beck's Philadelphia band was brought down on the boat with Mr. Clay. The old hotel register, which is still preserved, has upon it the names of the following Kentuckians, who came that day: Hon. Henry Clay (written in a big, round hand by one of the committee), Colonel John Swift, H. White and son, W. S. Smith, F. Lennig, Miss Riche, Miss Johns. Mr. Clay was given a rest on his arrival, but the day following was his busiest while on Cape May's grand beach. During the day many more arrived, and the Island was filled with country folks anxious to see the great man. Rev. Moses Williamson made the address of welcome, to which Mr. Clay fittingly responded in words that electrified his listeners. Among other things he remarked to a friend that Mr. Williamson made one of the best addresses of the kind he ever heard, and made many inquiries about the good and well-known divine. Mr. Clay's magnificent language, says one who heard him, held the crowds spell-bound. After the speech-making there was hand-shaking and a grand feast. The speech-making took place in the old "Kersal," the music pavilion and ball-room of the hotel, which had been built in the spring of that year. Mr. Clay was received on the part of the county of Cape May by Dr. Maurice Beesley. During his visit there were more arrivals each day than there had been for any previous day of that summer.

While at Cape May Mr. Clay loved bathing and went in as often as twice a day, and it was while enjoying it that he lost a great deal of his hair. The ladies would catch him and with a pair of scissors, carried for just that purpose, clip locks from his head to remember him by. When he returned to Washington his hair was very short, indeed.

In Beck's Band, which furnished the music, there was the father, six sons and three others, and as it was at Cape Island season after season their names are here given: Jacob

W. Beck, leader; L. Beck, C. Beck, H. Beck, J. M. Beck, G. Beck, A. Beck, J. W. Gaul, J. Leech, A. Fenner and B. Wilks.

Mr. Clay remained at Cape May for several days. "About seven o'clock this (Friday, August 20, 1847) morning," said the New York Herald, "the steamboat New Haven let fall her anchors opposite the place, having left New York the previous afternoon, with a number of eminent citizens, to invite Mr. Clay to visit that city. Among the visitors were Recorder Tallmadge, Nicholas Dean, M. G. Hart, Morris Franklin, Horace Greeley, Matthew L. Davis, James A. Coffin, Mr. Gammage and Mr. McCracken, of New Haven. A surf boat was sent off and brought the committee ashore, who waited on Mr. Clay and received his promise to meet them at the Mansion House at noon. During the morning all the passengers came ashore from the steamboat. The mode of transit created great amusement and many jokes. Some called it the landing before Vera Cruz, and to see dignity perched on the shoulders of the boatmen, who, wading through the surf, deposited their loads on the beach, was truly laughable.

"The New Yorkers stopped principally at the Columbia House. At the appointed time Mr. Ludlam sent down his band from the Mansion House to accompany the procession, which soon arrived at the place appointed for the reception. The hall was filled with ladies and gentlemen, and 'mute expectation spread its anxious hush,' interrupted only by the strains of the band, until Henry Clay made his appearance. Then ensued such a shouting and cheering, and applaudits from fair hands, and waving of handkerchiefs, as Cape May never saw before, and probably never will again. Old Ocean started from his noonday repose and lifted up his white locks to listen to the unwonted shout, and then there came wave after wave, spreading itself on the beach, as if doing joyous homage to 'the man and the hour.'

"Nicholas Dean, Esq., as chairman of the New York delegation, then arose, and in behalf of the citizens of New York, irrespective of party, expressed their appreciation of the long and eminent services of Mr. Clay, and requested an opportunity of tendering him an expression of their confidence and esteem. In the name of the half million citizens of New York, he invited Mr. Clay to visit the metropolis— he said thousands of tongues were waiting to give him welcome, and the entire aggregate heart and pulse of the city was beating and throbbing to bid him welcome—thrice welcome to the hospitality of New York.

"Mr. Clay, who had listened with much emotion to the glowing language and impassioned tone of Mr. Dean, after a silence of a few moments, arose to reply. Hushed then was every sound, lest one word that was to fall from those eloquent lips should be lost. He commenced by alluding to the presence of other committees, on similar errands to the one from New York—especially from Philadelphia, Trenton and New Haven—and then continued:

"'Fellow Citizens—The eloquent address which has just been delivered has had the effect almost to induce me to adopt the language which was used on a more solemn occasion. "Thou almost persuadest me" to go to New York. But in all that uprightness of my nature which I have ever endeavored to practice, I must tell you the objects and motives which brought me to the shores of the Atlantic. I returned to my residence, after passing the winter at New Orleans, on the 23d or 24th of March last and a day or two afterwards melancholy intelligence came to me. I have been nervous ever since, and was induced to take this journey, for I could not look upon the partner of my sorrows without experiencing deeper anguish.'

"(Mr. Clay was here completely overcome by his feelings, covered his face with his hands and was silent for several minutes. At length with an effort he recovered himself and resumed.)

"'Everything about Ashland was associated with the memory of the lost one: the very trees which his hands assisted me to plant seemed to remind me of his loss. Had the stroke come alone, I could have borne it with His assistance, and sustained by the kindness of my friends and fellow-citizens, with meekness and resignation. But of eleven children four only remain. Of six lovely and affectionate daughters not one is left. Finding myself in a theatre of sadness, I thought I would fly to the mountain top and descend to the waves of the ocean, and by meeting with the sympathy of friends, obtain some relief to the sadness which encompassed me. I came for private purposes, and for private purposes alone. I have not desired these public manifestations, but have rather desired to escape from them. My friend and traveling companion, Dr. Mercer, will tell you, that in Virginia, in every section of the State of my birth, I have been implored to remain if only for a few hours, to exchange congratulations with my friends, but I invariably refused and only remained in each place sufficiently long enough to exchange one vehicle for another. You may imagine that I made a visit to Philadelphia, but I was accidentally thrown into Philadelphia. When I arrived in Baltimore, I learnt that the most direct route to this place was by the Delaware. I had no public object in view in taking that route, and yet indifferent I am not nor cannot be to these manifestations of popular regard, nor to anything which connects me with the honor, welfare and glory of my country.

" 'Gentlemen of the Committee of New York, I have truly and sincerely disclosed the purpose of the journey, but I cannot but deeply feel this manifestation of your respect and regard. It is received with thankfulness, and excites the warmest feelings of my heart, that I, a private and humble citizen, without an army, without a navy, without even a constable's staff, should have been met at every step of my progress with the kindest manifestations of feelings—feelings of which a President, a monarch or an emperor might well be pround.

" 'No—I am not insensible to these tokens of public affection and regard, I am thankful for them all. To you, gentlemen of the Committee of New York, who, in behalf of the 400,000 individuals whom you represent, have taken so much trouble, I am deeply thankful for this manifestation of your regard, but I must reluctantly decline the honor of your invitation. And you, gentlemen of the other committees, to your fellow-citizens of Trenton, New Haven and Philadelphia, I must beg of you to excuse me, and trust to your affection to do so, for if I do not place myself upon the affection of my countrymen, whither should I go, and where should

I be?—on the wide ocean without a compass and without a guide!

"'I must beg of you, gentlemen of all these committees, to retrace your steps, charged and surcharged with the warmest feelings of gratitude—go back charged with warmest thanks from me, and tell my friends that nothing but the circumstances in which I am placed, nothing—for we may as well mingle a laugh with our tears, and borrow the words of the Irish Ambassador, "situated as I am and I may say circumstanced as I am"—prevents the honor of meeting you. Tell them—and I hope that general response will be considered as a specific answer to each of the committee—that you are charged with the expression of the best feelings of my heart. And you, gentlemen of New York, be assured that among the recollections of the incidents of this journey, this visit will be paramount, and the circumstances which led to it.

"'I wish you an agreeable voyage on your return, and pray make my apologies for being constrained to decline your kind invitation.'

"Mr. Clay then sat down, and from the tears which had been so copiously shed during his speech, the smiles of welcome and felicitation lit up a mellow radiance which fell with rainbow softening over the scene. Throughout the whole reply of Mr. Clay, he was deeply and powerfully affected, and it was with a giant effort that he succeeded in uttering his closing remarks."

Nathaniel Holmes, Jr., who served in the Assembly from 1847 to 1849, was the son of Captain Nathaniel Holmes. He was born July 7, 1782. He served in the Board of Freeholders from Dennis township from 1834 to 1841 and from 1847 to 1851, or eleven years, during all of which time was the director (chairman) of the board.

On April 25, 1848 the people by ballot decided to have a new court house built, and chose for its location Cape May Court House village. The Board of Freeholders selected as the committee to visit other counties and get ideas of public buildings James L. Smith and Samuel Fithian Ware. On the 6th of June following the board ordered the house built to be 48 by 35 feet, with the lower story to be twelve feet in the clear and the upper story to be nine feet in the clear. The court house was finished in 1850, and on May 7 the freeholders met at the new court house to settle the bills, and they all amounted to $6284.33. Richard Thompson was chosen to dispose of the old court house.

The song, "Cape May," was written about May 1, 1848, by Theophilus Townsend Price. The circumstances leading to its inception are here related:

Being one evening in company with some young people, his personal friends, they sang the minstrel song of "Dearest May," which at that time was very popular. He remarked that it was a pity that so sweet a melody should be wedded to such trifling words. They requested him to write a song for the music, which he accordingly did, and produced the song as printed at first. There was no paper published at Cape May at that time, and it was first printed in a Philadelphia paper.

Theophilus Townsend Price was born on the Price homestead plantation at Town Bank, Cape May county, on the 21st day of May, 1828. He was the seventh child of John Price and Kezia Swain, who was the daughter of Daniel Swain, and belonged to one of the oldest families in Cape May county. When he was three years old his father sold his interest in the homestead farm at Town Bank to his brother, Captain William Price, and bought one of the Swain farms of his father-in-law on the seaside road above Cold Spring.

Here the subject of our sketch grew up to manhood, engaged in the general work of the farm, and in going to school whenever opportunity offered. He was by nature a student and lover of books, and does not remember the time when he could not read. His education was obtained at the common schools and at the Cold Spring Academy, which at that time was furnishing an academic education for both sexes under the direction of Rev. Moses Williamson.

In his twentieth year he began teaching in the public schools of Cape May county, and continued in this occupation about three years. In 1850 he commenced the study of medicine, reading under direction of Dr. V. M. D. Marcy, of Cold Spring. He graduated in March, 1853, and in April settled at Tuckerton, N. J., where he has continued in active practice ever since.

In November, 1854, he married Eliza, youngest daughter of Timothy Pharo, of Tuckerton. By this union he had two children, one of which only is living, the Rev. Theophilus Pharo Price.

Soon after his settlement he became interested in and identified with the public affairs of the communities in which he lived. The township of Little Egg Harbor, in which the village of Tuckerton is located, was at that time a part of Burlington county. He became a member of the Burlington County Medical Society in 1854 and is still a member. He was township superintendent of the public schools of Little Egg Harbor for eight years, and until the law was passed abolishing town superintendents and creating county superintendents. He was postmaster of Tuckerton during the Lincoln and the Johnson administrations; was elected to the New Jersey Legislature in 1868. During this service he obtained a charter to build a railroad from Tuckerton to Egg Harbor City, and a supplement to a charter to build a railroad from Manchester to Tuckerton. The latter road was built in 1871, of which he was, elected a director and secretary, still holding these offices. He was a director of the National Bank of Medford, N. J., for thirty-five years.

In 1877 he wrote the descriptive and historical portions of the New Jesey Coast Atlas, published by Woolman & Rose, covering the first sixty-eight pages of that work.

In 1864 he organized and conducted for fourteen years a union mission Sunday school in a destitute neighborhood near Tuckerton; was instrumental and active in organizing the first Baptist church at West Creek, Ocean county, in 1876, of which he was chosen deacon, clerk and treasurer for fifteen years. In 1891 he was actively instrumental in organizing and constituting the Baptist church of Tuckerton, of which he is a licentiate, deacon and clerk.

He was a trustee of the South Jersey Institute, at Bridgeton, for nine years; a trustee of the New Jersey Reform School for Boys at Jamesburg for three years. He is now president of the Board of Trustees of the Camden Baptist

Association, president of the Board of Education of Little Egg Harbor, physician and secretary of the Board of Health, director and secretary of the Beach Haven Land Association, life member of the New Jersey Historical Society, president of the Board of Trustees of Tuckerton Library Association, and is a member of several other benevolent and charitable societies.

For seventeen years he held the office of United States Marine Hospital surgeon at the port of Tuckerton and until the office was abolished by the government, March, 1896. During this time he examined annually about one hundred and fifty life-saving men before they entered on their duties. He has contributed from time to time articles to the press, both in prose and verse, and has delivered many public addresses and lectures.

On the 9th of June, 1849, two additional postoffices were established in the county, one at Townsend's Inlet, with William Stiles as postmaster, and the other at Seaville, with John Gandy as postmaster.

Enoch Edmunds, of Cape Island, who was elected to the State Senate in 1849 and served three years, was born in Lower township in 1799. He was the son of Robert Edmunds. From 1844 to 1847 he was sheriff of the county. In 1851 he became an elder of the Cold Spring Presbyterian Church, and was such until he died, sixteen years later. In 1860 he was chosen overseer of poor of Cape Island, and served in the City Council in 1861 and from 1863 until his death, on March 30, 1867. He was a merchant.

CHAPTER XXI.
THE DECADE BEFORE THE REBELLION.

From 1845 the people of this county began to move into the then newly developing States of Indiana and Illinois, and after the gold fever of 1849 many went further. These two States, however, were the objective point of many of the emigrating families from Cape May. Dr. Maurice Beesley, in speaking of this fact, says (1857):

"The population meets with an unceasing annual drain in the way of emigration. Numerous families every spring and fall sell off their lands and effects to seek a home in the far West. Illinois has heretofore been the State that has held out most inducements to the emigrant, and there are at present located in the favored county of Sangamon, in that State, some sixty or seventy families which have removed from this county within a few years past, most of whom, be it said, are blessed with prosperity and happiness. Many of her people are to be found in the other free States of the West."

When the last half of the present century opened there were 6433 residents in this county, and it was estimated by the census takers that about one-fifth of the entire male population were engaged in seafaring, and a more hardy and adventurous band never sailed from any port; no sea or ocean where commerce floats a sail they did not visit if duty called.

The pilots of Cape Island were likewise renowned for their skill and enterprise in the way of their profession. They braved the tempest and the storm to relieve the mariner in distress, or to conduct the steamer, the ship, or the barque to the haven of her destination. There were about thirty-five of them living in the lower end of the county.

The Dias Creek postoffice, with Charles K. Holmes as postmaster, was established September 9, 1850, and on the

3d of March, 1851, another office was established at Beesley's Point, with Joseph D. Chatten in charge.

Captain Wilmon Whilldin, Sr., the first to establish steamboat communication between Philadelphia and Cape May, was a native of this county. He was born March 4, 1773, near Cape May City, on the estate possessed by his ancestors from the first settlement of the county. He was the son of Jonathan Whilldin (who is described as "gent" in old conveyances), by his wife, Hannah Crowell; grandson of James Whilldin, Esq., by his wife, Jane Hand; great grandson of Joseph Whilldin, by his wife, Mary; and great grandson of Joseph Whilldin, Esq., by his wife, Hannah. The last named Joseph was High Sheriff of the county from 1705 to 1708, and many years one of His Majesty's Justices of the Peace and of the Courts of Common Pleas. James Whilldin, Esq., the grandfather of Captain Whilldin, was commissioned a Justice of the Peace by Governor Belcher, June 7, 1753, and re-commissioned by Governor Hardy, September 24, 1762, and by Governor Franklin, August 21, 1767. On the two last occasions he was also commissioned a justice of the quorum. He was also commissioned Justice of the Court of Oyer and Terminer on March 13, 1773, in which capacity he served until he died. In 1779 he was a member of the Legislature, and during the Revolution he served on the County Committee of Safety. He was a prominent member of the Cold Spring Presbyterian Church, of which he was a ruling elder from 1754 until his decease, November 5, 1780. Captain Whilldin studied navigation, and early in life removed to Philadelphia, where he resided until his decease, April 2, 1852. He was one of the pioneers in steam navigation on the Delaware. In 1816 he built the steamer "Delaware," with which he established communication with Cape May. (A large portrait in oil of Captain Whilldin, now in the possession of his granddaughter, Mrs. J. Granville Leach, has a portrait of the "Delaware" in the background.) Captain Whilldin became the owner of several steamers, which plied to different points on the Delaware, also on the Chesapeake. At one time he was a partner of the elder Commodore Vanderbilt. The pilot boat John G. Whilldin, so familiar in our waters, was named in honor of Captain Whilldin's son, Dr. John Galloway Whilldin, a promising young physician of Philadelphia, who died of consumption in early life.

On the decease of Captain Whilldin his only surviving child, Captain Wilmon Whilldin, Jr., succeeded to the business of the father, and continued the line of steamers to Cape May until the civil war, when most of his boats were employed by the government in the transportation of troops and provisions to the army. At his decease, May 23, 1866, he was extensively engaged in transportation by steam, and was interested in lines running to many parts of the country.

The first town school superintendents were appointed in the county in 1851, and they were: Upper township, Barnabas Coffie; Dennis, Joshua Swain; Middle, Rev. N. B. Tindall; Lower, Joseph E. Hughes; Cape Island, Rev. Clark Polly. There were 2135 school children in the county, divided as follows: In Upper, 441; Dennis, 534; Middle, 609; Lower, 400; Cape Island, 151.

The old borough of Cape Island did not suit the inhabitants. Therefore, in 1851, a city charter for the place was secured from the Legislature. Since that time Cape May City has had two charters; one in 1867, and the last in 1875. From 1851 to 1867 the Councilmen (six in number), were elected yearly; and from 1867 to 1875 three Councilmen were elected each year, for a two-years' term, making six as before. Up to 1875 the Alderman and City Recorder were members of Council, and the Mayor was its president, but the latter had no vote only in case of a tie, while the two former were accorded that privilege. Council then elected its clerk. Since 1875 there has, each year, been three Councilmen elected for terms of three years each, making the body nine in number, and they choose their president from among their number. The Recorder is now the clerk of the city, and by ordinance superintendent of the water works and register of the bonded indebtedness. The Alderman is now simply justice of the peace, and, should the Mayor resign or die, acts as such until the next election.

Joshua Swain, Jr., who was elected to the State Senate

in 1852, was the son of Joshua Swain, who was a member of the Constitutional Convention of 1844. He was born June 2, 1804, and died March 23, 1866. He served in the Assembly from 1850 to 1852, and then in the Senate until 1854. He was continuously clerk of the Board of Chosen Freeholders from 1831 until he died. He was for six years a Judge of the Court of Errors and Appeals of the State of New Jersey. He died at Seaville, and his remains lie in

COURT HOUSE USED SINCE 1850.

Calvary Baptist Church Cemetery, Seaville. He was a Baptist in faith.

He was succeeded by his son, Edward Y. Swain, as clerk of the Board of Freeholders. The latter was prominent in county affairs, and was clerk from 1866 to 1871, when he died. He was born December 27, 1834, and died October 9, 1871.

Henry Swain, brother of Joshua, Jr., who was loan commissioner, was born May 12, 1806, and died September 24, 1877. He served the county as loan commissioner from 1854 to 1856, and from 1857 to 1862.

The first bank in the county to be established was that at Cape Island, known as the "Bank of Cape May County," which had subscribers to stock from every part of the county. Its certificate of association was filed in the County Clerk's office on September 26, 1853. It was a State bank. In 1855 it closed up its business. On October 17, this year, Joseph F. Leaming, its vice-president, gave notice that "all circulating notes issued must be presented to the State Treasurer within two years" for payment. On March 3, 1854, the act to incorporate the Cape May Turnpike Company became a law. The object of this company was to construct a thoroughfare between Cape Island and Cape May Court House. The incorporators were Richard C. Holmes, Dr. John Willey, Eli L. B. Wales, George Bennett, Joseph Ware, Richard Thompson and Clinton H. Ludlam. The work on it was not commenced until three years afterwards, and in 1858 it was completed.

The Cape Island Turnpike Company built the pike from the steamboat landing on the Delaware Bay to Cape Island for the accommodation of steamboat passengers. This pike was constructed between 1846 and 1848. The company is still in existence, and toll is still charged to those who drive vehicles over it.

The first President of the United States to visit Cape May was Franklin Pierce, who visited the island in the summer of 1855. He was welcomed by the City Council and held a public reception. People came from all parts of the county to see him.

In September (5th) of this year the famous Mount Vernon Hotel at Cape Island, which had been two years in building, was burned. And in June, of 1856, the Mansion House and Kersal were destroyed by fire also.

The first newspaper published in the county was the "Ocean Wave," which was established at Cape Island by one Colonel Johnson in June, 1855. The sizes of its four pages were twelve by eighteen inches. About three months after it was founded it was purchased by Joseph S. Leach, who edited and published it until 1863, when he sold it to Samuel R. Magonigle. When Mr. Magonigle died, in 1869, the "Wave" became the property of Christopher S.

Magrath and Aaron Garretson, Sr. In 1878 Mr. Magrath became sole owner, and remained so until he sold it, in 1883, to Thomas H. Williamson, son of Rev. Moses Williamson. In 1886 Mr. Williamson died, and it was then purchased from his estate by James H. Edmunds, who still (1897) owns it. It has been edited from 1883 by Henry W. Hand, who served in the United States Navy during the Civil War.

Joseph S. Leach, editor of the "Ocean Wave," was born in Shutesbury, Mass, March 30, 1816, and died at his residence in Cape May City, August 9, 1892. He was the son of Lemuel Leach, Jr., and Eilzabeth Smallidge, his wife. His grandfather, Lemuel Leach, Sr., was an officer in the Revolutionary Army, and his maternal grandfather, Rev. Joseph Smallidge, was a prominent clergyman of the Baptist faith in Western Massachusetts. His colonial ancestor, Lawrence Leach, a descendant of John Leche, surgeon to King Edward the Third, arrived in Massachusetts with Rev. Francis Higginson, in 1629. Mr. Leach also descended from John Washbourne, the first secretary of Massachusetts, and from Francis Cooke, one of the "pilgrims" who came in the Mayflower.

Mr. Leach was educated at New Salem High School, and at Franklin Academy, Shelburne Falls, Mass. He afterwards studied theology and entered the ministry, in which he was preceded by three elder brothers, Rev. Sanford Leach, Rev. William Leach and Dr. Elbridge G. Leach. Failing health compelled him to seek a milder climate, and, in 1840, he came to Cape May, and took up his residence at the county seat. Shortly after his arrival he was invited to take charge of the Seaville school, which position he accepted, and from that time until he became the proprietor of the "Ocean Wave" he was constantly and successfully engaged in teaching the youth of this county.

Foremost among those who were engaged in the Baptist Church of Cape Island was Mr. Leach. He was licensed to preach at Shutesbury Church, in Massachusetts, about 1838. He did not, however, unite with the local church until January, 1849. For nearly half a century Mr. Leach was one of the leading members of the church, was many years clerk of the church, and one of its trustees, and for forty-three years a deacon. The congregation was frequently without a settled pastor for months at a time, on which occasions he occupied the pulpit, but always declined compensation for his ministerial work.

In the early fall of 1855 Mr. Leach purchased the "Ocean Wave" and published it and edited it until he sold the paper to the late Samuel R. Magonagle. As editor he gained the reputation of being one of the ablest and strongest newspaper writers in the State, and by the use of his pen he was largely instrumental in advancing the social, educational, and material interests of the county. His writings were notedly valuable in aiding to secure the construction of the Cape May and Millville Railroad. The late Charles B. Dungan is known to have said that, "but for Mr. Leach's earnest and able support in this connection, the building of the road would doubtless have been delayed for years."

At the outbreak of the Civil War Mr. Leach warmly espoused the cause of the Union, not only with his pen, but with voice as well. He was recognized as one of our best public speakers, and his services in this direction were frequently in demand, particularly during the war, at "war meetings." He was concise in argument, clear in diction and fervid in utterance, and his eloquence stirred his hearers to the heartiest expressions of enthusiasm.

In 1851, on the granting of the charter creating Cape May (then Cape Island) into a city. Mr. Leach was elected the first Recorder, by virtue of which office he became a member of City Council and a justice of the peace. In 1852 and 1858 he was chosen a member of City Council, and in 1872 he was again chosen Recorder of the city. In 1862 he was town superintendent of public schools, and in 1863 President Lincoln appointed him postmaster of the city, which position he held until Andrew Johnson succeeded to the Presidency, when, entertaining views antagonistic to President Johnson's "policy," Mr. Leach resigned the office. He was a member of the County Board of Chosen Freeholders in 1863, 1864, 1865, 1867, 1868 and 1870. He was frequently urged to accept a nomination for the Assembly, as well as to the Mayoralty of Cape May, but declined these honors.

In his death Cape May lost one of its most prominent and highly-esteemed citizens, one who will long be remembered as a worthy representative of the "gentleman of the old school." The tablet erected to his memory in the Baptist Church bears this inscription:

"In Memory of
Joseph Smallidge Leach, Esq., a descendant of the Puritans. He preached to this people many years without compensation and served in the office of deacon forty-three years.
A Successful Educator.
An Able Editor.
An Exemplary Citizen.
He honorably filled many public offices. In all life's relations he merited and won universal respect and esteem.
A quiet and peaceable life in all godliness and honesty.
I Timothy, xi, 2."

Mr. Leach married, May 31, 1841, Sophia, daughter of Josiah Ball, Esq., of Worcester county, Mass. She still survives him, with seven of their nine children.

Petersburg's postoffice was first opened in April, 1856, with Peter Corson as postmaster. On the 6th of September following the Rio Grande postoffice was opened, with Jeremiah Hand as postmaster. This made the fifteenth postoffice established in the county. None were again established until after the close of the Civil War.

In 1856 a telegraph known as the Philadelphia and Cape Island Telegraph was doing business, and continued to do so until the outbreak of the Civil War, when it was abandoned by its proprietors.

In 1856 Jesse H. Diverty was chosen to represent Cape May in the State Senate, and served in the sessions of '57, '58 and '59, having served two preceding years as a member of the Assembly. His grandfather was William Diverty, who lived from 1744 to 1811, and was a native of Scotland. His father was James Diverty, born in Aberdeen, Scotland, in 1783. At the age of 10 the father came to Wilmington, Del., to live with an uncle. When 21 he came to Cape May to purchase hoop poles for the cooperage business of his uncle. He married afterwards Deborah Smith, the daughter of Mrs. Jesse Hand, wife of the Cape May patriot. The new couple began life at Dennisville, where the father became a lumber merchant and postmaster. He died in 1858.

Jesse H. Diverty was born there, December 22, 1822. He was educated in the village school and at Bridgeton Academy. For a time, when young, he was engaged in mercantile pursuits in Baltimore, and then with his father at Dennisville. In 1865 he began the ship building business,

JESSE H. DIVERTY.

building in his time about thirty vessels. When the shipbuilding died out, he entered into agricultural pursuits.

In public life he served as township collector, committeeman, justice of the peace, superintendent of schools, and for forty years was a school trustee. After serving in the Senate, he was made engrossing clerk of that body for the two following years. Governor Abbett appointed him one of the commissioners of State Charities and Corrections. He was at first a Whig, but later a Democrat. During the war he was a staunch Unionist. In 1877 he was appointed a

Judge of County Courts, and was reappointed in 1882 and 1887.

When 12 years of age he became a Methodist, and in 1843 was made a class leader. He was in 1844 made an exhorter, in 1847 a local preacher, in 1860 a deacon and in 1871 an elder. He was superintendent of the Sunday-school from 1843 until his death. He died at Dennisville March 9, 1890.

The county of Cape May owes to the memory of Dr.

DR. MAURICE BEESLEY.

Maurice Beesley, of Dennisville, as much, if not more, as to any man of recent times, for his preservation of the facts concerning the early settlers and the development of the county. In 1857 he had printed his "Sketch of the Early History of Cape May County," and it has proved a valuable document. Dr. Beesley was long connected with the welfare of the county. He first saw the light of day at Dennisville on May 16, 1804. His grandfather, Jonathan Beesley, was a Revolutionary soldier, being killed fighting in battle for American independence. His father was Thomas

Beesley. The doctor was an elder brother of Thomas H. Beesley, who succeeded him in public life a few years later. Young Maurice Beesley obtained a good education by his own diligent work, and then began the study of medicine with Dr. Theophilus Beesley, of Salem. He graduated in 1828, and shortly after began practicing his profession at Cape May Court House, remaining there about a year. Afterwards he removed to Dennisville, where he actively practiced for fifty-three years. Dr. Beesley was sent to the Legislature by the people from 1840 to 1842, and the two years following he served in the Legislative Council. He was actively interested in the laws perfecting the management of the insane institutions in the State. In 1845 he became a member of the New Jersey Historical Society, and contributed to its library often valuable historical records.

In 1866, upon the taking effect of the new school law, he was appointed superintendent of public instruction for Cape May county, and served efficiently in that capacity until 1881, when he resigned on account of failing health. He dearly loved nature. "His researches into the origin of the burned juniper forests of Dennis Creek are of great and lasting value," says a writer, "being the standard authority to this day." He died January 13, 1882, aged 78, and his remains lie in the cemetery at South Dennis.

William Smith Hooper, who, in 1856, was elected Sheriff and served three years, was born at Tuckahoe, September 10, 1816, and was the last male descendent of his line when he died. His father, who came from South Carolina, and who was a nephew of William Hooper, the signer of the Declaration of Independence, was drowned in the Delaware Bay when the lad was 4 years of age. His mother was Abagail Smith, a daughter of Captain William Smith, of the Revolutionary army. When young he was bound to Richard Smith Ludlam (Assemblyman in 1847 and cousin of his mother). Young Hooper served as clerk in Mr. Ludlam's store and mill at Dennisville, and afterwards at the Mansion House in Cape Island. When he became of age he went to the banks of the Ohio River, crossing the Allegheny Mountains by stage, and engaged in purchasing and selling lumber in the towns along the river, and, for a time, was clerk in a counting house in Covington. His health failing him, he came back to Cape May county and resided at Dennisville, where he held township offices. He came to Cape Island, and in 1853 he was a member of the City Council of Cape Island, and in 1855 was Recorder of the city, and at the same time a member of the Board of Freeholders. He enlisted for the war with Mexico, but did not go. At the breaking out of the Civil War he entered Company A, Seventh Regiment, New Jersey Volunteers, being mustered into service for three years and commissioned corporal August 23, 1861, and was promoted to sergeant July 15, 1863. He

WILLIAM S. HOOPER.

was in all the important battles with the regiment during the service, being mustered out October 7, 1864. He became an invalid in the service, and remained so until his death. In 1872 he was chosen tax collector of Cape May City, and was re-elected five times, serving until 1878. In 1884 he was chosen a member of the Board of Freeholders again, and served in the board from 1886 to 1891. He was a member of the Cape Island Lodge, Free and Accepted Masons, a director of the Cape Island Turnpike Company. In politics he was a Whig until the formation of the Republican party, when he became a believer in its principles. He died in Cape May City on August 20, 1896, being within twenty days of his 80th year. His remains are interred in Calvary Baptist Church Cemetery, Seaville.

The mail service in the year 1857 was irregular, the attempts being made to get two and sometimes three mails a week. The mails were all carried by the stage lines. The "Ocean Wave" of April 16, this year, tells of the need of a daily mail and of the delays in the following article:

"We need a daily mail. That we have no direct mail communication between Cape Island and Cape May C. H., our county seat, but once a week, is a fact known to all. A letter written here on Wednesday may go direct to the Court House on Thursday, and an answer be returned on Saturday, by the Bridgeton mail; but at any other time in the week our letters must be sent up by the Bayside mail, on Mondays, Wednesdays or Fridays to Tuckahoe, and there stopped till the next down mail to the Court House, thus performing a journey of nearly fifty miles, while the distance is only thirteen miles direct from here to the Court House."

The same source gives the facts that in Cape May county, from returns of assessors and statistics otherwise obtained, that farm products had increased by 1857 over the products in 1850 by 50 per cent., and that since the United States census of 1850 the price of land in the county had nearly doubled.

In the election of the fall of 1857 there were but 541 votes polled in the county. Downs Edmunds, Jr., was chosen Assemblyman; Elijah Townsend, Jr., Surrogate, and William S. Hooper Sheriff. In the election of the succeeding year the slavery question was beginning to agitate the people. There were the American, People's and Democratic parties. The result was that Downs Edmunds, Jr., American, and Abram Reeves, People's, were chosen Senator and Assemblyman respectively. In 1859 Reeves was re-elected to the Assembly on the American ticket.

In 1858 the Cape Island Gas Company had been established, and the rates charged for gas was $6.00 per one thousand feet burned, and the rent of the meters was $3.00 per year.

Downs Edmunds, Jr., served three years in the Assembly, 1856, 1857, 1858, and was elected and served a full term in the Senate, serving in the Legislatures of 1859, 1860 and 1861. He was born at Fishing Creek, October 29, 1813, and was the son of Downs Edmunds, an esteemed resident of lower Cape May county. He was a man of considerable business qualifications, being a farmer, merchant and, for a number of years, was agent at Cape May for the steamboats plying between Cape May and other places. He was a member of the Board of Freeholders for several years. On June 3, 1884, Governor Abbett appointed him a Judge of Common Pleas Court for Cape May county, and he served out the unexpired term of Abraham Reeves. He was an adherent of the Republican party. He died at his West Cape May home April 1, 1890, aged 77 years.

Abraham Reeves, who was elected to the Assembly when Mr. Edmunds was chosen Senator, was a son of Abijah Reeves, of the War of 1812, and was born in Lower township October 22, 1802. He was a man of commanding presence, six feet in height. He was known as "Uncle Abe" to every one. His educational advantages were limited, it being said of him that he never spent but three months in a school. He, however, was a man of good judgment and integrity. He served two terms in the Assembly and was twice appointed a Judge of Common Pleas Court, holding the position when he died. For a number of years he was a chosen Freeholder, and held many township offices. He served several years as president of the County Bible Society, was an elder of the Cold Spring Presbyterian Church. He was at first a Whig, and then a Republican in politics. He died May, 1884.

In the year 1860 Cape May was passing out of one epoch into another. The old stage coach was soon to give way to the railroad train. The impending conflict of affairs which terminated in the War of the Rebellion was becoming intense. No better way of ascertaining the condition of the county at this time can be had than by recourse to the statistics here presented. The population consisted of 7130 persons, divided as follows:

TOWNSHIPS.	WHITE.			FREE COLORED.			Aggre'te
	Male	Female	Total	Male	Female	Total	
Dennis	765	790	1555	2	1	3	1558
Lower, (including Cape Island)	826	849	1675	77	113	190	1865
Middle	1032	1053	2085	40	30	70	2155
Upper	788	754	1542	5	5	10	1552
Total	3411	3446	6857	124	149	273	7130

There were in the county 1465 families, 1600 dwellings, 523 separate farms and thirty-eight manufacturing establishments. The value of the assessable real estate in the county was $872,364.00, and the total taxes assessed in the county were $11,727.47, it being used for the following purposes: For support of the county, $3899.47; for schools, $6128.00, and for public roads, $1700.00.

Farming was the principal occupation of the residents, and the production for the year ending on June 1 is here given:

THE DECADE BEFORE THE REBELLION.

TOWNSHIPS	Acres of Land		Cash Value of Farms	Value of Farming Implements and Machinery	Live Stock							
	Improved	Unimproved			Horses	Asses & Mules	Milch Cows	Working Oxen	Other Cattle	Sheep	Swine	Value of Live Stock
Upper	3393	14448	$322,500	$13,780	159	0	449	55	626	419	458	$34,164
Dennis	3555	12462	260,600	10,985	142	11	413	53	678	526	508	33,070
Middle	7235	15347	512,950	21,785	312	4	685	45	868	1219	1225	64,579
Lower	5345	6163	366,350	20,200	250	6	441	0	430	453	641	43,090
Total	19528	48420	$1462,400	$66,750	863	21	1988	153	2602	2617	2832	$174,903

Produce during year ending June 1.

TOWNSHIPS	Wheat, bu. of	Rye, bu. of	Indian Corn, bu. of	Oats, bu. of	Wool, lbs. of	Peas and Beans, bu. of	Irish Potatoes, bu. of	Sweet Potatoes, bu. of	Buckwheat, bu. of	Value of Orchard Products	Wine, gallons of
Upper	3816	1282	20120	1550	904	64	6059	2769	646	$297	15
Dennis	3971	714	24560	2980	1152	39	8151	2889	742	150	0
Middle	7106	342	45480	8109	2495	21	13100	9942	1835	615	43
Lower	6415	73	30285	7350	720	133	9218	6100	790	775	0
Total	21308	2411	120445	19989	5271	257	36429	21700	4013	$1837	58

The average monthly wages of a farm hand was $12.00, the day laborer's, with board, seventy-five cents per day; the day laborer's, without board, $1.00; carpenter's average daily wages, $1.50; weekly wages of a domestic female, with board, $1.00, and without board, $2.25 per week.

The number of manufacturing establishments was thirty-eight, in which there was $79,658.00 invested. The value of material used in a year was $60,846.00, out of which the annual productions amounted to $75,320.00. Seventy-eight males and seven females were employed.

There were twenty-seven schools in which thirty-two teachers were employed, teaching 2373 scholars at an annual cost of $7586.00. There was one academy, the one at Cold Spring (M Williamson's), in which one teacher was engaged, and which had thirty students, which was run at an expense of $760 per year. There was one library in the county, in which there were 1550 books. Throughout the county there were twenty-one churches of various denominations, with an aggregate accommodation for 9056 persons, and valued at $58,900.

The mode of travel to and from the county was either by stage or vessel up to 1863. The steamers during the summer seasons made round trips from Philadelphia and New York once every two days, and sometimes there was a daily communication by water in this season with Philadelphia. But at other seasons of the year the water route was more uncertain.

The stages ran by way of Bridgeton and Tuckahoe. The "Bridgeton stage" passed through the bay shore towns from Cape Island to Bridgeton, while the "Tuckahoe stage" passed through the villages on the seashore side of the county, going to May's Landing and thence to Philadelphia These routes were subject to change. The stages, before the advent of the railroads, carried the mails, and, when approaching the villages, the driver would always herald their approach by tooting a big horn. Then the village folk would gather around the primitive postoffice to get a letter or hear the latest news from the "United States Gazette" (now the "North American"), of Philadelphia, which seemed to be the principal newspaper read in the county.

The fare between Philadelphia and Cape May, one way only, was $3.50 per passenger.

The Bridgeton stage, which in 1856 was owned by James Whitaker, left Cape May on Mondays and Thursdays at 5 in the morning, winter and summer, and passed through the villages of Cold Spring, Fishing Creek, Green Creek, Dyers Creek, Goshen, Dennisville, Leesbury, Dorchester, Port Elizabeth and Millville, arriving at Bridgeton on the same evening at 4 o'clock. There the passengers took another stage and went on to Philadelphia. The returning days were Wednesdays and Saturdays, which gave the team of horses a day's rest between times. Those who drove these stages the longest were Henry C. Mulliner, William Hebenthal, better known throughout the county and to his passengers at the time as "Dutch Billy."

The great centres of industries were about West Creek, and Dennis Creek, which was reached by water. At the latter place ship building was conducted on a large scale. Most of the store business of the county was done there, and these businesses did not decline until the railroad opened and made the means of transportation a more easy matter.

The people of this county held many meetings during the eight years preceding 1863, when the Cape May and Millville Railroad was finally opened to Cape May.

There were schemes and routes laid out for many roads, and during the year 1857 the proposed "Cape May and Atlantic" Road had meetings held all over the county. The directors of it were Ebenezer Westcott, Joshua Swain, Jr., Hezekiah W. Godfrey, Matthew Whilldin, Dr. Henry Schmoele, Daniel E. Estel, Abraham L. Iszard, William Schmoele and Lilburn Harwood. Elias Wright was the engineer in charge.

On September 2, at a public meeting at Cape Island, Downs Edmunds, Jr., David Reeves, John West, Waters B. Miller and Joseph Ware were appointed to confer with the West Jersey Railroad about building a road through the county. On the 7th of August, preceding, Dr. Schmoele, Matthew Whilldin, Waters B. Miller and Joseph Ware (then Mayor) were appointed at a public meeting to confer with the Camden and Atlantic Road for the same purpose.

The Council of Cape Island was asked to subscribe $10,000 for the enterprise, which it finally did on April 24, 1860. Matthew Whilldin was paid by this Council also to procure the right of way for a road from property owners.

Joseph S. Leach, editor of the "Ocean Wave," and Charles B. Dungan, who was president of the company which finally built the road and who was the contractor also, deserve, with others, a large share of gratitude from the present residents of Cape May county for their untiring efforts in getting the road here. On May 13, 1863, the Board of Freeholders passed a resolution allowing the Cape May and Millville Railroad the right to lay rails over Cape Island bridge, and within a few days thereafter the railroad was opened to Cape May. It was not until August 29, 1879, that it was united with the West Jersey Railroad. Since then the great Pennsylvania system has secured control and thus has given to Cape May unnumbered advantages, and cheap excursion rates from all over the country. The opening of the road caused much prosperity.

Charles B. Dungan was born in Holmesburg, Pa., in 1813. He remained there for twelve years, attending the public schools.

A blind gentleman from Brooklyn, N. Y., who was visiting Holmesburg, took a strong liking to him, and induced his mother, who was a widow, to allow him to take the boy with him upon his return home. Young Dungan remained with this gentleman until his death, a period of five or six years, acting as his clerk and companion. He was then apprenticed to Gideon Cox, a dry goods merchant, whose place of business was at the corner of Eighth and Market streets, Philadelphia. When he attained his majority he went in to business for himself in Philadelphia. His store was robbed, and everything of value carried off. Not being able to resume his business, he secured a clerkship in the office of the Northern Liberties Gas Works, eventually becoming one of its officers.

He then engaged in the business of building gas works, constructing those in the cities of Washington, D. C.; Fredericksburg, Va.; Reading, Pa.; Hartford and New Haven, Conn., and other cities, seventeen in all. In 1850, when, through ill health, he had virtually retired from business, he was the possessor of large means.

He was induced to take an interest in the construction the Hoosac Tunnel, in Massachusetts. This work was being successfully prosecuted, when the great panic of 1857 overtook them, and in consequence became so involved that he was never able to resume work on it, the State taking it up after the war and completing it.

He then became interested in the managements of city passenger railways in Philadelphia, and was for several years president of the Fairmount and Arch Street Road. He conceived and carried out its consolidation with the Hestonville Road.

His next venture was the building of the Millville and Cape May Railroad, in 1863, of which he was contractor and president. He was not only public-spirited, but whole-souled and generous to a fault. His purse was always open to the needs of others, to the church and to any worthy benevolence which claimed his attention. He was a member of the Presbyterian church and a consistent professor of Christianity.

He died at his home in Cape May City on Wednesday, January 11, 1888.

Thomas T. Townsend, who was a prominent sea captain before the war, has done a good work for posterity in preserving many historical records. He was born about 1812, and when young was a clerk in the store of Jeremiah Leaming at Dennisville. He then became a blacksmith, and later a sea captain, commanding at different times eleven vessels. He retired in 1863. His historical documents were gathered since then. He died April 24, 1894.

CHAPTER XXII.
OPENING OF THE CIVIL WAR.

The attention of our reader is now turned to the part our people took in the War of the Rebellion, in which Cape May men did honor to themselves and to their State and country. As soon as the Confederates seized Fort Sumter, in April, 1861, the spirit of patriotism spread over Cape May county in as great a degree as anywhere else in the Union. In the autumn previous the people of the county had voted by a large majority for Mr. Lincoln for President. In every village the people assembled in public meetings and pledged their support to the Union. Military organizations were formed throughout the county. The Cape Island Home Guards, under command of Captain John West; the Seaville Rangers, under the care of Captain Joseph E. Corson, and a company at Cape May Court House, under the command of N. N. Wentzell, were quickly organized. "Long Tom," the only cannon in the county, which had been used in the War of 1812, was brought out, and the Board of Freeholders, on May 7, were asked to repair its carriage, which they, however, refused to do, being composed at the time of men not in sympathy with President Lincoln. On the same day Captain West's communication, asking for aid for the "Home Guards," was also disregarded by the board. But, as more serious events happened in the border States, the Board of Freeholders at last realized that they must do something, and therefore their sympathies were turned in for the Union.

On May 1 Henry W. Sawyer, of Cape Island, offered his services to Governor Olden, and was subsequently given a commission in the First Cavalry. He had already performed service for the Governor and in Washington, which is told of later on.

On the 11th of June the Board of Freeholders gave N. N.

Wentzell permission to use the Grand Jury room in the Court House for drilling purposes. Immediately previous to this the board also passed a resolution giving to the family of Mr. Sawyer $6.00 per month as long as he remained in the service of either the United States or New Jersey.

Simultaneous with these movements for the recruitment and organization of troops, the State authorities were engaged in other important labors. Realizing the necessity of means of prompt and constant communication with all parts of the State, the telegraph line to Cape May, which had been abandoned by the company, was at once ordered to be put in working order at the expense of the State; and, as a further means of defense, a maritime guard was established along the line of the coast, consisting of patriotic citizens living adjacent thereto. Waters B. Miller, then a member of the Board of Freeholders from Cape Island, sent the following telegram to the Governor concerning the abandoned Philadelphia and Cape Island Telegraph Line:

"Philadelphia, April 21, 1861.

"Governor Olden:—The telegraph line to Cape Island has not been in operation for several months. The company, it is said, have abandoned it. The line should be put in working order to communicate with government vessels off the Capes. It will cost about $500. Shall I have it put in order? W. B. Miller, of Cape May."

The Governor forthwith ordered Mr. Miller to repair the line, which was quickly done, the work costing in all $779.08.

In order to prepare for an earnest Union meeting, on Friday, June 21, 1861, a meeting was held in Court House village, at which J. F. Craig presided and A. L. Haynes acted as secretary, to arrange for the celebration of the Fourth of July. The following Committee of Arrangements was appointed: Dr. John Wiley, Dr. Coleman F. Leaming, Dr. Jonathan F. Leaming, Hon. Thomas Beesley, Judges Holmes and Samuel Springer. The committee subsequently met and appointed a County Committee, consisting of the following persons: Thomas Williams, Joseph E. Corson, Richard B. Stites, Charles Ludlam, James L. Smith, **Henry Swain, Stephen Bennett, Franklin Hand,** John

Swain, William J. Bate, Abraham Reeves, Jacob Corson, Waters B. Miller, S. R. Magonagle and Colonel John West, Committee on Grounds and Seating were: William Ross, William H. Benezet, George Ogden, Joseph Holmes and Charles Mills. Committee for Obtaining Speakers and Music: Dr. J. F. Leaming, Dr. C. F. Leaming. Committee on Resolutions: Rev. Moses Williamson, Drs. Coleman F. and Jonathan F. Leaming.

This celebration was held and the residents of the whole county participated in it.

During the early summer Samuel R. Magonagle, editor of the "Ocean Wave," at Cape Island induced the following persons to enlist for the war, who signed the roll in the Baptist Church there: Samuel R. Magonagle, George W. Smith, Richard T. Tindall, Joseph Hand, David Reeves, Jr., Charles H. Weeks, William S. Hooper, Samuel R. Ludlam, Harry L. Gilmour, Walter S. Ware, W. S. Ware, William B. Eldredge, Albert J. Cassedy, James T. Smith, John W. Kimsey, Nicholas T. Swain, Stephen D. Bennett, Joseph W. Johnson, John Mecray, Townsend T. Ireland, Stephen Pierson, James Burns, Caleb Warner, Thomas S. Stevens, Benjamin Redheffer, Joseph W. Ireland, Charles S. Hays, Charles J. Silver, T. Fletcher Jacobs, Jonathan C. Stevens, John Stites, Owen S. Clark, Walter A. Barrows, Patrick Kerns, Swain S. Reeves, Edward Filkin and Lewis H. Cresse. Nearly all of them finally went to the front. Walter S. Ware was not accepted because of his youthfulness.

With those who went to Trenton from Cape May county to join the First Cavalry Regiment were Thomas S. Stevens and Joseph Hand, who were enrolled and mustered in as privates in Company F, Fourth Regiment Infantry, on August 15, for a period of three years. Mr. Stevens remained with his regiment until August 17, 1864, when he was mustered out at Trenton. Mr. Hand served until he was discharged from the service on account of disability at De Camp U. S. Army, General Hospital, David's Island, New York harbor, on October 7, 1862.

The Fourth Regiment arrived in Washington on August 21, and was assigned to the brigade of General Philip Kearney, known as the First Brigade. The regiment took part in the following engagements: West Point, Va., May 7, '62; Gaines Farm, Va., June 27, '62; Charles City Cross Roads, Va., June 30, '62; White Oak Swamp, Va., same day; Malvern Hill, Va., July 1, '62; Manassas, Va., August 27, '62; Chantilly, Va., Septemberber 1, '62; Crampton's Pass, Md., September 14, '62; Antietam, Md., September 17, '62; Fredericksburg, Va., December 13 and 14, '62; Fredericksburg, Va., May 3, '63; Salem Heights, Va., May 3 and 4, '63; Gettysburg, Pa., July 2 and 3, '63; Fairfield, Pa., July 5, '63; Williamsport, Md., July 6, '63; Funktown, Md., July 12, '63; Rappahannock Station, Va., October 12, '63; same place, November 7, '63; Mine Run, Va., November 30, '63; Wilderness, Va., May 5 to 7, '64; Spottsylvania, Va., May 8 to 11, '64; Spottsylvania C. H., Va., May 12 to 16, '64; North and South Anna River, Va., May 24, '64; Hanover C. H., Va., May 29, '64; Tolopotomy Creek, Va., May 30 and 31, '64; Cold Harbor, Va., June 1 to 3, '64; before Petersburg, Va. (Weldon Railroad), June 23, '64; Snicker's Gap, Va., July 18, '64, and other skirmishes and battles following, none of which the Cape May men were in as members of the Fourth Regiment.

In the Sixth Regiment of Infantry, which left the State for the scene of the war, was Dr. John Wiley, of Cape May Court House, who served as chief surgeon of the regiment during the war. He was commissioned and mustered into service on August 17, 1861, for three years, being mustered out September 17, 1864. He was born in Pennsgrove, N. J., in 1815, and graduated from Jefferson Medical College, Philadelphia, in 1837. Shortly after he settled at Cape May Court House, being for many years county physician. He was chosen by the Board of Freeholders in 1865 county collector and held the office for upwards of twelve years. He died at Cape May Court House on December 24, 1891.

Wilmon Whilldin enlisted as private in Company I, Sixth Regiment, on August 9, 1861, and was mustered into service twenty days later for three years, but, owing to disability, he was discharged at Washington on June 16, 1862. After this he entered the service again in the famous Wilson Raiders, which operated during the close of the war around Georgia. Upon the arrival of the Sixth in Washington it went into camp at Meridian Hill, and there remained until the early part of December, when the Second New Jersey Brigade, of which the regiment formed a part, was ordered to report under Joseph Hooker.

Company A, Seventh Regiment, as first organized, was composed largely of Cape May men, all of whom enlisted and were mustered into service on August 23 for three years, excepting Thomas Bush and John Reeves, who were enrolled and mustered into the company on September 15.

Those who entered the company were, and their records of promotion are, as follows:

George W. Smith, first sergeant; sergeant-major of regiment January 11, '62; second lieutenant of company, June 16, '62; first lieutenant, Company H, October 2, '62; captain Company C, February 23, '62; resigned January 7, '64. Was shot through cheek.

Joseph W. Johnson, private; corporal, June 9, '62; sergeant, March 1, '63; sergent-major of regiment June 1, '63; first lieutenant of company, October 27, '63.

Samuel R. Magonagle, private; quartermaster-sergeant of regiment, September 13, '61; discharged on account of disability, November 21, '61.

James T. Smith, private; corporal, October 12, '61; sergeant, July 22, '62; wounded in battle of The Wilderness.

William S. Hooper, corporal; sergeant, July 15, '63.

Charles H. Weeks, private; corporal, June 9, '62; sergeant, July 15, '63.

Thomas L. Van Wrinkle, private; corporal, January 1, '64; discharged as paroled prisoner at Trenton on February 1, '65. Was taken prisoner and confined in the "Pen" at Andersonville, Ga., suffering many privations.

Swain S. Reeves, private; corporal, June 18, '64.

Jonathan C. Stevens, private; corporal, July 15, '63.

Thomas Bush, private.

Moses W. Matthews, private.

John Reeves, private.

Nicholas T. Swain, corporal; discharged on account of disability at Division Hospital, Budd's Ferry, Md., June 13, '62.

Walter A. Barrows, private; discharged on account of

disability at U. S. Army General Hospital, Newark, N. J., November 10, '62.

Lewis H. Cresse, private; discharged on account of disability at Centre Street U. S. Army General Hospital, Newark, N. J., October 30, '62.

Edward Filkins, private; discharged on account disability at U. S. Army General Hospital, Philadelphia, October 24, '62.

Isaac H. Hall, private; discharged on account of disability at U. S. Army General Hospital, Philadelphia, September 13, '62.

Joseph W. Ireland, private; discharged on account of disability at Washington, May 16, '62.

Thomas Fletcher Jacobs, private; discharged on account of disability at U. S. Army General Hospital, Newark, N. J., August 18, '62.

Levi E. Johnson, private; discharged on account of disability at Baltimore, July 14, '62.

Thomas Keenan, private; discharged on account of disability at White House, Va., May 18, '62.

David T. Kimsey, private; discharged on account of disability at U. S. Army General Hospital, Philadelphia, January 24, '63.

John W. Kimsey, private; discharged on account of disability at Convalescent Camp, Alexandria, Va., September 4, '63.

Stephen Pierson, private; discharged on account of disability at New York city, October 29, '62.

Ulysses Receaver, private; discharged on account of disability at U. S. Army General Hospital, Philadelphia, November 19, '62.

David Reeves, Jr., private; discharged on account of disability at Budd's Ferry, Va., June 18, '62.

William H. Kirby, private; transferred to Veteran Reserve Corps; re-enlisted May 6, '64; discharged therefrom August 18, '64.

Richard T. Tindall, sergeant; died of typhoid fever at Washington, October 8, '61.

Stephen D. Bennett, private; died at Cape May, May 28

'62, of wounds received in battle at Williamsburg, Va., May 5, '62.

Owen S. Clark, private; died at Baltimore, July 20, '63, of wounds received in battle at Gettysburg, Pa.

Townsend Ireland, private; killed in battle at Williamsburg, Va., May 5, '62.

John Mccray, private; killed in battle at Williamsburg, Va., May 5, '62.

John F. Shaw, private; died of congestion of lungs and measles at Camp Baker, Md., March 12, '62.

Charles J. Silver, private; died at Cape May, May 28, '62, of wounds received in battle at Williamsburg, Va., May 5, '62.

Of these men of Company A the following few remained to the end and were mustered out of service on October 7, 1864: Joseph W. Johnson, James T. Smith, William S. Hooper, Charles H. Weeks, Swain S. Reeves, Jonathan C. Stevens, Thomas Bush, Moses W. Matthews and John Reeves.

J. Howard Willetts, of Cape May county, was, on October 18, 1861, appointed captain of Company H, Seventh Regiment, with which he remained until he was appointed lieutenant-colonel of the Twelfth Regiment, on August 11, '62. He was born at Dias Creek, November, 18, 1834, and removed to Port Elizabeth, Cumberland county, in 1845. He was educated at Pennington Seminary and at West Point Military Academy. He is a grandson of Nicholas Willets, who was in the Legislature in the early part of the century.

He studied medicine after leaving West Point, and graduated from Jefferson Medical College, Philadelphia, in 1858. In 1852 and 1853 he was a member of the Assembly from Cumberland county, and from 1855 to 1858 was State Senator.

At the request of the government that the Seventh Regiment be forwarded to the seat of war, seven companies, including Company A, were dispatched to Washington September 19, 1861, and reported for duty the following day. Upon arrival at Washington the regiment went into camp at Meridian Hill, D. C., and there remained until the early part of December, at which time, in connection with the

Fifth, Sixth and Eighth Regiments, they were ordered to report to General Joseph Hooker, near Budd's Ferry, Md., where they were brigaded and designated the Third Brigade, Hooker's Division.

In the spring of 1862 the work of the regiment began in earnest. "During the month of April," says John Y. Foster, "General McClellan having determined his plans for an offensive movement, the brigade was transferred (with its division) to the Peninsula, General F. E. Patterson being placed in command shortly after its arrival. On the night of the 3d of May Yorktown was evacuated by the enemy, and on the following morning the army was promptly ordered forward in pursuit, Stoneman leading the advance. * * * About noon Hooker's Division advanced on the Yorktown road to Williamsburg, where the enemy was expected to make a stand, having a strong fort in front of that place, at the junction of several roads, which commanded, with some thirteen connecting works, all the roads leading further up the Peninsula. The Jersey brigade, leaving Yorktown at 2 o'clock, pushed forward with all possible rapidity until 11 o'clock, when it bivouacked in a swamp some five miles from Williamsburg. The night was intensely dark and rainy, the roads were muddy and difficult, and the men were sorely exhausted by labor in the trenches and want of sleep; but, notwithstanding all obstacles and discouragements, the troops pressed eagerly forward, all anxious to participate in the struggle which was felt to be imminent. At 2 o'clock on the morning of the 5th the brigade, being in advance, resumed its march, and three hours after, emerging from a forest, came in sight of the enemy's works. The position of the enemy, as described in General Hooker's report, was one of great strength. * * * After a careful survey of the position, Hooker decided to attack at once, and at half-past 7 o'clock advanced his skirmishers on both sides of the road by which he had come up, at the same time throwing forward two batteries on the right, and sending in the Fifth New Jersey as their support. Almost simultaneously the remaining regiments of the brigade—Sixth, Seventh and Eighth—were sent into the left of the road, occupying a wood in front of a line of field-works.

At this time the rain was falling in torrents, and the men stood half-leg deep in mire and water. Steadily advancing through the underbrush, the gallant regiments soon came upon the enemy's forces, and at once opened a vigorous fire. Here, for three hours, the conflict raged with desperate fury. Commanding the ground at every point, the fire of the enemy was pitilessly destructive, and did not slacken for a moment. But the brave fellows into whose faces it was poured stood firmly and unflinchingly—sometimes, indeed, pushed back a little space, but as surely hurling the rebels, bleeding and shattered, back to their works. From the nature of the ground there was no opportunity for the bayonet, but the rapid volleys of the heroic troops were scarcely less effective. And thus the battle raged, the enemy reinforced again and again, directing against these three regiments all the fury of their attack; but still for hours the little column stood immovable. At last, however, the enemy, driven now to desperation, rushed forward in overwhelming numbers, pouring a terrific fire into our whole line. Then, at last, that brave line wavered. The ammunition exhausted, their muskets rusted by the drenching rain, their ranks terribly thinned, exhausted by want of food and a difficult march, these heroes of the day, before this last overwhelming onset, fell slowly back. But they were not defeated. They had held the enemy in check, had frustrated every attempt to flank our position, and so had saved the division, which, but for this stubborn resistance, would have been swept in disaster from the field."

Samuel Toombs, in his account of the "Jersey Troops in the Gettysburg Campaign," says of the second day of the battle at Gettysburg:

"The Seventh New Jersey Regiment suffered considerably from the artillery fire of the enemy while lying in support of the batteries, a number of men being killed and wounded. * * * At last, when the fighting was the fiercest at Little Round Top, the Devil's Den and the Wheatfield, the Seventh became exposed to a shower of flying bullets at their backs. The regiment changed front to the left by the right flank, bringing them to face in the lane and moving a few hundred feet over towards the Emmetsburg road, and nearer to Trostle's lane. Just at this time the artillery, in order to escape the advancing lines of Longstreet's hosts, limbered up and came hastening to the rear from the Peach Orchard and from the field. One battery, coming straight toward the Seventh Regiment, caused the right four companies to separate from the line, thus causing a gap, and, to avoid being crushed to death by the reckless drivers of the battery, were forced across Trostle's lane. The artillery became temporarily blocked in the lane, the anxiety of the drivers caused them to lap their horses over the pieces and caissons in front of them, thus effectually preventing the right four companies of the Seventh from rejoining their colors and the other six companies on the south side of the lane. Simultaneously with this blockade in Trostle's lane came the rebel lines into the sunken road, running from the Emmetsburg pike to Round Top, and, with colors planted on this natural breastwork, they opened a galling fire upon the Seventh New Jersey and the Second New Hampshire, which, falling back from its first position at the extreme angle in the Peach Orchard, had made this its last stand, in the field, about midway between the two roads. The right of the Seventh, which was then the color company of the regiment commanded by Captain Hillyer, rested under a single tree that still stands on the fence line of Trostle's lane. The regiment could not return with any effect the fire of the rebel line, as nothing but the slouch hats of their men were visible; they were unable to lie down in the lane, owing to the blockade of the artillery, and there was no other shelter for the gallant veterans of the Seventh, who had no thought of leaving the field without firing one shot at the enemy, at least, before the guns were safely drawn. Colonel Francine, Lieutenant-Colonel Price and Major Cooper in a few moments saw that it would be impossible to hold the men together inactive, exposed to this concentrated and galling fire, which in a few moments would become deadly, when the rebel riflemen had a more accurate range. Believing that a charge on the double-quick, with hearty Yankee cheers, would check the advance of the enemy's line and draw his fire from the retreating batteries, at the same time destroying his range, the order was quickly given: 'Fix bayonets; forward, double-quick, charge!' and this devoted little band swept across the field with shouts of confidence. As they reached about the prolongation of the line of the Second New Hampshire—which stood like a wall, hopelessly watching its spent, feeble and almost exhausted fire against the long line of battle confronting it—the hopelessness of the Seventh's effort was apparent, and all knew that any further advance meant certain annihilation for the brave Jerseymen. A halt, a hasty adjustment of the line and a volley at the line of dirty slouch hats in front, was the work of but a minute, and the rattle of the musketry drowned all other sounds, while the smoke totally obscured the rebel hats and colors.

"At this point Colonel Francine, Lieutenant Mullery, Adjutant Dougherty and over one-third of the Seventh were quickly placed hors de combat. The few who were still able to get away (wounded and unhurt) fell back beyond the Trostle house, where they joined the other four companies, under the command of Lieutenant-Colonel Price, who rallied the scattered fragments and made another stand nearTrostle's dwelling, until he himself fell, shot through the thigh, when the command devolved upon Major Frederick Cooper. In falling back from its most advanced position many more were struck by the shower of balls. * * * The losses of the Seventh were severe. * * * wounded and missing as follows:

"Company A.

"Killed.—Corporal Parker S. Davis, Martin Van Houten, James Flaveger.

"Wounded.—Lieutenant Robert Allen, First Sergeant Frederick Laib (died July 7), Corporal Swain S. Reeves, William H. Kirby, Thomas Brady, Lewis Hoag, Jonathan C. Stevens, Owen S. Clark (died July 20), John Geckler."

These two regiments (the Sixth and Seventh) constituted two of the four regiments composing what was generally known as the Second Brigade, New Jersey Volunteers, and was first attached to the Third Brigade, Hooker's Division; afterwards to the Third Brigade, Second Division, Third Corps; then to the First Brigade, Fourth Division, Second Corps; then to the Third Brigade, Third Division, Second

Corps, and at the close of the war was attached to what was known as the Provisional Corps, Army of the Potomac.

The regiments took part in the following engagements (while Cape May men were in them): Siege of Yorktown, Va., April and May, '62; Williamsburg, Va., May 5, '62; Fair Oaks, Va., June 1 and 2, '62; Seven Pines, Va., June 25, '62; Savage Station, Va., June 29, '62; Glendale, Va., June 30, '62; Malvern Hill, Va., July 1, '62; Malvern Hill, Va., August 5, '62; Bristow Station, Va., August 27, '62; Bull Run, Va., August 29 and 30, '62; Chantilly, Va., September 1, '62; Centreville, Va., September 2, '62; Fredericksburg, Va., December 13 and 14, '62; Chancellorsville, Va., May 3 and 4, '63; Gettysburg, Pa., July 2 and 3, '63; Wapping Heights, Va., July 24, '63; McLean's Ford, Va., October 15, '63; Mine Run, Va., November 29, 30 and December 1, '63; Wilderness, Va., May 5 to 7, '64; Spottsylvania, Va., May 8 to 11, '64; Spottsylvania C. H., Va., May 12 to 18, '64; North Anna River, Va., May 23 and 24, '64; Tolopotomy Creek, Va., May 30 and 31, '64; Cold Harbor, Va., June 1 to 5, '64; before Petersburg, Va., June 16 to 23, '64; Deep Bottom, Va., July 26 and 27, '64; mine explosion, Va., July 30, '64; North Bank of James River, Va., August 14 to 18, '64; Fort Sedgwick, Va., September 10, '64, and Poplar Spring Church, Va., October 2, '64.

Of Captain George W. Smith it is said that he was a brave soldier. He was born in Cincinnati in 1828, being the grandson of Thomas Smith, who came from England to Maryland in 1750. The oldest son was Thomas, father of the captain, who died in Cincinnati from cholera in 1832. The youth was then left to toil for himself with his two brothers, James T. and William. In 1844 the widowed mother and sons removed to Philadelphia, where George learned the painter's trade. In 1850 they came to Cape Island. In 1861 he was elected Alderman of Cape Island, but went to war before serving out his term. On June 17 he became first lieutenant of the "Cape Island Home Guards," and shortly after entered the service, as noted before. He was wounded at Chancellorsville May 3, 1863, which was the cause of his resignation from the service on January 7, 1864. When the advance was being made upon

OPENING OF THE CIVIL WAR.

Richmond and just before the Seven Days' battle, he was in command of Companies A and G. At the battle of Malvern Hill he commanded the regiment because every other commissioned officer had been killed or wounded. He brought the regiment safe to Harrison's Landing.

Shortly after resigning Captain Smith came home, and was, in March, elected a member of the City Council. In 1871 and 1872 he was Sergeant-at-Arms of the New Jersey Senate.

He organized Company H, Sixth Regiment, New Jersey

GEORGE W. SMITH.

State Guards, and was made its first captain, June 4, 1875, He was elected major of the regiment on September 21, 1882, and lieutenant-colonel on October 11, 1885. He resigned the last-named position on March 14, 1887, and has since been in private life. He was postmaster at Avalon during his brief residence there. He was for twenty-five years superintendent of the Methodist Episcopal Church Sunday-school at Cape May City. In politics he was a Republican, but in later years has been a member of the Prohibition party. His brother, William, who was one time captain of the "Cape Island Home Guards," served in a Pennsylvania regiment, and was killed in the battle of Gettysburg.

Company C, of the Ninth Regiment Infantry, New Jersey Volunteers, contained the following persons, who enrolled and were enlisted on September 20, 1861, for three years of service: David D. Burch, Samuel D. Corson, Joseph F. Craig, Enoch W. Hand, Job Heritage, Richard Heritage and Augustus Spalding, all privates. Burch reenlisted January 18, '64, and was appointed corporal December 3, '64, and sergeant May 14, '65. Corson and Spalding also re-enlisted on January 18, '64, and Richard Heritage two days following. Benjamin B. Garrison was mustered into the service on May 22, 1863, and Jeremiah Garrison on April 13, 1864, each as a private, for three years. Samuel Hearon and John High, of Cape May county, who had enlisted, and were mustered in Company E, same regiment, on April 8, 1865, for one year, were transferred to Company C, while John C. Garrison, who enlisted on March 16, '65, for one year in Company B, was transferred to Company C also. Benjamin B. Garrison died of typhoid fever at the hospital of the Third Division, Twenty-third Army Corps, Greensboro, N. C., May 17, 1865, and was buried at Raleigh National Cemetery, N. C., Section 23, Grave 6. All the others served out their enlistments or were mustered out of service as follows: Enoch W. Hand, December 7, '64; Joseph F. Craig and Job Heritage, the next day; David D. Burch, Samuel D. Corson, Jeremiah Garrison, John C. Garrison, Richard Heritage, Samuel Hearon and John High, July 12, '65, and Augustus Spalding, August 7, '65.

The Ninth Regiment took part in the following engagements: Roanoke Island, N. C., February 8, '62; Newberne, N. C., March 14, '62; Fort Macon, N. C., April 25, '62; Young's Cross Roads, N. C., July 27, '62; Rowells' Mills, N. C., November 2, '62; Deep Creek, N. C., December 12, '62; South West Creek, N. C., December 13, '62; before Kinston, N. C., December 13, '62; Kinston, N. C., December 14, '62; Whitehall, N. C., December 16, '62; Goldsboro, N. C., December 17, '62; Comfort Bridge, N. C., July 6,

'63; near Winton, N. C., July 26, '63; Deep Creek, Va., February 7, '64; Deep Creek, Va., March 1, '64; Cherry Grove, Va., April 14, '64; Port Walthall, Va., May 6 and 7, '64; Procters, Va., May 8, '64; Swift Creek, Va., May 9 and 10, '64; Drury's Bluff, Va., May 12 to 16, '64; Cold Harbor, Va., June 3 to 12, '64; Free Bridge, Va., June 16, '64; before Petersburg, Va., June 20 to August 24, '64; Gardner's Bridge, N. C., December 9, '64; Foster's Bridge, N. C., December 10, '64; Butler's Bridge, N. C., December 11, '64; South West Creek, N. C., March 7, '65; Wise's Fork, N. C., March 8, 9 and 10, '65; Goldsboro, N. C., March 21, '65.

Colonel James Stewart, Jr., of the Ninth, in a letter to Governor Joel Parker from Carolina City, N. C., October 15, 1864, says of Enoch W. Hand, who, with others, were bearers of State colors, that they "were severely wounded by bearing them at the battles of Newberne and Goldsborough, N. C., and Drury's Bluff, Cold Harbor and Petersburg, Va."

In the Tenth Regiment, which was raised under authority from the War Department, and without the consent of the Governor of New Jersey, and was recruited at Beverly, were Richard H. Townsend, in Company B, and Silas Hoffman, in Company I. Townsend enlisted on September 28, 1861, and two days later was mustered in as first sergeant of the company. He enlisted for three years, but was commissioned April 9, '63, and was mustered in as second lieutenant of Company C, Twelfth Regiment, on June 30, '63. Hoffman enlisted and was mustered in as a private in Company I on November 8, 1861, for three years. He re-enlisted on January 3, 1865, and served until July 1, 1865, when he was mustered out of service. The earlier services of the regiment were around Washington. After May 15, 1863, the regiment took part in the principal engagements in which the Sixth and Seventh Regiments participated.

CHAPTER XXIII.

FIRST NEW JERSEY CAVALRY.

In the First New Jersey Cavalry the following from Cape May county enlisted: Henry W. Sawyer, William B. Eldredge, Caleb L. Warner, John H. Warner and Harry L. Gilmore, in Company D, and Jacob E. Johnson, in Company B.

Henry W. Sawyer was commissioned second lieutenant of Company D, and mustered into service on April 14, 1861, for three years, and on April 7, 1862, was promoted to first lieutenant; was promoted to captain of Company K on October 8, 1862, and commissioned major of the regiment October 12, 1863, but was not mustered into this office until August 31, 1864. He was mustered out of service on July 24, 1865.

Henry Washington Sawyer was born in Lehigh county, Pa., May 16, 1829. In youth he received a plain education, and, as he was advanced in years, he learned the carpenter's trade. In 1848 he removed to Cape Island, where he worked at his trade until the Rebellion broke out. On April 15, 1861, when President Lincoln issued his proclamation calling for volunteers, he was among the first to offer his services. As there was no regimental organization or company ready, or likely to be ready for two weeks in this State at that time, Mr. Sawyer went to Trenton, saw Governor Olden, and offered his services to the Union cause. At that time the rebels had possession of Baltimore, and intercepted all mail and telegraphic communications with Washington city. Governor Olden accepted his services and sent him to the latter city, with dispatches to Simon Cameron, then Secretary of War, which Sawyer faithfully delivered. On the 19th of April (midnight) he was chosen one of the guards to protect the Capitol, there being but one company of regular cavalry in Washington. On the 20th five companies of Pennsylvania three-months' men arrived, to one of which Mr. Sawyer was attached as private. Ere thirty days had passed he was appointed a second sergeant, and in sixty days from the time of his enlistment he was promoted second lieutenant. The time of the three-months' men having expired in August, 1861, he returned home.

He had not been home long when he again offered his services to Governor Olden for a position in a New Jersey regiment, and his record having been found so meritorious, he was, on the 19th of February, 1862, commissioned as second lieutenant in Company D, First New Jersey Cavalry, in which position he served with such marked credit that, on April 7, 1862, he was promoted first lieutenant, and so meritorious had been his conduct from the time he first entered the regiment that he was promoted captain of Company K on the 8th of October, 1862.

Captain Sawyer made a most gallant fight with his company on the 9th of June, 1863, at the battle of Brady's Station—one of the great cavalry battles of the Rebellion. Unfortunately, he received two wounds in this battle, was taken prisoner and held for nine months in Libby Prison.

In order to do justice to him, we copy at length from the "Appended Notes" in Foster's "History of New Jersey and the Rebellion" that portion in reference to Captain Sawyer. It reads:

"In the battle of Brandy Station, June 9, 1863, Captain Sawyer was taken prisoner, and, after remaining a short time at Culpepper, was carried to Richmond and placed in Libby Prison. Here he remained until the 6th of July, when all the captains among the prisoners were summoned by General Winder from their quarters into a lower room of the prison. No exchanges having taken place, the men generally supposed that they were to be paroled and sent home; but no such good fortune awaited them. Instead of receiving an order for their release, they were informed that an order had been issued by the rebel War Department directing that two captains should be selected by lot from among the prisoners to be shot in retaliation for the execution by General Burnside of two rebel officers, who had been detected in recruiting within the Union lines. The consternation occasioned by this announcement may be imagined. They had hoped for release, and here was an order which in a moment clouded the whole prospect. Escape, of course, was impossible. The drawing was inevitable. After being formed in a hollow square, a slip of paper, with the name of each man written upon it, and carefully folded up, was deposited in a box, whereupon Captain Turner informed the men that they might select whom they pleased to draw the names, the first two names drawn to indicate the men to be shot.

"Captain Sawyer, who alone seemed to retain his selfpossession, suggested that one of the chaplains should be appointed. Three of the chaplains were called down from an upper room, and the Rev. Mr. Brown, of the Sixth Maryland, accepting the task, amid a silence almost deathlike the drawing commenced. The first name taken out of the box was that of 'Captain Henry Washington Sawyer, of the Second New Jersey Cavalry,' and the second that of 'Captain Flynn, of the Fifty-first Indiana.' 'When the names were read out,' says the Richmond Dispatch, 'Sawyer heard it with no apparent emotion, remarking that some one had to be drawn, and he could stand it as well as any one else. Flynn was very white and depressed.' The drawing over, the prisoners were returned to their quarters, the condemned meanwhile poceeding under guard to the headquarters of General Winder, Provost Marshal-General. Here they were warned not to delude themselves with any hope of escape, as retaliation must be and would be inflicted, it being added that the execution would positively take place on the 14th, eight days hence. Sawyer, however, desperate as the situation seemed, did not despair, but, reflecting that if by any means his situation could be brought to the knowledge of the government, he might still be rescued, he asked permission to write to his wife, which, being granted on condition that the authorities should read the letter, he immediately wrote the following, which none other than a brave and true-souled man, thus standing in the shadow of death, could pen:

"'Provost-General's Office,
"'Richmond, Va., July 6th, 1863.

"'My Dear Wife:—I am under the necessity of informing you that my prospects look dark.

"'This morning all the captains now prisoners at the Libby Military Prison drew lots for two to be executed. It fell to my lot. Myself and Captain Flynn, of the Fifty-first Indiana Infantry, will be executed for two captains executed by Burnside.

"'The Provost-General, J. H. Winder, assures me that the Secretary of War of the Southern Confederacy will per-

HENRY W. SAWYER.

mit yourself and my dear children to visit me before I am executed. You will be permitted to bring an attendant. Captain Whilldin, or Uncle W. W. Ware, or Dan, had better come with you. My situation is hard to be borne, and I cannot think of dying without seeing you and the children. You will be allowed to return without molestation to your home. I am resigned to whatever is in store for me, with the consolation that I die without having committed any crime. I have no trial, no jury, nor am I charged with any crime, but it fell to my lot. You will proceed to Washington. My government will give you transportation for Fortress Monroe, and you will get here by a flag of truce, and return the same way. Bring with you a shirt for me.

"'It will be necessary for you to preserve this letter to bring evidence at Washington of my condition. My pay is due me from the 1st of March, which you are entitled to. Captain B—— owes me fifty dollars, money lent to him when he went on a furlough. You will write to him at once, and he will send it to you.

"'My dear wife, the fortune of war has put me in this position. If I must die, a sacrifice to my country, with God's will I must submit; only let me see you once more, and I will die becoming a man and an officer; but, for God's sake, do not disappoint me. Write to me as soon as you get this, and go to Captain Whilldin; he will advise you what to do.

"'I have done nothing to deserve this penalty. But you must submit to your fate. It will be no disgrace to myself, you or the children; but you may point with pride and say: "I give my husband;" my children will have the consolation to say: "I was made an orphan for my country."

"'God will provide for you; never fear. Oh! it is hard to leave you thus. I wish the ball that passed through my head in the last battle would have done its work; but it was not to be so. My mind is somewhat influenced, for it has come so suddenly on me. Write to me as soon as you get this; leave your letter open, and I will get it. Direct my name and rank, by way of Fortress Monroe.

"'Farewell! farewell!! and I hope it is all for the best. I remain yours until death, "'H. W. Sawyer,
"'Captain First New Jersey Cavalry.'

"After penning this letter, with a conflict of feeling which we may well imagine, Sawyer and his companion were placed in close confinement in a dungeon under ground. Here they were fed on corn bread and water, the dungeon being so damp that their clothing mildewed. The 14th came at last, but still they remained unmolested. Sawyer had estimated aright; his letter had saved him from the rebel clutch. Immediately upon receiving it, his true-hearted wife hastened to lay the matter before influential friends, and these at once proceeded to Washington, presented the case to the President and Secretary of War, who, without delay, directed that General Lee, son of General

Robert E. Lee, and General Winder, son of the rebel Provost Marshal-General, then prisoners in our hands, should be placed in close confinement as hostages, General Butler being at the same time ordered to notify the Confederate Government that immediately upon receiving information, authentic or otherwise, of the execution of Sawyer and Flynn, he should proceed to execute Winder and Lee. This action, prompt and unmistakable, and more significant, perhaps, to the enemy, because of General Butler's known resolution of purpose, produced the desired effect. Sawyer and Flynn were not executed.

"After remaining twenty-one days in the dungeon to which they were assigned, they were relieved and placed on the same footing with other prisoners. Still, however, the Richmond papers vehemently insisted that the execution must and would take place, and the fate of the condemned remained some time longer a matter of speculation and doubt. But the days lengthened into weeks, the winter passed, and at length, in March, 1864, the prison doors were opened, Sawyer being exchanged for General Lee. The satisfaction with which the brave captain once more walked forth a free man, and found shelter under the old flag, was such as only a man coming from death into life, from dismal bondage into joyous and perfect liberty, can ever experience, and none other, certainly, can appreciate. It should be added that Captain Sawyer, after this sad experience, as before it, fought gallantly and effectively for the good cause, coming out of the war a major and with scars 'more honorable than the highest rank.'"

Captain Flynn, who never got over his long confinement in Libby Prison, seven weeks of which were spent in a dungeon, died six months after his release.

The Philadelphia Inquirer of Wednesday, March 23, 1864, said of Captain Sawyer's confinement in Libby:

"Captain Sawyer, of the First New Jersey Cavalry, who has been a prisoner in the Libby Prison for nine months, arrived in this city on Monday. Captain Sawyer was taken prisoner in the cavalry combat at Brandy Station in June last. This was the closest cavalry fight of the war. Towards the conclusion Captain Sawyer received two wounds from pistol bullets, one of which passed through his thigh and the other striking his right cheek, passed out of the back of the neck on the left side of the spine. Notwithstanding his wounds, he still kept the saddle until his horse was shot, when the latter sprang up into the air and fell dead, throwing his rider with such force as to render him insensible. When he recovered consciousness Captain Sawyer saw Lieutenant-Colonel Broderick lying near, and crawled up to him, but on examination found that he was dead. A short distance further on he saw Major Shellmire, while all around him were men of his own or other companies, either killed or wounded.

"While by the side of Colonel Broderick, Captain Sawyer was seen by two rebel soldiers, who took him prisoner, and, after washing the blood from his face with water from a neighboring ditch, conveyed him to the rear. His wounds were pronounced very dangerous, if not mortal, but in a few weeks he improved so much he was sent to Richmond and confined in Libby Prison. In that dismal prison he remained until about a week ago. Early in June all the captains who were prisoners were assembled in a room by a Captain Turner, their jailor. These officers, of course, did not know of the object of these unusual proceedings, but supposed it was in order that they might be pardoned. The reader can judge of the painful surprise they experienced when Captain Turner said: 'Gentlemen, it is my painful duty to communicate to you an order I have received from Genera Winder (provost marshal of Richmond), which I will read.' The order was then read, ordering Captain Turner to select, by lot, two Federal captains for immediate execution, in retaliation for the execution of two Confederate officers in Kentucky by General Burnside.

"The order having been read, it only remained to decide who the lot should fall upon, and Captain Turner asked the Union officers to select a man to draw the ballots as the names were called. After a brief silence Captain Sawyer suggested a chaplain of the United States Army, who was present. This was acceded to, and the drawing commenced. Nearly half the roll had been called and neither of the fatal

FIRST NEW JERSEY CAVALRY. 323

ballots had been drawn; but when the name of Captain Henry W. Sawyer was called the ballot drawn responded 'execution.'

"The two victims were separated from their comrades and ordered to prepare for death. The Richmond papers, in their published accounts of this scene, all agreed in saying that Captain Sawyer met the trial with unfaltering courage. There was no bravado, no affectation of recklessness, but there was no faltering; only the steady, calm courage of a brave man; to use the captain's own words (if we may do so without impropriety), he was determined that New Jersey should have no cause to be ashamed of his conduct.

"The prisoners thus sentenced to death were removed to a dungeon, a vault in the cellar of the Libby Prison, where they remained until about the middle of August. The vault was only about six feet wide, and had no place for light or air, except a hole about six inches square cut in the door. In front of this door a sentry was constantly stationed whose duty it was to challenge the inmates once in each half hour and receive a reply. This, of course, rendered it impossible for both the inmates to sleep at one time. That, however, would have been impossible without this, for it was necessary for one to remain awake to keep away the rats, which swarmed in the cell, off his comrade. About the 10th of August the prisoners were removed from this vault to the upper rooms among the other prisoners, where 1100 men were confined in six rooms, averaging about 37 by 100 feet each.

"We should have stated above that shortly after being sentenced, Captain Sawyer asked for a respite sufficient to permit his wife to visit him. This procured a respite for fifteen days. During this time the Richmond papers clamored for the execution of the two Union officers, with a spirit worthy the bloodiest barbarians. But during the fifteen days the Government had received information, and General Lee, a son of General Robert E. Lee, and Captain Winder, a son of the Richmond jailor, were ordered into close confinement as hostages for Sawyer and Fynn. This was effectual, and it is hardly probable that the Rebel Government, after that event, ever really intended to carry their sentence into effect. At all events, last week Captains Sawyer and Flynn were exchanged for Lee and Winder, and both are now safe.

"Captain Sawyer, from long and close confinement (being entirely without meat for the last forty days of his imprisonment), is, of course, somewhat weak; but he is in good spirits and hopes to rejoin his regiment at an early date."

After the close of the war he was breveted lieutenant-colonel by United States Commission, and remained in that position until September, 1865, when the regiment was discharged. At the close of the Rebellion, the rank of the regular army being recruited up, he was offered by Edwin M. Stanton, Secretary of War, having been recommended by a division officer, a lieutenantcy in the regular army, which position he declined. During the time that he was in the field he received four wounds, two of which were of a serious character. One ball he carried in his body until he died. For being one of the guards at the Capitol on April 19, 1861, he was granted a medal by the Pennsylvania Legislature in recognition of his services.

In 1867 Colonel Sawyer became proprietor of the Ocean House, Cape May City, and held it until April, 1873, when he removed to Wilmington, Del., and became proprietor of the Clayton House, which he conducted for about three years. He again returned to Cape May and built the "Chalfonte," which he managed and owned for several years, when he sold it.

Colonel Sawyer was for a number of years a valued member of the City Council, and served in that capacity during the years 1876, '77, '78, '80, '81, '82, '85, '86 and '87, and was at one time superintendent of the United States Life Saving Service for the coast of New Jersey and a member of the New Jersey State Sinking Fund Commisison from 1888 to 1891. He died suddenly of heart failure at Cape May City on October 16, 1893.

The records of the other Cape May men in the First Cavalry Regiment are:

William B. Eldredge, private Co. D.; enlisted August 13,

FIRST NEW JERSEY CAVALRY.

'61; mustered in August 20, '61; transferred to Company K June 2,'63; mustered out of service September 16, '64.

Caleb L. Warner, private Company D; enrolled August 13, '61; mustered into service August 24, '61; re-enlisted January 1, '64; mustered out of service July 24, '65.

John H. Warner, corporal Company D; commissioned August 13, '61; mustered into service August 20, '61; re-enlisted as a sergeant January 1, '64; first sergeant December 12, '64; commissioned second lieutenant July 18, '65, but not mustered into office; mustered out of service July 24, '65.

Harry L. Gilmore, sergeant Company D; commissioned August 13, '61; mustered into service August 20, '61; transferred to United States Army as hospital steward June 1, '62; discharged threfrom July 24, '65.

Jacob E. Johnson, private Company B; enrolled and mustered into service September 5, '64 for one year; discharged at camp near Cloud's Mills, Va., May 31, '65.

Johnson also served in Company K, Twenty-third Infantry Regiment, previously. He enrolled on August 28, 1862, and was mustered into service as a corporal for nine months on September 13, 1862. He became a private October 25, 1862, and was mustered out of service with his company on June 27, 1863.

The First New Jersey Cavalry was organized by authority of the War Department, and was not under the control of the State, and was first known as Halstead's Cavalry. It proceeded to Washington on September 1, 1861, where it encamped until February, 1862. On February 19 an order was issued placing it under the State authority, and it was then thoroughly organized. The regiment was first attached to the Cavalry Division, Army of the Potomac, then to the military district of Washington; then to the Department of the Rappahannock; then to the Army of Virginia; then to the defenses of Washington; then to the Army of the Potomac, and again to the Department of Washington. This regiment was probably in as many encounters during the war as any other regiment, the following being the list: Pohick Church, Va., December 29, '61, and January 15, '62; Seddons' Farm, Va., May 1, '62; Gray's Farm, Va., May 9;

Rappahannock Station, May; Strasburg, June 1; Woodstock, June 2; Harrisonburg, June 6; Cross Keys, June 8; Madison C. H., July 27; Barnett's Ford (Rapidan), July 29, August 4 and August 7; Cedar Mountain, August 9; Rappahannock Station, August 18; Brandy Station, August 20; Rappahannock Station, August 20 and 21; Warrenton, August 23; Waterloo Ford, August 24; Snicker's Gap, August 28; Bull Run, August 29 and 30; Chantilly, September 1; Warrenton, September 24; Aldie, October 31; Port Conoway, November 19; Fredericksburg, December 11 to 13; Rappahnnock Station, April 7, '63; Stoneman's road, April 30; Rappahannock Station and Kelly's Ford, May 19; Brandy Station, June 9; Aldie, June 17; Middleburg, June 19; Upperville, June 21; near Aldie, June 22; Westminster, Md., June 30; Gettysburg, Pa., July 2 and 3; Emmettsburg, Md., July 4 and 6; Tettersburg, Pa., July 7; Cavetown, Md., July 8; Harper's Ferry, Va., July 14; Sheppardstown, Md., July 16; Barryville, Va., July 31; Salem, Va., August 15; White Plains, August 16; Sulphur Springs and Brandy Station, October 12; Bristow Station, October 14; near Warrenton, November 12 and 18; Mountain Run, November 27; Mine Run, November 27; Parker's Store, November 29; Custer's raid, February 18, '64; Ravenna River, February 21; Ely's Ford (Rapidan), May 3; Todd's Tavern, May 5 and 7; Sheridan's raid, May 9; Beaver Dam Station, May 10; Yellow Tavern and Ashland Station, May 11; fortifications of Richmond, May 12; Church of the Messiah, May 12; North Anna River, May 24; Hawes' shop, May 28; Emmons Church, May 29; Cold Harbor, June 1; Gaines' Mills, June 2; Chickahominy River, June 2; Bottom's Bridge, June 4 and 5; Pamunky River, June 8; Trevillian Station, June 12 and 14; White House, June 20 and 21; St. Mary's Church, June 24; near Petersburg, June 29 and July 12; raid through the Shenandoah, July; Deep Bottom, July 28; Malvern Hill, July 28 to 30; Deep Bottom, August 14; Charles City Cross Roads, August 16 and 17; Reams Station, August 26; Malvern Hill, September 5; Charles City, September 11; Jerusalem plank road, September 17; Reams Station, September 29 and 30; Vaughn's road, October 1;

FIRST NEW JERSEY CAVALRY.

Boydton plank road, October 6; Stony Creek, November 27; Bellefield Station, December 9 and 10; Dinwiddie C. H., February 6, '65; Hatcher's Run, February 6 and 7; before Petersburg, March 20; Dinwiddie C. H., March 30; Five Forks and Chamberlain's Creek, March 31; Amelia Springs and Jettersville, April 5; Sailors' Creek, April 6; Farmville, April 6 and 7; Appomattox C. H. (Lee's surrender), April 9.

CHAPTER XXIV.

THE ENLISTMENTS OF 1862.

Not until the second year of the war did any more men go to the front from Cape May county, but in the meanwhile the Board of Freeholders prepared for the relief of the families of those who went to help save the Union. On August 28, 1861, a committee consisting of one person from each township and Cape Island, were appointed to look after the wants of the soldiers' families: Thomas Williams, Upper township; William S. Townsend, Dennis; Smith Townsend, Middle; Samuel F. Ware, Lower, and Waters B. Miller, Cape Island. These committeemen each had his own territory to look after, and was authorized to give each soldier's family six dollars per month as long as the head of the family was in service. This committee served until May, 1862, when a new one was appointed, consisting of Thomas Williams, of Upper; Richard S. Leaming, of Dennis; Aaron Miller, of Middle; Samuel F. Ware, of Lower, and Dr. Samuel S. Marcy, of Cape Island.

Samuel Fithian Ware, of Lower township, who served with great credit on the Relief Committee during the war, was born on October 16, 1800, and was a brother of Wilmon W., Maskel, John G. W., and Joseph. He served in the Board of Freeholders many years. He was a carpenter and an undertaker, and buried during his time about fifteen hundred persons. He died in 1876.

In the meanwhile the Seaville Rangers, which were known as Company B, of the Atlantic Brigade, did duty and drilled at home under the care of Captain Joseph E. Corson. They were given by the State for use on October 26, 1861, thirty sets of arms and equipment and 1000 rounds of elongated ball cartridges.

On the 23d of December the Board of Freeholders provided for the transporting of volunteers to the State rendezvous and appointed as a committee to take charge of the work Clinton H. Ludlam, of Dennisville, and Samuel R. Magonagle, of Cape Island.

The Twelfth Regiment was one of the quota of five regiments charged upon New Jersey under the call for 300,000 volunteers for three years made by President Lincoln on July 7, 1862. It was rendezvoused at Woodbury, and left the State on September 7 for service. In it were J. Howard Willetts, formerly of Cape May, who had served in the Seventh Regiment, as before noted; Richard S. Thompson and Albert Walker, of Cape May Court House. J. Howard Willetts was commissioned lieutenant-colonel of the regiment on August 11, 1862, and served as such until he was promoted to the colonelcy of the regiment, February 27, 1863. He was discharged on December 19, 1864, on account of wounds received in the battle of Chancellorsville, Va.

Richard S. Thompson was commissioned captain of Company F on August 14, 1862, and mustered into service on September 4. He was promoted major of the regiment on February 25, 1864, and commissioned as lieutenant-colonel on July 2, 1864, and sixteen days later mustered into that position. On account of wounds received in the action at Ream's Station, Va., where he commanded the regiment, he was discharged from the service February 17, 1865.

Lieutenant-Colonel Richard S. Thompson was born December 27, 1837, at Cape May Court House. His father was Richard Thompson, a prominent citizen of this county. His mother, Elizabeth, was the daughter of Major Nathaniel Holmes, also of this county. After nine years' study in seminaries and under private tutors, he entered Harvard College in 1859, graduated in 1861. He was admitted to the Philadelphia bar early in 1862. He was a member of Captain Biddle's Artillery Company, of Philadelphia.

In July, of 1862, he raised a company in Cumberland county, N. J., and enlisted as captain of Company K, Twelfth N. J. Vols. He was mustered with his regiment September 4, 1862. His regiment was shortly after stationed at Ellicott's Mills, Md., where he was appointed assistant provost-marshal under General Wool. In December, 1862, with his regiment, he joined the Army of the Potomac, and was placed in the Second Army Corps.

February 16, 1864, he was appointed judge advocate of a division court-martial. He remained with his regiment (excepting a few months in 1864, while he was on detached service) until August 25, 1864, when he was severely wouned in the battle of Ream's Station, Va. He commanded his regiment as captain, major and lieutenant-colonel.

Among the general engagements in which he took part were Chancellorsville, Gettysburg, Auburn Mills, Bristow Station, Robinson's Tavern, Mine Run, Deep Bottom and Ream's Station.

In December, 1864, while still on crutches, he was appointed president of a general court-martial for trial of officers in Philadelphia. February 17, 1865, he was honorably discharged on account of wounds received in battle. June 7, 1865, he married Miss Catherine Scovel, daughter of the Rev. Alden Scovel, of Bloomington, Ill.

In November, 1865, he changed his residence from Cape May county to Chicago, where he entered upon the practice of his profession, in which he is still engaged.

In November, 1872, Colonel Thompson was elected Senator of the Illinois General Assembly.

Albert Walker was enrolled for service on August 9, '62, and mustered into service (in Company K) on September 4. He was promoted to corporal on June 4, '64, and served until mustered out, on June 15, '65.

On April 9, 1863, Richard Townsend, of Cape May, who was then a sergeant in Company B, Tenth Regiment, was commissioned second lieutenant of Company C, this regiment, and mustered into service on June 30, and on July 3, in the battle of Gettysburg, was killed. His remains were buried at the National Cemetery, Gettysburg, in Section A, Grave 1. Samuel Tombs, in his work on Gettysburg, says:

"In the height of the fight Lieutenant Richard H. Townsend, of Cape May county, fell, shot through the heart. Promoted from the Tenth Regiment, New Jersey Volunteers, he had been able to join his new command only three days before, and thus died in his first battle."

On the 28th of August the Board of Freeholders passed a resolution "That, for the purpose of filling the requisition made on the county of Cape May," under the call for the 300,000 volunteers, they would give to each volunteer who enlisted in the United States service the sum of fifty dollars. The county collector, at the same time, was authorized to borrow on the credit of the county the sum of ten thousand dollars to pay this bounty, and Richard S. Leaming, of Dennisville, was authorized to go to Beverly, where the Twenty-fifth Regiment was being rendezvoused, to give the volunteers their orders.

The Twenty-fifth Regiment Infantry was organized under the provisions of an act of Congress, approved July 22, 1861. A draft for 10,478 men to serve for nine months, unless sooner discharged, had been made upon the Governor of this State by the President of the United States, August 4, 1862, and soon after full instructions for conducting it were received from the War Department. The draft so ordered, was not to interfere with orders governing recruiting, and all enlistments up to September 1, 1862, would be placed to the credit of the State. A general desire manifested and expressed by the State authorities, as well as by prominent citizens throughout the State, to avoid the draft, gave an enthusiasm to recruiting, which caused the entire quota to be raised by voluntary enlistment, and in camp, by the 3d day of September, 1862, the time appointed for commencing the draft. The organization of the regiment was immediately commenced, and soon after fully completed, officered and equipped. It was then duly mustered into the service of the United States for nine months. Companies F, G and I, composed principally of men from Cape May county, were mustered in at Beverly, N. J., September 26, 1862, by William B. Royall, captain Fifth Cavalry, U. S. Army. The headquarters of the regiment were established at Beverly, from which place it left the State October 10, 1862, en route to Washington, D. C. Upon arrival at Washington it was assigned to the Second Brigade, Casey's Division, defenses of Washington, and went into camp at East Capitol Hill, and immediately began to prepare for active service. It remained in this vicinity until the 30th day of November, when, under orders, it marched to the front and joined the Army of the Potomac, having been assigned to the Ninth Army Corps. On the 11th of February, 1863, the regiment, in connection with the Ninth Corps, was detached from the Army of the Potomac and proceeded to Newport News, Va. On the 13th of March it proceeded to Suffolk, Va., to assist in repelling a threatened invasion by the enemy at this point. The regiment continued its organization and remained in active service until the expiration of its term of service, when it was ordered to return to New Jersey for discharge. It was mustered out at Beverly, N. J., June 20, 1863. After leaving Casey's Division it was attached to the First Brigade, Third Division, Ninth Army Corps. It took part in the engagements at Fredericksburg, Va., December 13 and 14, '62, and at "Near Suffolk," Va., May 3, '63.

Company F was composed entirely (excepting Captain Blenkow) of residents of Dennis and Lower townships and Cape Island. All the members were enrolled for service on September 1, '62, and mustered into service on September 26. When the company left with its regiment it was composed of the following officers and men:

Captain, David Blenkow, shoe dealer.

First lieutenant, Nicholas W. Godfrey, carpenter.

Second lieutenant, Henry Y. Willetts, carpenter.

First sergeant, Reuben Foster.

Sergeants, John F. Goff, Edwin Ludlam, J. Granville Leach.

Corporals, Coleman F. Ludlam, William T. Stevens, Abijah D. Reeves, Joseph Garrison, Virgil D. Schellenger.

Musician (drummer), George S. Cresse.

Privates—Charles Abrams, Skidmore Abrams, William Armstrong, Jerome Bowker, Joseph Brewton, Elias Camp, Daniel Chambers, John Chambers, John W. Corson, Frederick W. Cradol, Thomas M. Creamer, Anthony Cresse, Daniel F. Crowell, Samuel S. Cummings, Evan Edmunds, Jonathan H. Edwards, George H. Eldredge, James S. Eldredge, Clark Elliott, Samuel R. Stites, Ezekiel Voss, Joseph Elliott, Owen Endicott, Seely Ernest, James Ewing, Livingstone Ewing, Thomas S. Foster, Elbridge G. Goff,

Albert Grace, James S. Grace, Matthew W. Hall, Jeremiah Hampton, Philip Hand, Samuel Hand, Seth L. Hand, Thomas H. Hand, Charles Heisles, Joseph S. Higbee, John T. Hoffman, Samuel Honn, Joseph B. Hughes, Joshua Johnson, Alphonso A. Jones, James H. Kimsey, Henry Langley, Alphonso D. Lee, Richard F. Lloyd, Walter S. Peterson, Josiah Powell, William L. Pritchard, Charles P. Riel, William C. Rutherford, Charles T. Shaw, Francis W. Sheldon, William F. Smith, William Snyder, Israel S. Townsend, John Trout, Samuel F. Ware, Jr., Maurice V. Warner, Leaming Weatherby, George T. Weeks, John Weeks, Jeremiah Weldon, Eva E. Westcott, Joseph Whitaker, Josiah Whitaker, Thomas B. Williams, Stacy M. Wilson, Jonathan G. Fidler, Thomas Morton, Jesse S. Godfrey, Furman Barnett, Theodore Church, Elwood Devaul, John W. Reeves, John P. Sutton, David E. Swain, Albert S. Edmunds, Thomas Beckwith, Albert F. Brewton, Hugh Edmunds David E. Hand, Thomas P. Hand, John B. Robinson, Jeremiah F. Tyler and Daniel H. White. The occupations and professions of the company were as follows: Artists, 2; carpenters, 8; clerks, 2; farmers, 40; laborers, 33; shoemaker, 1; seamen, 9; miller, 1, and printers, 2. This company had five men wounded and one (Albert S. Edmunds) killed in the battle of Fredericksburg, and two men wounded at Suffolk.

Nicholas W. Godfrey resigned as first lieutenant on December 22, and three days later Henry Y. Willetts was commissioned and mustered into that position. On the same day Reuben Foster was commissioned second lieutenant, and on January 3, 63, mustered into the office. John F. Goff was made first sergeant January 3. Coleman F. Ludlam and William T. Stevens were made sergeants January 1. Samuel R. Stites was promoted to corporal December 29, '62, and to sergeant two days later. J. Granville Leach was promoted to sergeant-major of the regiment on January 1, '63, and then commissioned second lieutenant of Company I March 20, '63. John Chambers was made corporal November 15, while Ezekiel Voss, Anthony Cresse and John W. Corson were promoted to corporals on January 1, '63.

The records of the men who, owing to disability and other

causes, did not stay with the company until the close of its service, were:

Jonathan G. Fidler—Discharged at Suffolk, Va., April 15, '63; disability.

Thomas Morton—Discharged at camp near Falmouth, Va., December 29, '62; disability.

Jesse S. Godfrey—Discharged at Fortress Monroe, Va., April 9, '63; disability.

Furman Barnett—Discharged at Fifth Street U. S. Army Hospital, Philadelphia, Pa., February 4, '63; disability.

Theodore Church—Discharged at Convalescent Camp, Alexandria, Va., February 4, '63; disability.

Elwood Devaul—Discharged at U. S. Army General Hospital, Philadelphia, February 23, '63; disability.

John W. Reeves—Discharged at Philadelphia, Pa., February 14, '63; disability.

John P. Sutton—Discharged U. S. Army General Hospital, Philadelphia, February 4, '63; disability.

David E. Swain—Discharged U. S. Army General Hospital, Philadelphia, January 28, '63; disability.

Albert S. Edmunds—Killed in action at Fredericksburg, Va., December 13, '62.

Thomas Beckwith—Died of measles at Emory U. S. Army Hospital, Washington, D. C., November 9, '62.

Albert S. Brewton—Died of typhoid fever at Regimental Hospital, near Suffolk, Va., April 15, '63; buried at National Cemetery, Hampton, Va., Row 22, Section C, Grave 19.

Hugh Edmunds—Died of disease at Regimental Hospital, near Suffolk, Va., March 26, '63; buried at National Cemetery, Hampton, Va., Row 21, Section B, Grave 5.

David E. Hand—Died of typhoid fever at U. S. Army General Hospital, Newark, N. J., January 27, '63.

Thomas P. Hand—Died of chronic diarrhoea at Hampton U. S. Army General Hospital, Fortress Monroe, Va., May 3, '63.

John B. Robinson—Died of congestion of brain in camp near Suffolk, Va., March 19, '63; buried at National Cemetery, Hampton, Va., Row 19, Section B, Grave 26.

Jeremiah F. Tyler—Died at U. S. Army General Hospital, Newark, N. J., January 6, '63; wounds received in action at

Fredericksburg, Va.; buried at Fairmount Cemetery, Newark, N. J.

Daniel H. White—Died at St. Elizabeth U. S. Army General Hospital, Washinton, D. C., December 23, '62, of wounds received in action at Fredericksburg, Va.; buried at Military Asylum Cemetery, D. C.

The following remained in the service of the company until it was mustered out, on June 20, 1863: Henry Y. Willetts, Reuben Foster, John F. Goff, Coleman F. Ludlam, William T. Stevens, Edwin Ludlam, Samuel R. Stites, Abijah D. Reeves, Joseph Garrison, Virgil D. Schellenger, John Chambers, Ezekiel Voss, Anthony Cresse, John W. Corson, George S. Cresse, Charles Abrams, Skidmore Abrams, William Armstrong, Jerome Bowker, Joseph Brewton, Elias Camp, Daniel Chambers, Frederick Crandol, Thomas M. Creamer, Daniel F. Crowell, Samuel S. Cummings, Evan Edmunds, Jonathan H. Edwards, George H. Eldridge, James S. Eldridge, Clark Elliott, Joseph Elliott, Owen Endicott, Seely Ernest, James Ewing, Livingstone Ewing, Thomas S. Foster, Elbridge G. Goff, Albert Grace, James S. Grace, Matthew W. Hall, Jeremiah Hampton, Philip Hand, Samuel Hand, Seth L. Hand, Thomas H. Hand, Charles Heisler, Joseph S. Higbee, John T. Hoffman, Samuel Honn, Joseph B. Hughes, Joshua Johnson, Alphonso A. Jones, James H. Kinsey, Henry Langley, Alphonso D. Lee, Richard F. Lloyd, Walter S. Peterson, Josiah Powell, William L. Pritchard, Charles P. Riel, William C. Rutherford, Charles T. Shaw, Francis W. Sheldon, William F. Smith, William Snyder, Israel S. Townsend, John Trout, Samuel F. Ware, Maurice V. Warner, Leaming Weatherby, George T. Weeks, John Weeks, Jeremiah Weldon, Elva E. Westcott, Joseph Whitaker, Josiah Whitaker, Thomas B. Williams and Stacy M. Wilson.

Company G was made up mostly of upper Cape May county men and of men who lived at Tuckahoe, on the Atlantic county side, and men from Marshallville, in Cumberland county, since made a part of Cape May county. They enlisted on September 2, and were mustered into service on the 26th of the month. When they left the State for service they held these ranks:

Captain, Charles R. Powell, blacksmith.
First lieutenant, Ewing W. Tibbles, painter.
Second lieutenant, Nicholas Corson, school teacher.
Sergeants—Maurice B. Stites, John S. Cole, Enoch S. Willetts.
Corporals—John W. Shoemaker, Charles W. Corson, Benjamin Weatherby.
Musician (drummer), Lewis S. Williams.
Privates—Charles S. Corson, Matthew Hughes, George Baner, Samuel Barnes, Jonathan Borden, John L. Buzby, Aaron B. Clark, Jonathan Cliver, John Collins, Joseph Collins, Lucien B. Corson, Daniel Creamer, Reuben Creamer, Robert M. Dare, John Dayton, Nicholas Frambers, Howard M. French, George E. Gandy, Thomas Garron, James H. Gifford, Abraham Hayes, Mahlon Horton, David T. Ingersoll, Richard Ingersoll, Levi E. Lippincott, James Little, Charles Lloyd, John Lloyd, Leaming Lloyd, John Magee, Furman Mannery, Frederick Marshall, Hollis Mickel, Adam Moore, Samuel Morris, Thomas W. Pettitt, George M. Searse, Reuben Searse, Ezekiel Stevenson, Gabriel G. Surran, John Thornton, Richard S. Townsend, Stephen Williams, Townsend S. Williams, Evan Armstrong, Thomas R. Gandy, William Gruff, Richard Jarman, Adam Kerrick, Mark Cook, William W. Cook, Charles H. Coombs, Frederick Creamer, Joseph W. Lee, Samuel T. Surran, Theophilus Vannaman, Hezekiel Veach, George Trader.

The occupations and professions of this company was apportioned as follows: Bricklayers, 2; blacksmith, 1; carpenters, 2; clerks, 3; cigarmaker, 1; sheetiron worker, 1; seamen, 14; carriage trimmer, 1; mason, 1; machinist, 1; moulder, 1; shoemaker, 1; school teacher, 1; farmers, 5; millwright, 1; miller, 1; printer, 1; harness makers, 2; painters, 2; laborers, 50; glasscutter, 1; glassblower, 1.

Captain Powell resigned on December 22. Enoch S. Willetts was promoted to first sergeant on September 30. Charles H. Corson was promoted to corporal on October 16, and Matthew Hughes to the same rank on January 1, 1863.

THE ENLISTMENTS OF 1862.

Those who did not remain with the regiment until it was mustered out and the reasons therefor were:

John S. Cole—Discharged at U. S. Army General Hospital, Philadelphia, Pa., January 24, '63; disability.

Evan Armstrong—Discharged at Washington, D. C., January 5, '63; disability.

Thomas R. Gandy—Discharged at Regimental Hospital, near Fairfax Seminary, Va., November 28, '62; disability.

William Gruff—Discharged at Regimental Hospital, near Fairfax Seminary, Va., November 28, '62; disability.

Richard Jarman—Discharged February 23, '63; wounds received in action at Fredericksburg, Va.

Adam Kerrick—Discharged at Newport News, Va., March 8, '63; disability.

Maurice B. Stites—Died of typhoid fever at Regimental Hospital, camp near Falmouth, Va., Febuary 1, '63.

Mark Cook—Died of measles at Emory U. S. Army General Hospital, Washington, D. C., November 5, '62; buried at Military Asylum Cemetery, D. C.

William W. Cook—Died of measles at Emory U. S. Army General Hospital, Washinngton, D. C., November 1, '62; buried at Military Asylum Cemetery, D. C.

Charles H. Coombs—Died at Richmond, Va., January 7, '63, of wounds received in action at Fredericksburg, Va.; prisoner of war.

Frederick Creamer—Died of typhoid fever at Chestnut Hill U. S. Army General Hospital, Philadelphia, March 2, '63.

John W. Lee—Died of measles at Emory U. S. Army General Hospital, Washington, D. C., November 28, '62; buried at Military Asylum Cemetery, D. C.

Samuel T. Surran—Died of heart disease at Harewood U. S. Army General Hospital, Washington, D. C., January 11, '63; buried at Military Asylum Cemetery, D. C.; Tuckahoe, Atlantic side.

Theophilus Vanneman—Died of typhoid fever at Regimental Hospital, camp near Suffolk, Va., March 28, '63.

Hezekiah Veach—Died of typhoid fever at Regimental Hospital, camp near Falmouth, Va., January 25, '63; buried at National Cemetery, Fredericksburg, Va., Division D, Section C, Grave 277.

George Trader—Absent, sick in U. S. Army General Hospital, Fairfax Seminary, Va., December 1, '62; final record unknown.

Those who remained to the end with the company and were mustered out, on June 20, 1863, were:

Ewing W. Tibbles, Nicholas Corson, Enoch S. Willetts, John W. Shoemaker, Charles W. Corson, Benjamin Weatherby, Charles H. Corson, Matthew Hughes, Lewis S. Williams, George Baner, Samuel Barnes, Jonathan Borden, John L. Buzby, Aaron B. Clark, Jonathan Cliver, John Collins, Joseph Collins, John Magee, Furman Mannery, Frederick Marshall, Lucien B. Corson, Daniel Creamer, Reuben Creamer, Robert M. Dare, John Dayton, Nicholas Frambes, Howard M. French, George E. Gandy, Thomas Garron, James H. Gifford, Abraham Hayes, Mahlon Horton, David T. Ingersoll, Richard Ingersoll, Levi E. Lippincott, James Little, Charles Lloyd, John Lloyd, Leaming Lloyd, Hollis Mickel, Adam Moore, Samuel Morris, Thomas W. Pettitt, George M. Searse, Reuben Searse, Ezegiel Stevenson, Gabriel G. Surrann, John Thornton, Richard S. Townsend, Stephen Williams, Townsend S. Williams.

All but twenty-five of the men in Company I were Cape May men, and enlisted either from the county or Atlantic county. These men all enlisted on August 30, 1862, and were mustered into service on September 26. When they went to the front they ranked as follows:

First lieutenant, John F. Tomlin, farmer.

Second lieutenant, Samuel E. Douglass, farmer.

First sergeant, James Whitaker.

Seargeants—William Ogden, Enos R. Williams, John Spalding, Edward L. Townsend.

Corporals—David Hildreth, Joseph H. Holmes, Charles G. Mills, Willoby Snyder, Malachi High.

Privates—Elmer Edwards, Reuben Smith, Adam Abrams, Henry Bennett, Henry Brown, Daniel Chambers, James F. Chambers, James Chester, George W. Corson, James Crandol, Page R. Crawford, Joseph E. Dickinson, William Early, Joseph Elberson, Daniel Eldredge, Charles S. Elwell, George Errickson, John Errickson, William Farrow, Joseph Foster, Jesse Grace, Elias Hand, Aaron Hewitt, Freling F Hewitt, John Hewitt, Gabriel H. Holmes, Francis Katts, Aaron Leaming, John D. Leaming, Joseph McCarty, William H. McKeag, Richard Nott, Jonathan Rash, Clayton G. Sapp, Martin Selover, William Smith, Charles H. Stephens, Charles W. Townsend, Embury Townsend, James Weeks, Elmer Willetts, Jonathan Willetts, George L. Williams, Enos R. Williams, John Spalding, Alexander Corson, Edmund Y. Godfrey, Thomas D. Sayers, Elmer Taylor, Alonzo Willis, Edward L. Townsend, David Hildreth, Henry Rudolph, John Russell, David Norton, Benjamin Conover.

The occupations and professions of the members of the company were apportioned as follows: Blacksmith, 1; butchers, 2; carpenters, 7; farmers, 36; hucksters, 1; cotton spinner 1; mason, 1; painters, 2; moulders, 2; seamen, 37; shoemakers, 4; sheetiron workers, 2.

John F. Tomlin was promoted to captain on March 20, '63, and at the same time Samuel E. Douglass was made first lieutenant and J. Granville Leach promoted from the non-commissioned staff (sergeant-major) to second lieutenant of the company. Joseph H. Holmes was promoted to sergeant on December 15, '62, and Charles G. Mills on April 15, '63. Elmer Edwards was made a corporal January 29, '63, and Reuben Smith on April 15.

Those who did not remain in service with the company until it was mustered out and the causes therefor are as follows:

Enos R. Williams—Discharged at camp near Falmouth, Va., January 29, '63; disability.

John Spalding—Discharged at camp near Suffolk, Va., April 15, '63; disability; corporal August 30, '62; sergeant October 2, '62.

Alexander Corson—Discharged at camp near Falmouth, Va., January 9, '63; disability.

Edmund Y. Godfrey—Discharged at U. S. Army General Hospital, Washington, D. C., April 12, '63; disability.

Thomas D. Sayers—Discharged at Summit House U. S.

Army General Hospital, Philadelphia, Pa., February 4, '63; disability.

Elmer Taylor—Discharged at U. S. Army General Hospital, Portsmouth Grove, R. I., June 26, '63; disability.

Alonzo Willis—Discharged at Ward U. S. Army General Hospital, Newark, N. J., March 2, '63; disability.

Edward L. Townsend—Died at hospital, Fredericksburg, Va., December 14, '62, of wounds received in action at Fredericksburg, Va.; buried at National Cemetery, Fredericksburg, Va., Division A, Section A, Grave 54.

David Hildreth—Died of typhoid fever at camp near Falmouth, Va., December 29, '62.

Those who remained in service until the regiment was mustered out, June 20, 1863, were:

John F. Tomlin Samuel E. Douglas, J. Granville Leach, James Whitaker, William Ogden, Joseph H. Holmes, Charles G. Mills, Willowby Souder, Malachi High, Elmer Edwards, Reuben Smith, Adam Abrams, Henry Bennett, Henry Brown, Henry Rudolph, John Russell, David Norton, Benjamin Conover, Embury Townsend, James Weeks, Elmer Willetts, George L. Williams, Daniel Chambers, James F. Chambers, James Chester, George W. Corson, James Crandol, Page R. Crawford, Joseph E. Dickinson, William Early, Joseph Elberson, Daniel Eldridge, Charles S. Elwell, George Errickson, John Errickson, William Farrow, Joseph Foster, Jesse Grace, Elias Hand, Aaron Hewitt, Freling F. Hewitt, George Hewitt, John Hewitt, Gabriel H. Holmes, Francis Katts, Aaron Leaming, John D. Leaming, Joseph McCarty, William H. McKeag, Richard Nott, Jonathan Rash, Clayton G. Sapp, Martin Selover, William Smith, Charles H. Stephen and Charles W. Townsend.

Josiah Granville Leach, eldest son of Joseph S. Leach, was born at Cape May Court House July 27, 1842. He received his education in our public schools. at the classical school of Rev. Mr. Julien, and under private tutors. In his eighteenth year he began writing for the newspapers, and continued to write largely until the summer of 1862, when he enlisted in the Twenty-fifth New Jersey Volunteers, where he served as sergeant, sergeant-major and second-liutenant, receiving his promotion at the hands of Colonel Derrom, to the sergeant-majorship, for gallant conduct at the battle of Fredericksburg. For some months previous to his military service he devoted much of his time in organizing soldiers' aid societies, by which he was instrumental in providing a large amount of clothing and hospital stores for the sick and wounded.

On leaving the army he removed to Philadelphia, and began the study of law; was graduated LL. B. by the University of Pennsylvania, and in March, 1866, was admitted to the bar in Philadelphia, where he has since continued the practice of his profession. During the summer of 1865, at the instance of S. R. Magonagle, Esq., Colonel Leach organized and edited the "Cape May Daily Wave."

He has ever taken a deep interest in public affairs, and has been active in almost every political campaign since his nineteenth year, when he took the stump in support of Lincoln and Hamlin. He is said to have been the first to formally present Mr. Blaine's name for the Presidency. In the fall of 1875 he was elected to the Pennsylvania Legislature from Philadelphia, and served in the House during the session of 1876. Declining a renomination, he became a candidate for the Senate, but failed of a nomination. In 1878 he was nominated for the Legislature by the Greenback-Labor party, but declined the honor. In April, 1887, Governor Beaver appointed him Commissary-General of the National Guard of Pennsylvania, with the rank of colonel, which position he retained until January, 1891.

At the beginning of President Harrison's administration a strong movement was on foot to secure the appointement of Colonel Leach as Minister Resident and Consul-General to Switzerland, but before his claims were presented to the President the mission was filled by the appointment of his kinsman, Colonel Washburne, of Massachusetts. A few days later (March 18) the President appointed him appraiser of the United States at the port of Philadelphia, this being the President's first apointment in Philadelphia. The office had not been sought, but was accepted, and filled for four years with marked ability.

Colonel Leach has long devoted much time to literary

pursuits, largely of a historical and genealogical character. His contributions to "Appleton's Cyclopaedia of American Biography" were more numerous than those of any other contributor, aside from its editorial staff. Among his publications is "Memoranda Relating to the Ancestry and Family of Levi P. Morton, Vice-President of the United States," a work of 190 pages. He is a member of the American Bar Association, the American Academy of Social and Political Sciences and the Historical Society of Pennsylvania, and was for some years the historiographer of the latter. He was one of the founders of the Genealogical Society of Pennsylvania, of which he has been a vice-president since its organization; a member of the Society of Colonial Wars; a founder of the Pennsylvania Society of Sons of the Revolution and its historian, and is also historian of the Pennsylvania Society of Descendants of the Mayflower, and a member of many other organizations of a literary and social character.

Reuben Foster was born in Lower township October 28, 1839. He received a common school education, and when eighteen years of age went to Southwestern Iowa, where he remained with his uncle, Rev. Dr. Daniel L. Hughes, for four years, being engaged in agricultural pursuits. In 1861 he returned home, and entered the Twenty-fifth Regiment, and was promoted for meritorious conduct at Fredericksburg. After the close of the war he attended a business college in Philadelphia, and in 1867 he entered into the transportation business. He shortly afterwards located at Baltimore. He became connected with the Southern Steamship Line, and is now one of the wealthiest men in the Monumental City. He was at one time receiver of the Richmond and Danville Railroad, and is also agent of the North River line of steamers.

The Relief Committee for the years 1863-4, as appointed by the Board of Freeholders on May 13, 1863, was composed of Thomas Williams, of Upper; William S. Townsend, of Dennis; Dr. Alexander Young, of Middle; Samuel F. Ware, of Lower, and Joseph S. Leach, of Cape Island. Besides the money distributed by the board, the State contributed to the relief of the soldiers' families a total of $5449.40, through County Collector Charles Hand.

By the calls made by the State for troops in July and October, this year, Cape May county was to furnish eighty-three on the first call and eighty-eight on the second call. These men were to be recruited by January 4, 1864. On December 22, '63, the Board of Freeholders voted a bounty of $300 to each volunteer who would enlist, and this offer was to last until the 171 men had been secured. Dr. Coleman F. Leaming was appointed to distribute the bounty among the volunteers. The townships' committees and Cape Island City Council also passed resolutions giving bounties in addition to further aid in the recruiting. The Freeholders recommended recruiting officers for each township, which they asked the Governor to appoint, as follows: Thomas Williams, Upper; Clinton H. Ludlam, Dennis; Dr. Coleman F. Leaming, Middle; Waters B. Miller, Lower, and George W. Smith, Cape Island. By the same body it was agreed that each volunteer would get seventy-five dollars before leaving camp, and, in addition to regular pay, be given every six months an additional sum of fifty dollars. On January 13, 1864, the Freeholders passed a resolution making the $300 bounty apply to colored as well as white persons, and the rule was to hold good until the 171 men had entered the service. The bounty ceased on May 7, 1864.

CHAPTER XXV.

THE CAMPAIGNS OF 1864 AND 1865.

On the 4th of January, 1864, the time set for the filling up of the quota for Cape May, a number of persons volunteered and entered Company A, Third New Jersey Cavalry. Most of these men had served in the Twenty-fifth Regiment, Infantry.

The Third Cavalry was organized under the provisions approved July 22, 1861, and in pursuance of a proclamation issued by the President of the United States, dated October 17, 1863. The organization of the regiment was to be effected under the requirements of existing orders for the enrollment of troops. The organization of the regiment was immediately commenced, and the authorities to raise companies were issued to individuals in different parts of the State. The headquarters of the regiment were established at Camp Bayard, Trenton, and, to insure an early completion of the organization, it was designated the First Regiment, United States Hussars, and a uniform pertaining to this branch of service was adopted, which gave an enthusiasm to recruiting, and the required number of men to complete the regiment was soon obtained. As soon as the companies were raised they reported at camp, and were immediately mustered into the service of the United States for three years, unless sooner discharged. Company A was mustered in January 26. The regiment left the State April 5, 1864, and marched overland to Annapolis, Md., having been assigned to the Ninth Army Corps. It remained at this point but a short time, when, under orders, it proceeded to Alexandria, Va., and joined the Army of the Potomac. The regiment continued its organization and remained in active service until the close of the war, and the most of the officers and men were mustered out August 1, 1865, at Washington, D. C. The regiment was first attached to the Ninth Army

Corps; then to the Third Brigade, First Division, Cavalry Corps; Army of the Potomac; then to the First Brigade, Third Division, Cavalry Corps, Army of the Potomac. It took part in the following engagements, all in Virginia: United States Ford, May 19, 1864; Ashland Station, June 1; North Anna River, June 2; Haines' Shop, June 3; Bottom's Bridge, June 4; White Oak Swamp, June 13; Smith's Store, June 15; before Petersburg, July 25; Lee's Mills, July 27; Winchester, August 17; Summit Point, August 21; Kearneysville, August 25 and 26; Berryville Turnpike, September 13; Opequan, September 19; Front Royal, September 21 and 22; Fisher's Hill, September 22; Winchester, September 24; Waynesboro, September 28; Bridgewater, October 2; Tom's Brook, October 9; Cupp's Mills, October 13; Cedar Creek, October 19; Back Road (near Cedar Creek), November 12; Mount Jackson, November 22; Lacey's Spring, December 21; Moorefield, February 22, 1865; Waynesboro, March 2; Dinwiddie C. H., March 31; Five Forks, April 1; capture of Petersburg, April 2; Deep Creek, April 3; Sailor's Creek, April 6; Appomattox Station, April 8, and at Appomattox C. H. (Lee's surrender), April 9.

When the company was mustered into service the Cape May men ranked as follows:

Second lieutenant, John F. Tomlin.

Sergeant, Joseph H. Holmes.

Blacksmith, German Corson.

Privates—David S. Townsend, Isaac W. Mulford, Daniel H. Wheaton, Thomas H. Taylor, Shamgar C. Townsend, Lewis Gooden, John W. Hand, Andrew Kramer, George W. Lester, John W. McCarty, Joseph A. McCarty, Isaac W. McCormick, William H. McKeag, Francis G. Springer, John Thornton, Edgar Voss, Elva E. Westcott, Josiah Whittaker, George L. Williams, Willets Corson, Charles Grace, Alfred Warwick.

John F. Tomlin was promoted to first lieutenant of Company M on May 6, '64, and assumed the place five days later. May 3, 1865, he was commissioned captain of Company E, and on the 17th mustered into that office and remained as such until the regiment was mustered out on August 1, 1865.

Joseph H. Holmes was, on May 3, 1865, commissioned second lieutenant of Company F, and mustered into that position on May 18, 1865, in which he served until mustered out of service on August 1, 1865.

David S. Townsend was promoted to sergeant January 1, 1865, and Isaac W. Mulford to corporal on June 11, 1864. Daniel H. Wheaton was made a corporal on January 4, 1865; Shamgar C. Townsend, April 26, 1864, and Thomas H. Taylor, March 1, 1865.

Those who did not remain with the company during their entire service and the reasons therefor were:

Shamgar C. Townsend—Prisoner of war and confined in Andersonville Prison; paroled and discharged at U. S. Army General Hospital, York, Pa., May 12, 1865.

Andrew Kramer—Discharged at Armory Square, U. S. General Hospital, Washington, May 3, 1865.

Edgar Voss—Discharged at same time and place.

Willitts Corson—Died at Douglass U. S. Army General Hospital, Washington, D. C., June 9, 1864; buried at National Cemetery, Arlington, Va.

Charles Grace—Died at U. S. Army General Hospital, Fairfax Seminary, Va., June 19, 1864; buried at National Cemetery, Alexandria, Va., Grave 2191.

Alfred Warwick—Died October 6, 1864; buried at Poplar Grove National Cemetery, Va.; prisoner of war; died of starvation in Saulsbury Prison.

Those who remained with the company until it was mustered out, August 1, 1865, were: David S. Townsend, Isaac W. Mulford, George L. Williams, German Corson, Lewis Go:den, John W. Hand, Elva E. Westcott, Joshua Whittaker, Daniel Wheaton, Thomas H. Taylor, George W. Lester, John W. McCarty, Joseph A. McCarty, Isaac W. McCormick, William H. McKeag, Francis G. Springer, John Thornton.

The next companies in which Cape May men served were Companies H and K, Thirty-eighth Regiment Volunteers. This regiment was organized under the provisions of acts of Congress of July 22, 1861, and July 4, 1864, and under authority of the War Department for the raising of two regiments of infantry. The recruiting was commenced and headquarters of the regiment were established at Camp Bayard, Trenton, and active measures were pursued to complete the organization at an early date. The required number of men to complete the regiment was raised and mustered into the service of the United States by companies, for one year, by the 1st day of October, 1864. Company H was mustered into service September 30, 1864, and Company K September 15, at Camp Bayard. The regiment was fully officered and completed by October 3. It

WILLIAM J. SEWELL.

left the State in three detachments. Company K left in the first detachment on September 20, and Company H October 4, under Colonel William J. Sewell, whose name has since become a household word in the county by reason of his prominence in Cape May's improvement, his summer residence in the county and his twice serving the State in the United States Senate. Each detachment proceeded to Baltimore, Md., thence by transports to City Point, Va. Upon its arrival it was assigned to garrison and other duties, the headquarters of the regiment being at Fort Powhattan, on the James River, having been assigned to a provisional brigade, Army of the James. It remained in this vicinity during its entire period of service, which lasted until the end of the war. It was mustered out of service at City Point, Va., June 30, 1865, and started immediately for its return to New Jersey, where it arrived on July 4. It took part in the operations of the army before Petersburg, Va., which resulted in its capture April 2, and the surrender of General Robert E. Lee, April 9.

Those who enlisted in Company H on September 20 were: George Aumack, Richard Aumack, Jr., Samuel Barnes, John G. Sheppard, Edward F. Townsend, Joseph W. Whitaker, and on the 27th were John C. Camp, James Chambers, Frederick W. Crandol and Franklin Scull. They all served as privates. All but Franklin Scull were mustered out on June 30, 1865, he having died of pleurisy at Post Hospital, Fort Pocohontas, Va., on November 22, 1864.

The Cape May men in Company K all enlisted on September 6, excepting William Hoffman, who enlisted on the following day. When the company was mustered into service the Cape May men ranked as follows:

First lieutenant, Albert E. Hand.
Sergeant, Samuel E. Douglass.
Corporal, Eleazer F. Hankins.
Privates—Isaac Heritage, Enoch T. Abrams, Skidmore Abrams, Elijah D. Batts, Henry Brown, James F. Chambers, Jacob S. Corson, Joseph Cresse, George Eldridge, James Estell, Robert Garrison, Benjamin A. Hankins, William H. Heritage, William Hoffman, David Lloyd, Albert Norton, David Norton, Uriah Norton, Henry Rudolph and Socrates J. Smith.

Samuel E. Douglass was made first sergeant October 1, 1864; sergeant-major of the regiment on November 1, and was on May 16, 1865, promoted to be second lieutenant of Company E, with which company he served until the regiment was mustered out.

Eleazer F. Hankins was made sergeant on October 1, 1864, and Isaac Heritage a corporal on November 1. All the men remained with the company until it was mustered out, on June 30, 1865, excepting Samuel E. Douglass and

Henry Rudolph, the latter being discharged at Camp Parole, Annapolis, Md., May 1, 1865.

Cape May men did excellent service in the navy, the more prominent of these men being:

Henry W. Hand, acting master; appointed November 13, '61; discharged February 21, '66; served on U. S. steamship "Vermont" during 1863 and 1864.

James Mecray, Jr., acting assistant surgeon; appointed November 5, '62; resigned April 1, '64; served in East Gulf Blockading Squadron, '62; U. S. bark "James L. Davis," 1863,

Henry Bennett (records unknown); drowned in Charleston Harbor, S. C.

Edward D. Springer, acting ensign; appointed August 11, '64; dischaged December 11, '65; served in Mississippi Squadron.

Eli D. Edmunds, acting master; appointed May 8, 1865; discharged September 9, 1865; acting master's mate September 9, '62; U. S. steamer "Crusader," '62; acting ensign September 9, '63; Potomac Flotilla, '63 and '64; commanding coast survey steamer '66.

Seth L. Hand, landsman; appointed September 2, '64; discharged June 11, '65; served on U. S. receiving ship "Princeton."

Theodore F. Hildreth, seaman; appointed December 14, '63; discharged December 7, '64; served on U. S. steamer "Niphon."

Elijah Hand, Jr., ordnance seaman; appointed September 5, '64; discharged June 8, '65; served on U. S. steamer "Pontoosuc."

Andrew J. Tomlin, U. S. Marine Corps.

Henry Walker Hand is of colonial stock, being a lineal descendant of Mark Hand, a soldier in the army of Oliver Cromwell. He is a son of Christopher Smith Hand, and was born at Green Creek on July 8, 1833. After obtaining such educational advantages as were to be had in his native neighborhood, he began a life upon the sea at seventeen years of age. At twenty-one he was a master in the merchant marine. When in Mobile, Alabama, in 1856, he was arrested for carrying off a negro slave, but upon trial was acquitted. He was, however, an ardent Abolitionist and strong Union man during the war. He entered the navy at the outbreak of the conflict, on November 13, 1861, and as master was ordered to the U. S. steamship "Keystone State" as division and watch officer. He was on this vessel when it made its long cruise after the Confederate blockade runner "Nashville." He was in Admiral Du Pont's squadron when his fleet captured the Southern ports south of Port Royal, South Carolina. He operated with the divisions of sailors and marines for shore duty and was prize master of the Confederate privateer "Dixie," captured by the "Keystone State." He was attached to the monitor "Passaic" in New York during the celebrated draft riots, and had command of her turret division. He was afterwards transferred to the U. S. ships "Vermont" and "New Hampshire," and was executive officer of each of them in succession from July 28, 1863, to November, 1865. He did service at the blockade at Charleston, S. C., and with the naval brigade, under Brigadier General Hatch, operated in South Carolina in February, 1865, in the division which acted as a diversion to General Sherman in the march to the sea.

After the war Captain Hand made a three years' cruise in the U. S. steamship "Lackawanna," on the Pacific station, as watch officer. This ship did surveying in the Pacific Ocean with headquarters at Honolulu, Sandwich Islands. This was the first U. S. war vessel to reach that port after the war. He was honorably discharged in 1869, and returned home. Since that time he was connected with the public schools as teacher until he devoted his whole time to editorial duties as editor of the "Wave," in which capacity he has acted since 1883.

In 1862 the total value of property in the county was $2,638,028, divided as follows: Upper township, $536,775; Dennis, $520,871; Middle, $580,180; Lower, $498,476, and Cape Island, $474,726. In 1865 the total value had decreased, according to estimate, a half million dollars. The following table shows the condition of the county as estimated at the close of the war (June, 1865):

TOWNSHIPS.	Number of Acres.	Value of Lands.	Value of Real and Personal Estate.	Quota of State Tax.	Quota of Co. Tax.	Quota of War Tax.
Upper	23,545	$246,675	$435,000	$ 582.26	$1357.45	$ 160.00
Dennis	26,162	295,870	430,000	575.58	1341.84	240.00
Middle	28,476	424,760	530,000	709.42	1653.90	666.66
Lower	13,516	265,000	360,000	481.87	1123.41	622.22
Cape Island	240	281,000	360,000	481.87	1123.40	311.12
Total	91,939	$1513,305	$2,115,000	$2831.00	$6600.00	$2000.00

In 1866 the war debt of Cape May county had reached about twenty thousand dollars, and it was reduced at the rate of about thirty-five hundred dollars per year until extinguished.

Frederick Ricard, State superintendent of public schools, in his report of January 15, 1862, says of the Cape May county schools:

"The tax per child raised here for the purpose of education is exceeded by only three other counties in the State. * * * There is no charge made for tuition in any of the public schools, though I regret to say that the average number of months which they are kept open does not compare favorably with that of other counties. The teachers here are, with very few exceptions, spoken of in the highest terms."

Cape May county's war Senator was Jonathan F. Leaming, A. M., M. D., D. D. S., who served from 1862 to 1865. He was born in Cape May county September 7, 1822. His family is of English extraction, he being the sixth in his line from Christopher Leaming, who migrated from England in 1670 and settled in Cape May county in 1691. He was a great-grandson of Aaron Leaming, second. He pursued his collegiate course at Madison University, New York, and subsequently at Brown University, Rhode Island, and graduate at the Jefferson Medical College, in Philadelphia, in 1846. In 1847 he commenced the practice of medicine in his native county, which he pursued for fourteen years, compelled to relinquish it for the kindred but less arduous profession of dentistry on account of impaired health. In 1860 he graduated at the Pennsylvania Dental College, Philadelphia, and has since practiced dentistry in Cape May county. He has taken an active part in public affairs, educational, political and religious. For several years he was township superintendent of public schools, for fifteen years county school examiner; served two terms as trustee of the State Normal School, of which he was always a firm advocate and supporters.

In 1861 he was elected as a Republican to the New Jersey House of Assembly, and in 1862 he was elevated to the

State Senate, where he served three years. He was chairman of the committee of the Senate on the establishment of the New Jersey Agricultural College, and was largely interester in securing for Rutger's College her agricultural endowment fund.

In 1868 he was elected surrogate of Cape May county for five years, and re-elected in 1873, but in 1877 resigned that position on January 1 to accept a seat in the State Senate again, to which he had been elected by the people for a term of three years.

Religiously, he is a Baptist, and has been affiliated with church work for sixty years, either as teacher, trustee, dea-

DR. JONATHAN F. LEAMING.

con and clerk, and for a great many years was a Sunday-school superintendent.

A prominent citizen of Cape May during the war period was Dr. Coleman F. Leaming, of Court House. He was the second son of Jeremiah Leaming, who was in the Legislative Council in 1832 to 1834, and elder brother of Richard S. Leaming, who was a Senator in 1874 to 1877. The doctor was born on June 6, 1818. He was loan commissioner of Cape May county from 1863 to 1880. He was a member of the Board of Freeholders from Middle township in 1863, '64, '65. Previous to the war he practiced medicine in New York. For a number of years he has been a director of the West Jersey Railroad, and was for some years superintendent of schools in Middle township.

The war Assemblyman was Wilmon W. Ware, who served from 1862 to 1865, and who was State Senator from 1865 to 1868. He was born at Cape May City, where he always resided, in 1818, and was a brother of Joseph, Daniel C., Maskel and John G. W., all of whom held public offices of trust in Cape May City. He was a member of Cape Island Ctiy Council during the years 1854, 1864, 1870 and 1878. He served as city clerk from 1858 to 1861, and was a member of the Board of Freeholders in 1870. In politics he was Republican, having formerly been a Whig. He died at Cape May City on August 25, 1885.

CHAPTER XXVI.
LIFE FOLLOWING THE REBELLION.

John Wilson was elected sheriff in 1865 and served until 1868. He was born at East Creek, where his father, then a lad of nineteen, had settled, June 13, 1809. His father came from the north coast of Ireland to America. He always lived in that village, where he was a leading citizen. He was a merchant, and engaged largely in the shipping of cord wood. He was the first postmaster of his village, having been appointed in 1842, and occupying the position until he died, December 23, 1875. He was prominently identified with the Methodist Episcopal Church of his neighborhood and a devout Christian. In politics he was at first a Whig and then a Republican.

On June 14, 1865, the Board of Freeholders concluded to build a new surrogate's and clerk's office, and selected a committee to visit other counties and examine the public offices. Dr. Coleman F. Leaming, Sylvanus Corson and Joseph E. Hughes were chosen as the committee. On December 28 they reported to the Board that they had had the offices built at a cost of $5100 and that they were finished on December 1.

By the census of this year, and in spite of the war, the population had increased to 7625 persons, or a gain in five years of 495. The population was apportioned among the townships as follows: Upper, 1575; Dennis, 2019; Middle, 2077; Lower, 1355, and Cape Island, 599.

On September 10, 1866, the New Jersey Legislature, in special session, ratified the Fifteenth Amendment to the Constitution of the United States. Wilmon W. Ware was Senator and Thomas H. Beesley was the Assemblyman.

On January 16, 1767, a postoffice was established at Belle Plain, which was then in Cumberland county, but which is now within the bounds of Cape May county. On the 7th of September of this year the postoffice at South Seaville was opened, with Remington Corson as postmaster.

Samuel R. Magonagle, who was a member of the Assembly in 1868, and the fifth and seventh Mayor of Cape Island, was born in 1829 at Mifflin, Juniata caunty, Pa., where he was brought up and went to school. His mother died when he was ten years of age, and he was left much of the time to look out for himself. Early in life he apprenticed himself to a printer, and learned that trade, and so industrious was he that, when nineteen years of age, or in 1848, he was the publisher of a newspaper in his native town, known as the "Pennsylvania Register." He published the journal for a number of years, and during his editorial management was a power for the Democratic party, to the principles of which Mr. Magonagle always clung. After disposing of his paper, the young and ambitious man hunted for new fields, and traveled all over the West, working his way at the printer's case, until, in 1859, we find him in Philadelphia. At that time he became an employe at the printing establishment of Crissy & Markley, and afterwards became an employe of the "Philadelphia Inquirer." In 1856 he came to Cape May, or Cape Island, as the place was then called, and became an employe and assistant to Mr. Joseph S. Leach, at that time proprietor and publisher of the "Cape May County Ocean Wave," when the paper was a power both editorially and in a business way. While in the employ of Mr. Leach he did not waste any time, but between hours learned to manipulate the telegrapher's keyboard, and was shortly made the manager of the Western Union Telegraph Company for Cape Island.

On December 5, 1859, President Buchanan made him postmaster of the town, which office he held until June 26, 1863, when he was succeeded by Mr. Joseph S. Leach.

In May, 1860, he married Mrs. Mary E. Tindall, widow of Rev. N. B. Tindall, a Baptist clergyman, and a daughter of Richard Thompson, of Court House.

In March, 1861, Mr. Magonagle was elected Mayor for one year, and, although his place was never filled by another appointment, the office was virtually vacant, because Mr. Magonagle had, shortly after election, volunteered his

LIFE FOLLOWING THE REBELLION.

services to the country and gone off with the brave boys of Company A, Seventh Regiment, New Jersey Volunteers. He was only away a short time, during which time he was quartermaster-sergeant. He was taken ill and never crossed the Potomac, and the illness never left him entirely.

He purchased the "Wave" in 1863 from Mr. Leach, and was its proprietor until his death. In 1865 he began the summer-time daily issue, which has been continued by successive proprietors of the paper since.

He was elected Mayor for the second time in March, 1863,

SURROGATE'S AND CLERK'S OFFICE, BUILT IN 1865.

and re-elected in 1864, 1865, 1866 and 1867 for terms of a year each. He would have probably been elected in 1868, but he was elected to the House of Assembly in the fall of 1867. Before he had served to the end of his session, in 1868, he was elected a member of City Council, and died before that term was served out. He was the first Democrat elected to the Assembly from the county.

In 1859 he united with the First Methodist Episcopal Church of this city, and remained a faithful member and worker and Sunday-school teacher during the balance of his life.

While in Trenton attending to getting some amendments to the city charter, which were finally passed in 1869, he was taken ill at a reception at the home of Hon. John P. Stockton, a firm friend of Mr. Magonagle, who has since that time been United States Senator and Attorney-General of the State. This illness, caused by the illness contracted in the army, became worse, and he died in his apartments in the American House, in Trenton, on the evening of January 22, 1869. The body was brought home, and, after a large funeral, it was placed in its last resting place in the Cape May Court House Cemetery. He left a widow, who died in 1894.

At the time of his death he was a member of the Soldiers' Union, the Masonic Order and of the Good Templars.

In speaking of him in its obituary, the Philadelphia "Evening Bulletin" said:

"* * * Mr. Magonagle was a gentleman of varied abilities, and of the most estimable character. Generous and humane in his nature, his affections and sympathies were always enlisted on the side of mercy. These traits were eminently developed throughout the seven years he occupied the position of chief magistrate of Cape Island.

"In the adjudication of the varied cases which came before him, Mr. Magonagle exhibited signal ability. His quick appreciation of legal duty and unmistakable power of analysis always guided his decisions and led him to a correct determination of the cases that came before him. In the discharge of his duties on these principles he won for himself the warmest attachments of all who came in social and political contact with him. A community loses much when it loses such a man. Mr. Magonagle had been a resident of Cape Island for many years, and had grown almost with the growth of that popular seaside resort.

"He had been successful in establishing his newspaper, the 'Ocean Wave,' on a firm and quite prosperous basis, and was an active spirit in advancing all the essential interests and improvements of that city.

"Mr. Magonagle was a gentleman of pleasing and affable manners; a well-known Democrat, but of moderate political views; was a member of the Legislature in 1868, and was esteemed by his colleagues for his honorable traits of character, and by the members of the press throughout the State for his social qualities, business enterprise and energy."

Anthony Steelman, Sheriff from 1868 to 1871, was born in Atlantic county December 23, 1823, his father being Jonas Steelman. He attended the public schools until he was eighteen years of age. Then he worked on his father's farm until 1845, when, on October 6, he became a partner of Elijah Ireland, at Tuckahoe, in the mercantile business, and in August, 1847, became a partner of James Shoemaker, remaining with him twenty-three years. He then became sole owner, and conducted the business until he retired in 1895, having been in business then forty-nine years. He was a member of the Board of Freeholders nine years, and of the Upper Township Committee fifteen years.

The "Star of the Cape," the second newspaper established in the county, first appeared at Cape May Court House about 1868, its publishers being J. Alvin Cresse and one Cheever. In less than two years' time it was moved to Cape May City by W. V. L. Seigman, who purchased it of its original owners, and who conducted it until 1883, when it was purchased by Thomas R. Brooks. Mr Brooks edited it until May, 1889, when he sold it to Aaron W. Hand and N. Perry Edmunds. In February, 1890, Mr. Brooks purchased of Mr. Edmunds his interest, and finally the whole paper in 1894, but in September, 1895, he sold it to the Star of the Cape Publishing Company, who are the present owners. It is now managed for this company by Aaron W. Hand.

Thomas Rezo Brooks, a grandson of Rev. Thomas Brooks, a Baptist clergyman who preached at West Creek, was born at Heislerville, Cumberland county, N. J., October 4, 1838. His grandfather was a Revolutionary soldier, and he was one of those who were confined in the prison ship in New York harbor by the British for his ardent patriotism. His father was Samuel Brooks, a prominent official member and exhorter in the Methodist Church of Cumberland county. His mother is Loraina, a daughter o.

Barlow Williams, who was licensed as a local minister in the Methodist Church at the beginning of the present century. Mr. Brooks' parents removed to Philadelphia in the spring of 1839 and it was in the public schools of that city that he was mainly educated. In December, 1861, he married Miss Emma T. Brooks, of Smyrna, Delaware. In 1859 he began teaching school in his native county, and in 1869 closed his career as a teacher at Dennisville, this county, and accepted a position tendered him by the West Jersey Railroad Company. He was with this company for fourteen years. While yet with the company, in 1876, he be-

THOMAS R. BROOKS.

came associate editor of the "Wave," and in 1883 resigned his position with the company and purchased the "Star of the Cape," from which he retired in the fall of 1895. Under his editorial control the "Star of the Cape" became one of the most popular and successful journals in South Jersey. He now resides in Cape May City.

Dr. Edmund Levi Bull Wales, of Tuckahoe, was, about 1866, appointed a judge of the New Jersey Court of Errors and Appeals, to succeed Joshua Swain, Jr., who had died. He served in that capacity until 1881. Dr. Wales was a son of Dr. Roger Wales, and was born March 15, 1805. He was a graduate of Jefferson Medical College, Philadelphia, and practiced medicine at Tuckahoe for many years. He was the wealthiest man of the county at the time of his death, on August 19, 1882.

His brother, Dr. Eli B. Wales, of Cold Spring, was for many years a judge of the Court of Common Pleas of Cape May county. He was born July 10, 1798, and died September 24, 1883.

In 1870 Cape May's acreage was divided as follows: Beaches, 4424; marsh on which tide rose and fell, 58,824; bays and sounds and creeks, 10,443; fast upland, 96,480; total, 170,171 acres. Twenty-one thousand four hundred and two acres of this fast land were under cultivation and known as "improved land." The estimated total value of farms was $1,683,430. The total value of all farm productions, including betterments and addition to stock, was $318,609. The live stock in the county (valued at $196,000) was divided as follows: Horses, 816; mules and asses, 4; milch cows, 1545; working oxen, 13; sheep, 382, and swine, 1751. The productions were as follows: Bushels of winter wheat, 19,064; bushels of rye, 171; bushels of Indian corn, 86,218; bushels of oats, 6648; bushels of buckwheat, 157; pounds of wool, 1095; bushels of Irish potatoes, 22,360; bushels of sweet potatoes, 21,193, and pounds of butter, 68,310.

The assessed valuation of real and personal estate was $3,800,810; true value of real and personal estate, $5,599,383; total amount raised by taxation, $36,637; State tax, $2228; county tax, $11,529; town and city tax, $22,870; county public debt, nothing; township and city public debt, $50,600.

The population of the county was apportioned as follows:

TOWNSHIPS.	WHITE	COLORED	TOTAL
Cape May City,	1245	148	1393
Dennis,	1598	2	1600
Lower,	1602	211	1813
Middle,	2128	67	2195
Upper,	1521	7	1528
	8094	435	8529

In the beginning of the present century whale boats were used on the Cape May county coast for the saving of lives and merchandise from wrecks. These boats were built for such purposes in conjunction with use for fishing purposes of shore. They were owned by private parties, and the crews were necessarily volunteers. About 1840 Jonathan J. Springer, of Middle township, brother of Samuel Springer, sheriff, built a boat for the purpose, which was named "Insurance." This craft was built for the Vessel Insurance Company, for which Judge Richard C. Holmes was agent in Cape May county. The "Insurance," owing to its unseaworthy qualities, was abandoned, and about 1852 the "Relief" was built by Mr. Springer for a company of nine. Some of those who served as volunteers in the crew were Richard Ludlam, Aaron D. Hand, George Hildreth, Isaac Isard, Jonathan Fifield, Elijah Townsend, Enoch Hand and James Crowell. About 1860 "The Rescue" was built and manned by Henry Y. Hewitt, captain; Richard Holmes, Enoch Hand, Cornelious Bennett, Swain, Church, Somers, Isard, William McCarty, Sr.

In 1857 Judge Holmes built his self-righting life-saving boat, and in the summer of that year it was exhibited on the beach at Cape Island. This boat, however, never proved successful.

Judge Richard C. Holmes was born in Cape May county September 17, 1813. He was educated in Philadelphia, and the early part of his life was spent in the employ of Captain Joseph Hand, an extensive shipping merchant (who was also born in Cape May county). While in Captain Hand's employ young Holmes gained a full knowledge of vessels, boats and seamen, and afterwards used his knowledge in saving hundreds of lives on the coast. He was an officer of both the State and the United States and agent for Philadelphia and New York insurance companies. He was collector of the Port of Cape May about 1852. Judge Holmes died at his home, near Cape May Court House, January 25, 1863, aged 49 years.

The attention to establishing life-saving stations on the coast was first given by the United States Government in

LIFE FOLLOWING THE REBELLION.

1848, when William A. Newell, of New Jersey, was in Congress. He urged the expediency of action, and secured an appropriation of $10,000 to "provide surf boats, rockets, carronades and other necessary appurtenances for the better preservation of life and property from shipwreck. In 1849 boats were first placed on Cape May beaches for life-saving stations by the authority given above. The boats and appurtenances were not placed in the hands of persons held accountable. In December, 1854, Congress authorized the appointment of captains, who were paid $200 per year salary, while the crews were to be volunteers. In 1871 the present organized service was established. New stations were built and equipped with boats and with rooms for living and sleeping, a code of signals adopted and full crews employed.

Geographical positions of United States life-saving stations in Cape May county:

No. 30, Beasley's—South side Great Egg Harbor Inlet.

No. 31, Peck's Beach—Three and one-half miles above Corson's Inlet.

No. 32, Corson's Inlet—Near inlet, north side.

No. 33, Ludlam's Beach—Three and one-half miles above Townsend's Inlet.

No. 34, Townsend's Inlet—Near the Inlet, west side.

No. 35, Stone Harbor—Three and one-half miles above Hereford Inlet.

No. 36, Hereford Inlet—Near Hereford Light.

No. 37, Turtle Gut—Six and one-quarter miles above Cape May City.

No. 38, Two-Mile Beach—Four miles above Cape May City.

No. 39, Cold Spring—One hundred feet west Madison avenue, Cape May City.

No. 40, Cape May—Near Cape May Light.

No. 41, Bay Shore—Two and one-half miles west Cape May City.

Thomas Beesley, of Dennisville, who was chosen State Senator in 1870 and served in 1871, '72 and '73, was a younger brother of Dr. Maurice Beesley. Thomas Beesley was born in Cape May county August 22, 1815, and, after receiving a moderate education, engaged himself in mercantile pursuits. He became prominent as a counselor among men. He was five times chosen to the Assembly, serving in the years 1865, '66, '67, '69 and '70. He held local offices and was an ardent Union man. He was at first allied with the Whig party, and then with the Republican, and as such was elected to public office. He died on October 16, 1877.

Nelson T. Eldredge, of Lower township, who was chosen sheriff in 1871, was a son of Jeremiah L. Eldredge, a prominent pilot who lived in the county. He was born in Lower township October 13, 1833. He served as sheriff from 1871 to 1874. He died in Lower township on June 16, 1886.

In 1872 postoffices were at Ocean View and Palermo, the former on May 6 and the latter on December 11. February 24, 1873, the office at South Dennis was first opened.

In 1872 the State Legislature passed a law authorizing the building of life saving stations along the beaches.

In 1875 the International Cape May Ocean Regatta came off, and the Cape May Cup, which was then won, has been carried all over the world and raced for many times since by those yachts famous both in Europe and America.

The cup was raced for by the New York Yacht Club from a buoy off Sandy Hook to Five-Fathom Beach, off Cape May.

The third **President to visit Cape May** county was General Grant, who came for four different seasons for short visits. On Saturday evening, June 13, 1873, he arrived at Congress Hall, Cape Island, and was at the opening of the hotel for the season. He brought with him several Cabinet officers and prominent citizens, among whom were General George H. Williams, Attorney-General; Hon. Benjamin Bristow, Secretary of the Treasury; Hon. R. B. Cowen, Assistant Secretary of the Interior; ex-Vice-President Hannibal Hamlin, then United States Senator from Maine; General O. E. Hancock, United States Army, and Private Secretary to the President; Hon. A. G. Cattell, ex-United States Senator from New Jersey, and who was afterwards president of the local banking institution, the New Jersey Trust and Safe Deposit Company; Governor A. R. Sheppard, of the District of Columbia; Hon. John Goforth, Assistant Attorney-General; General Edward McCook, Governor of Colorado; Thomas H. Dudley, Consul to Liverpool, and others. The party was received by Company H, Sixth Regiment, the local military organization, and welcomed to the city by Mayor Waters B. Miller. During that season Hon. Frederic T. Frelinghuysen, afterwards Secretary of State under President Arthur, was a guest at the Stockton with his family. The following season Governor Thomas A. Hendricks, afterwards Vice-President of the United States, was a Stockton guest.

Frank Willing Leach, who left Cape May for other fields about this time, is the youngest surviving son of Joseph S. Leach, and was born at Cape May August 26, 1855. He was educated primarily at the local schools and by private tutor. Having read law with his brother, J. Granville Leach, he was admitted to the Philadelphia bar March 31, 1877. He immediately began the practice of his profession in that city, where he has resided since January, 1873. Mr. Leach, at an early age, even before attaining his majority, evinced an appetite for journalism and literature. When a youth he was president of the Philadelphia Amateur Press Association and critic of the Eastern Amateur Press Association. About this time he was editor of "The Literary Gem," a monthly journal, published by the Crescent Literary Society, of which organization, made up chiefly of college students, he was the president. Soon afterward he began contributing to current periodicals, his first story, a novelette, having been published in the "Waverly Magazine," when he was twenty-two years of age. Before this he had done work as a correspondent for the Philadelphia "Press" and Philadelphia "North American." For a number of years Mr. Leach has been engaged upon a biographical and genealogical work entitled "The Signers of the Declaration of Independence: Their Ancestors and Descendents."

Mr. Leach's tastes and inclinations ran to politics while he was yet a young man. In 1881 he was a delegate to the Republican State Convention, of which, also, he was the secretary. The same year he followed the political fortunes of Hon. Charles S. Wolfe, who ran as an independent candidate for State Treasurer. Mr. Leach was secretary of the Independent Republican State Committee that year, as well as in 1882, when Hon. John Stewart was the independent candidate for Governor, and he was also secretary of the convention which placed the latter in nomination, May 24, 1882. In 1883 he was chief auditor in the office of the City Controller of Philadelphia, and the following year he was chief clerk, at the same time serving as secretary to the Commissioners of the Sinking Fund of that city. In 1885 he became the secretary of the Republican State Committee of Pennsylvania, which position he held until the summer of 1893. From 1886 to 1892, and again in 1895, he was secretary of the Republican State Committee. He was also a delegate to the State Convention of 1893. In 1888 he was secretary of the Republican National Convention, which met at Chicago, and from 1888 to 1892 he was assistant secretary of the Republican National Committee, and he conducted the campaign of that year. As a political organizer he has few equals in Pennsylvania.

Mr. Leach is a member of the Pennsylvania Society Sons of the Revolution and of the Pennsylvania and New York Societies of Mayflower Descendants; also a member of the Historical Society of Pennsylvania, the American Academy of Political and Social Science, the Numismatic and Antiquarian Society of Philadelphia, the University Archeological Association, the American Folk Lore Society, the Civil Service Reform Association of Philadelphia and the Gealogical Society of Pennsylvania; also of Mt. Moriah Lodge, No. 55, F. A. M., and Damascus Council, No. 536, Jr. O. U. A. M.; also of the Markham and Penrose Clubs of Philadelphia, and the Harrisburg Club, of Harrisburg, Pa.

Hereford Inlet Light was established in 1874.

This light is located on the north end of Five-Mile Beach, in latitude 39°00′00″ and longitude 74°47′00″. Its height of tower is 49½ feet and elevation of light 57 feet above sea level. It has a fourth-order lens and fixed red light, visible at a distance of thirteen nautical miles. Arc of illumination, N. E. by N. ¾ N., around eastward to S. W. ½ S. This structure is of wood and placed in a grove. The tower surmounts the dwelling. Both are painted straw color. Distant 10¾ nautical miles north of Cape May Lighthouse.

Richard S. Leaming, Senator from 1874 to 1877, was a prominent man of the county. He was a son of Jeremiah Leaming, who was Senator from 1834 to 1836, and was born in Cape May county July 16, 1828. In early life he evinced business capacity, and began business as a ship builder at Dennisville, where he was successful in his opera-

RICHARD S. LEAMING.

tions. During the war he became a staunch Union man, and was active in moving supplies and securing volunteers. He became a member of the Republican party upon its formation. He was a member of the Board of Freeholders from Dennis township during the years 1862, '69, '70,'71 and '72. He served as a member of the Assembly in 1871, '72 and '73. The latter year he was chosen to the Senate and served during the years 1874, '75 and '76. He was a candidate for Presidential elector in 1888 on the Harrison and Morton ticket. He was a prominent Baptist and many years superintendent of his Sunday school. He died at Dennisville on May 25, 1895.

In 1874 Dr. Alexander Young, of Court House, served in the Assembly. He was a grandson of Henry Young, who was surrogate of Cape May from 1743 to 1768. Dr. Young was born at Beesley's Point March 27, 1828. After getting a primitive education, he entered Jefferson Medical College, in Philadelphia, in 1857, and two years later was graduated an M. D. He settled at Goshen and practiced there until 1873, when he removed to Court House. Early

DR. ALEXANDER YOUNG.

in life he became a member of the Petersburg M. E. Church, and was some years a class leader. While at Goshen he gave attention also to cranberry growing and had one of the largest bogs in the county.

Beginning in 1868, he served in the Board of Freeholders for about fifteen years from Middle township, and from 1870 until he retired he was the director (president) of that body. He died at Court House on May 17, 1887.

In 1874 Joseph E. Hughes was appointed a judge of county courts by Governor Joel E. Parker. Judge Hughes, who was a son of James R. Hughes, a well-known local educator of his day, and a grandson of Aaron Eldredge, surrogate from 1802 to 1803, was born in Lower township July 31, 1821. In his thirteenth year he became a member of the Cold Spring Presbyterian Church. He grew to manhood on his father's farm and was studious and acquired a moderate education. He entered upon farming, and for fifteen years taught the district school. For many years superintendent of the Cold Spring Sunday-school, and was

JOSEPH E. HUGHES.

made an elder of the church in 1835, where he remained until 1875, when he united with the church in Cape May City, of which he is to-day an elder. He was clerk of the Township Committee and town superintendent of schools. In 1865 he was a member of the Board of Chosen Freeholders, and was its clerk in 1871 and 1872. During the latter year he removed to Cape May City, and was in 1874 elected to the City Council. In 1874 he was appointed judge, and served until 1882, when he was appointed postmaster of Cape May City by President Arthur. He held this position four years. In 1886 he was chosen alderman, and served two years. In

1893 he was appointed again a judge of the courts by Governor Werts, and served until the law was changed in 1896. In politics he is a moderate Republican. He was in private life engaged in mercantile pursuits and the hotel business.

By the State census of 1875 Cape May had a population of 8190, of which 354 were colored persons. The population, according to townshis, was: Upper, 1569; Middle, 2355; Lower, 1480; Dennis, 1585, and Cape May City, 1201.

In 1875 Cape Island was given a new charter by the Legislature, and its name changed to Cape May City. The new charter provided for a mayor, an alderman, and a recorder, elected every two years; nine councilmen for three year terms, three going out of office each year, and a collector of taxes, assessor of taxes, treasurer and overseer of poor, each elected anually. The limit of indebtedness was fixed at $100,000.

Richard D. Edmunds, who served in the Assembly in 1875, was a son of Robert Edmunds, a soldier in the War of 1812. He was born in Lower township in 1814, where he spent his boyhood days. He obtained an education as best he could, and then entered into mercantile pursuits and farming. He served in the Board of Freeholders from Lower township in 1857. In 1862 he was chosen loan commissioner of the county, and held that office for a year, having that autumn been chosen sheriff. He served in that capacity until 1865. Afterwards he removed to Cape Island, and, in 1871, was chosen from there a member of the Board of Freeholders. In 1875 he was elected recorder of Cape May City under its new charter, and served one year. He was a judge of the Court of Common Pleas for some years previous to his death. For fifteen years he was an elder of the Cold Spring Presbyterian Church. He died on October 8, 1879.

In 1875 Sea Grove, now Cape May Point, was founded as a Presbyterian summer resort by Alexander Whilldin, of Philadelphia, and others. The idea of such a place had been in the minds of Mr. Whilldin for some years. The first move towards its founding was the organizing of the West Cape May Land Company, which was chartered by the Legislature in March 8, 1872. The incorporators were Alexander Whilldin, Colonel James Pollock, George H. Stuart, H. R. Wilson, S. A. Mutchmore, Nicholas Murray, James H. Stevens, George W. Hill, G. H. Huddell, J. P. Reznoo, John Wanamaker, Robert J Mercer, Hon. M. Hall Stanton and Joseph Freas, of Philadelphia; Return B. Swain, Franklin Hand, Richard S. Leaming, Thomas Beesley, Downs Edmunds and Virgil M. D. Marcy, of Cape May county, and former United States Senator Alexander G. Cattell, of Camden county. On the 18th of February, 1875, the Sea Grove Association was chartered by the Legislature, with Alexander Whilldin, Dr. V. M. D. Marcy, Downs Edmunds, Dr. J. Newton Walker and John Wanamaker as directors.

Under their supervision Sea Grove was laid out on the most northerly point of the State, and on what was originally known as Stites' Beach. The town prospered for a about fifteen years. A postoffice was established there on March 27, 1876, with Alexander Whilldin Springer, nephew of the above, as postmaster. In 1878 the name of the office was changed to Cape May Point, by which it is still known. Shortly after the town was settled a borough government was established, which lasted until 1894.

Alexander Whilldin was born in Philadelphia in 1808, his father being a Cape May pilot, who was drowned in 1812. The mother and son then came to Cape May and lived here until young Alexander was sixteen years of age. He then became a clerk in a Philadelphia store, and did the chores. Gradually rising in his position, he was, in 1832, able to begin business for himself as a wool merchant. He prospered until he became one of the first men in the financial world of Philadelphia. He was for years president of the American Life Insurance Company. He died in Philadelphia in April 16, 1893.

John Wanamaker, a merchant and philanthropist, of Philadelphia, was born in that city on July 11, 1837. He was educated in the public schools there, and began business in 1861, and now owns the greatest retail establishment in the United States. He has also a large retail store in New

York city. He is a prominent Presbyterian, and in 1857 organized Bethany Sabbath-school, of which he has ever since been superintendent. For many years he was president of the Young Men's Christian Association of Philadelphia. From 1889 to 1893 he was Postmaster-General of the United States under the administration of President Benjamin Harrison. He owns a handsome summer residence at Cape May Point, where he built Beadle Memorial Chapel.

Virgil M. D. Marcy was the son of Dr. Samuel S. Marcy, and was born in Lower township January 5, 1823. At ten years of age he was sent to Connecticut to school, and there prepared for college. At sixteen he was prepared for college, but, being young, waited a year and then entered Yale College, from which he graduated in 1844. He became a member of the Phi Beta Kappa Literary Society. He then returned to Cape May and studied medicine under his father and Dr. Edmund L. B. Wales, of Tuckahoe. In 1846 he received the degree of M. D. from the University of Maryland, at Baltimore. He then settled in Gloucester county, Va., and practiced three years, and then, in 1849, removed to Cold Spring, and took up his father's practice, where he resided until 1876, when he removed to Cape May City. He was a charter member of Cape Island Lodge, F. and A. M., organized in 1866. He became a member of Cold Spring Church in 1840, and has been an elder for thirty-five years. He is a member of the firm of Marcy & Marcy, druggists.

In the summer of 1876 ten commissioners of the Methodist Church South and Methodist Church North met at Cape May City to settle on a basis of fraternal union between the two organizations, which had been divided by the Civil War, and they originated a plan which was subsequently agreed upon by the two bodies.

On June 4, 1875, a company of the State National Guard was organized in Cape May City, which was known as Company H, Sixth Regiment, until it was disbanded in May 16, 1893. Its membership was composed of residents of all parts of the county. The records of the officers of this company are as follows:

LIFE FOLLOWING THE REBELLION. 373

Captains.

George W. Smith—Elected June 4, 1875; commissioned June 22, 1875; promoted major September 21, 1882.

Christopher S. Magrath—Elected October 10, 1882; commissioned January 23, 1883; resigned January 15, 1884; afterwards became adjutant of the regiment.

Edwin P. Clark—Elected April 17, 1884; commissioned May 20, 1884; resigned March 21, 1885.

George W. Reeves—Elected July 18, 1885; commissioned September 22, 1885; resigned February 5, 1889.

Herbert W. Edmunds—Elected March 14, 1889; commissioned April 19, 1889; resigned September 30, 1890.

H. Freeman Douglass—Elected February 9, 1891; commissioned May 2, 1891; retired May 16, 1893.

First Lieutenants.

Christopher S. Magrath—Elected June 4, 1875; commissioned June 22, 1875; elected captain October 10, 1882.

William Farrow—Elected October 10, 1882; commissioned January 23, 1883; resigned April 24, 1884.

James T. Bailey—Elected July 4, 1884; commissioned August 5, 1884; resigned March 21, 1885.

Robert C. Hill—Elected July 18, 1885; commissioned September 22, 1885; resigned January 24, 1888.

Herbert W. Edmunds—Elected March 26, 1888; commissioned April 24, 1888; elected captain March 14, 1889.

H. Freeman Douglass—Elected April 13, 1889; commissioned August 20, 1889; elected captain February 9, 1891.

James T. Bailey—Elected February 9, 1891; commissioned May 2, 1891; retired May 16, 1893.

Second Lieutenants.

John Henry Farrow—Elected June 4, 1875; commissioned June 22, 1875; resigned December 25, 1877.

William Farrow—Elected February 4, 1878; commissioned May 2, 1878; elected first lieutenant October 10, 1882.

Edwin P. Clark—Elected October 10, 1882; commissioned January 23, 1883; elected captain April 17, 1884.

Charles G. Clark—Elected April 17, 1884; commissioned May 20, 1884; resigned March 21, 1885.

James T. Bailey—Elected March 24, 1886; commissioned April 29, 1886; elected first lieutenant February 9, 1891.

William F. Williams—Elected February 9, 1891; commissioned May 2, 1891; retired May 16, 1893.

CHAPTER XXVII.
FIFTEEN YEARS OF PROSPERITY.

In 1876 William Doolittle, of Ocean View; W. V. L. Seigman, of Cape May City; Dr. John Wiley, of Court House, and Downs Edmunds, of Lower township, were appointed by the State Centennial Commission as a local committee to gather agricultural and horticultural specimens from Cape May county for exhibition at the Centennial Exposition, held that year in Philadelphia. They asked the Board of Freeholders for one hundred dollars, with which to accomplish their purpose. It was refused, and Cape May was, therefore, not represented officially.

In 1876, '77 and '78 William T. Stevens, of Cape May City, was the member of the Assembly. He was born in Lower township on November 13, 1841, and was a great grandson of Henry Stevens and of Henry Young Townsend, both captains in the Revolution, and a grandson of Joshua Townsend, lieutenant in the War of 1812, and afterwards a member of both branches of the Legislature. He obtained his education in the public schools and under Rev. Moses Williamson and James R. Hughes. He served in Company F, Twenty-fifth Regiment, during the Civil War, and, after being mustered out, as a recruiting officer. Having learned the carpenter's trade, he was employed after the war in the rebuilding of light houses in the South. In 1871 and '72, and again from 1886 to 1892, he was a member of the City Council of Cape May City. In 1888 he was president of the body. He was a member of the Board of Freeholders from 1893 to 1896, and was chosen in 1897 for an additional term of three years. He has been building inspector of Cape May City for two years. In politics he has always been a Republican. He is a deacon of the Baptist Church, with which he united when a young man.

In 1877 William Hildreth, of Court House, was appointed

surrogate to succeed Dr. Jonathan F. Leaming, who resigned. He was that year elected for five years, and has been three times re-elected, holding the office at the present time. He is a son of Joshua Hildreth, who was born in 1774 and died in 1859, and who was a judge of the Court of Common Pleas. Surrogate Hildreth is also a grandson of John Dickinson, colonel of the Cape May regiment in the War of 1812. He was born at Court House on June 10, 1828. He was first chosen assessor of Middle township.

WILLIAM T. STEVENS.

On March 26, 1878, a part of Maurice River township was set over into Cape May county by act of the Legislature. The new boundaries were as follows: Beginning at a stone on the old Cape road, on the division line between Cape May and Cumberland, thence along the several courses of the said Cape Road to the intersection with the Dorchester and Estelleville road. Following that highway to the Cumberland and Tuckahoe road, the line ran thence along said road to a point on Hunter's Mill Dam in the Cumberland and Atlantic line, thence along the latter line to the terminus of the present Cumberland and Cape May line, thence to beginning. This land was made a part of Upper township.

In 1879 Ocean City, on Peck's Beach, the most northerly in Cape May county, was founded by three brothers, Samuel Wesley Lake, James E. Lake and Ezra B. Lake, all ministers of the Methodist Episcopal Church. During that summer, while sailing across Great Egg Harbor Bay, they conceived the idea of selecting the place as a Methodist and temperance resort. In October, that year, the Ocean City Association was formed. In February following, William Lake, another brother, made survey, and in May an auction was held. The next year a postoffice was established there, with Rev. W. H. Burrell as postmaster.

In 1877 William H. Benezet, of Court House, was chosen sheriff, serving three years. In 1883 he was again elected sheriff, and served as such until he died, in 1886. He was a descendant of Anthony Benezet, the famous Philadelphia philanthropist, who lived there before the Revolution. He was born at Court House on March 27, 1841, where he obtained his education. He was apprenticed to a carriage builder and learned that trade. He afterwards became a shoe merchant at Court House. After his second election as sheriff he removed to Cape May City, and opened a shoe store there. He died August 10, 1886, at Cape May City.

By the census of 1880 the population of the county was 9765, of which 570 were colored persons. The number of males living in the county over twenty-one years of age were: Native white, 2465; foreign white, 101; colored, 144. The population was divided among the political divisions as follows: Cape May City, 1699; Cape May Point, 198; Dennis township, 1812; Lower, 1779; Middle, 2575, and Upper, 1702. The population of the villages reported were: Court House, 570; Dyers (Dias Creek), 356; Goshen, 464; Green Creek, 362; Mayville, 273; Rio Grande, 241; Townsend Inlet, 309.

Waters Burrows Miller, who was State Senator from 1880 to 1886, and was the ninth and eleventh mayor of Cape Island, was born in Gloucester county, N. J., in 1824, and, when eleven years of age, his father, Jonas Miller, a prominent hotel man of his day, and who, as proprietor of Congress Hall, entertained President Buchanan when that distinguished official visited Cape May, moved with his family to Cape Island, where young "Burr," as he was familiarly called, grew up. Miller, as soon as he was old enough, began his life as a partner with his father in the management of Congress Hall, which was a most famous place in its day, being known in almost every part of America. His sister, Miss Pauline, married Jacob Frank Cake, who afterward became famous as a Congress Hall and Stockton Ho-

WATERS B. MILLER.

tel proprietor, who entertained both Grant and Arthur, and numerous Cabinet officers and statesmen. After Mr. Cake's death Mrs. Cake continued to manage Congress Hall.

When the city of Cape Island was made a municipality, he was elected at its first election, in March, 1851, the first alderman of the city, and for the forty years succeeding was one of the foremost citizens, not only of the city, but of the county and State.

FIFTEEN YEARS OF PROSPERITY.

In the fall of 1852 Mr. Miller was elected a member of the New Jersey Assembly, and served in the seventy-seventh Legislature. In 1854 the people of this city elected him a member of the Board of Chosen Freeholders, and he was successively re-elected in 1855, 1856, 1857, 1858, 1859, 1860 and 1861, and, after being out a year, was again elected to the same office in 1863. In 1865 he was elected a member of the City Council for one year, and again made a member of the Board of Freeholders in 1866 and 1868.

In March, 1869, he was elected mayor of the city for a term of two years. In 1871 he was a candidate for the office, but was defeated by Mayor Joseph Ware by a few votes, two other candidates, Messrs. Richard R. Thompson and Joseph Q. Williams, being in the field and dividing the vote. But in 1873 Mr. Miller was again a candidate and elected for a two-year term. He was again, in 1878 and 1879, made a member of the Board of Freeholders. He was a leading Democrat of the county, and was a power in politics. He tried five times to get into the State Senate, being successful twice. He made his first trial in 1855, and was defeated by Jesse Diverty, Know Nothing, afterwards a leading Democrat and judge of the county courts. He tried for the place again in 1873, and was defeated by Senator Richard S. Leaming. Not discouraged, he was again made the Democratic nominee in 1879, and was successful, defeating his former opponent, Senator Leaming, being the second Democrat elected to the Senate from the county. He was re-elected in 1882 for three more years. In 1891 he was defeated in the convention by one vote by Lemuel E. Miller, who was elected.

When the Cape May and Millville Railroad, now the West Jersey, was being built to Cape May, its projection seemed to be a failure, when, by mortgaging his property, he aided materially in its completion to this city.

In 1886 he was the originator of the first electric light company in this county. He was largely instrumental in the securing of the Cape May City charter of 1875. He was postmaster of Cape May City from March 12 to April 16, in 1886.

He has three sons, Richard T. Miller, appellate judge of the New Jersey Supreme Court; Jonas S. Miller, prosecutor of the pleas in Cape May county, and Lafayette Miller. He died at Cape May in September, 1892.

Richard T. Miller, his son, was born in Cape May City December 16, 1845. He studied law with Thomas P. Carpenter, then a justice of the Supreme Court of New Jersey. He was admitted to the bar as an attorney in 1867 and as counsellor in 1870. He was city solicitor of Cape May in 1869 and 1870, and again from 1890 to 1893. He was district court judge of Camden city from March 3, 1877, to July 11, 1888, and was prosecutor of the pleas for Cape May county from 1889 to 1892. On April 1, 1892, he was made president judge of the Camden County Common Pleas and resigned from that position on March 11, 1893, to go on the Circuit Court bench of the New Jersey Supreme Court, to which he had been appointed by Governor Werts for a term of seven years, which will expire in 1900. In politics he is a Democrat.

Jesse D. Ludlam, who was elected Assemblyman in 1879, and who served in the Assembly in 1880, 1883, 1884 and 1885, was a grandson of Henry Swain, who, with Joshua Swain, patented the centre-board in 1811. He was born at Dennisville, February 28, 1840. He was educated in the public schools and at Pennington Seminary. He was for ten years a member of the Dennis Township Committee, and for five years its chairman. He was a member of the Board of Freeholders from Dennis township from 1881 to 1884. He served for many years on the School Board. He is engaged in farming and in selling and shipping cedar. In 1890 Governor Abbett appointed him a judge of the Court of Common Pleas, and he served as such until 1896, when the law was passed reducing the number to one law judge. In politics he is a Democrat.

Remington Corson, of South Seaville, was sheriff from 1880 to 1883, was born about 1846 and died at his home at South Seaville on April 21, 1894, aged 48 years. He held township offices and postmaster at South Seaville, where he was a leading merchant from 1867 to 1881, and from 1889 to 1893. He was a member of Calvary Baptist Church. His father, Baker Corson, also postmaster from 1881 to 1885, died one day before Remington—on April 20, 1894, aged 78 years. He was for forty years a member of Calvary Baptist Church. He was formerly a sea captain and merchant.

The third newspaper established in the county was the "Cape May County Gazette," which was printed at Cape May Court House. The first number appeared on March 6, 1880. It was and still remains a weekly. The first issue contained four pages, each 15 by 21 inches. It was issued

ALFRED COOPER.

by Alfred Cooper, who is still its publisher. Alfred Cooper is a son of George B. Cooper, of Cumberland county, who was a clerk of the New Jersey Assembly in 1865 and 1866. He was born at Kinderhook, N. Y., September 6, 1859. He obtained his education in Millville, N. J.; Valatia, N. Y., and at Pierce's Business College, Philadelphia. After graduating he learned the printer's trade at Millville, where he remained until establishing the "Gazette." Since 1890 he has been on the Count Board of Elections. In politics he is a Republican.

On January 3, 1881, Thaddeus Van Gilder, of Petersburg,

died. He was one of the most noted merchants in the county. He was born April 6, 1830. He conducted a ship-building business and had hundreds of men chopping and shipping wood.

During the session of our Legislature of 1881 a bill was passed entitled "An act to encourage the manufacture of sugar in the State of New Jersey." This act provided that a bounty of one dollar per ton could be paid by the State to the farmer for each ton of material out of which crystallized cane sugar was actually obtained; it provided also a bounty of one cent per pound to the manufacturer for each pound of cane sugar made from such materials. After the passage of this act, the Senate requested the Agricultural College to experiment on the sorghum plant in order to further its cultivation by the farmers of this State.

Mr. Hilgert, an enterprising business man of Philadelphia, member of the firm J. Hilgert's Sons, sugar refiners, built and fitted up an extensive sugar house at an expense of at least $60,000 at Rio Grande. This house during the first fall worked the cane of about 700 acres. The product of crystallized sugar was sold to refiners at seven and eight cents per pound. The yield, though not as large as expected, was regarded as satisfactory. The farmers of that section who calculated on an average yield of ten tons of cane and thirty bushels of seed were disappointed, the average yield per acre being about five tons of cane and twenty bushels of seed, which sold readily for sixty-five cents per bushel. Lemuel E. Miller, who was perhaps the largest cane grower on the cape, raised, on 120 acres, 641 tons of cane and 2500 bushels of seed. The total amount realized by him is reported to be $3648. The cost of growing this crop is not known at present, but the reported cost for Iowa in the year 1873, is, exclusive of fertilizers, $12.50 per acre.

The bounties offered for the production of sorghum cane and sugar encouraged the Rio Grande Sugar Company, which had succeeded the Hilgerts, to invest large sums, and in the purchase of lands upon which to grow sugar cane. This enterprise was continued until 1885. Good crops were grown and much sugar made. The difficulties in establishing a new business was fairly overcome. The ruinously low prices of sugar in the latter years, however, took away all chances of profit in a mill which, at the best, could express only half the sugar in the cane. The process of diffusion, or soaking out the sugar by water, was tried upon a large scale, but difficulties incident to a new business delayed the realization of the hopes of the company, and work by the Rio Grande Sugar Company ended with 1886. The bounties offered by the State ended with 1885. The whole amount of bounties paid to encourage this industry was $43,723.

Henry A. Hughes, of Cape May City, who had been the superintendent of the works from the beginning, and who was largely interested in overcoming the difficulties experienced in the above enterprise, at the beginning of 1887 organized the Hughes Sugar Company, and, with the assistance of the United States Department of Agriculture, built and equipped a small sugar house, to work fifteen or twenty tons of cane per day. The machinery in the house was mainly of his own invention, and included machines for topping, stripping and shredding the cane, and for extracting the sugar by diffusion. The results of the work in 1887 were, in many respects, satisfactory, and the experience gained showed where and how many savings of time, labor and expense could be made.

At the beginning of 1888 numerous changes were planned so as to produce effective work, and a large sum of money was appropriated by the New Jersey Agricultural Experiment Station to carry them into operation. But these plans for the expenditure of the money were not carried through.

The United States Government latterly assisted, but in 1890 the attempt to raise sorghum cane was abandoned.

Henry A. Hughes was a grandson of Captain Humphrey Hughes, of the War of 1812. He was for years an employe of Edward C. Knight in the Philadelphia Sugar Refinery.

Rev. Edward Patrick Shields was appointed county superintendent of public schools in 1881 to succeed Dr. Maurice Beesley, who had resigned.

Edward Patrick Shields, D. D., was born August 31, 1833, at New Albany, Ind., and was the third son of Henry B. and Jeanna D. Shields. He joined the Presbyterian Church there on profession of faith in 1849, in the sixteenth year of his age. He received an academical training at New Albany in an eight years' course of superior schooling in the classical institute. From 1848 he was employed in a wholesale hardware store in Louisville, Ky., remaining three years. He graduated at Miami University, at Oxford, O., in 1854, during the presidency of Rev. William C. Anderson, D. D.

He then took a three years' course (1854-57) in the New Albany Theological Seminary, now the McCormick Seminary, at Chicago, Ill. Another year was added in theology with the class which graduated at Princeton Theological Seminary in April, 1858. He served as a stated supply of the Presbyterian Church at Bloomington, Ind., in 1856, while his studies at New Albany were in progress. He was ordained a minister of the gospel in the Presbyterian denomination by the Presbytery of West Jersey, at Pittsgrove, N. J., June 2, 1858. He was settled over the church there from 1858 to 1870. During this time a very handsome brick church was erected by the congregation at a cost of $25,000. He removed on January 1, 1871, to Cape May City, and was installed pastor over the Presbyterian Church, where he remained until March 1, 1884, the longest pastorate in the history of the county of Cape May, with the exception of the very long pastorate of Rev. Moses Williamson, at Cold Spring, viz., forty-six years.

He was called to the pastorate of the Presbyterian Church at Bristol, Pa., being installed May 1, 1884, where he remained until 1897, when he resigned. His three pastorates averaged thirteen years. He received the honorary degree of D. D. from Miami University, his alma mater, in 1887.

He served a full three years' term as superintendent of public instruction in Cape May county from 1881 to 1884, by appointment of the State Board of Education. His removal to Pennsylvania required a change in the office.

Furman L. Richardson, who served in the Assembly from 1881 to 1883, was born in Middle township February 23, 1842. He is a grandson of Aaron Leaming, who was sheriff of the county from 1812 to 1815. He attended the public schools at Rio Grande. In 187- he entered into the grocery and provision business with J. Henry Farrow under the firm name of Richardson & Farrow, which continued until Mr. Farrow died, in 1883. He served in the Cape May City Council in 1875 and 1876, and was treasurer in 1879 and 1880. After serving in the Assembly in 1881 and 1882, he was sergeant-at-arms of the State Senate in 1887 and 1888. In 1889 he was appointed postmaster of Cape May City and served five years. He has for several years past conducted summer hotels. In politics he is a Republican.

The fourth newspaper, a weekly, established in Cape May county was the" Ocean City Sentinel," first issued at Ocean City on April 21, 1881, by W. H. Boyle & Bros. In 1885 this paper was purchased by R. Curtis Robinson and W. H. Fenton, but a couple of years later Mr. Robinson purchased Mr. Fenton's interest and has since been sole proprietor.

R. Curtis Robinson was born in Atlantic county in 1862. At sixteen years of age he entered a wholesale dry goods house in Philadelphia. Finding this distasteful, he engaged to learn the printing business in the "Banner" office, Beverly, N. J. Shortly after he became connected with the "Atlantic Review," of Atlantic City, where he remained six years. During this time he was also editor of the "May's Landing Record" and associate editor of the Philadelphia publication, "Over the Mountains and Down by the Sea." In 1885 he removed to Ocean City. In 1888 he was a member of the Board of Freeholders from Ocean City. He was postmaster there from 1889 to 1893.

In 1882 the town of Sea Isle City, on Ludlam's Beach, which had been founded by Charles K. Landis, had grown large enough to have a post-office established there on June 20, with George Whitney as postmaster. In 1883 another postoffice was established at Anglesea, a new town on the north end of Five-Mile Beach. A week later an office was established at Holly Beach, which had been founded on the south end of the same beach.

President Arthur visited Cape May City in the Summer of 1883. With a party of friends, he arrived at the steamboat landing at Cape May Point on Monday, July 23, at 11 o'clock in the morning. He had come there on the government steamer "Dispatch." He was received there by United States Marshal McMichael, of Washington; Colonel Henry W. Sawyer and J. Frank Cake, proprietor of the Stockton Hotel. They were conveyed by carriage along the ocean front to the hotel, where, as they entered, Simon Hassler's orchestra and the Weccacoe Band played "Hail to the Chief." In the afternoon the President was driven over the town. In the evening a reception was given to Mayor Melvin and Council, followed by a banquet and ball at the Stockton, in honor of the President. At 9 o'clock President Arthur appeared, with United States Marshals William H. Kern, of Philadelphia, and McMichael, of Washington, leading the way. During the evening President Arthur shook the hands of over 2500 persons.

The President left about 12 o'clock at night, amid a grand display of fireworks, and was rowed through the billows in the surfboat, manned by the crew of Life Saving Station No. 39, to the "Dispatch," which had then steamed around in front of the city.

In 1884 West Cape May was created a borough out of Lower township, and has remained a political division ever since. In 1885 Holly Beach, on the south end of Five-Mile Beach, and Anglesea, on the north end of the same beach, were made boroughs.

In 1884 Vincent O. Miller, of Dennisville, was appointed County Superintendent of Public Instruction, to succeed Rev. Edward P. Shields. He was born at Goshen on May 5, 1852. He attended the public schools at Goshen and at Bridgeton, N. J., finishing his education at Fort Edward Collegiate Institute, Fort Edwards, N. Y., in 1870. He taught in the public schools of Cape May county for sixteen years. On June 26, 1883, he was appointed county superintendent, and held that position until September 29, 1896. He also held other local offices. He is engaged at present in manufacturing fertilizers and in sawing and selling cedar lumber.

By the census of 1885 there were 10,744 persons living in the county, of which 9856 were white natives, 591 colored and 297 white foreign born. The population of the political divisions of the county were as follows:

Cape May City, 1610; Cape May Point, 200; Dennis township, 1770; Holly Beach, 210; Lower township, 1208; Middle township, 2605; Ocean City, 465; Sea Isle City, 558; Upper township, 1500: West Cape May, 618. The villages had the following number of residents: Ocean View, 191; South Seaville, 408; North Dennisville, 487; South Dennis, 308; East Creek, 111, and West Creek, 175.

In 1885 the Cape May County Medical Society was organized, and during the same year West Cape May was created a borough out of Lower township.

During this year Ludlam's Beach Lighthouse was built at Sea Isle City, its latitude being 39°09′42″ north, and longitude 74°41′05″ west from Washington. The light flashes white every quarter minute, and is of the fourth order. The light stands 36 feet above mean high water, and is visible a distance of $11\frac{1}{4}$ miles.

Joseph H. Hanes, who was elected Senator in the fall of 1885, was born at Woodstown, Salem county, on September 20, 1845. He learned the blacksmith trade when young and subsequently became a successful contractor. He served nine years in the Cape May City Council, from 1878, and was president of that body during the first three years of his service. He served in the Senate during the sessions of 1886, 1887 and 1888. In 1895 he was again elected to Council for three years, but resigned after a month's service, owing to the pressure of his private business. In politics he is a Republican.

Alvin P.. Hildreth, who this same year was elected to the Assembly, was born at Cold Spring, June 13, 1830. He attended the public schools, and then attended a private academy in Central Pennsylvania, and during the years 1846-7 and 1847-8 was a student in Yale College. Owing to ill health he returned home and subsequently taught school. In private life he was connected with many large hotels afterwards in Cape May, Philadelphia and Washington. He was city clerk of Cape Island in 1856 and 1857 and served in the City Council from 1859 to 1863. He was assessor from 1859 to 1873, and a member of the Board of Freeholders from Cape May City from 1880 to

1886. He served in the Assembly in the sessions of 1886 and 1887. He was appointed a Riparian Commissioner of the State in 1892 and served two years. For several years he has been a member of the Democratic State Committee.

In 1886 the fifth newspaper established in the county was the "Cape May County Times," published by Thomas E. Ludlam, at Sea Isle City. It contained four pages, size 15x 21 inches. He continues to be its publisher. Thomas E. Ludlam was born at Dennisville, on January 30, 1855. He obtained his education there. For eight years he taught

THOMAS E. LUDLAM.

school in different sections of the county, and then removed to Sea Isle City, and at its first election, in 1882, was made a member of the Board of Freeholders. He was six years agent of the West Jersey Railroad at Sea Isle City, and from 1884 to 1896 Mayor of the borough. He was interested in the formation of the M. E. Church there and has for a number of years been on the Board of Education, being now its president. As a real estate dealer he was largely instrumental in the development of Sea Isle City. He is a director of the South Jersey Railroad.

In 1886 postoffices were established at Burleigh (formerly Mayville), and at Clermont.

The valuation of real and personal property as assessed in the county in 1887 was as follows: Upper, $456,740; Dennis, $416,215; Middle, $614,125; Lower, $259,850; Cape May City, $1,700,000; Cape May Point, $200,000; West Cape May, $133,430; Anglesea, $150,000; Sea Isle City, $237,365; Ocean City, $200,073; Holly Beach, $175,000; total, $4,542,798.

On July 9, 1888, a postoffice was established at Avalon, a newly laid-out town on the north end of Seven-Mile Beach, and in September, 1889, one established at the new town of Wildwood on the centre portion of Five-Mile Beach. In June, 1890, the office at Marmora was opened.

On September 5, 1888, the people voted upon the question of "local option," or for and against the granting license for the sale of liquor as a beverage. The following townships and boroughs voted for granting licenses: Sea Isle City, Cape May City, Holly Beach, Anglesea, Middle, Upper and Lower. Those voting against were: West Cape May, Ocean City, Dennis and Cape May Point. The combined majority in the county for license was 222. This was the only time in the history of the county when the question was decided by ballot.

The 175th anniversary of the founding of the Cold Spring Presbyterian Church was celebrated in 1889. Rev. Daniel L. Hughes, D. D., read the historical address.

In 1888 Dr. Walter S. Leaming was elected State Senator. He is a son of Dr. Jonathan F. Leaming, who twice had been State Senator. He was born at Seaville on March 4, 1854, and there passed his boyhood days. For a time he was a law clerk in New York city. In 1867 his father removed to Court House. After that time the Doctor attended the Mayville Academy. He entered the Pennsylvania College of Dental Surgery in 1876, graduating two years later with honors. Later on he entered Jefferson Medical College, Philadelphia, and was graduated as M. D. in 1881. He became a partner of his father and remained so until moving to Cape May City in 1891, where he still practices dentistry. In 1887 he was elected to the Assembly and served in the session of 1888.

It was during this session of the House that in a speech, ably made, he broke the then prevailing political Republican combination, and succeeded in electing Colonel Henry W. Sawyer Sinking Funk Commissioner of the State.

That year he was chosen Senator, and served three years in the upper house. In 1891 he was the Republican caucus nominee for President of the Senate, receiving the full Re-

DR. WALTER S. LEAMING.

publican vote. In 1895 he was elected a member of the Cape May City Council for three years, during all of which time he was president of the body. In politics he is a Republican, and in religion a Baptist.

Eugene Conrad Cole, who was Assemblyman in the sessions of 1889, 1890, and 1891, was born at Seaville, June 23, 1851. He was of Revolutionary stock, and his ancestors were Massachusetts people, and was also a direct maternal descendant of Henry Young, surrogate and surveyor-general of the county in the last century. He was educated in the public schools, and studied military tactics at West Point in 1869. In 1871 he began teaching school, and taught until about 1894. He was for years up to 1897 a county examiner. He was admitted to the bar in 1886. He was Coroner of the county from 1881 to 1884, and was a Justice of the Peace for several years. In politics he is a Republican, but not a partisan, and one in whom men of every party have confidence.

Charles E. Nichols, of Court House, who was Sheriff from 1889 to 1893, was born at Kingston, New Hampshire, on August 27, 1849. His forefathers fought in the Revolution. For a time he attended school there, and later at Oswego, New York. For two years he was a drug clerk in the latter place. In 1865, when sixteen, he came to Cape

EUGENE C. COLE.

May Court House, where he has since resided. He completed his education at Mayville Academy. In 1885 he was appointed postmaster by President Cleveland, and served until 1889, when he was elected Sheriff. In 1893 he was again appointed postmaster by President Cleveland. He has been a Justice of the Peace for several years. He is a Democrat politically. For thirty-two years he has been a member of the Baptist Church, twelve years of which time he has been a teacher in the Sunday school.

The condition of the county in 1890 was prosperous. Its total debt was $7000, which had been incurred three years before in the building of a new almshouse, which cost $10,000. The population of the county was 11,268, divided as follows: Anglesea, 161; Cape May City, 2136; Cape May Point, 167; Dennis township, 1707; Holly Beach, 217; Lower, 1156; Middle, 2368; Ocean City, 452; Sea Isle City, 766; Upper, 1381; West Cape May, 757. The number of farms were 505; area of farms, 47,066 acres; area of improved land, 26,491 acres; unimproved, 20,575 acres; value of farms, including lands, fences and buildings, $1,312,530; value of implements and machinery, $68,330; value of live stock, $141,580; value of farm products, $235,800.

In June, 1890, the "Five-Mile Beach Journal," at Wildwood, was first printed by Samuel P. Foster. It contained four pages of six columns each. Mr. Foster published it until the autumn of 1895, when it was sold to Jedediah Du Bois, who continues to publish it.

CHAPTER XXVIII.
DISTINGUISHED VISITORS.

Soon after Cape May Point was established, John Wanamaker, of Philadelphia, bought property there and erected a summer residence. When President Harrison was inaugurated, he appointed Mr. Wanamaker his Postmaster-General. They became warm friends. During a few weeks in June, 1889, Mrs. Harrison and the family were guests of the Wanamaker cottage, and liking Cape May well, she so expressed herself. The President also paid one visit. During the winter of 1889-1890 the friends of the President built a handsome $10,000 summer cottage, and through Postmaster-General Wanamaker and William V. McKean, editor of the Philadelphia "Public Ledger," presented the cottage to Mrs. President Harrison, by handing her the deed and keys in the White House, at Washington, on June 6, 1890. In three weeks the family took possession, where they resided from June 20 until August 28. The President passed about four weeks of the season with his family.

Hon. James G. Blaine, the Secretary of State of Presidents Garfield and Harrison, visited the Cape during the summer. General William Tecumseh Sherman visited his daughter, who resided in a Columbia avenue cottage.

On the 24th of August, that day being Sunday, the President, accompanied by Mrs. Harrison and Mrs. Dimmick, his wife's niece, who afterwards became the second Mrs. Harrison, visited the Cold Spring Church for worship. While on their way home, Coachman William Turner, who had grown up in the neighborhood, was directed to drive by the cottage of "Uncle Dan" and "Aunt Judy" Kelly, on the "thunpike," in Lower township, to whom the attention of Mrs. Harrison had been drawn by a photograph she had seen of the aged couple, and the vine clad cottage in which they had lived for years. Through Mrs. Harrison the President became interested, and that occasion was taken for viewing it.

The carriage drove up to the garden gate and the President alighted and entered. Aunt Judy, who was asleep inside the cottage, was aroused, and President Harrison requested a drink of water, which was furnished clear and cool from the depths of the old well, and which was drawn up by the "old oaken bucket," hung upon a rope. As he stood drinking Judy's bright eyes watched him closely. As he finished he remarked, "I have a photograph of you and your husband."

"What might you name be?" asked Judy.

"I am General Harrison," replied the President.

"The saints be praised," cried Judy. "I have lived to see a President and talk to him. Dan'l! Dan'l! Coom out here, old man. Sure an the President has coom to us."

The old man, who was a cripple, hobbled out, and, dropping his hat, seemed too awe-struck at the great honor to talk. Judy, however, had her tongue wagging, and, turning to the President, said:

"Sure if you have my picter, can't I have one of yourn?"

"I have no picture of myself with me," answered the President. "But," and his eyes twinkled as he felt in his pocket, and drawing something therefrom, which he handed to Judy, "this is the picture of another President."

Judy's hand closed over the gift, and she grasped the President's hand, shouting her thanks as he moved toward his carriage, which he entered with a farewell, lifting his hat, and was whirled out of sight.

Only then did Judy stop to look at what had been given her, and her surprise and delight can be imagined when she discovered a new and crisp five-dollar bill, containing the likeness of President Jackson.

During the summer of 1891 President Harrison and family again passed the season at Cape May Point, while the President established his executive office at Congress Hall, in Cape May, which was open from July 3 until September 15.

The President and family came on July 3 to their cottage, but the President himself did not remain there all the season. From August 18 to 29 he was away at Saratoga, N. Y. In the season of 1892 the family did not come to Cape May Point. That fall Mrs. Harrison died. During the summer of 1893 General Harrison, who had on the 4th of March preceding retired from the Presidential chair, passed part of his summer at the cottage. In 1896 he disposed of the cottage to a Philadelphian.

In the fall of 1889 Edward L. Rice, son of Leaming M. Rice, who had previously been State Senator, was elected county clerk, to succeed Jonathan Hand, after fifty years of service. Edward L. Rice was born at Dennisville on January 25, 1864. He attended school at Dennisville and at Rutgers College, New Brunswick, N. J. Before he entered college and before reaching his eighteenth year he began teaching school. When elected clerk he was principal of the Cape May City School. He is a natural orator, and has written some poetry. In 1894 he was chosen by the people for another term of five years. In politics he is a Democrat.

The Jewish colony at Woodbine was founded in 1891. It was early in the spring of that year that the American trustees of the Baron Hirsch Fund closed negotiations by purchasing 5100 acres of land in and around Woodbine from Mr. John M. Moore, the Clayton, N. J., glass manufacturer, for $39,000. Before the purchase was completed the titles were searched back to the days of the "West Jersey Society."

In April, 1891, work was commenced at the colony. A number of small dwelling houses were erected for the accommodation of the men who came to the place to clear the land and build homes. A survey of the land was made and sixty-two farms of thirty acres each were laid out. These farms are now occupied by as many families. They were sold to the settlers on terms which were extremely liberal, and yet not calculated to make the buyers entirely dependent. By the terms of purchase the refugees upon their arrival in this country were brought direct to Woodbine and placed on their farms, which were thirty acres each in extent.

In August the colony was settled. To every family were

allotted a neat house, barn and all necessary outbuildings; one cow, twenty-five chickens, farming implements and seeds.

Ten acres of the thirty were cleared and ploughed and sown with rye or wheat. For the farm complete, the trustees asked $1200, the cost price. Every settler was given ten years' time in which to pay for his purchase, and in order to give him a start, the fund only required the interest on the principal to be paid during the first three years. After that time the purchase price was to be paid off in yearly payments.

Immediately after the founding of the colony a large number of refugees were brought to the colony and employed in the large cloak factory the trustees had erected.

During the summer of 1892 the crops were very large and farming proved a success far beyond all expectations. The town site was laid out near the depot and within six months thirty-five new houses, costing over $50,000, were built and occupied by those who worked in the cloak factory. A new factory for the manufacture of trousers was completed and the two industries gave employment to over five hundred people.

The management of the colony devolved upon Professor H. L. Sabsovich, who is yet superintendent. Professor Sabsovich is a native of Southern Russia and is about forty-seven years of age. His title comes from the "Agricultural College of Russia," of which institute he is a graduate. In 1888 he left Russia on account of aggressive laws with his family and came to New York. Shortly after arriving in America he accepted a position as professor of chemistry in the Colorado State Experimental College, at Denver, where he remained until he came to Woodbine to superintend the newly-established colony. Within a year nearly seven hundred persons settled there.

In 1891 the Legislature again passed an act changing Cape May's boundary line, by adding a portion of Maurice River township, in Cumberland township, to Dennis township. It was during this year that Avalon became a borough.

The first woman physician to settle in Cape May county

was Anna M. Hand, who began the practice of medicine in Cape May City in January, 1892. She was of Revolutionary stock, having had maternal and paternal ancestors in the Revolution. Dr. Hand was born near Cape May Court House, where she obtained her education in the public schools and with private teachers. This was supplemented by two years of study in the New Jersey State Normal School. After graduating she taught school for seven years in Eastern Pennsylvania. The idea of studying medicine then took hold of her, and she matriculated in the Women's

DR. ANNA M. HAND.

Medical College, Philadelphia, in 1886, and took an extended or four years' course. Afterwards she took a post graduate course in the Philadelphia Polyclinic. Her career of preparation was concluded with nearly two years more of practical experience in the Maternity Hospital and Nurse School, of Philadelphia. She then settled at Cape May City and acquired a large practice.

The first move towards establishing a second railroad through Cape May county was by Logan M. Bullitt, of Philadelphia, and James E. Taylor, of Cape May City. They secured an agreement with the Central Railroad of New Jersey, the Atlantic City Railroad Company and Vineland Railroad Company to operate a proposed road in connection with these companies. On January 14, 1893, a public meeting was held in Hand's Hall, Cape May, which was presided over by James M. E. Hildreth. At that meeting $5300 was subscribed toward the project. The road was built from Winslow Junction in Camden county to Sea Isle City, and the first train ran there on July 27, 1893. The next day a regular train service was established.

On June 23, 1894, the road having been completed from Tuckahoe to Cape May, the first train arrived with a large party of invited guests, and a public holiday was the consequence. In July regular service was established. The road's projectors had had many financial difficulties. It was first known as the Philadelphia and Seashore Railroad, and afterwards reorganized as the South Jersey Railroad. On August 22 a receiver was appointed for the road, who still manages it. The officers of the company at the time of the appointment of the receiver were: William S. Fox, president; Logan M. Bullitt, vice-president; Thomas H. Willson, secretary; Thomas Robb, James E. Taylor, Charles K. Landis, J. H. Wheeler, James M. E. Hildreth, Morris Boney, Thomas E. Ludlam, John Halpin, H. W. Sawyer, Edward A. Tennis, Dr. James Mecray and Dr. V. M. D. Marcy.

Logan M. Bullitt is a son of John C. Bullitt, of Philadelphia, a large land holder of Cape May. He was born in Philadelphia in 1863, and was graduated from the University of Pennsylvania in 1883. After graduating he was appointed superintendent of Dunbar Furnace Company, Dunbar, Pa. In 1884 he became manager of the Northern Pacific Coal Company and remained in Dakota and Montana until 1888. In 1889 he was admitted to the Philadelphia bar.

James E. Taylor was born in Cape May, and after obtaining an education he studied civil engineering. He was at one time head of the contracting department of the Edison Electric Company, New York city. In 1888 and 1889 he was collector of Cape May city.

Lemuel E. Miller, who was State Senator from 1892 to 1895, was born at Green Creek, August 1, 1854, and was a son of Aaron Miller, one time Sheriff. When fifteen his father died and he was left to care for himself. He became a gneral contractor, doing work in all parts of the country, such as building railroads, bulwarks, etc. He served in the Cape May City Council from 1875 to 1878, and in 1876 was the president of the council.

On the fourth of July, 1893, the celebration was participated in by ex-President Benjamin Harrison, who made the principal address from the piazza of the Stockton Hotel, Cape May City. Those who took part in celebration were Mayor James M. E. Hildreth; General William J. Sewell,

COUNTY PRISON, BUILT IN 1894.

of Camden; Congressman John E. Reyburn, of Philadelphia; Hood Gilpin, Esq., of Philadelphia, and Rev. James N. Cockius, pastor of the Presbyterian Church.

The one hundred and eighty-second anniversary of the founding of the First Baptist Church of Cape May was held at Cape May Court House on June 16, 17, 18, 19, 20 and 21, 1894.

In 1894 South Cape May was created a borough out of West Cape May.

The first hanging which ever took place in Cape May county was that of the murderer Richard Pierce, a colored man, of Goshen, aged about 24. The hanging took place in the court house yard on the afternoon of July 13, 1894. Sheriff Robert E. Hand was in charge of the execution. Pierce had killed his wife on February 19.

In 1894 the present county prison was erected.

By the census of 1895, the school property in the county was valued at $64,000; public property, $46,150; church and charitable institutions, $173,450; cemeteries, $2,100. The total number of residents in the county was 12,855; each political division containing the following inhabitants: Anglesea,

EDMUND L. ROSS.

247; Avalon, 105; Cape May City, 2452; Cape May Point, 136; Dennis township, 2370; Holly Beach, 300; Lower township, 1063; South Cape May, 65; Middle township, 2500; Ocean City, 921; Sea Isle City, 424; Upper township, 1420; West Cape May, 742; Wildwood, 109. There were 3367 dwelling houses in the county, occupied by 3193 families.

Edmund L. Ross, who represented Cape May county in the Senate during the sessions of 1895, '96 and '97, was born at Cape May Court House, March 10, 1852. He was educated in the public schools and at Mayville Academy. He followed the sea for some years and then entered into the mercantile business. He has been nine years county collector. He was a member of the Assembly in the sessions of 1892, '93 and '94.

Furman L. Ludlam, who was Assemblyman in 1895 and 1896, was born at South Dennis, on November 23, 1832, and is a farmer. In early years he was a sea captain.

Andrew J. Tomlin, of Goshen, was in 1895 elected Sheriff for a three-year term. He was a brother of John F. Tomlin, who was a distinguished soldier from Cape May county during the war of the rebellion. He was born at

ANDREW J. TOMLIN.

Goshen, March 15, 1845. He grew up on the farm and went to the village schools. In 1862 he went to Philadelphia, where he enlisted in the United States Marine Corps, and was detailed for duty at the Washington Navy Yard. After remaining there for one year, he was sent with a battalion to Morris Island, participating in the attack upon Fort Sumter in September, 1863. He was then detailed to the revenue cutter "Cuzler," and later to the U. S. steamer "Wabash," being with the latter in the Fort Fisher campaign. He helped to storm the breastworks and for his personal bravery received a medal from Gideon Welles, Secretary of the Navy. At the close of the war he was transferred to the U. S. steamship "Mohongo," of the Pacific squadron, upon which he remained until his five years' enlistment expired. He returned home, remained a short while, and enlisted again, being detailed to the U. S. steamship "Plymouth," of the European squadron. While on the "Plymouth" he was in Europe during the Franco-German war of 1870, and was also enabled to visit the Holy Lands and ports on both sides of the Mediterranean Sea. He,.

SYNAGOGUE AT WOODBINE.

upon returning home, allied himself with the Republican party. He was township committeeman of Middle township for ten years, school trustee fourteen years.

By reason of the unconstitutionality of the State borough laws, all the boroughs in Cape May county ceased to exist, but the Legislature, in 1896, passed an enabling act to allow boroughs to hold on to their government until legislation could be enacted. They all continued their existence excepting Cape May Point, which became again a part of Lower township. Ocean City was incorporated as a city in 1897, and on April 13 held its first election under its new charter.

On Sunday, November 29, 1896, the Synagogue at Woodbine was consecrated. Every part of the structure was made by the colonists themselves. It cost about six thousand dollars. The day was made a memorable one, a large number of visitors being present.

In September, 1896, Aaron W. Hand, of West Cape May, was appointed County Superintendent of Public Instruction by the state Board of Education, and entered into the performance of the duties of the office with an earnestness which greatly stimulated interest in the public schools. He was of Cape May stock, and born at Camden, N. J., February 10, 1857. He

AARON W. HAND.

was educated in the public schools of Camden and Philadelphia, and was for a considerable time a student at the U. S. Military Academy at West Point, N. Y. He began teaching school in 1877, and taught twelve years, being stationed at Dennisville, Rio Grande, Cape May Point and Cape May City. He was one of the most efficient principals of the schools of the latter place, and resigned the position to enter into the newspaper business in 1889. From 1880 to 1887 he resided at Cape May Point, and was tax collector and teacher there six years. He was also a merchant there. In 1887 he removed to West Cape May and began a mercantile business. He was assessor of the borough in 1895 and 1896. He was associate editor of the Daily Star in the summer season from

1881 to 1889. In 1889, in company with N Perry Edmunds, he purchased the Star of the Cape, and in 1890 Mr. Edmunds sold out to Thomas R. Brooks, who became a partner. In 1894, Mr. Hand sold his interest to Clarence R. Brooks, son of Thomas R. When the Star of the Cape Publishing Company purchased the paper in 1895, Mr. Hand became its editor and manager. In his newspaper career he has been fearless as an editor and successful as manager.

Robert E. Hand, who served in the Assembly in the session of 1897, was born at Erma, Cape May county, June

ROBERT E. HAND.

28, 1854, and still resides there. He was educated in the public schools. He owns large tracts of lands, is engaged in cultivating and shipping oysters. He was a member of school board for twelve years. He was a member of the Board of Freeholders from Lower township from 1887 to 1892. In the latter year he was elected Sheriff and served three years. In politics he is a Republican. In June, 1896, he was a delegate to the Republican National Convention at St. Louis, which nominated McKinley and Hobart for President and Vice-President.

CHAPTER XXIX.
CAPE ISLAND.

All that portion of Cape May county, beginning at a point in the Atlantic Ocean opposite the mouth of Cold Spring Inlet, as far southerly as the jurisdiction of the State extends, and running a westerly course until opposite an inlet (now filled up) between Cape Island and the lighthouse; thence following the several courses of the inlet, or creek, to Mount Vernon Bridge, and Broadway; thence along the northwest side of Broadway to the north side of its junction with the Cape Island turnpike; thence along the north side line of the turnpike to Cape May Island Bridge and creek; thence, following the several courses of the creek down the main channel to the place of beginning, is by law of 1875 declared to be the City of Cape May. Previous to this the territory was called Cape Island.

The first reference to Cape Island was when George Eaglesfield in 1699 built the causeway. The first reference to the island by law was in 1796, when a law was passed to make a road on which boats could be stowed. The old way of getting to Cape May, formerly called Cape Island, was by carriages, the visitors from Philadelphia driving down. In 1815, a sloop was built to convey passengers. Sometimes it would take two days to get down. The old Atlantic, the only hotel, was at the foot of Jackson street, and was the resort of men of prominence and wealth for many years. Commodore Decatur, the gallant and lamented American naval officer, for years was a visitant of Cape Island and was a constant habitue of the old Atlantic. Among its proprietors may be mentioned Ellis Hughes, William Hughes, Dr. Roger Wales, Aaron Bennett, Alexander McKenzie, Daniel Saint and Mr. McMackin.

The old Congress Hall did not occupy the site of the present brick structure, but in 1812, when built by Thomas

H. Hughes, its rotunda stood where Drs. Marcy & Mecray's Palace Pharmacy now stands. It was a wooden building, of extensive exterior, being 108x140, but not as elegant as the newer class of hotels. Thomas Hughes, Joseph Hughes, Jonas Miller, W. Burr Miller, Richard Thompson, John West and Jacob F. Cake were among the proprietors before its destruction in 1878. Jackson street was the first regularly laid out thoroughfare.

The reason why Cape Island was not laid out in squares, like he more modern towns, is because streets were only made when they were needed. Jackson street was the first made street in the town, and that was more than one hundred years ago. Lafayette street was a cow path for the most part, and for convenience it was made a wagon road, and finally adopted as a street. Washington street was made to run parallel with Lafayette. Delaware avenue is probably the next oldest. Franklin, Jefferson and Queen are also very old streets.

There was a hotel on the lot north of the old Atlantic, built in 1822, and kept by Ephraim Mills. The first steamboat began to run in 1828. Before that freight was brought to Cape May in sloops up to Schellenger's Landing. Old Captain Whilldin ran the first steamboat to the present landing place on the bay side. The boat stopped at New Castle to take up the Baltimoreans and Southerners who would come down on the old Frenchtown and New Castle Railroad—the first railroad ever run in this country. They would come over in carriages from Baltimore to Frenchtown, in Maryland, on the Susquehanna, near Havre de Grace.

The hotel next erected after Congress Hall was the Mansion House, raised in 1832, covering four acres of ground. It was the first lathed and plastered house on the island. Richard S. Ludlam built it, and also opened a street fifty feet in width, called Washington, between Perry and Jackson. The first summer cottage was put up by Thomas Hart, of Philadelphia. "The Kersal," meaning a place of amusement, was a wing or extension of the Mansion House, 124 feet long, built in 1849, had hops and concerts in it; also used as a large dining room. Among the proprietors of the Mansion House were Ephraim Mills, Isaac Schellenger, Eli B. Wales, Daniel Saint, John Sturtevant, Richard Smith Ludlam in 1839; William S. Hooper and Albert H. Ludlam from 1850 until the house was burned in 1856.

The Ocean House was erected about 1832 by Israel Leaming, and was located on the east side of Perry street, between Washington street and the beach.

After the old Mansion House, the next house was built by Mrs. Reynolds, called the American, with accommodations for 125 guests.

About 1834 the steamer "Portsmouth" began to make weekly trips to Cape May and Lewestown. In later years she was followed by the "Wilmon Whilldin," "Kent," "Rip Van Winkle," "Zephyr," "Wave," "Mountaineer" and others.

The first Methodist Episcopal society in Cape May City was formed in December, 1837, and fourteen years after this, 1843, the first church was erected near the site of the present one, and it is now the A. M. E. Church, on Franklin street. Socrates Townsend, Israel Townsend, Jonas Miller, Israel Leaming and Jeremiah Church were the most active workers for its foundation. Joseph Ware was the builder, and Rev. Clark Polley was the first preacher. He was also the first town Superintendent of Schools for Cape Island. The church is now located on Washington street, having been last rebuilt in 1893.

In 1846 the Old Columbia Hotel was built, extending from Ocean to Decatur street, erected by George Hildreth. Messrs. Harwood and Bolton were its proprietors.

The Merchants was built on the site of the New Columbia and Messrs. Mason and Eldredge were its proprietors before it was swept away in 1878.

The Centre House, erected in 1840, was kept by Jeremiah Mecray on the corner of Jackson and Washington streets, until the fire destroyed it with the rest in 1878.

The New Atlantic was built in 1840, and conducted by Benjamin, Joe and John McMackin until its destruction in 1878.

On Decatur street stood the Madison, whose construction dated from 1845.

The Washington Hotel was first erected on Washington street and was built in 1840. It now stands at Beach and Madison avenues. White Hall was erected in 1850, by Dr. Samuel S. Marcy, and the Delaware in 1840.

National Hall was erected in about 1850 by Aaron Garretson.

The first Baptist Society was formed about 1844, and a church was erected in the spring of 1845. It was replaced in 1879 by the present one, costing some $19,000. The first pastor was Rev. M. B. Tindall. The following were the original members of the church: Isaac Church, Philip Hand, George Stratton, Stephen Mulford, Alexander A. Shaw, John Price, Thomas McKain, William Price, John K. Church, Aaron Schellenger, Rebecca H. Church, Sarah H. Hand, Abigail F. Stratton, Hetty Barnett, Elnor Fisher, Jane E. Shaw, Elizabeth McKain, Phoebe Webb, Louisa M. Schellenger, Elizabeth Brooks, Eliza Burch, Mary Leaming, Keziah Price, Isabella Stevens and Hannah Robertson.

The need of local government was apparent and Assemblyman Richard S. Ludlam began a movement in the Legislature which on March 8, 1848, terminated in the passage of the act "to incorporate Cape Island into a borough." This instrument named James Mecray chief burgess; James Clark, assistant burgess; Thomas B. Hughes, high constable, and William Cassedy, borough clerk; and these men were to constitute the government, with an assessor and collector of taxes, until the first Tuesday of May, 1849, when the people were from year to year to choose their successors. The government existed until 1851, when in March the Legislature incorporated the "City of Cape Island." There was a mayor, six councilmen, an alderman and a recorder, who as a body were legislators for the new city.

The first Council met in the school house on the corner lot of Franklin and Lafayette streets (south side), on Saturday evening, March 15, 1851. There were present Isaac M. Church, Mayor; Waters B. Miller, Alderman; Joseph S.

Leach, Recorder, and James S. Kennedy, David Pierson, John G. W. Ware, Joseph Ware, Aaron Garretson and James Mecray, Councilmen. The only thing done that evening was the election of Charles T. Johnson, a carpenter, as City Clerk.

On the following Saturday evening, March 22, Mayor Church delivered his inaugural address, in which he said:

"Gentlemen and Fellow Citizens:
"Allow me the privilege of congratulating you upon the happy auspices under which we are now convened.

"Our unfeigned gratitude is due the Great Author of all good, for the bounties of Providence we so largely enjoy. In addition to wealth, peace and plenty, our 'lines have fallen to us in pleasant places.' Situated as we are, upon one of the most delightful spots to be found within the fair domain of our beloved country, from this location we may look out upon the heaving bosom of the broad and fathomless Atlantic, and listen to the ceaseless roar of its rolling billows as they dash upon our sandy beach. This island prominence is worthily noted for its unsurpassed beauty and salubriousness, and has lately become truly celebrated for the pleasantness of its climate, and the invigorating influence of its summer sea breezes. These advantages, together with the convenience and safety of its bathing-grounds, contribute so many attractions that it is often thronged by thousands of the wealthy and fashionable from various and even remote parts of the Union. And their anticipations are usually more than realized in the agreeableness of the retreat from the sultry and sickly atmosphere of crowded cities and inland towns. It is our good fortune here to have our dwelling places, as free and independent citizens, and to enjoy uninterruptedly the privileges of the Gospel, with the rights and immunities of the civil and social institutions of our highly favored land.

"But this occasion requires especially that I should congratulate you upon the success of your late application to the Legislature of our State for the rights and privileges of a city charter. We have, for a few years past, been witnessing with much gratification the unparalleled growth and prosperity of our place, which has only been equalled by its widening notoriety and increasing popularity as a desirable summer resort. A large amount of capital is annually expended in the erection and furnishing of commodious and magnificent hotels and boarding-houses for the comfortable entertainment of the multitudes who visit us during each successive bathing season. So that, in point of fact, our former village is rapidly assuming the real appearance of a splendid city. And to maintain the respectability to which the rapid progress of the place entitles it, as well as for the security of the stock invested in its improvement, it was deemed expedient to procure a city charter. For this, and other reasons, such as the preservation of just rights and good order among us, it was thought indispensable that an efficient municipal government should be organized.

"Moved by a commendable spirit of enterprise, you, my fellow citizens, after mutual and mature deliberation, prepared a bill which, in the dictates of your best judgment, should meet the exigencies of the case. This bill was in due time presented to the Legislature by your committee appointed for that purpose, through whose efficiency it secured the early attention of that body. And being duly considered, with the circumstances which called for its enactment, it was slightly amended to meet the views of the members interested, and finally secured the Legislative sanction by a passage through both houses, and was approved and signed by the Governor. And by our bill thus becoming law, we were constituted a chartered corporation. On the tenth of the present month, Cape Island took her place among her older sisters of the Union as a legally incorporated city. And though she may be the least among the thousands of America bearing such a title, yet the vigor of her infancy promises well for a speedy, a propitious and a far-famed maturity. The realization of this result, however, depends very much upon the spirit with which our chartered privileges are improved and carried out to their practical operations.

"In this responsible business we have just embarked.

CAPE ISLAND. 411

Agreeably to the provisions of the charter, the polls were legally opened on the eleventh instant, for the election of municipal officers; and our citizens, with a zeal worthy the cause, came forward to the enjoyment of their right of suffrage. The voice of the sovereign people, spoken through the medium of the ballot-box, has summoned us, the officers-elect, to take the first administration of the public affairs of this municipality.

"In accepting the honor to which my fellow citizens have called me—that of serving them as chief magistrate of the city—it may not be amiss for me to remark that at the late election was the first time I ever allowed my name to be used as a candidate for a public civil office. And notwithstanding the misgivings I may have respecting my capability for the duties devolved upon me, I should still be an ingrate, indeed, not to feel and express the emotions of unaffected gratitude to my friends for placing me in this honorable position, by such a decided expression of the public will. Yet I should be reluctant to obey even this summons to official duty, were it not that I have the fullest confidence in the abilities of my compeers in office. Feeling satisfied that they are every way competent to meet and discharge the respective duties assigned them, and to grapple successfully with every emergency that may arise, and, moreover, cherishing the assurance that they will give me their cordial co-operation in all measures that concern the public weal; with such coadjutors, and with entire dependence upon the direction and assistance of God, I venture cheerfully into the new department of civil obligations. And we feign hope the public will be prepared to make all reasonable allowance for errors in judgment that may arise through inadvertency or inexperience on the part of their official servants.

"And now, gentlemen, you who have the honor to be the elected functionaries of this body politic, and especially the members of the City Council, permit me with due deference to your respective views and abler judgment, to state in brief the principles I wish to be governed by and would recommend to you as the basis of our official administration.

"We are placed by the favor and confidence of our constituents in a position that will call forth our best energies to sustain satisfactorily all the interests of this corporation. To us is committed the responsible work of setting in operation a new form of government for a newly constituted city. And this is to be done with very limited financial resources, amid the paralyzing influence of fear on one side, prejudice on another, and perhaps derision on the third. And this responsibility is necessarily laid upon those altogether inexperienced in the work they have to perform. A government is to be established and kept in effective motion, with the least possible friction in its machinery, although its operators be unused to many of its delicate wires.

"With such raw material, both as agents and principals, it will be difficult to prevent some creaking in the contact between new rules and old usages. For, no doubt, it will be expected of us, as a condition of our public approval, that all the varied and somewhat conflicting interests that here concentrate, be maintained and promoted. Yet I trust we shall not be deterred from launching the ship, though the channel be narrow, shallow and difficult to navigate; for if we do our duty, we think she will float out to good sailing; at all events it will be satisfaction enough to be conscious of having done the best we could under the circumstances. Among the several interests that will demand our attention, the first are those of a local character, confined within the limits and to the inhabitants of the city itself. Embraced in this class will be internal improvements, proper care of health and cleanliness, the preservation of peace and good order, the protection and fostering of moral institutions, the detection and punishment of vice and misdemeanor, the judicious management and suitable encouragement of educational interests, with the prudent direction of finances. To these things we must carefully look, in order that the city, so far as its internal police is concerned, may be kept in a thriving and prosperous condition. By these means it will present a standing invitation to its visitors to continue their periodical visitations; and to those who are in search of a location to make it their permanent residence. And this evidently will be the surest and quickest way of increasing the value of city property, by which all are benefited.

"The next claim upon the deliberations of the Council is the interest of the surrounding vicinity, and the county at large. With these our municipal enactments should conflict as little as possible. It is an obvious fact that the pecuniary interest of the adjacent country is closely identified with the prosperity of this city. The more rapid and permanent its growth, and the greater number that can be induced to visit it during the summer, the longer and better market it will afford for their produce, and the more employment it will provide for their teams and carriages. While the effect of wholesome restraints and regulations in the city will go far to prevent a poisonous influence of immorality from spreading around, which otherwise would have a tendency to contaminate the whole region. It is to their advantage, therefore, not to fight against, but to assist in promoting the interests of the city. Yet, on the other hand, there is a reciprocal dependence upon them in securing and perpetuating the advantages of the corporation. We want their marketing, their fish, their hay, their wood, their labor, their teams, and their vehicles. Hence it will be but prudent economy for both city and country, far as practicable, to give mutual encouragement to each other's interests.

Next, and the last that we shall name, though perhaps not the least in its bearing upon the ultimate success of our municipal enterprise, is to be considered the interests, comfort and wishes of the annual visitors to the city. Some of them own property here, and are actual residents with us during the summer season, while the vast majority only remain a few weeks in the capacity of boarders, at the hotels and private houses. That it will be an important point with the authority of the city to consult their advantages and preferences is evident from the fact that from this class of people has come the principal part of the money that has thus far built up our city; and from them must still come the funds indispensable to the continued life and activity of our business operations. If, therefore, through carelessness or an arrant disregard of the comfort, safety, and gratification of these visitors, they should be turned off in some other direction, our hope of prosperity to our youthful city must end in bitter and remediless disappointment. Such a catastrophe we should not only deprecate, but endeavor to avoid.

"Having thus presented to your consideration some of the leading objects at which I hope it will be our united purpose to aim, in our administration of the public affairs of the city, your indulgence is asked while I take the liberty of recommending the means which to me seem best adapted to attain these desirable ends. Not only is the public good as a whole to be sought by us, but it is to be sought in the easiest and best way we can devise. And first of all, it will be essential to an effective government that each officer connected with it acquaint himself thoroughly with the duties, privileges, and responsibilities of his office. And that he hold himself ready at all times to act expeditiously and decidedly as occasion may require. Without prompt and energetic action on the part of officers, no stability or force can be given to the municipal transactions; and the whole organization would soon be treated with the disrespect its childish indecision would merit. But we will not give place to the fear that any one has, or will take upon him, an office merely for its honor or emoluments, who are still unresolved as to its duties. For may the Lord deliver me from an association with men in office who wilfully neglect the duties they are sworn to perform.

"Another point of importance will be a vigilant endeavor to preserve unanimity of sentiment and concert of action in the deliberations and decisions of Council. United counsel will be the best guarantee that the city government can give for the perpetuity and practical benefits of our charter. Of course, it will be both proper and expedient, when different views are entertained on subjects under consideration, to compare and discuss their relative merits, to advocate measures with all your several abilities. Only let this be done in a friendly manner, and with due respect to each other's judgment. And though majorities should always be submitted to cheerfully, yet they should never carry points with an overbearing and exulting spirit; rather let a conservative spirit predominate and regulate the whole proceedings. To secure this, compromises will sometimes require to be made to minority views, which is well enough, where it can be done without encroaching upon important rights and principles. But if sectional or personal prejudices and jealousies are allowed to produce embittered controversies, and control the consultation and enactments of the Council, the arm of its strength will be palsied. 'For a house divided against itself cannot stand;' while its wranglings will soon become the by-word of those who will treat its ordinances with contempt. In your legislative movements, you will have a noble trio of well-established landmarks by which to steer your course. The highest and broadest of these is the Constitution of the United States, which it will ever be the duty and pride of every good American citizen, whether in office or private life, to preserve inviolate by a faithful adherence to its requisitions, prohibitions and principles. Next to this is the Constitution of our own State, which expresses the fundamental laws by which we are governed as Jerseymen. And where is the Jerseyman worth the name that does not regard it an honor either to live under or assist in maintaining, unimpaired, the majesty of that purely republican document. Then as the inside directory of our enactments, we have our city charter, which defines our rights, privileges, and duties as citizens of Cape Island, and more particularly as officers chosen by said citizens to take the supervision and prosecution of their public concerns. In our enactment and execution of local law, therefore, it will be indispensable to keep our eye upon the limitations of those higher and more general laws already established. These we are bound to respect as supreme, to obey them faithfully, to abide by them immovably; in doing which we shall not be liable to overreach our proper jurisdiction, but will secure all due reverence to the city authority.

"I will now detain you, gentlemen, no longer than will be necessary to make a few special recommendations. Your independent and judicious judgment will need to be immediately exercisd in the choice of a Councilman to fill the vacant seat, the election of a City Clerk, and Street Commissioner. After these selections are made, it will be requisite to draft and adopt suitable Rules of Order, By-Laws, etc., for your own convenience in expediting the correct transaction of business. These preliminaries disposed of, I would recommend the early appointment of an efficient police, with definite instructions as to their duties, that they may be ready to operate whenever needed; but that they be not called into service until actual occasion requires. It will be well for the Council, soon as practicable, to take measure for ascertaining the amount of money sufficient to meet the ordinary expenses of maintaining the poor, repairing the streets, supporting the schools, etc., which, together with the State and county tax, will constitute the sum which the Assessor will have to raise by a tax levied on the inhabitants and property holders of the city, according to a fair valuation of their respective possessions. The amount needed to meet the current expenses of the City Government, and for internal improvements, I would recommend to be derived from a revenue that shall be produced from various sources. Of these, the following are proposed: First, let a light tax be laid upon all vehicles that come from without the bounds of the city, to be used here as pleasure carriages during the boarding season. I would suggest that the owners or drivers of all such be required to obtain a written permit from the Mayor, or City Clerk, for the season before commencing operation. The sum to be paid for said permits will be fixed by the wisdom of the Council. Probably something like the following rates might be an equitable demand: for each two-horse carriage belonging to the line, one dollar; for each of the same description not connected with the line, two dollars, and for each of like kind coming from without the county, five dollars. As a further source of revenue, let all transient shop-keepers of whatever kind, before opening for sale, be required to procure license of the city authorities, to pay therefor such sum as the discretion of the Council shall designate. I would also recommend that all kinds of exhibitions, farces, shows, fireworks, etc., be prohibited, except they first procure license in like manner, and that the respective charges be adjusted to their probable income. And further, that the same principle be undeviatingly applied to all bowling alleys, pistol galleries, archeries and whatever other places of amusement the Council may see proper to allow within the limits of the city. In their number and character, we hope the Council will not overlook the moral interests of the community. You are aware that the Legislature have seen fit in the passage of the bill to authorize the Council to grant license to inns, bars, etc., within the city, and this right shall be discretionary, sole and exclusive, and that it may also be applied to defining the period of such license to any term not exceeding one year. Now, if the Council shall deem it expedient to grant license for the sale of ardent spirits, I recommend that the term of said license be fixed to three months only, from the tenth of June. You will find by a reference to the statutes of the State that in determining upon the amount demanded for tavern licenses, you have the range between ten and seventy dollars to select in.

"We confidently think that the revenue derived from these several sources will be sufficient to meet the necessary expenditures. We earnestly recommend that immediate action be taken by the Council for the prevention of the destruction of property by fire. Let the Marshal be authorized to institute a speedy and thorough examination of all chimneys, stovepipes, flues, etc., in the city, and report those he regards as unsafe. It might be well to pass an ordinance requiring every house to be furnished with a certain number of leather fire-buckets, according to its number of rooms, to be kept in good repair and in a conspicuous place. We should entertain the plan favorably, of your encouraging the formation of a hook and ladder company, who could operate to good advantage in case of fire.

"Regulations will be needed also, in regard to suitable wagon-stands, that the public passage way to boarding and other houses be not obstructed. It is further recommended that timely and stringent measures be adopted to prevent any indecent or improper behavior on or about the bathing-grounds at any time, especially during bathing hours. While from the necessity of the case, the observance of economy will be required in arranging your expenditures, still we hope that a due degree of public spirit will characterize your appropriations. Some improvements will doubtless be expected and demanded by the public; and it is hoped that they will not be altogether disappointed in their wishes. Our streets and sidewalks need repairing. But as to Public Buildings, I would suggest that for the present the Council rent or lease some suitable room, that will answer all practical purposes for a city hall. In addition to this, I should favor your proceeding at once to build a small jail. We think the time is not far distant when a market-house will be needed. I would merely notify you that some of the stockholders have proposed to offer the school house and lot on which it stands, for sale, which would be a very good site for city buildings. Especially do we recommend that the educational interests of the city receive your liberal patronage. 'Better pay for the tuition of the boy than for the ignorance and vice of the man!' We hope that school appropriations will be made to such an extent as will render it an object of interest to the Superintendent of Common Schools to look well to its judicious and profitable outlay. This he can do by giving his sanction only to competent teachers, visiting the schools, giving lectures, etc.

"As to the salaries and fees of officers, a proper medium between meanness on one hand and extravagance on the other should be preserved. While it is not reasonable to expect that men can devote their time and energies to the public benefit without compensation, neither is it to be supposed that office-holding in an infantile city like ours can be a very lucrative employment. Equity and good policy would dictate that paid officers receive a fair and proper remuneration for the time they occupy and the services they render in public affairs. And as this cannot at present be ascertained in the case of most of them, I would recommend that the Council defer their decision upon this question until the first of October, and that they require each officer to keep a faithful account of the time they have been in actual service during the interim, and present said accounts to the Council at the time specified.

"It will add much to the respectability and comfort of the

city that no horses, cattle, sheep, goats or swine be allowed to roam at large as commoners within the incorporated bounds.

"In conclusion, allow me to express my fond hope that a year's trial of the new arrangements under which we now enter will prove to the satisfaction of all concerned the utility and advantage of our city charter. And it is our earnest desire that all who have been chosen by the suffrages of their fellow citizens to bear a part in the government of our young city will honorably acquit themselves in meeting the responsibility under which they are laid, and thereby creditably sustain the confidence reposed in them. If this is done, voters will have no occasion to regret the result of their choice.

"We should now fervently invoke upon you, and the city you represent, the continued and special blessing of Him, without whose favor and protection the 'watchmen of a city but waketh in vain.'"

Isaac Miller Church, the first Mayor of Cape Island, and a Baptist clergyman, was born in Philadelphia, Pa., April 8, 1814. He was taken by his father, Isaac Church, in 1818, to Lancaster, Ohio. The lad returned to Philadelphia alone and on foot in 1834, being followed shortly by his father, who settled near the steamboat landing in Lower township, now Cape May Point. Mr. Church was ordained at the meeting house of the West Creek Baptist Church, Cumberland county, N. J., Saturday, April 24, 1841, as licentiate of the First Baptist Church of Cape May.

He had been laboring for a few years before as a missionary under the patronage of the State Convention in the West Creek field.

On June 11, 1848, he was extended a call to become pastor of the Cape Island Baptist Church, accepting the call on the 7th of October, and remained its pastor until he left Cape May in October, 1851. On the 20th of October he delivered his valedictory to the Council, having resigned as Mayor, and a resolution of "thanks" was tendered him "for the judicious manner in which he had conducted the affairs of the city." On October 27, the new Mayor, James Clark, was sworn into office.

Mr. Church commenced his pastorate with the First Baptist Church of South Kingston, Washington county, R. I., April 1, 1853, and continued for one year to April 1, 1854. Mr. Church continued to reside in Rhode Island until he died.

Mr. Church, who was a chaplain in the Civil War, entered Company E, Second Rhode Island Infantry, as second lieutenant, and on June 6, 1861, was made first lieutenant of Company H, same regiment. On July 21, 1861, he was taken prisoner at the battle of Bull Run and borne as a prisoner of war to Richmond, Va., where he was confined in Libby Prison for about a year. He afterwards published a diary of three hundred pages on his confinement in that nefarious place. He was afterwards made captain of Company G, Fourth Regiment, Rhode Island Infantry.

Mr. Church was a very industrious and useful man; besides his work as a minister in South Kingston, R. I., he carried on the business of house painting, photographing, taught school, was agent, committee, manager and counsel for the town in road cases and other important matters. He was town surveyor, then chairman of their School Committee and in 1859 and 1860 was president of the town Council. He died at his son-in-law's house in Davisville, R. I., October 28, 1874, and is buried at Riverside Cemetery, in Wakefield, R. I. He married Judith Swayne Thompson, of Cape May, N. J., October 16, 1834, who died at Millville, N. J., August 19, 1887.

The Presbyterian Church was organized June 25, 1851, by a committee of the Presbytery of West Jersey. The present church was erected in 1853. St. Mary's Roman Catholic Church was erected about 1848, on the opposite side of Washington street from where it stands to-day. It was in about 1870 removed to its present location.

James Clark, the second Mayor of Cape Island, was born June 7, 1798, at Cedarville, Cumberland county, New Jersey. He lived some years in Philadelphia before coming to Cape May, where he passed the remainder of his life, identifying himself with all that pertained to the welfare of the place. He was related to the Fithian and Bateman families, of Cumberland county. His father was Charles Clark, born January 1, 1772. His first office was that of postmaster of the village of Cape Island, which he held by appointment of President Polk from July 7, 1845, to May 9, 1849, when he was succeeded by George W. Hughes. This was before the city was incorporated.

At the meeting of Council on October 20, 1851, when Isaac M. Church tendered his resignation as Mayor, M.. Clark was chosen by Council on the fifth ballot to fill the

CAPE MAY CITY BAPTIST CHURCH.

unexpired term. His opponents on that occasion were John K. F. Sites and Dr. Samuel S. Marcy. He was sworn in and assumed the duties of his office on October 27, 1851, and served as Mayor until March, 1853, having been elected by the people in 1852.

He was an ardent Democrat of his time, and was appointed postmaster a second time by President Buchanan, and served from March 13, 1857, to December 5, 1859, being succeeded by Samuel R. Magonagle. Five days after, on December 10, 1859, he passed from this earth to the world beyond, aged 61 years and 6 months.

It is said of him that he was very fond of music and interested in the improvement of church music. To that end he worked in the Baptist Church here, having charge of the choir for quite a period. He married Eliza Bennett, a sister of Jeremiah and Stephen Bennett, Delaware River pilots of their day.

John Kake Church, the third Mayor of Cape Island, was born at Lancaster, Ohio, on Christmas Day, in the year 1818. He was a son of Isaac Church, a prominent Baptist and preacher, who removed with his family to Cape May when John was a lad of sixteen years. With them came his elder brother, Rev. Isaac M. Church, the first Mayor. Both the father and John K. Church on April 6, 1844, at the organization of the Cape Island Baptist Church, became members of the church, with twenty-three others. The father was blind, but nevertheless was the first regular pastor of the church, and served from May 17, 1844, to October 7, 1848.

While young, the subject of our sketch learned the carpenter trade and followed it throughout his life.

The first office which Mr. Church held was that of City Clerk, to which he was elected by Council in March, 1852. At the charter election, in the following year, he was chosen Mayor of the city, and re-elected in 1854 and 1855.

In 1856 he was elected to the City Council, and held the office for a year.

He died of apoplexy in his boat at Schellenger's Landing, while returning from a pleasure trip in the sounds with a party of men, on Saturday afternoon, July 30, 1859, being in his 41st year. His widow still lives.

The Cape May Ocean Wave of the Thursday following his death said of him:

"Mr. Church was respected and esteemed by every one who knew him for his calmness of disposition, his honesty, uprightness and veracity of character in all his dealings and intercourse with the world; and, above all, his consistent Christian walk. He needed but to be known to be appreciated. He was for several consecutive years (formerly) elected Mayor of Cape Island, which office he filled with the same uprightness with which he has ever performed all the other duties of life."

Joseph Ware, the fourth and tenth Mayor of Cape Island, was a son of Joseph Ware, who came from Cumberland county, and a brother of Samuel Fithian, of Lower township, and of James W., Mashel, John G. W., Daniel C., Wilmon W., of Cape May City. He was born May 16, 1809. In early life he learned the carpenter's trade. In 1851 he was a member of the Board of Freeholders, in 1852 Assessor, 1854 Recorder, and 1855 Assessor. In 1856 he was chosen Mayor and re-elected three times, serving until 1861. Again he was chosen in 1871, and served a term of two years. He died on April 30, 1890, in the Mount Vernon Hotel, the latter at the time being the largest hotel in the United States. It was never completed, being burned in 1855. The Mansion was destroyed by fire, in 1856, and the Atlantic, United States and American hotels were burned in 1869. The proprietors of the Mount Vernon Hotel were Samuel Woolman and M. Cain, who was burned to death in the fire, with five others.

In the advertisement of summer resort hotels in 1858 the following were the houses and their proprietors: Columbia House, L. Harwood; Atlantic House, J. and B. McMackin; Ocean House, Israel Leaming; Delaware House, James Mecray; National Hall, Aaron Garretson; Washington Hotel, S. G. Woolman; Merchants' House, John Lyons; Tontine Hotel, George L. Ludlam; White Hall Hotel, S. S. Marcy. In 1859 Congress Hall and the Morphy House were added to the list of advertisers.

A writer in "The Knickerbocker Magazine," New York, of August, 1859, says: "The neighborhood of which we are speaking is none other than that most charming of ocean summer resorts and watering places, that famous refuge from the heat and dust of the weary city—the beach at Cape May. * * * We speak literally, for it is a city, and not a village or town merely, at which the traveler will land when he debarks at Cape May. In this census we speak, of course, of the permanent residents only, and not of the summer visitants. These may, in their season, be counted not only by hundreds, but by thousands, and with their help and that of the dozen to twenty imposing hotel edifices, and the infinite tail of restaurants, barber shops, ice cream saloons, bowling alleys, billiard rooms, pistol galleries, bathing houses and temporary houses of all names —the little city really grows metropolitan in aspect; and the 'gas works' and the 'Mayor's office,' which at other times seem to have been sent there merely on storage, now appear quite in place."

James S. Kennedy, M. D., who was one of the first druggists of Cape May City, was born in Philadelphia, January 16, 1807, and came to Cape May when a small boy. He studied medicine under Dr. Brooks, of Philadelphia, and graduated at the Pennsylvania College of Medicine, Philadelphia, March 7, 1843.

The same year he opened the first drug store kept in Cape May City, in a small building on Washington street, near Jackson street, where he continued the practice of his profession for one year, when he built a drug store on Lafayette street, near Decatur street, which he afterwards moved to Washington street, near Decatur street. On September 3, 1844, he married Miss Charlotte R. Swain, a daughter of Lemuel Swain, Sr. For many years he was owner and proprietor of the Franklin House, and during the early days of the incorporation of the city he was an influential member of Council, and well known and highly respected citizen. When Isaac M. Church, the first Mayor of Cape Island, resigned in October, 1851, Dr. Kennedy came within one of being elected Mayor by the City Council. In 1851 he was elected he first Assessor of the city, and also a member of the first Council, and was twice again elected to the position of Assessor in 1856 and 1857. He was for many years continuously a member of Council, being first elected in 1855, and served during the years of 1857, 1861, 1862, 1869, 1870 and 1875. He was chosen Alderman in 1863, and five years continuously. At that time the Alderman was a member of Council, as well as a committing magistrate. He was a member of the county Board of Freeholders from Cape May City during the years 1864 and 1865. He served as Overseer of the Poor six years from March, 1862. In 1868 he associated with himself in business his son, Dr. Henry A. Kennedy, and they afterwards conducted the business under the name of Dr. J. S. Kennedy & Son, in the same place, until 1873. That year they purchased the ground at the corner of Decatur street, where the United States Hotel had formerly stood, which was destroyed by fire August 29, 1869. He, Dr. Kennedy, remained in business a the United States Pharmacy until he died, June 20, 1876. He was a prominent member of the Presbyterian Church of Cape May City, and a member of Evening Star Lodge of Odd Fellows, which then flourished in Cape May.

Samuel S. Marcy, M. D., was born at Willington, Tolland county, Conn., December 7, 1793, and passed his boyhood days in that section, where he availed himself of the advantages of the schools, and acquired a thorough English education. At the age of twenty-one years he entered the office of Joseph Palmer, Jr., M. D., at Ashford, Conn., where he read and practiced for three years. He then attended lectures at the medical department of Yale College, and received his first diploma from the State Medical Society of Connecticut, and subsequently received the degree of M. D. from the faculty of Yale College. He migrated to Cape May county in 1817, and located at Cold Sprirgs. On April 3, 1822, he married Miss Thankful Edmunds, a daughter of Robert Edmunds, of Fishing Creek, at one time judge of the Court of Common Pleas, and an elder in the Cold Spring Presbyterian Church. Doctor Marcy moved to Cape May long before the place was incorporated, where he followed his profession until he retired, owing to his advanced age. He held many local offices, being a member of the Board of Freeholders during the years 1854, 1856, 1857, 1858, 1859, 1860, 1861, 1862 and 1869. He was a member of City Council in 1856 and 1857; Recorder in 1861, and Alderman in 1858, 1859 and 1860.

He was a director and treasurer of the Cape Island Turnpike Company for a long time, and one of the charter members of Cape Island Lodge, No. 30, F. and A. M.

He died in Cape May City February 13, 1882.

In 1862 the Legislature passed an act allowing Cape Island to issue $20,000 in bonds for the purpose of erecting a water works, subject to the vote of the people.

The West Jersey Railroad was opened to Cape May in 1863. Then things soon took a start and people began to build cottages. The value of lots ranged according to fancy, and speculation was for a long time rife and much money was made.

St. John's Protestant Episcopal Church was incorporated in 1863.

In 1866 the charter of Cape Island was changed so that Councilmen were elected for two years instead of one.

On March 28, 1866, the "Cape Island Lodge, No. 30, Free and Accepted Masons," was incorporated, with Virgil M. D. Marcy, Alvin P. Hildreth, Samuel R. Ludlam, Joseph Q. Williams, Samuel R. Stites, Samuel S. Marcy and their associates as members.

The third disastrous fire on the island occurred on the last day of August, 1869, which destroyed that entire portion of the island lying between Washington street and the ocean, and between Ocean and Jackson streets, with the exception of the Columbia House and two or three other small buildings. Among the hotels burned were the United States Hotel, American House and the Atlantic and other small houses. The Atlantic was rebuilt.

About this time St. John's Protestant Episcopal Church was built at Washington and Franklin streets through the influence of Bishop Coleman, of Delaware.

In 1869 the mammoth Stockton Hotel, which stands to-day, was built by the Pennsylvania Railroad Company, at a cost of $600,000. This company owned it for about twenty years.

George Hildreth was born at Rio Grande, May 28, 1822. At sixteen he was employed in vessels carrying coal between Philadelphia and New England ports. In 1839 he was wrecked at sea in the "Reaper," of Cape May. He was picked up by a passing vessel and carried to New York. He then became an employee of Richard C. Holmes in the wrecking business. After a period of such service he was engaged in buying and selling lumber. In 1846 he built the Columbia Hotel, and sold it in 1851. That year he built the West End.

From 1861 to 1863 he was engaged in fishing and in 1864 entered into the feed business, which he still conducts. In 1874 he built the Wyoming Hotel. On April 12, 1870, he was appointed keeper of Cold Spring Life Saving Station, and held the position for about fifteen years.

Military organizations have been numerous at Cape May during the summer seasons. The Fifth Maryland encamped here during the summer of 1873, and has been here several times since. The Baltimore Light Infantry, the Washington Light Infantry, Sixth, Seventh and Second New Jersey Brigades, the Philadelphia State Fencibles, the First Pennsylvania Regiment, and various civic societies, such as St. John's Commandery of Knights Templar, have been here during various seasons.

Henry Hand, a leading citizen, is a son of Recompence Hand, a pilot, and brother of Joseph Hand and Enoch W. Hand, who have been Councilmen. He was born in this city January 31, 1826, and was a cousin of General Scheuch, once U. S. Minister to England. He was educated in the public schools here. At sixteen he entered as a carpenter's apprentice at Philadelphia, learned his trade and returned home. He was chosen City Clerk and served from 1853 to 1855. In 1856, his health failing him, he went to Minnesota and remained there three years, working at his trade. His health being restored, he returned to Cape May again, and entered into partnership with Mashel Ware, under the firm name of Hand & Ware. This firm built many cottages here, the Pennsylvania Railroad Station at Newark, and in 1872 twenty-six life-saving stations along the New Jersey coast for the United States Government. He is a prominent member of the Cape Island Presbyetrian Church, and has been an elder since 1869. From 1861 to 1863 he was a second time City Clerk, and from 1863 to 1866 was City Recorder. From 1869 to 1872 he was Tax Collector, and served as Assessor from 1872 to 1876, from 1878 to 1883, and from 1884 to 1891. In 1895 he was chosen City Treasurer, which office he still holds.

On March 22, 1872, the act to incorporate the Cold Spring and Cape May Water Company became a law, and John C. Bullitt, General William J. Sewell, Jacob F. Cake, James Leaming and Return B. Swain were the incorporators. The works, which were finally in possession of the city, were started in 1874.

Return B. Swain was born in Middle township, now near Swain's Station, on the West Jersey Railroad, February 19, 1826. He was raised on a small farm, and educated in the district public school until the completion of his sixteenth year, at which period he commenced self education through the medium of text-books, with accompanying keys. At nineteen he commenced life on his own account as teacher in the public schools. When twenty years of age he went into the employ of E. T. Randolph & Co., iron manufacturers, at Millville, N. J., where he was a bookkeeper for two years. The confinement impaired his health, and he returned to a farm near his birthplace, where his time was passed in farming and surveying in summer, and in teaching the district school in winter. This he did until 1865. In February, 1848, he had married Miss Rachel Reeves, a daughter of Benjamin F. Reeves, of Cumberland county. The completion of the West Jersey Railroad to Cape May, in 1863, gave an impetus to improvement in Cape May City, and in 1865 Mr. Swain moved to the place, where he became largely interested in many public enterprises, being a Master in Chancery, Notary Public, surveyor and conveyancer. He was for a number of years a large real estate operator, and a long time superintendent of the Cape Island Gas Company. He was a member of the City Council in 1874. About 1880 he removed to Philadelphia, where he entered into the plumbing business and manufacturing of bath tubs.

CHAPTER XXX.
CAPE MAY CITY.

John G. W. Ware, the twelfth Mayor of the city of Cape May, was born at Cape May City in 1825, and lived at Cape May all his life, being identified with nearly every public enterprise. He was known during his life as "Uncle John," because of the kindness he did in sickness and in aiding in ever public enterprise. He was a brother of Wilmon W. Ware, who was once State Senator; Daniel C. Ware, who served as a Councilman; of Joseph Ware, who was twice Mayor of Cape May, and Maskel Ware, a chosen Freeholder of Cape May City.

When the first city charter went into effect in 1851 he was chosen a member of Council for one year. He was elected to the same office in 1857, 1858, 1859, 1864, 1865, 1866 and 1867 for one-year terms.

He was elected Alderman in 1870, and served until 1875, when he was elected Mayor for a term of two years. He was chosen again Alderman in 1877, and served until 1879. In 1881 he was again elected Alderman, and served until 1886. In 1888 he was again elected and served until his death, on September 8, 1894, which was caused by heart disease.

Dr. James Mecray, son of James Mecray, pilot, and first Burgess of Cape Island, was born at Cape May in 1842. He attended school in Cape May and at Philadelphia. After graduating at the University of Pennsylvania as a physicin he entered the navy as a surgeon and served during the civil war. In 1866 he entered into partnership with Dr. Samuel Marcy, and established a drug business. After ten years Dr. Marcy retired, and his son, Dr. V. M. D. Marcy, became Dr. Mecray's partner, and the firm remains the same to this day. He seved in the City Council in 1868, and when the charter of 1875 went into effect he was elected a member of Council for three years, serving as president during his entire term. He served a second three-year term from 1881 to 1884, and was again president during the whole of his term. He was City Treasurer from 1869 to 1871. He enjoys a large medical practice, and is a member of the Presbyterian Church.

John H. Benezet, merchant, is a descendant of Anthony Benezet, who was a patriot resident of Philadelphia during the Revolution. He was born at Cape May Court House in 1844. When sixteen his father died, and he then began working on the plantations of different farmers until he

DR. JAMES MECRAY.

went to Woodbury, N. J., where he learned the tinman's trade. By 1863 he had finished his trade, and then began business at Court House on his own account. He then began a housefurnishing business. In 1866 he opened an establishment at Cape Island. He afterwards, with his brother, Alfonso, established stores at Dennisville and Sea Isle City. He was a member of City Council in 1872 and 1873.

Joseph Q. Williams, the sixth, eighth and thirteenth Mayor of this city, was born in Philadelphia, November 2, 1827, and came to Cape May about 1850, just previous to the incorporation of the city. Mr. Williams is a carpenter by trade, and began his career here as a builder and built many of the residences about the Cape. He married Miss Sarah E., a daughter of William Stites, one time Treasurer of Cape Island. His first office was that of Alderman, to which he was elected in March, 1856. It was for a term of one year. At that time the Alderman was a member of the Council and a justice of the peace. During the years beginning in March of 1857 and 1858 he served the city of Cape Island as Councilman. In 1860 he was elected Recorder, and served for a year. This was virtually the same as an Alderman, and in this capacity was again Councilman and Justice of the Peace.

In 1862 he was put forward for Mayor, and was elected for one year. He introduced the system of paying over fines to the city treasury, a rule which his predecessors had not complied with. It was during this term also that the police were uniformed for the first time in this city.

In 1865, 1866 and 1867 he was successively elected a member of the City Council and performed also the duties of two other offices in the last of these three years. He was a triple office holder in that he was Councilman, Tax Collector and a Representative of Cape Island in the County Board of Freeholders. His colleague in the Freeholder Board was Joseph S. Leach.

At the spring election in 1868 he was again chosen Mayor for one year, and was a candidate for re-election, but was defeated by a close vote by Waters B. Miller, who succeeded him. During the year the Legislature passed a bill and made Mr. Williams, together with General William J. Sewell, of Camden, afterwards United States Senator from 1881 to 1887, and from 1895 to 1901; Col. J. Frank Cake, a prominent hotel proprietor of his day in Washington, Baltimore and Cape May; Hon. John C. Bullitt, a large property owner, but a resident and eminent lawyer of Philadelphia, who framed the famous Bullitt bill, or charter granted to Philadelphia in 1886; and Captain George Hildreth, of Cape May, the commission to improve the highways of the place. This commission lasted five years and four months, and during its existence the magnificent Beach avenue, or boulevard, was built, the work of superintending which almost wholly devolved upon Mr. Williams. For this service Mr. Williams never received any pay.

In 1874 he was again elected Recorder for one year, and of course was a member of the Council and Justice of the Peace. In the spring of 1875 the new charter of the city of Cape May went into effect, changing the name from the

JOSEPH Q. WILLIAMS.

City of Cape Island, and at the election he was elected Alderman for one year. The duties of this office were purely judicial, and its holder virtually vice-Mayor.

In 1877 Mr. Williams was again elected Mayor for a term of two years, and in March, 1889, he was re-elected for two more years. He was succeeded in 1881 by Mayor Melvin.

In 1884 he was again elected to office, this time as a Councilman. He was re-elected in 1887 and 1890 and served until 1893, since which time he has given up office holding. In 1884 he was chosen as President of Council, and again was its president in 1887. He was a valuable member and in 1886 was one of the five who saved to Cape May her valuable water works franchise.

Mr. Williams has been a consistent Presbyterian and active in church work the greater part of his life. In 1854 he was elected superintendent of the Sunday school of the First Presbyterian Church, and for twenty-seven years labored in the same position. For a number of years he has been an elder in the church, and was twice elected a member of the Presbyterian General Assembly of the United States for the New Jersey Synod—that of St. Paul in 1888, and of Saratoga in 1894. It is very seldom that a layman is twice honored in this way. Mr. Williams is a fluent speaker. His son, J. Ashton Williams, has been City Recorder since 1891.

One of the most disastrous fires which has ever visited this seaside resort burned over the most interesting and profitable part of the ocean front of Cape May City on Saturday, November 9, 1878. The fire broke out in the Ocean House about 8 o'clock in the morning, amid excellent elements, and lasted until night. The wind was an ally, and the limited fire apparatus was of no avail. At half past five in the afternoon it had crossed Ocean street, and taken everything clean on Beach avenue from Congress street to Stockton Row, and the mammoth Stockton seemed in the clutches of the fiend when the efforts of the Cape May, Vineland and Camden firemen, and the steamers which the two latter companies had brought with them, finally subdued it. All night long and Sunday the people were storing away their goods which they had saved. Trains came down crowded the next day from Philadelphia. The burned district covered an area of over thirty acres, divided as follows: Congress Hall property, five acres; the block bounded by Perry, Jackson and Washington streets and the beach, eight acres; the block bounded by Jackson, Decatur and Washington streets and the beach, eight acres; the property destroyed between Decatur and Ocean streets, from east of Washington street to ocean, five acres; the property annihilated between Ocean and Guerney (Stockton Row) streets, five acres. The Star of the Cape, of the Thursday following the fire, said: "The ravages of the fire can scarcely be appreciated from a pen description. Where on Saturday morning stood thirty acres covered with magnificent hotels, gems of cottages and thousands of bath houses is now a blackened waste, swept by the besom of destruction, leaving nothing in its wake but spectre chimneys and smouldering ruins." The property destroyed was estimated at $600,000, and included nine hotels: Congress Hall, Centre House, Ocean House, Avenue House, Merchants', Centennial, Atlantic, Knickerbocker and Columbia, all frame buildings. The principal cottages burned were Fryer's Bluff and Ocean Cottages, on Perry street; J. E. Mecray's, Peterson's, Fenlin's, Eliza Miller's, King's Ocean Villa, Hildreth's Wyoming Cottage, Chill's, McConnell's two, and Rudolph's, on Jackson street; Judge Hamburger's, King's three, Denizot's and Columbia's two on Decatur street; Smart's, Fisher's, Bullitt's and Wolfe's on Ocean street.

When the fire fiend had finished its work it left the following hotels: Stockton, Arctic, National, St. Elmo, Sea Breeze, United States, Chalfonte, Arlington, Clarendon, Cape May House, Delaware House, White Hall, Chester County House, Mineral Spring, Tremont House, Baltimore, American, Washington, Greenwood, and Young's.

In the place of the burned ones Congress Hall was rebuilt of brick on the ocean part of the property where it stands now. Congress place was laid out, and where the main building of Old Congress Hall stood is now the Elberon and several private properties.

The New Columbia was built of brick on Jackson street, occupying the block in which six of the burned hotels stood. Cottages have gradually taken the places of the ruins, and Cape May has not to-day those large hostelries, but the more modern houses are of the smaller class. Nearly thirty cottages were burned, whose places were taken inside of three years by forty-six new ones.

On February 11, 1880, John Mecray Post, No. 40, Grand Army of the Republic, was organized, with twenty-one old soldiers as members, as follows: George W. Barnes, Samuel C. Barton, James H. Carman, James V. Clark, James Crandol, John B. Davis, James J. Doak, Francis K. Duke, P. J. Donnelly, William B. Eldredge, William Farrow, Augustus C. Gile, Thomas Lemmon, Christopher S. Magrath, William W. Messich, John N. Reeves, Mitchell Sandgran, Charles Sandgran, Henry W. Sawyer, Henry P. Seaman and John D. Speace.

FREDERICK J. MELVIN.

Frederick J. Melvin, the fourteenth Mayor of Cape May, was born at Lumberton, North Carolina, February 28, 1848. When only six months old his parents removed with him to Philadelphia, where he resided until he was sixteen years of age. Young Melvin attended the public schools there until he came to Cape May, being employed for several summer seasons by the Harlan and Hollinsworth Steamboat Company, of Wilmington, on their line of small steamers which plied between Philadelphia and Cape May, traveling in those known as "Lady of the Lake," "Felton,"

"Sue" and others. During the winter seasons he was employed in the gas fixture business in Philadelphia.

When he attained his twentieth year he entered the employ of George B. Cake as clerk in the old Washington House, which stood where the Knickerbocker Building now stands, and was later a clerk at the Sherman House, previously called the Tontine, but now the United States Hotel, at Jackson and Lafayette streets. After this Mr. Melvin entered the employ of the firm of Richardson & Farrow, who during their time were the most prominent provisioners in the city of Cape May.

During the years 1874 and 1875 Mr. Melvin travelled for a New York firm, and in the latter year and early in 1876 superintended for a glass firm their part of the construction of the big main building of the Centennial Exposition in Philadelphia. During the Centennial he also ran a restaurant near the Exposition grounds. In 1877 he began business for himself in Cape May, opening a paint warehouse at the corner of Mansion and Jackson streets, which he conducted for about five years. In the spring of 1880 he was chosen by the people Alderman for a term of two years. After serving one year of his term, in 1881, he was elected Mayor for a term of two years, and was re-elected in 1883 for another term. He retired from the chair in 1885, after an administration which was a credit to his adopted city and to himself. Through his influence in the summer of 1881 St. John's Commandery, No. 4, Knight Templars, of Philadelphia, visited the Cape for four days, and the city was gay and festive. The commandery came again in 1882, and were royally entertained through the efforts of Mayor Melvin and the committee he selected. On this occasion the commandery presented him with a magnificent Templar's charm, and conferred upon him the rare honor of making him an honorary member of the commandery. In 1883 he entertained President Chester A. Arthur, who was a visitor.

In the summer of 1881 the Washington Light Infantry, through his efforts, came to Cape May for their first encampment. This famous organization was commanded by

Colonel William G. Moore, chief of police of Washington city, who had previously been private secretary to President Andrew Johnson. The infantry was composed of the cream of Washington's male population. In 1883 they came again to Cape May, and were again royally entertained. Before going home the infantry presented to Mayor Melvin, at the Stockton Hotel, in the presence of a large assemblage, a gold-headed cane, on the head of which was inscribed, "To Hon. F. Melvin, August, 1883, from the Washington Light Infantry, Washington, D. C." When the regiment was about to depart for their homes on that visit Mayor Melvin went to the depot to bid them goodbye and a safe return. In appreciation of his kindness he was arrested and carried by them to Washington, and received by a grand ovation, a military reception, and with fireworks en route. A grand banquet was given there in his honor, at which were in attendance nearly all the prominent citizens and officers in Washington.

For nine years previous to 1894 he was proprietor of the Sea Breeze Hotel, the property of the great Pensylvania Railroad.

President Cleveland appointed him postmaster of Cape May City on April 16, 1886, which office he held until April 16, 1889, when he resigned and was succeeded by Postmaster F. L. Richardson. In 1890 he entered the hotel business in Washington, which he successfully carried on for three years.

In 1884 he purchased the grocery business of Stillwell Hand, in Cape May City, and has successfully managed it. In 1888 he was the Democratic nominee for State Senator, but while polling a full Democratic vote was defeated in the landslide which carried President Cleveland into temporary retirement and made General Harrison President. He is a prominent Free Mason.

Isaac H. Smith, merchant, is a son of Isaac Smith, pilot (1805-1881), was born in Lower township on October 12, 1830. He passed his boyhood days there, and then learned to be a tailor in Philadelphia. Afterwards he established himself in the clothing business here, and became a successful merchant. He is an elder of the Presbyterian

Church. He is a director of the New Jersey Trust and Safe Deposit Company, and his advice in financial matters has always been considered wise by a large number of people who consult him frequently. He has served the city in various capacities creditably. He was Tax Collector in 1868, and member of Council from 1873 to 1878, and again from 1879 to 1882. He was chosen Treasurer of the city from year to year, often without opposition, from 1883 to 1895.

Eldridge Johnson, also a prominent merchant, was born January 1, 1838, in West Cape May. He attended the old cape school, and then began business life as a clerk in the stores of Enoch Edmunds, and later was a partner with W. Burr Miller in the general store business. For many years Mr. Johnson has devoted himself to his shoe business and to the management of his property. He is a trustee of the Presbyterian Church, and has for years been president of the Cape May Saving Fund and Building Association. Mr. Johnson was seveteen times elected City Treasurer, serving from 1860 to 1869 and from 1871 to 1879. He was a member of City Council from 1880 to 1883 and from 1895 to the present.

The iron ocean pier was erected at the foot of Decatur street in 1885 at a cost of $60,000.

James Henry Edmunds, the fifteenth and seventeenth Mayor of Cape May, was born in Lower township, Cape May county, August 7, 1847. He is a son of Hon. Richard D. Edmunds, who has been Sheriff, Assemblyman and Recorder of Cape May City. The first office which he held was that of Overseer of Poor in 1874. When the new charter went into effect in March, 1875, he was elected a member of the City Council for a term of two years. In March, 1878, he was again elected to Council for a term of two years to fill a vacancy, and again in 1883 he was elected for a term of three years. When he had served two years of this term, in March, 1885, he was elected Mayor for a term of two years, and was successively re-elected in 1887, 1889 and 1891. In 1893 he was defeated. He became a candidate in 1895, and was elected for a two-year term. He has been superintendent of the local beach front railroads, superintendent of the local gas company, and publisher of the Cape May Wave since 1887.

In 1886 a scheme was gotten up to sell the valuable franchise of the city water works to a company headed by General W. W. Taylor, a brother of the literateur, Bayard Taylor, for $22,000. At the head of the scheme was the Mayor, James H. Edmunds, who was a pronounced corporation man. At the time there were six hold-over members of Council, four for the sale, one against it, Joseph Q. Williams, and one who did not define his position, Charles H. Dougherty. After a three-days' campaign the people almost unanimously elected F. Sidney Townsend, Enos R. Williams and William T. Stevens as colleagues of Mr. Williams. Charles H. Dougherty, who was the president for year beginning in 1885, resigned, and there was a tie in the body over the matter—4 to 4. Subsequently Thomas H. Williamson was elected to the vacancy. He voted with the people's representatives, and thus the works were saved to their rightful owners.

In the autumn of 1889 the New Columbia Hotel, built on the site of the Atlantic (burned in 1878), was burned down. It was a brick structure, valued at $200,000.

In 1879 the present Baptist Church was erected at the corner of Franklin and Lafayette streets, but was not dedicated until August 14, 1892, when it was out of debt.

Francis K. Duke, who was president of the City Council during the year 1890, was born at Harper's Ferry, Va., December 7, 1830, where he remained until he was ten years of age, after which he lived in Pennsylvania and New Jersey, and when the Mount Vernon Hotel was being built in 1847, he came to Cape May. He had learned the carpenter's trade, and worked on that famous hotel. While here he married Miss Louisa Eldredge, a sister of Coroner Daniel C. Eldredge. Before the Rebellion he moved to Delaware, and when the war broke out he entered the Union army in the Second Delaware Regiment, serving as second lieutenant of Company F, and was promoted for meritorious service at the battle of Savage Station. He was bushwhacked at Drummondstown, Va., and his horse being shot from under him he was thrown, and the horse falling upon his leg crippled him so that he has never since had its free use. He came to Cape May again in 1868, where he has ever since resided, taking an active part in politics and Grand Army affairs. He has always been a Republican, is past commander of John Mecray Post, No. 40, G. A. R., and is a builder of note. For ten years he served as Justice of the Peace in Lower township, and in 1886 he was elected by City Council to the vacancy caused by the death of the late Thomas H. Williamson, and re-elected by the people for the unexpired term for one year. In 1888 he was chosen for a full term of three years, and was the president of the body during the year beginning March, 1890. In the fall of 1893 he was elected Coroner for Cape May county, and served three years.

James M. E. Hildreth, the sixteenth and eighteenth Mayor of the city of Cape May, is a son of Hon. Alvin P. Hildreth, who has served his city in various public offices, and served his county as a member of the State Legislature and the State as a Riparian Commissioner under the administration of Governor George T. Werts. The younger Hildreth was born in Cape May City, December 9, 1858, and for twelve years as a child lived in this city. His maternal ancestors were of the Wales family, whose history is well known, his great uncle, E. L. B. Wales, being at one time a judge of the New Jersey Court of Errors and Appeals, the highest tribunal in the State.

When Mr. Hildreth reached his twelfth year he was taken to Mount Holly, where he remained, finishing his education at the Mount Holly Academy, which has been a famous institution of its kind. After leaving school he studied law in the offices of Hon. Walter A. Barrows, an uncle, and Hon. Joseph H. Gaskell, now President Judge of Burlington county. After being admitted to the practice in the courts of New Jersey, in 1881, he removed to his native city again, where he has since resided, and become a prominent practitioner and enjoys a large clientage. It is said of Mr. Hildreth that he never advises any one to take up a law fight unless they have a wrong to right, and that his cases are nearly always won by his thorough research.

In 1883 Mr. Hildreth was chosen by the City Council Solicitor, and that he conducted the office in a way that bespoke praise to himself was known by every one who remembers the time. He held the office for one year, and then did not hold another office until elected Mayor in March, 1893, for a term of two years. He was always on hand to receive all visiting delegations. It was through his efforts mainly that the Fourth of July celebration of 1893 was a success. The principal speaker was Benjamin Harrison, ex-President of the United States. The ceremonies took place on the Stockton Hotel piazza and Mayor Hil-

JAMES M. E. HILDRETH.

dreth had the honor of introducing the famous visitor, and every one remarked on the occasion of the gracefulness by which it was done. During that year of Mr. Hildreth's administration, by his efforts, City Council secured as much for the city in the improvement line as any preceding Council, and yet so economical was the city's affairs managed that each taxpayer was saved fourteen per cent. of his usual net amount of tax.

In 1895 the City Council again elected Mr. Hildreth City Solicitor for a term of one year. In 1897 he was again chosen Mayor. He is a member of the First Presbyterian

Church of this city, and since January, 1885, has been a trustee and treasurer of the church. Since 1886, when the company was organized, he has been general manager of the Franklin Electric Light Company, of this city. He is also a director in the South Jersey Railroad Company, which opened a competing line to Cape May in 1894 during his term as Mayor.

He is an active member of the Cape May City Athletic Club, which was organized August 15, 1887, and had for its directors, besides himself, General William J. Sewell, of Camden, State Senator (afterwards Congressman) John E. Reyburn, of Philadelphia; George W. Boyd, assistant general passenger agent of the great Pennsylvania Railroad; Max Riebenack, the auditor of freight receipts of the same great corporation; W. S. P. Shields, the Philadelphia builder; Charles A. Hart, of Philadelphia; General Clinton P. Paine, of Baltimore, and Nathan C. Price, of this city. Mr. Reyburn was president; General Sewell, vice-president; Mr. Hildreth, secretary and attorney, and Mr. Riebenack, treasurer.

James J. Doak, president of Council from 1892 to 1894, was born in the First ward of Philadelphia, November 7, 1844. He was educated in the public schools of that city, principally at the Weccacoe and Mount Vernon Grammar Schools. Between school hours he was clerk in a grocery and provision store. Early in 1862, when not yet eighteen years of age, he enlisted as a private in the Nineteenth Pennsylvania Regiment, but was not accepted because of his youthfulness. He enlisted a second time early in 1863 in the Fifty-ninth Pennsylvania Regiment, and served in it four months, the time for which the regiment was mustered. After being discharged therefrom he again entered the army as a private in the One Hundred and Ninety-sixth Regiment, serving a full enlistment. He then learned the carpenter's trade, and in 1868 came to Cape May, where he has ever since resided. He followed his trade here for a while, but in 1869 became a member of the police force, in which he served eighteen years, being chief for eight years from 1870. He became a hotel detective and served in the Stockton

Hotel and Congress Hall, Cape May, and Willard's, Washington. He was for some years a detective of the Pennsylvania Railroad, operating on the New Jersey Division. In 1887 he was elected for a full term of three years as a member of the City Council, and has since been three times reelected, holding the position at the present time. He has been for several years assistant chief of the Cape May Fire Department. In politics he is a Republican, and a leader in the party.

Alonzo L. Leach, M. D., second son of Joseph S. Leach, was born at Cape May City March 19, 1845; received his education at our public schools and under private tutors; began the study of medicine at Harvard Medical College and completed the same at Jefferson Medical College, from which he was graduated with honors in 1868. Upon his graduation he was appointed Demonstrator of Anatomy in the Philadelphia School of Anatomy. In 1869 he was commissioned first assistant surgeon of the First Regiment, Pennsylvania National Guard, and was with his command on the several occasions it was called into service to quell formidable riots in Pennsylvania. During the railroad riots at Pittsburg in 1877 he was in charge of the division hospital, and on his return home was promoted surgeon for his meritorious service with rank as major. He resigned his commission after a service of thirteen years in the Guard, and after practicing medicine in Philadelphia with marked success for twenty years he was obliged to relinquish his work there on account of impaired health. Returning to Cape May in 1887 to recuperate his health, he here, later, resumed practice. While in Philadelphia he wrote on medical subjects, his writings being published in the then current medical magazines. One article published in the American Medical Journal on "The Influence of Close Confinement in Prisons on the Production of Phthisis" was translated into many of the leading magazines of Europe. He was a member of the Pathological Society and of the Philadelphia County Medical Society. He is president of the Board of Health of Cape May City, being elected in 1892, and was elected member of the Board of Education of the same city in 1896, and vice-president of the Cape May County Medical Society in 1897.

Lewis T. Stevens, president of Council in 1894, was born in West Cape May, August 22, 1868, and is a son of William T. Stevens, and grandson of William S. Hooper. He obtained his education in Cape May public schools and at Princeton College. Early in life he became an amateur journalist, then learned the trade of a printer, and finally became a newspaper correspondent. In 1892 he was elected to City Council for three years, serving as president the last year.

F. Sidney Townsend was born at Seaville, this county, June 21, 1849, and is a grandson of Joshua Townsend, Legislator. He obtained his educotion in Seaville, and in 1875 removed to Cape May City, where he has since resided. He was a member of Council from 1883 to 1892, and was chosen in 1896 for another full term of three years. He was president of Council in 1889 and in 1891. He was Alderman from 1894 to 1896.

CHAPTER XXXI.
THE BOROUGHS.

Ocean City, on Peck's beach, came into existence as a temperance and Methodist summer resort in 1880. It grew rapidly and is second now only to Cape May City in prosperity. It was beautifully laid out. In 1884 it was organized as a borough government. In 1897 it was made a city, and with the following as its bounds: Beginning at a point in the line of low-water mark on the northerly side of Corson's Inlet at the intersection of low-water mark to said Corson's Inlet with low-water mark of the Atlantic Ocean; thence northwesterly along and in line of low-water mark of said Corson's Inlet to the intersection thereof with Beach Thoroughfare; thence northeasterly along said Beach Thoroughfare to the most easterly channel of Peck's Bay; thence still northeasterly in and along the most easterly channel of Peck's Bay and Great Egg Harbor Bay to the dividing line between Cape May county and Atlantic county; thence following said dividing line in a southeasterly direction down Great Egg Harbor Bay and Great Egg Harbor Inlet to the Atlantic Ocean; thence extending into the Atlantic Ocean as far as the jurisdiction of the State of New Jersey extends; thence southwesterly along and in the said jurisdictional line of the State to a point in said line at right angles to low-water mark on the north side of Corson's Inlet aforesaid; thence northwesterly to the place of beginning.

It has a water works, by which water is obtained from artesian wells driven nearly 800 feet in the earth. A sewage and drainage system has been introduced. The town is lighted by electricity. The leading hotels are the Brighton, Illinois, Emmett, Wesley House, Vandalia, Strand, Lafayette, Traymore, Excursion and Adams' Casino. It has a public school, a Methodist church, built in 1890; St. Augustine's (Catholic) Church, built in 1895, and an Episcopal church, built in 1897.

The West Jersey Railroad was opened to Ocean City in 1884.

Gainer P. Moore, the first Mayor, was born in Chester county, Pa., in 1836, where he obtained his education. He served honorably in the civil war on the Union side. In 1866 he became a merchant in Philadelphia, and in 1881 he came to Ocean City, and has since been an energetic public citizen. He is a Methodist in religion.

James E. Pryor, the second Mayor, was born near Logansport, Indiana, April 24, 1861, and was educated in the public schools there and at nineteen became a teacher in them. He fitted himself for the medical profession in the University Medical College at Detroit, Mich., graduating in 1888. He then came to Ocean City.

Harry G. Steelman, fourth Mayor, was a native of Weymouth, N. J., and settled in Ocean City in 1888.

Robert Fisher, fifth Mayor, is a real estate agent of considerable activity.

Wildwood was founded by Philip Pontius Baker, of Vineland, N. J., about 1890.

"Wildwood" is situated on the famous "Five Mile Beach," about six miles northeast of Cape May City. The tract comprises 100 acres and it lies between the ocean and the "thoroughfare." About fifty acres are in woods, grand timber, some of the trees being nearly one hundred feet high, and two to five in diameter. They include pine, red, white and black oak, sassafras—six feet in circumference—red and white cedar, holly, magnolia, wild cherry, persimmon, sweet gum, beech, plum and other varieties, and from the branches of many of them hang festoons of beautiful green mosses, three to six feet in length. Gigantic grape vines here flourish, one monster nearly a yard in circumference ten feet from the ground, spreading away over the branches of the oaks a distance of two hundred feet. All underbrush, undesirable vines and bushes have been cleared away, bringing to view the innumerable variety of beautiful wild flowers which cover the ground in every direction. An authority on the subject states that

THE BOROUGHS. 447

every variety of flower that grows along the coast from Maine to Florida is here to be found.

In the centre of the forest is a charming little body of fresh water appropriately called Magnolia Lake. It is about three feet in depth and is fed by a small stream that rises a mile or so away. It is one of the prettiest spots on the tract, and is especially popular with the children who are never happier than when navigating the lake in boats.

Here and there in the woods are rare and interesting specimens of nature's handiwork, to see which is alone worth a visit to the "Beach." There is, for example, an immense huckleberry bush growing from the trunk of a tree twenty feet from the ground, and which has for years borne large crops of fine fruit.

The town was developed rapidly, and laid out in squares. It is situated on the central portion of Five Mile Beach. There are water works, a Baptist church, a Presbyterian church and a public school there. The water is derived from two artesian wells, one 1000 feet deep and the other 700 feet. The latter alone has a capacity of 500,000 gallons per day. The leading hotels of the place are Hotel Dayton, Marine Hall, The Latimer, Sea View, Ocean Villa, Tower Villa, Silver Dean, Brighton, Woodland, Selina, Stewart, Ivy and Wildwood. The West Jersey Railroad runs there. The borough was incorporated first on May 1, 1895.

Philip P. Baker, its founder, was born at Cowan, Union county, Pa., January 14, 1846. He went to school there, and at sixteen when his father died, managed the farm there.

In 1869, with his brother, L. R., he removed to Vineland, N. J., and there conducted a general store. The Baker Brothers, as their firm was known by name, built the Baker House Block there. He was a member of Assembly from Cumberland county in 1882, and in 1886 was elected State Senator from that county. He was a prominent mover in having the law passed introducing manual training in the public schools. Being a Democrat, he was a delegate-at-large from New Jersey to the National Democratic convention in 1888 and in 1892 was a Presidential elector, casting a vote for Grover Cleveland. In 1891 he was receiver of the Philadelphia and Seashore Railroad. He was interested in Sea Isle City's foundation.

In 1896 he was made New Jersey's member of the Democratic National Committee.

Avalon was founded by the Seven-Mile Beach Company, at the head of which was Frank Siddall, of Philadelphia, in 1887, and in 1891 a borough was created. It is situated on the north end of Seven Mile Beach, and has several hotels. The West Jersey Railroad is opened through it.

Thomas Bray, who has been Mayor since its incorporation, was born in New York city on September 5, 1843. He lived there until four years of age, when he was taken to Philadelphia, where he resided until 1857. He then returned to New York, where he was educated. In 1861 he came back to Philadelphia and was with the Lockwood Manufacturing Company two years. He then went to New York again, remaining for eight years. Soon after this he became manager of Dr. J. H. Schenck's medicine manufactory, in Philadelphia, and removed there until he became secretary of Seven-Mile Beach Company, in 1886, since which time he has devoted his entire time to its success.

Sea Isle City includes the whole of Ludlam's Beach, and was first laid out about 1880. Charles K. Landis was its founder. The island fronts six and one-quarter miles in length on the Atlantic Ocean, and varies from one-quarter to one and one-quarter miles in width, extending from Corson's Inlet, on the north, to Townsend's Inlet, on the south, and is bounded on the west by Ludlam Bay and a navigable channel, called the Thoroughfare, furnishing excellent advantages for fishing, sailing, or still-water bathing.

Sea Isle City is brilliantly illuminated at night with electric light, and the cottages and hotels are lighted by electricity. As to good water, Sea Isle City is supplied from an ever-flowing well of water. All the cottages are supplied with this water.

Two systems of railroads, West Jersey and Seashore, and the South Jersey.

It has thirty hotels, an electric railroad, ice plant, school house, a Methodist church, built in 1888, and a Catholic church, built in 1890.

Its first Council was composed of James P. Way, Roger Dever, William L. Peterson and Hudson Ludlam.

Cape May Point was set off as a political division in 1878, and continued to be a borough until 1896. Its borough government, after 1890, became a matter of uncertainty, its final abandonment of local government being the outcome of the unconstitutionality of the law under which it existed. It is now a part of Lower township. It has an electric light works, a water plant, four or five hotels, several boarding houses, a public school, a Baptist, a Catholic and an Episcopal church.

Anglesea was made a borough in 1885. It is a great resort for fishermen, who go to sea to fish. It contains several hotels and boarding cottages.

Holly Beach was also made a borough in 1885, and has several hotels and boarding cottages.

West Cape May was made a borough and came out of Lower township in 1884. Out of it was made South Cape May Borough ten years later.

APPENDIX A.
MEMBERS OF THE LEGISLATURE.

A list of the Members of the Legislature from the first record of them after the surrender of the Government in Queen Anne's reign in 1702 to the present time.

DATE.	COUNCIL.	ASSEMBLY.
1702 to 1707	....	Peter Fretwell.
1707 to 1708	....	Peter Corson.
1708 to 1709	....	Ezekiel Eldredge.
1709 to 1716	....	Jacob Spicer, Peter Fretwell.
1716 to 1717	....	Jacob Spicer, Jacob Huling.
1717 to 1723	....	Jacob Spicer, Jeremiah Bass.
1723 to 1733	....	Humphrey Hughes, Nath'l Jenkins.
1733 to 1740	....	Aaron Leaming, 1st, Henry Young.
1740 to 1743	....	Aaron Leaming, Aaron Leaming, Jr.
1743 to 1744	....	Aaron Leaming, John Willets.
1744 to 1745	....	Henry Young, Jacob Spicer, 2d.
1745 to 1769	....	Aaron Leaming 2d, Jacob Spicer 2d.
1769 to 1771	....	Aaron Leaming 2d, Nicholas Stillwell.
1771 to 1773	....	Aaron Leaming 2d, Jonathan Hand.
1773 to 1776	....	Eli Eldredge, Jonathan Hand.
1776 to 1778	Jonathan Hand.	Eli Eldredge, Joseph Savage, Hugh Haythorn.
1778 to 1779	Jonathan Jenkins.	Eli Eldredge, Richard Townsend.
1779 to 1780	Jesse Hand.	Henry Y. Townsend, James Whillden, Jonathan Leaming.
1780 to 1781	Jesse Hand.	Joseph Hildreth, Jeremiah Eldredge, Matthew Whillden.
1781 to 1782	Elijah Hughes.	Richard Townsend.
1782 to 1783	Jesse Hand.	Matthew Whillden, John Baker, Elijah Townsend.
1783 to 1784	Jesse Hand.	John Baker, Joseph Hildreth.
1784 to 1785	Jeremiah Eldredge.	Elijah Townsend, Levi Eldredge.
1785 to 1786	Elijah Hughes.	Elijah Townsend, John Baker, Nezer Swain.
1786 to 1787	Jeremiah Eldredge.	Matthew Whillden, John Baker, Elijah Townsend.
1787 to 1789	Jeremiah Eldredge.	Matthew Whillden, Richard Townsend, Elijah Townsend.
1789 to 1790	Jeremiah Eldredge.	Eli Townsend, Nezer Swain, Elijah Townsend.
1790 to 1791	Jeremiah Eldredge.	Richard Townsend, Nezer Swain, Elijah Townsend.
1791 to 1793	Jeremiah Eldredge.	Richard Townsend, Matthew Whillden, Elijah Townsend.

MEMBERS OF THE LEGISLATURE. 451

DATE.	COUNCIL.	ASSEMBLY.
1793 to 1794	Jeremiah Eldredge.	Richard Townsend, Matthew Whillden, Ebenezer Newton.
1794 to 1795	Matthew Whillden.	David Johnson, Richard Townsend.
1795 to 1796	Matthew Whillden.	Richard Townsend, Reuben Townsend, Eleazer Hand.
1796 to 1797	Parmenas Corson.	Abijah Smith, Elijah Townsend, Richard Townsend.
1797 to 1798	Parmenas Corson.	Persons Leaming.
1798 to 1799	Parmenas Corson.	Elijah Townsend.
1799 to 1801	John Townsend.	Abijah Smith.
1801 to 1803	Parmenas Corson.	Persons Leaming.
1803 to 1804	Ebenezer Newton.	Joseph Falkenburge.
1804 to 1805	Parmenas Corson.	Matthew Whillden.
1805 to 1806	William Eldredge.	Thomas Hughes.
1806 to 1807	Matthew Whillden.	Nicholas Willets.
1807 to 1808	Ebenezer Newton.	Thomas H. Hughes.
1808 to 1809	Joseph Falkenburge	Nicholas Willets.
1809 to 1810	Matthew Whillden.	Thomas H. Hughes.
1810 to 1811	Matthew Whillden.	Joseph Falkenburge.
1811 to 1812	Nathaniel Holmes.	Nicholas Willets.
1812 to 1813	Joseph Falkenburge.	Thomas H. Hughes.
1813 to 1814	Joseph Falkenburge.	Joshua Swain.
1814 to 1815	Furman Leaming.	Robert H. Holmes.
1815 to 1819	Joshua Swain.	Nicholas Willets.
1819 to 1821	Thomas H. Hughes.	Joshua Townsend.
1821 to 1822	Thomas H. Hughes.	Nicholas Willets.
1822 to 1823	Thomas H. Hughes.	Joshua Townsend.
1823 to 1824	Joshua Swain.	Israel Townsend.
1824 to 1825	Thomas H. Hughes.	Israel Townsend.
1825 to 1827	Joshua Swain.	Israel Townsend.
1827 to 1830	Israel Townsend.	Joshua Townsend.
1830 to 1831	Israel Townsend.	Jeremiah Leaming.
1831 to 1834	Joshua Townsend.	Jeremiah Leaming.
1834 to 1836	Jeremiah Leaming.	Richard Thompson.
1836 to 1838	Richard Thompson.	Amos Corson.
1838 to 1840	Amos Corson.	Thomas P. Hughes.
1840 to 1842	Thomas P. Hughes.	Maurice Beesley.
1842 to 1844	Maurice Beesley.	Reuben Willets.

Session Dates	SENATE.	House of Assembly.
1845	Reuben Willits.	John Stites.
1846	Reuben Willits.	Samuel Townsend.
1847	James L. Smith.	Richard S. Ludlam.
1848 and 1849	James L. Smith.	Nathaniel Holmes, Jr.
1850 and 1851	Enoch Edmunds.	Mackey Williams.
1852	Enoch Edmunds.	Joshua Swain.
1853	Joshua Swain, Jr.	Waters B. Miller.
1854 and 1855	Joshua Swain, Jr.	Jesse H. Diverty.
1856, 1857 and 1858	Jesse H. Diverty.	Downs Edmunds, Jr.
1859 and 1860	Downs Edmunds.	Abram Reeves.
1861	Downs Edmunds.	Jonathan F. Leaming.
1862, 1863 and 1864	Jonathan F. Leaming	Wilmon W. Ware.

452   HISTORY OF CAPE MAY COUNTY.

Session Dates.	SENATE.	House of Assembly.
1865, 1866 and 1867	Wilmon W. Ware.	Thomas Beesley.
1868	Leaming M. Rice.	Samuel R. Magonagle.
1869 and 1870	Leaming M. Rice.	Thomas Beesley.
1871, 1872 and 1873	Thomas Beesley.	Richard S. Leaming.
1874	Richard S. Leaming.	Alexander Young.
1875	Richard S. Leaming.	Richard D. Edmunds.
1876	Richard S. Leaming.	William T. Stevens.
1877 and 1878	Jonatnan F. Leaming.	William T. Stevens.
1879	Jonathan F. Leaming.	Daniel Schellinger.
1880	Waters B. Miller.	Jesse D. Ludlam.
1881 and 1882	Waters B. Miller.	Furman L. Richardson.
1883, 1884 and 1885	Waters B. Miller.	Jesse D. Ludlam.
1886 and 1887	Joseph H. Hanes.	Alvin P. Hildreth.
1888	Joseph H. Hanes.	Walter S. Leaming.
1889, 1890 and 1891	Walter S. Leaming.	Eugene C. Cole.
1892, 1893 and 1894	Lemuel E. Miller.	Edmund L. Ross.
1895 and 1896	Edmund L. Ross.	Furman L. Ludlam.
1897	Edmund L. Ross.	Robert E. Hand.

DIRECTORS OF THE FREEHOLDERS.

1827—Joseph Falkinburge.
1830—Richard Thompson.
1831—Joseph Falkinburge.
1833—Samuel Matthews.
1834—Nathaniel Holmes.
1841—Franklin Hand.
1842—Jonathan J. Springer.
1844—Franklin Hand.
1845—Stephen Young.
1846—John Smith.
1847—Nathaniel Holmes.
1851—William S. Townsend.

1855—Hezekiah W. Godfrey.
1859—Samuel F. Ware.
1861—Thomas Williams.
1869—Aaron Miller.
1870—Alexander Young.
1878—Alexander Corson.
1888—John W. Reeves.
1893—William Lake.
1894—Andrew Weeks.
1895—William T. Bate.
1896—A. Carlton Hildreth.

APPENDIX B.

BOARDS OF FREEHOLDERS.

Members of the Boards of Chosen Freeholders from 1827 to 1897:

1827—Ezekiel Stevens, Thomas P. Hughes, Lower; Ephraim Hildreth, Joseph Falkenburg, Middle; Jacob G. Smith, Samuel Bishop, Dennis; John Williams, Amos Corson, Upper.

1828—John Williams, Amos Corson, Upper; Samuel Bishop, Christopher Ludlam, Dennis; Joseph Falkenburg, Ephraim Hildreth, Middle; Ezekiel Stevens, Reuben Foster, Lower.

1829—Stephen Young, Parmenas Corson, Upper; Christopher Ludlam, Samuel Bishop, Dennis; Joseph Falkenburg, Ephraim Hildreth, Middle; Ezekiel Stevens, Spicer Leaming, Lower.

1830—Parmenas Corson, Stephen Young, Upper; Amos C. Moore, Elijah Robinson, Dennis; Richard Thompson, Swain Townsend, Middle; Ezekiel Stevens, Downs Edmunds, Lower.

1831—Parmenas Corson, Stephen Young, Upper; John Smith, Elijah Robinson, Dennis; Joseph Falkenburg, Samuel Springer, Middle; Ezekiel Stevens, Alexander McKean, Lower.

1823—Parmenas Corson, Stephen Young, Upper; John Smith, Elijah Robinson, Dennis; Joseph Falkenburg, Samuel Springer, Middle; Ezekiel Stevens, Alexander McKean, Lower.

1833—John Williams, Stephen Young, Upper; Samuel Matthews, James L. Smith, Dennis; Jeremiah Hand, Samuel Springer, Middle; Ezekiel Stevens, Joseph B. Hughes, Lower.

1834—Parmenas Corson, David Kinsey, Upper; Jacob Souder, Nathaniel Holmes, Dennis; Ephraim Hildreth,

John Townsend, Middle; Joseph B. Hughes, David Cresse, Lower.

1835—John Stites, David Kinsey, Upper; Nathaniel Holmes, James L. Smith, Dennis; John Townsend, Ephraim Hildreth, Middle; Israel Townsend, David Cresse, Lower.

1836—David Kinsey, John Stites, Upper; Nathaniel Holmes, Jacob G. Smith, Dennis; Joseph Falkenburg, Ephraim Hildreth, Middle; Israel Townsend, David Cresse, Lower.

1837—John Williams, Eli Bunnell, Upper; Jacob G. Smith, Nathaniel Holmes, Dennis; Samuel Springer, Franklin Hand, Middle; Ezekiel Stevens, David Cresse, Lower.

1838—John Williams, Eli Bunnell, Upper; Nathaniel Holmes, James L. Smith, Dennis; Franklin Hand, Samuel Springer, Middle; Ezekiel Stevens, David Cresse, Lower.

1839—David Kimsey, Miles Corson, Upper; Nathaniel Holmes, James L. Smith, Dennis; Franklin Hand, Jonathan J. Springer, Middle; Ezekiel Stevens, David Cresse, Lower.

1840—John Williams, John Stites, Upper; Nathaniel Holmes, William S. Townsend, Dennis; Franklin Hand, Jonathan J. Springer, Middle; Ezekiel Stevens, David Cresse, Lower.

1841—Randolph Marshall, John Stites, Upper; James L. Smith, Amos C. Moore, Dennis; Franklin Hand, Jonathan J. Springer, Middle; David Cresse, Ezekiel Stevens, Lower.

1842—Eli Bunnell, Hezekiah W. Godfrey, Upper; Amos C. Moore, James L. Smith, Dennis; Jonathan J. Springer, Jonathan Hewitt, Jr., Middle; Ezekiel Stevens, David Cresse, Lower.

1843—Eli Bunnell, Hezekiah W. Godfrey, Upper; John Smith, James L. Smith, Dennis; Jonathan J. Springer, Franklin Hand, Middle; Israel Townsend, Ezekiel Stevens, Lower.

1844—Hezekiah W. Godfrey, Daniel Corson, Upper; Jame L. Smith, John Smith, Dennis; Franklin Hand, Thomas Hewitt, Middle; Israel Townsend, Ezekiel Stevens, Lower.

1845—Stephen Young, Reuben Gandy, Upper; James L.

Smith, John Smith, Dennis; Eli Townsend, Thomas Hewitt, Middle; Spicer Hughes, Abraham Reeves, Lower.

1846—Thomas Van Gilder, Ezra Corson, Upper; James L. Smith, John Smith, Dennis; Thomas Hewitt, Stephen Hand, Middle; David Cresse, Abraham Reeves, Lower.

1847—Hezekiah W. Godfrey, Stephen Young, Upper; Nathaniel Holmes, James L. Smith, Dennis; Richard Thompson, Stephen Hand, Middle; Israel Townsend, Samuel Fithian Ware, Lower.

1848—Stephen Young, Hezekiah W. Godfrey, Upper; Nathaniel Holmes, James L. Smith, Dennis; Richard Thompson, Stephen Hand, Middle; Israel Townsend, Samuel F. Ware, Lower.

1849—Stephen Young, Hezekiah W. Godfrey, Upper; Nathaniel Holmes, James L. Smith, Dennis; Richard Thompson, Richard C. Holmes, Middle; Israel Townsend, Samuel F. Ware, Lower.

1850—Hezekiah W. Godfrey, Levi Corson, Upper; Nathaniel Holmes, William S. Townsend, Dennis; Richard Thompson, Richard C. Holmes, Middle; Israel Townsend, Lemuel Swain, Lower.

1851—Levi Corson, Townsend Stites, Upper; James L. Smith, William S. Townsend, Dennis; Stephen Hand, Matthew Marcy, Middle; Abraham Reeves, Israel Townsend, Lower; Joseph Ware, William Cassedy, City of Cape Island.

1852—Townsend Stites, Hezekiah W. Godfrey, Upper; William S. Townsend, James L. Smith, Dennis; Stephen Hand, Matthew Marcy, Middle; Israel Townsend, Abram Reeves, Lower; William Cassedy, Charles Downs, Cape Island.

1853—Hezekiah W. Godfrey, Thomas Van Gilder, Upper; William S. Townsend, James L. Smith, Dennis; Matthew Marcy, Stephen Hand, Middle; Israel Townsend, Abraham Reeves, Lower; William Cassedy, Richard S. Ludlam, Cape Island.

1854—Hezekiah W. Godfrey, Stephen Young, Upper; William S. Townsend, James L. Smith, Dennis; Matthew Marcy, Stephen Hand, Middle; Downs Edmunds, Jr., Samuel F. Ware, Lower; Samuel S. Marcy, Waters B. Miller, Cape Island.

1855—Hezekiah W. Godfrey, Amos S. Corson, Upper; David T. Smith, Clinton H. Ludlam, Dennis; Stephen Hand, Aaron Miller, Middle; Samuel F. Ware, Richard D. Edmunds, Lower; William S. Hooper, Richard S. Ludlam, Cape Island.

1856—Hezekiah W. Godfrey, Townsend Stites, Upper; Matthew Marcy, Stephen Hand, Middle; Clinton H. Ludlam, William S. Townsend, Dennis; Andrew H. Reeves, Samuel F. Ware, Lower; Dr. Samuel S. Marcy, Waters B. Miller, Cape Island.

1857—Hezekiah W. Godfrey, Townsend Stites, Upper; William S. Townsend, Clinton H. Ludlam, Dennis; Stephen Hand, Aaron Miller, Middle; Samuel F. Ware, Richard D. Edmunds, Lower; Samuel S. Marcy, W. B. Miller, Cape Island.

1858—Hezekiah W. Godfrey, Townsend Stites, Upper; Clinton H. Ludlam, William S. Townsend, Dennis; Stephen Hand, Smith Townsend, Middle; Samuel F. Ware, Andrew H. Reeves, Lower; Samuel S. Marcy, W. B. Miller, Cape Island.

1859—Townsend Stites, Thomas Williams, Upper; William S. Townsend, Clinton H. Ludlam, Dennis; Stephen Hand, Smith Townsend, Middle; Samuel F. Ware, Andrew H. Reeves, Lower; Samuel S. Marcy, W. B. Miller, Cape Island.

1860—Thomas Williams, Joseph D. Chattin, Upper; William H. Townsend, Clinton H. Ludlam, Dennis; Smith Townsend, Aaron Miller, Middle; Samuel F. Ware, Andrew H. Reeves, Lower; Waters B. Miller, Samuel S. Marcy, Cape Island.

1861—Thomas Williams, Townsend Stites, Upper; William S. Townsend, Clinton H. Ludlam, Dennis; Aaron Miller, Smith Townsend, Middle; Samuel F. Ware, Andrew H. Reeves, Lower; Samuel S. Marcy, Waters B. Miller, Cape Island.

1862—Thomas Williams, Townsend Stites, Upper; Clinton H. Ludlam, Richard S. Leaming, Dennis; Aaron Miller, Smith Townsend, Middle; Samuel F. Ware, Andrew H.

BOARDS OF FREEHOLDERS.

Reeves, Lower; Samuel S. Marcy, Richard S. Ludlam, Cape Island.

1863—Thomas Williams, Townsend Stites, Upper; Clinton H. Ludlam, William H. Townsend, Dennis; Coleman F. Leaming, Alexander Young, Lower; Waters B. Miller, Joseph S. Leach, Cape Island.

1864—Thomas Williams, Sylvanus Corson, Upper; William S. Townsend, Clinton H. Ludlam, Dennis; Coleman F. Leaming, Alexander Young, Middle; Andrew H. Reeves, Samuel F. Ware, Lower; Joseph S. Leach, James S. Kennedy, Cape Island.

1865—Thomas Williams, Sylvanus Corson, Upper; William S. Townsend, Clinton H. Ludlam, Dennis; Coleman F. Leaming, Alexander Young, Middle; Joseph E. Hughes, Andrew H. Stevens, Lower; Joseph S. Leach, James S. Kennedy, Cape Island.

1866—Thomas Williams, Sylvanus Corson, Upper; William S. Townsend, Clinton H. Ludlam, Dennis; Aaron Miller, John W. Swain, Middle; Samuel F. Ware, Andrew H. Reeves, Lower; Waters B. Miller, Thomas B. Hughes, Cape Island.

1867—Thomas Williams, Sylvanus Corson, Upper; William S. Townsend, Clinton H. Ludlam, Dennis; Aaron Miller, John W. Swain, Middle; Andrew H. Reeves, Samuel F. Ware, Lower; Joseph Q. Williams, Joseph S. Leach, Cape Island.

1868—Thomas Williams, Sylvanus Corson, Upper; Clinton H. Ludlam (John Grady, to fill vacancy), William S. Townsend, Dennis; Aaron Miller, Alexander Young, Middle; Samuel F. Ware, Andrew H. Reeves, Lower; Joseph S. Leach, Waters B. Miller (Joseph Q. Williams, to fill vacancy), Cape Island.

1869—Sylvanus Corson, James Shoemaker, Upper; Richard S. Leaming, Thomas Townsend, Dennis; John W. Swain, Aaron Miller, Middle; Samuel F. Ware, Andrew H. Reeves, Lower; Samuel S. Marcy, Joseph Schellenger, Cape Island.

1870—James Shoemaker, Sylvanus Corson, Upper; Thomas Townsend, Richard S. Leaming, Dennis; Alexander Young, Thomas Douglass, Middle; Andrew H. Reeves, Daniel Schellenger, Lower; Wilmon W. Ware, Aaron Miller (died, and Joseph S. Leach), Cape Island.

1871—James Shoemaker, Richard B. Stites, Upper; Richard S. Leaming, Leaming M. Rice, Dennis; Alexander Young, Thomas Douglass, Middle; Andrew H. Reeves, Daniel C. Eldredge, Lower; J. Stratton Ware, Joseph Schellenger, Cape Island.

1872—James Shoemaker, Sylvanus Corson, Upper; Richard S. Leaming, Leaming M. Rice, Dennis; Alexander Young, Thomas Douglass, Middle; Andrew H. Reeves, Daniel C. Eldredge, Lower; J. Stratton Ware, Richard D. Edmunds, Cape Island.

1873—James Shoemaker, Alexander Corson, Upper; Leaming M. Rice, James Henderson, Dennis; Alexander Young, Thomas Douglass, Middle; Daniel C. Eldredge, Daniel Schellenger, Lower; J. Stratton Ware, J. Henry Farrow, Cape Island.

1874—Lewis S. Williams, Alexander Corson, Upper; James Henderson, Leaming M. Rice, Dennis; Alexander Young, Thomas Douglass, Middle; Daniel C. Eldredge, Daniel Schellenger, Lower; J. Stratton Ware, J. Henry Farrow, Cape Island.

1875—Alexander Corson, Lewis S. Williams, Upper; Leaming M. Rice, John Tyler, Dennis; Alexander Young, Thomas Douglass, Middle; Daniel C. Eldredge, Daniel Schellenger, Lower; J. Stratton Ware, J. Henry Farrow, Cape May City.

1876—Alexander Corson, Anthony Steelman, Upper; Leaming M. Rice, John Tyler, Dennis; Alexander Young, Thomas Douglass, Middle; Daniel Schellenger, William L. Cummings, Lower; J. Henry Farrow, Maskel Ware, Cape May City.

1877—Alexander Corson, Anthony Steelman, Upper; Leaming M. Rice, John Tyler, Dennis; Dr. Alexander Young, Thomas Douglass, Middle; William L. Cummings, John W. Reeves, Lower; J. Henry Farrow, J. Stratton Ware, Cape May Ciy.

1878—Alexander Corson, Anthony Steelman, Upper; Leaming M. Rice, John Tyler, Dennis; Franklin Hand,

BOARDS OF FREEHOLDERS.

Cornelius Townsend, Middle; Daniel Schellenger, Joseph C. Eldredge, Lower; Waters B. Miller, Maskel Ware, Cape May City; George W. Barnes, C. B. Reeves, Cape May Point.

1879—Alexander Corson, Anthony Steelman, Upper; Leaming M. Rice, John Tyler, Dennis; Franklin Hand, John W. Swain, Middle; Joseph C. Eldredge, Samuel Townsend, Lower; Waters B. Miller, Maskel Ware, Cape May City; George W. Barnes, Samuel W. Wiley, Cape May Point.

1880—Alexander Corson, Anthony Steelman, Upper; Leaming M. Rice, John Tyler, Dennis; Franklin Hand, John W. Swain, Middle; Joseph C. Eldredge, Samuel Townsend, Lower; Alvin P. Hildreth, Maskel Ware, Cape May City; Samuel W. Wiley, Cape May Point.

1881—Alexander Corson, Anthony Steelman, Upper; Leaming M. Rice, Jesse D. Ludlam, Dennis; Franklin Hand, Townsend W. Garretson, Middle; Joseph C. Eldredge, Samuel Townsend, Lower; Alvin P. Hildreth, Maskel Ware, Cape May City; C. Simpson, William H. Keeler, Cape May Point.

1882—Alexander Corson, Anthony Steelman, Upper; Leaming M. Rice, Jesse D. Ludlam, Dennis; Townsend W. Garretson, Nathaniel Newton, Middle; Joseph C. Eldredge, Samuel Townsend, Lower; Alvin P. Hildreth. Maskel Ware, Cape May City; C. Simpson, Howard Finley, Cape May Point; Thomas E. Ludlam, William L. Peterson, Sea Isle City.

1883—Alexander Corson, Anthony Steelman, Upper; Leaming M. Rice, Jesse D. Ludlam, Dennis; Townsend W. Garretson, Nathaniel Newton, Middle; Joseph C. Eldredge, William S. Harris, Lower; Alvin P. Hildreth, Micajah Smith, Cape May City; C. Simpson, Cape May Point; Crawford Buck, Sea Isle City.

1884—Alexander Corson, Anthony Steelman, Upper; Leaming M. Rice, John W. Young, Dennis; Townsend W. Garretson, Nathaniel Newton, Middle; Joseph C. Eldredge, William S. Harris, Lower; Alvin P. Hildreth, William S. Hooper, Cape May City; Page Crowell, Cape May Point;

Crawford Buck, Sea Isle City; William Lake, Ocean City; John W. Reeves, West Cape May.

1885—Alexander Corson, Benjamin H. Marshall, Upper; Leaming M. Rice, Henry T. Corson, Dennis; Townsend W. Garretson, Nathaniel Newton, Middle; Joseph C. Eldredge, William S. Harris, Lower; Alvin P. Hildreth, Micajah Smith, Cape May City; Page Crowell, Cape May Point; Martin Wells, Sea Isle City; William Lake, Ocean City; John W. Reeves, West Cape May; John Measy, Holly Beach; Hewlett Brower, Anglesea.

1886—Alexander Corson, Benjamin H. Marshall, Upper; Leaming M. Rice, Henry T. Corson, Dennis; Townsend W. Garretson, Nathaniel Newton, Middle; Joseph C. Eldredge, James H. Shaw, Lower; Micajah Smith, William S. Hooper, Cape May City; William Lake, Ocean City; Martin Wells, Sea Isle City; Hewlett Brower, Anglesea; L. M. Pancoast, Holly Beach; John W. Reeves, West Cape May; Henry Jacoby, Cape May Point.

1887—Alexander Corson, Benjamin H. Marshall, Upper; Leaming M. Rice, Lewis Edwards, Dennis; Townsend W. Garretson, Nathaniel Newton, Middle; Micajah Smith, William S. Hooper, Cape May City; Joseph C. Eldredge, William T. Bate, Lower; William Lake, Ocean City; Martin Wells, Sea Isle City; Hewlett Brower, Anglesea; L. M. Pancoast, Holly Beach; John W. Reeves, West Cape May.

1888—Alexander Corson, John Wallace, Upper; Leaming M. Rice, Charles J. Devitt, Dennis; Townsend W. Garretson, Jacob G. Hand, Middle; William T. Bate, Robert E. Hand, Lower; Micajah Smith, William S. Hooper, Cape May City; R. Curtis Robinson, Ocean City; Crawford Buck, Sea Isle City; Hewlett Brower, Anglesea; L. M. Pancoast, Holly Beach; John W. Reeves, West Cape May; Richard C. Stevenson, Cape May Point.

1889—Alexander Corson, John Wallace, Upper; Leaming M. Rice, Charles J. Devitt, Dennis; Townsend W. Garretson, Jacob G. Hand, Middle; William T. Bate, Robert E. Hand, Lower; Micajah Smith, William S. Hooper, Cape May City; Youngs Corson, Ocean City; Crawford Buck, Sea Isle City; Hewlett Brower, Anglesea; L. M.

Pancoast, Holly Beach; John W. Reeves, West Cape May; Richard C. Stevenson, Cape May Point.

1890—Alexander Corson, Theophilus Corson, Upper; Charles J. Devitt, Michael Swing, Dennis; Townsend W. Garretson, Jacob G. Hand, Middle; William T. Bate, Robert E. Hand, Lower; William S. Hooper, Lewis T. Entrikin, Cape May City; John W. Reeves, West Cape May; James P. Spofford, Holly Beach; Andrew Weeks, Anglesea; Thomas Whittington, Sea Isle City; William Lake, Ocean City.

1891—Alexander Corson, Theophilus Corson, Upper; Charles J. Devitt, Leaming M. Rice, Dennis; Townsend W. Garretson, Jacob G. Hand, Middle; William T. Bate, Robert E. Hand, Lower; Lewis T. Entrikin, Albert L. Haynes, Cape May City; John W. Reeves, West Cape May; James P. Spofford, Holly Beach; Andrew Weeks, Anglesea; Thomas Whittington, Sea Isle City; William Lake, Ocean City.

1892—Alexander Corson, Theophilus Corson, Upper; Charles J. Devitt, Leaming M. Rice, Dennis; Townsend W. Garretson, Jacob G. Hand, Middle; William T. Bate, Robert E. Hand, Lower; Lewis T. Entrikin, Albert L. Haynes, Cape May City; John W. Reeves, West Cape May; Andrew Weeks, Anglesea; Crawford Buck, Sea Isle City; William Lake, Ocean City; Frank E. Smith, Holly Beach.

1893—Alexander Corson, Theophilus Corson, Upper; Leaming M. Rice, Charles J. Devitt, Dennis; Townsend W. Garretson, Jacob G. Hand, Middle; William T. Bate, J. Durell Hoffman, Lower; Albert L. Haynes, William T. Stevens, Cape May City; William Lake, Ocean City; Crawford Buck, Sea Isle City; Andrew Weeks, Anglesea; Frank E. Smith, Holly Beach; Samuel E. Ewing, West Cape May.

1894—Alexander Corson, Theophilus Corson, Upper; Charles J. Devitt, Joseph C. P. Smith, Dennis; A. Carlton Hildreth, Townsend W. Garretson, Middle; J. Durell Hoffman, William T. Bate, Lower; Albert L. Haynes, William T. Stevens, Cape May City; James W. Lee, Ocean City; Crawford Buck, Sea Isle City; Andrew S. Weeks, Anglesea;

Frank E. Smith, Holly Beach; Samuel E. Ewing, West Cape May.

1895—Alexander Corson, Theophilus Corson, Upper; Joseph C. P. Smith, Charles J. Devitt, Dennis; Townsend W. Garretson, A. Carlton Hildreth, Middle; J. Durell Hoffman, William T. Bate, Lower; Albert L. Haynes, William T. Stevens, Cape May City; James W. Lee, Ocean City; Crawford Buck, Sea Isle City; Edward M. Shivers, Anglesea; Charles Bridges, Holly Beach; Samuel E. Ewing, West Cape May.

1896—Alexander Corson, Theophilus Corson, Upper; Joseph C. P. Smith, Charles J. Devitt, Dennis; Townsend W. Garretson, A. Carlton Hildreth, Middle; J. Durell Hoffman, Enoch J. Hitchner, Lower; Albert L. Haynes, Robert S. Hand, Cape May City.

1897—Alexander Corson, Theophilus Corson, Upper; Joseph C. P. Smith, Douglass J. Robinson, Dennis; Townsend W. Garretson, A. Carlton Hildreth, Middle; J. Durell Hoffman, Enoch J. Hitchner, Lower; Robert S. Hand, William T. Stevens, Cape May City; Frederick P. Canfield, Lewis S. Smith, Ocean City.

APPENDIX C.

COUNTY OFFICIALS.

SHERIFFS.

1693—Timothy Brandereth.
1695—John Townsend.
1697—Ezekiel Eldredge.
1700—Edmund Howell.
1701—Caesar Hoskins.
1704—John Taylor.
1705—Joseph Whilldin.
1711—Humphrey Hughes.
1711—John Townsend.
1714—Richard Downs.
1715—Robert Townsend.
1721—Richard Downs.
1722—Henry Young.
1723—Richard Downs.
1740—Constant Hughes.
1744—Jacob Hughes.
1748—Jeremiah Hand.
1751—Thomas Smith.
1754—John Shaw.
1757—Jeremiah Hand.
1760—Ebenezer Johnson.
1762—Henry Hand.
1765—Sylvanus Townsend.
1768—Daniel Hand.
1771—Eli Eldredge.
1772—Jonathan Jenkins.
1774—Henry Y. Townsend.
1777—Isaiah Stites.
1780—Richard Townsend.
1781—Nathaniel Hand.
1782—Daniel Garretson.
1783—Jonathan Hildreth.
1784—Benjamin Taylor.
1787—Philip Hand.
1788—Henry Stites.
1791—Eleazer Hand.
1796—Jacob Godfrey.
1797—Jeremiah Hand.
1798—Jonathan Leaming.
1801—Thomas H. Hughes.
1804—Joseph Hildreth.
1807—Cresse Townsend.
1808—Jacob Hughes.
1809—Joshua Swain.
1812—Aaron Leaming.
1815—Spicer Hughes.
1818—David Townsend.
1821—Spicer Hughes.
1824—Swain Townsend.
1827—Thomas P. Hughes.
1830—Richard Thompson.
1833—Ludlam Pierson.
1834—Joshua Swain, Jr.
1835—Ludlam Pierson
1835—Samuel Matthews.
1838—Samuel Springer.
1841—Thomas Vangilder.
1844—Enoch Edmunds.
1847—Peter Souder.
1850—Thomas Hewitt, Jr.
1853—Elva Corson.
1856—William S. Hooper.
1859—Richard D. Edmunds.
1862—Aaron Miller.
1865—John Wilson.
1868—Anthony Steelman.
1871—Nelson T. Eldredge.
1874—Albert Adams.
1878—William H. Benezet.
1881—Remington Corson.
1884—William H. Benezet.
1886—Stillwell H. Townsend.
1886—James Shoemaker, Jr.
1889—Charles E. Nichols.
1892—Robert E. Hand.
1895—Andrew J. Tomlin.

COUNTY CLERKS.

1693—George Taylor.
1697—Timothy Brandreth.
1705—John Taylor.
1730—Aaron Leaming, 1st.
1740—Elijah Hughes, Sr.
1762—Elijah Hughes, Jr.
1777—Jonathan Jenkins.
1768—Jeremiah Eldredge.
1779—Eii Eldredge.

1802—Jeremiah Hand.
1804—Abijah Smith.
1824—Richard Thompson.
1829—Levy Foster.
1831—Jonathan Hand, Sr.
1834—Jacob G. Smith.
1835—Swain Townsend.
1840—Jonathon Hand, Jr.
1890—Edward L. Rice.

SURROGATES.

1723—Jacob Spicer, 1st.
1741—Henry Young.
1768—Elijah Hughes, Jr.
1787—Jesse Hand.
1793—Jeremiah Eldredge.
1796—Ebenezer Newton.
1802—Aaron Eldredge.

1803—John Townsend.
1831—Humphrey Leaming.
1852—Elijah Townsend.
1863—Peter Souder.
1871—Jonathan F. Leaming.
1877—William Hildreth.

COUNTY COLLECTORS.

1827—Robert M. Holmes.
1840—Charles Hand.
1865—Dr. John Wiley.

1880—David T. Smith.
1888—Edmund L. Ross.

LOAN COMMISSIONERS.

1837—Robert M. Holmes.
1840—Richard Thompson.
1844—Franklin Hand.
1854—Henry Swain.
1856—Richard Thompson.

1857—Henry Swain.
1862—Richard D. Edmunds.
1863—Dr. Coleman F. Leaming.
1880—John B. Huffman.

CLERKS OF BOARDS OF FREEHOLDERS.

1827—James Townsend.
1831—Joshua Swain, Jr.
1866—Edward Y. Swain.

1871—Joseph E. Hughes.
1873—W. V. L. Seigman.
1884—Samuel Townsend.

SUPERINTENDENTS OF PUBLIC SCHOOLS.

1866—Maurice Beesley, M. D.
1881—Rev. Edward P. Shields.

1884—Vincent O. Miller.
1896—Aaron W. Hand.

APPENDIX D.
POST MASTERS.

A list of postmasters of Cape May county, and the times of their appointments:

CAPE MAY COURT HOUSE.
Jeremiah Hand, January 1, 1803.
Jonathan Jarman, July 1, 1804.
Nathaniel Holmes, February 15, 1808.
Mark A. Carroll, August 18, 1810.
Joseph Fifield, August 27, 1829.
James Hildreth, October 18, 1838.
John M. Hand, March 7, 1844.
James Hildreth, November 12, 1846.
Elijah Townsend, Jr., April 19, 1847.
John Farrow, July 15, 1853.
Nicholas A. Wentzell, April 16, 1858.
James McCartney, September 10, 1860.
Charles E. Nichols, September 21, 1885.
Harry S. Douglass, April 17, 1889.
Charles E. Nichols, December 20, 1893.

CAPE ISLAND.
Ellis Hughes, January 30, 1804.
Alexander Mackenzie, March 8, 1820.
Joseph B. Hughes, April 4, 1833.
Jonas Miller, June 18, 1835.
James Clark, July 7, 1845.
George W. Hughes, May 9, 1849.
John K. F. Stites, July 28, 1851.
Samuel S. Marcy, January 20, 1853.
James Clark, March 13, 1857.
Samuel R. Magonagle, December 5, 1859.
Joseph S. Leach, June 26, 1863.
Joseph Ware, July 10, 1866.
Name changed to Cape May, January 15, 1869.

CAPE MAY.
Joseph Ware, January 15, 1869.
Jonathan S. Garrison, January 13, 1871.
Joseph E. Hughes, February 3, 1882.
Waters B. Miller, March 12, 1886.
Frederick J. Melvin, April 16, 1886.
Furman L. Richardson, April 16, 1889.
John W. Thompson, April 9, 1894.

SEA ISLE CITY.
George Whitney, June 20, 1882.
John S. Morris, August 29, 1883.
William R. Bryant, September 15, 1885.
J. Monroe Chester, April 17, 1889.
Lewis Steinmeyer, May 1, 1894.

SEA GROVE.
Alexander W. Springer, March 27, 1876.
Name changed to Cape May Point, August 8, 1878.

CAPE MAY POINT.
Alexander W. Springer, August 8, 1878.
Amnon Wright, September 21, 1885.
John N. Reeves, May 25, 1889.
Amnon Wright, July 14, 1893.

FISHING CREEK.
Robert Edmunds, June 20, 1818.
Jonathan Cummings, April 16, 1822.
Reuben Foster, May 20, 1825.
Robert E. Foster, April 3, 1834.
Leonard Cummings, October 18, 1838.
Aaron H. Snyder, December 6, 1886.
Washington Hemingway, February 15, 1887.

OCEAN CITY.
William H. Burrell, March 2, 1881.
R. Howard Thorn, October 15, 1887.
R. Curtis Robinson, April 25, 1889.
R. Howard Thorn, September 16, 1893.

GOSHEN.
Richard Thompson, Jr., June 5, 1818.
James Maguire, September 18, 1820.
Bernard Murphy, October 20, 1829.

Mackey Williams, March 29, 1834.
James Waters, March 5, 1836.
Thomas Wible, March 24, 1837.
James Maguire, July 11, 1840.
Edward Price, July 7, 1845.
John W. Swain, April 2, 1853.
Moses S. Dalbey, December 18, 1856.
James Wiley, July 13, 1861.
Griffin Smith, January 30, 1865.
William Oliphant, May 10, 1870.
Smith Champion, December 14, 1870.
Robert P. Thompson, January 25, 1872.
Edward J. Mixner, July 2, 1885.
Anna H. Grace, April 13, 1889.

COLD SPRING.
Aaron Eldredge, October 1, 1809.
Daniel Hughes, September 8, 1813.
Ezekiel Stevens, October 10, 1815.
Joseph Eldredge, June 15, 1849.
Richard D. Edmunds, February 21, 1855.
Joseph Eldredge, July 13, 1861.
John M. Russell, December 7, 1877.
Harry B. Marcy, November 13, 1885.
Joseph C. Eldredge, October 24, 1889.
Furman Barnett, November, 1893.

HOLLY BEACH.
Jennie L. Osborn, November 26, 1883.
Frank E. Smith, September 5, 1893.

BEESLEY'S POINT.
Joseph D. Chatten, March 3, 1851.
Joseph Baner, February 7, 1872.
James A. Chatten, March 6, 1884.
James C. Ross, October 10, 1887.
Frank S. Ashmead, June 17, 1889.

TOWNSEND'S INLET.
William Stiles, June 9, 1849.
Chauncey M. Brower, April 9, 1861.
William Hewitt, August 19, 1867.
Tabitha Brower, April 12, 1872.

Rockliff Morris, June 22, 1882.
Isaac Swain, Jr., September 18, 1885.
George Eldridge, August 16, 1889.
Luther M. Swain, September 5, 1893.
Name changed to Swainton, July 1, 1896.

SWAINTON.
Luther M. Swain, July 1, 1896.

GREEN CREEK.
Matthew Marcy, August 27, 1829.
Office discontinued, March 26, 1836.
Office re-established, September 9, 1850.
Seth Miller, September 9, 1850.
John T. Price, January 12, 1854.
James W. Johnson, May 14, 1855.
Matthew Marcy, June 15, 1857.
William Hildreth, October 3, 1861.
Aaron Miller, June 9, 1863.
James T. Miller, June 22, 1870.
Henry Schellinger, Jr., February 12, 1886.

ANGLESEA.
William A. Thompkins, November 19, 1883.
Sarah D. Thompkins, February 1, 1886.
John J. Sturmer, Jr., July 5, 1887.
Jason Buck, June 17, 1889.
John Taylor, August 8, 1893.

CLERMONT.
Chester J. Todd, February 4, 1886.
Martha G. Kates, January 16, 1889.

DENNIS CREEK.
Jeremiah Johnson, October 9, 1802.
James Diverty, February 8, 1816.
Jacob G. Smith, June 19, 1829.
Jacob Souder, June 14, 1840.
John L. Chance, January 20, 1848.
Name changed to Dennisville, January 12, 1854.

DENNISVILLE.
John L. Chance, January 12, 1854.
Richard Crawford, May 30, 1861.
Francis Williams, March 26, 1869.

Eleazer Crawford, January 19, 1874.
John W. Young, July 26, 1880.
Jonas Shaw, April 23, 1886.
Thomas Ludlam, May 26, 1886.
Herbert M. Carroll, October 9, 1890.
Thomas Ludlam, January 1, 1895.
Frank Earnest, January 1, 1897.

OCEAN VIEW.
William Doolittle, May 9, 1872.
Stephen T. Coleman, November 25, 1885.
Shamgar C. Townsend, August 16, 1889.
Belle S. Coleman, September 12, 1893.

SOUTH DENNIS.
Robert Hutchinson, February 24, 1873
Rhoda L. Hutchinson, July 23, 1877.
Margaret C. Carll, November 9, 1891.

PALERMO.
James S. Willetts, December 11, 1872.
Luther Corson, September 30, 1878.
Eleanor W. Corson, March 29, 1887.
Amos T. Gandy, April 5, 1887.
Sallie Young, July 29, 1889.
Seth W. Corson, October 17, 1893.

MARMORA.
James H. Corson, June 21, 1890.
Stephen H. Young, February 1, 1895.

BELLE PLAIN.
George W. Blinn, January 16, 1867.
Rettie M. Goff, October 8, 1879.
George W. Blinn, October, 1883.
Albert T. Peacock, December 12, 1890.
George W. Blinn, May, 1893.

RIO GRANDE.
Jeremiah Hand, September 6, 1856.
William K. Palmer, October 18, 1867.
Joseph H. Richardson, June 24, 1873.
Ichabod C. Compton, August 3, 1885.
Howard C. Buck, December 6, 1886.

EAST CREEK.

John Wilson, April 22, 1842.
Bell P. Wilson, January 5, 1876.
Asbury Goff, January 23, 1879.

TUCKAHOE.

John Williams, January 14, 1828.
Edward Middleton, May 11, 1835.
Mackey Williams, July 15, 1836.
Martin Madden, April 2, 1844.
Hosea F. Madden, March 20, 1846.
Thomas Williams, April 21, 1848.
Lewis L. Dunn, July 15, 1853.
Ephraim Westcott, August 16, 1853.
Elijah Ireland, January 30, 1858.
William J. Royal, February 8, 1859.
Peter Turner, May 9, 1864.
Thomas M. Seeley, June 4, 1875.
Charles H. Blizzard, August 29, 1883.
William B. Brown, August 3, 1885.
Thomas M. Seeley, May 11, 1889.
Otis Madden, August 14, 1893.
Jennie Madden, January 25, 1897.

SOUTH SEAVILLE.

Remington Corson, September 7, 1867.
Baker Corson, December 6, 1881.
Edwin F. Westcott, September 21, 1885.
Remington Corson, May 11, 1889.
Edwin F. Westcott, April 28, 1894.
Marietta Westcott, March 21, 1896.

SEAVILLE.

John Gandy, June 9, 1849.
John Jones, June 29, 1863.
Ellis H. Marshall, October 18, 1867.
Thomas C. Sharp, November 25, 1885.
Ellis H. Marshall, July 23, 1889.

AVALON.

George W. Smith, July 9, 1888.
Platt Brower.
Walter G. Smith.

STONE HARBOR.
Godfrey, 1894.
S. S. Hand, December 26, 1896.
ERMA.
Reuben T. Johnson, April 7, 1893.
DIAS CREEK.
Charles K. Holmes, September 9, 1850.
Alexander Springer, September 12, 1870.
Thomas H. Leaming, November 5, 1874.
Lizzie N. Errickson, January 11, 1886.
Thomas H. Leaming, August 16, 1889.
E. S. Erricson, August 31, 1893.
WILDWOOD.
Reuben W. Ryan, September 14, 1889.
PETERSBURG.
Peter Corson, April 14, 1856.
Thaddeus Van Gilder, June 22, 1865.
Hannah Van Gilder, February 7, 1881.
William R. Van Gilder, February 13, 1882.
Harrison J. Corson, August 3, 1885.
William R. Van Gilder, April 15, 1889.
Harrison J. Corson, October 13, 1893.
BURLEIGH.
Deborah Carey, May 13, 1886.
Maggie A. McPherson, December 6, 1895.
ELDORA.
Howard Goff, July, 1892.
Isaac W. Dawson, January, 1894.

APPENDIX E.
MUNICIPAL OFFICERS.

Anglesea.

MAYORS.
1885—Dr. Thompkins.
1885—Peter J. Munro.
1888—Edwin S. Hewitt.
1890—Edward M. Shivers.
1894—Edwin S. Hewitt.

COLLECTORS AND TREASURERS.
1885—John J. Sturmer.
1888—Hewlett Brower.
1890—Edwin S. Hewitt.
1893—Joseph Douglass, Jr.
1896—Wilbur E. Young.

ASSESSORS.
1885—Edwin S. Hewitt.
1886—John Taylor.
1887—E. Ellsworth Hewitt.
1890—Richard D. Shimp.
1891—E. Ellsworth Hewitt.
1897—Thomas Corson.

Avalon.

MAYORS.
1891—Thomas Bray.

CLERKS.
1891—Charles M. Preston.

ASSESSORS.
1891—James M. Corson.
1895—Hugh H. Holmes.

COLLECTOR AND TREASURER.
1891—George W. Kates.

Cape May City.

MAYORS.
(Presided over Council until 1875.)

1851—Isaac M. Church.
1851—James Clark.
1853—John K. Church.
1856—Joseph Ware.
1861—Samuel R. Magonagle.
1862—Joseph Q. Williams.
1863—Samuel R. Magonagle.
1868—Joseph Q. Williams.
1869—Waters B. Miller.
1871—Joseph Ware.
1873—Waters B. Miller.
1875—John G. W. Ware.
1877—Joseph Q. Williams.
1881—Frederick J. Melvin.
1885—J. Henry Edmunds.
1893—James M. E. Hildreth.
1895—J. Henry Edmunds.
1897—James M. E. Hildreth.

MUNICIPAL OFFICERS.

ALDERMEN.

(Were both a member of Council and Justice of the Peace until 1875, but now only a Justice of the Peace.)

1851—Waters B. Miller.
1852—George Stratton.
1853—William Cassedy.
1854—Isaac W. Buck.
1855—John K. F. Stites.
1856—Joseph Q. Williams.
1857—Christopher Leaming.
1858—Samuel S. Marcy.
1861—George W. Smith.
1862—Christopher Leaming.
1863—James S. Kennedy.
1868—John W. Lycett.
1870—John G. W. Ware.

1875—Jeremiah H. Townsend.
1875—Joseph Q. Williams.
1876—Henry F. Doolittle.
1876—Robert Gibson.
1877—John G. W. Ware.
1879—Samuel F. Ware.
1880—Frederic J. Melvin.
1881—John G. W. Ware.
1886—Joseph E. Hughes.
1888—John G. W. Ware.
1894—William T. Stevens.
1894—F. Sidney Townsend.
1896—Charles Sandgran.

RECORDERS.

(Were both a member of City Council and Justices of the Peace until 1875, since which time they have been City Clerk.)

1851—Joseph S. Leach.
1853—Charles T. Johnson.
1854—Joseph Ware.
1855—William S. Hooper.
1856—William Bennett.
1858—John W. Blake.
1860—Joseph Q. Williams.
1861—Samuel S. Marcy.
1862—Thomas B. Hughes.
1863—Henry Hand.
1866—Thomas B. Hughes.
1871—William Eldredge.

1872—Joseph S. Leach.
1873—Samuel R. Stites.
1874—Joseph Q. Williams.
1875—Richard D. Edmunds.
1876—Harry C. Thompson.
1881—George S. Ware.
1881—Harry C. Thompson.
1883—Samuel R. Stites.
1885—Harry C. Thompson.
1887—H. Freeman Douglass.
1891—J. Ashton Williams.

COUNCILMEN.

1851—James S. Kennedy, David Pierson, John G. W. Ware, Joseph Ware, Aaron Garretson, James Mecray.

1852—David Pierson, Aaron Garretson, Charles Downs, Lemuel A. Shaw, William Schellenger, Lemuel Swain, Jr.

1853—Israel Leaming, Richard R. Thompson, Philip Hand, Jr., William S. Hooper, George L. Ludlam, William Townsend.

1854—Richard R. Thompson, David W. Pierson, Wilmon W. Ware, Joseph S. Leach, Jeremiah Schellenger, Isaac W. Buck.

1855—David W. Pierson, Humphrey Leaming, Joseph Hall, James S. Kennedy, Maskel Ware, Joseph Schellenger.

1856—Daniel C. Ware, Aaron Schellenger, Jr., John K. Church,

James Leaming, Jr. (resigned, and Joseph Schellenger elected to vacancy), John K. F. Stites, Samuel S. Marcy.

1857—Samuel S. Marcy, William Townsend, John G. W. Ware, George Roseman, Joseph Q. Williams, James S. Kennedy.

1858—John G. W. Ware, Joseph Q. Williams, Joseph Schellenger, Joseph S. Leach, Aaron Garretson, Thomas B. Hughes.

1859—John G. W. Ware, Joseph Schellenger, Aaron Garretson, Alvin P. Hildreth, William Schellenger, Daniel C. Ware.

1860—Aaron Garretson, Daniel C. Ware, Charles A. Shaw, Jeremiah Schellenger, Alvin P. Hildreth, Thomas B. Hughes.

1861—Aaron Garretson, Alvin P. Hildreth, Enoch Edmunds, John West, Humphrey Leaming, James S. Kennedy.

1862—Aaron Garretson, James S. Kennedy, John W. Blake, George L. Ludlam, George Roseman, Aaron Schellenger, Jr.

1863—Aaron Garretson, Peter McCollum, Enoch Edmunds, Joseph S. Leach, Joseph Schellenger, Alvin P. Hildreth.

1864—Enoch Edmunds, Joseph Schellenger, Wilmon W. Ware, James Leaming, Jr., George W. Smith, John G. W. Ware.

1865—Enoch Edmunds, Joseph Schellenger, John G. W. Ware, Waters B. Miller, James Mecray, Joseph Q. Williams.

1866—Enoch Edmunds, Joseph Schellenger, John G. W. Ware, Joseph Q. Williams, Lemuel Swain, Jesse M. Smith.

1867—Enoch Edmunds (died, and George B. Cake put in vacancy), John G. W. Ware, Joseph Q. Williams, William S. Schellenger, John West, Samuel R. Ludlam.

1868—George B. Cake, William S. Schellenger, Samuel R. Ludlam, John W. Blake, James Mecray, Jr., Samuel R. Magonagle.

1869—John W. Blake, Samuel R. Ludlam, Thomas D. Clark, James S. Kennedy, James Mecray, Sr., Richard R. Thompson.

1870—Samuel R. Ludlam, Thomas D. Clark (died, and Henry W. Sawyer elected to vacancy; Sawyer failing to qualify, Wilmon W. Ware was chosen to vacancy), James S. Kennedy, James Mecray, Sr., Richard R. Thompson, J. Stratton Ware.

1871—James Mecray, Sr., Richard R. Thompson, J. Stratton Ware, Micajah Smith, William T. Stevens, Matthew Beardwood.

1872—Richard R. Thompson, Micajah Smith, William T. Stevens, Matthew Beardwood, John H. Benezet, William F. Cassedy.

1873—Richard R. Thompson, John H. Benezet, William F. Cassedy, Isaac H. Smith, Nathan C. Price, Christopher S. Magrath.

1874—Isaac H. Smith, Nathan C. Price, Joseph E. Hughes, Richard D. Edmunds, Jeremiah B. Schellenger, Return B. Swain.

1875—Isaac H. Smith, Matthew Whilldin (died, and James S. Kennedy elected to vacancy), James Mecray, Jr., Furman L.

Richardson, James H. Edmunds, James Leaming, William Townsend, William Bennett. John L. Lansing.

1876—Isaac H. Smith, James Mccray, Jr., Furman L. Richardson, James H. Edmunds, James Leaming, William Townsend, William Bennett, John L. Lansing, Henry W. Sawyer.

1877—Isaac H. Smith, James Mccray, Jr., James Leaming, William Bennett, John L. Lansing, Henry W. Sawyer, Sammuel R. Ludlam, Micajah Smith, Richard R. Thompson.

1878—James Leaming, John L. Lansing, Henry W. Sawyer, Samuel R. Ludlam, Micajah Smith, Richard R. Thompson (died, and Wilmon W. Ware elected to vacancy), James H. Edmunds, James C. Bennett, Joseph H. Hanes.

1879—Samuel R. Ludlam, Micajah Smith, James H. Edmunds, James C. Bennett (resigned, and John Bennett elected to vacancy), Joseph H. Hanes, Isaac H. Smith, Christopher S. Magrath, Eldridge Johnson, Victor Denizot.

1880—John Bennett, Joseph H. Hanes, Isaac H. Smith, Christopher S. Magrath, Eldridge Johnson, Victor Denizot, John Stuart, Henry W. Sawyer, Samuel R. Stites.

1881—Joseph H. Hanes, Isaac H. Smith, Christopher S. Magrath, Eldridge Johnson, Victor Denizot, John Stuart, Henry W. Sawyer, James Mccray, Jr., William F. Cassedy.

1882—Joseph H. Hanes, Eldridge Johnson, John Stuart, Henry W. Sawyer, James Mccray, Jr., William F. Cassedy, John Bennett, Joseph Hand, Robert E. Hughes.

1883—Joseph H. Hanes, James Mccray, Jr., William F. Cassedy, John Bennett, Joseph Hand, Robert E. Hughes, James H. Edmunds, Henry F. Doolittle, F. Sidney Townsend.

1884—Joseph H. Hanes, John Bennett, Joseph Hand, Robert E. Hughes, James H. Edmunds, Henry F. Doolittle, F. Sidney Townsend, Victor Denizot, Joseph Q. Williams.

1885—Joseph H. Hanes, Henry F. Doolittle, F. Sidney Townsend, Victor Denizot, Joseph Q. Williams, Charles A. Shaw, Lemuel E. Miller, Henry W. Sawyer, Charles H. Dougherty.

1886—Joseph H. Hanes, F. Sidney Townsend, Victor Denizot, Joseph Q. Williams, Lemuel E. Miller, Henry W. Sawyer, Charles H. Dougherty (resigned, and Thomas H. Williamson elected to vacancy, who afterwards died, and whose seat was then given to Francis K. Duke), William T. Stevens, Enos R. Williams.

1887—F. Sidney Townsend, Joseph Q. Williams, Lemuel E. Miller, Henry W. Sawyer, Francis K. Duke, William T. Stevens, Enos R. Williams, Albert L. Haynes, James J. Doak.

1888—F. Sidney Townsend, Joseph Q. Williams, Francis K. Duke, William T. Stevens, Enos R. Williams (resigned, and Robert E. Hughes elected to vacancy), Albert L. Haynes, James J. Doak, John Akins. W. Frank Shaw.

1889—F. Sidney Townsend, Joseph Q. Williams, Francis K. Duke, William T. Stevens, Albert L. Haynes, James J. Doak, John Akins, W. Frank Shaw (seat declared vacant because of absence, and Robert E. Hughes chosen to vacancy). Joseph Hand.

1890—F. Sidney Townsend, Joseph Q. Williams, Francis K. Duke, William T. Stevens, James J. Doak, John Akins, Joseph Hand, Joseph P. Henry, Augustus C. Gile.

1891—F. Sidney Townsend, Joseph Q. Williams, William T. Stevens, James J. Doak, John Akins, Joseph Hand, Joseph T. Henry, Samuel R. Stites, Charles P. Foster.

1892—Joseph Q. Williams, James J. Doak, John Akins, Joseph Hand, Joseph P. Henry, Samuel R. Stites, Charles P. Foster, Lewis T. Stevens. Stites York.

1893—James J. Doak, John Akins, Joseph Hand, Samuel R. Stites, Charles P. Foster, Lewis T. Stevens, Stites York, Enoch W. Hand, John Halpin.

1894—James J. Doak, Joseph Hand, Lewis T. Stevens, Stites York, Enoch W. Hand, John Halpin, Joseph Hand (jeweler), E. Swain Hildreth, Benjamin F. Poinsett.

1895—James J. Doak, Enoch W. Hand, John Halpin, Joseph Hand (jeweler), E. Swain Hildreth, Benjamin F. Poinsett, Walter S. Leaming, Eldridge Johnson, Joseph H. Hanes (resigned, and Augustus C. Gile elected to vacancy).

1896—James J. Doak, Joseph Hand (jeweler), E. Swain Hildreth, Benjamin F. Poinsett, Walter S. Leaming, Eldridge Johnson, F. Sidney Townsend, Stephen B. Wilson, Henry S. Rutherford.

1897—James J. Doak, Joseph Hand (jewelry), Walter S. Leaming, Eldredge Johnson, F. Sidney Townsend, Stephen B. Wilson, Henry S. Rutherford, Edward F. Townsend, Joseph Hand.

CITY CLERKS.
(From 1851 to 1875.)

1851—Charles T. Johnson.
1852—John K. Church.
1853—Henry Hand.
1855—Lemuel Swain, Jr.
1856—Alvin P. Hildreth.
1858—Wilmon W. Ware.
1858—Jesse M. Smith.
1861—Henry Hand.
1863—Jesse M. Smith.
1866—John M. Sullivan.
1867—Joseph B. Hughes.
1868—Samuel R. Stites.
1869—Christopher S. Magrath.
1869—Jesse McCollum.
1871—Samuel R. Stites.
1871—Richard D. Edmunds.
1872—George S. Ware.
1873—Jesse McCollum.
1874—John W. Blake.

MUNICIPAL OFFICERS. 477

PRESIDENTS OF COUNCIL.

1875, '76, '77—James Mecray, Jr.
1778, '79, '80—Joseph H. Hanes.
1861, '82, '83—James Mecray, Jr.
1884—Joseph Q. Williams.
1885—Charles H. Dougherty.
1886—Lemuel E. Miller.
1887—Joseph Q. Williams.
1888—William T. Stevens.
1889—F. Sidney Townsend.
1890—Francis K. Duke.
1891—F. Sidney Townsend.
1892, 1893—James J. Doak.
1894—Lewis T. Stevens.
1895, '96, '97—Walter S. Leaming.

TREASURERS.

1851—Lemuel Swain.
1852—James Mecray.
1858—William Stites.
1860—Eldridge Johnson.
1869—James Mecray, Jr.
1871—Eldridge Johnson.
1879—Furman L. Richardson.
1884—John Henry Farrow.
1883—Isaac H. Smith.
1895—Henry Hand.

COLLECTORS OF TAXES.

1851—Aaron Schellenger, Sr.
1852—Aaron Schellenger, Jr.
1861—Joseph Schellenger.
1867—Joseph Q. Williams.
1868—Isaac H. Smith.
1879—Henry Hand.
1872—William S. Hooper.
1878—Thomas H. Williamson.
1883—J. Swain Garrison.
1884—William F. Cassedy.
1885—Albert B. Little.
1887—Jeremiah E. Mecray, Jr.
1888—James E. Taylor.
1890—Albert B. Little.
1891—George L. Levett.
1894—David W. Redan.

ASSESSORS OF TAXES.

1851—James S. Kennedy.
1852—Joseph Ware.
1853—William Cassedy.
1854—Christopher Leaming.
1855—Joseph Ware.
1856—James S. Kennedy.
1858—John K. F. Stites.
1859—Alvin P. Hildreth.
1872—Henry Hand.
1876—William C. Miller.
1878—Henry Hand.
1883—Joseph H. Hughes.
1884—Henry Hand.
1891—Joseph M. Schellenger.
1893—Willim H. Elwell.
1894—Charles Sandgran.
1894—William H. Elwell.
1895—Joseph M. Schellenger.

Ocean City.

MAYORS.

1884—Gainer P. Moore.
1890—James E. Pryor, M. D.
1892—Gainer P. Moore.
1894—Harry G. Steelman.
1895—Robert Fisher.
1896—Gainer P. Moore.
1897—Wesley C. Smith.

CLERKS.

1884—Simeon B. Miller.
1889—John S. Waggoner, M. D.
1891—Simeon B. Miller.
1892—Harry B. Adams.
1894—E. A. Bourgeois.
1897—Ira S. Champion.

ASSESSORS.

1884—Reuben Ludlam.　　1897—Herbert C. Smith and B. English.

COLLECTORS AND TREASURERS.

1884—Edward Borie, Jr.　　1890—Harry G. Steelman.
1885—James W. Lee.　　1894—Samuel Schurch.

COLLECTORS.

1897—Samuel Schurch.

TREASURERS.

1897—George O. Adams.

Sea Isle City.

MAYORS.

1882—Martin Wells.　　1896—John G. Woertz (died).
1884—Thomas E. Ludlam.　　1896—Augustus H. Sickler.

CLERKS.

1882—Jacob L. Peterson.　　1887—R. H. Lee.
1883—William H. Davis.　　1897—James T. Chapman.
1885—William R. Bryant.

ASSESSORS.

1882—Thomas E. Ludlam.　　1890—Robert S. Muller.
1884—Isaac A. Hues.　　1891—Charles H. Clouting.
1885—Robert S. Muller.　　1896—Charles S. Schick.
1889—Uriah H. Huntley.　　1897—Charles H. Clouting.

COLLECTORS AND TREASURERS.

1882—James P. Way.　　1888—H. W. Fackler.
1883—John Telford.　　1891—Lewis S. Chester.
1884—James P. Way.　　1895—Daniel H. Wheaton.
1885—Lewis S. Chester.

South Cape May.

MAYORS.

1894—James Ritchie, Jr.

ASSESSORS.

1894—A. J. Rudolph.

COLLECTORS AND TREASURERS.

1894—Henry H. Walton.

Holly Beach.

MAYORS.

1885—Franklin J. Van Valin.　　1891—William E. Forcum.
1887—William E. Forcum.　　1892—Frank E. Smith.
1890—J. B. Osborn.

MUNICIPAL OFFICERS. 479

ASSESSORS.

1885—Frank E. Smith.
1886—Charles Bridges.
1887—Frank E. Smith.
1888—William E. Dedrick.
1889—Charles Bridges.

1890—Martin L. Harrison.
1891—Charles Bridges.
1894—William A. Shaw.
1896—Charles Bridges.
1897—John H. Smith.

COLLECTORS AND TREASURERS.

1885—Benjamin F. Barker.
1892—William E. Forcum.

1895—William H. Bright.

West Cape May.
MAYORS.

1884—Lemuel Swain.
1886—John Spencer.
1890—George H. Reeves.

1890—John Spencer.
1892—George H. Reeves.
1896—Samuel E. Ewing.

CLERKS

1884—Joseph H. Brewton.   1890—William G. Blattner.

ASSESSORS.

1884—William H. Reeves.
1895—Aaron W. Hand.

1897—Henry H. Eldredge.

COLLECTORS AND TREASURERS.

1884—John Spencer.
1885—Samuel E. Ewing.

1888—John Reeves.
1891—Enos S. Edmunds.

Wildwood.
MAYORS.

1895—Latimer R. Baker.

CLERKS.

1895—William Prentiss.   1897—Jedediah Du Bois.

ASSESSORS.

1895—Burgher V. Van Horn.   1897—W. H. Washburn.

COLLECTORS AND TREASURERS.

1895—Charles H. Leaman.   1897—Burgher V. Van Horn.

APPENDIX F.

The population of Cape May, at different periods since the year 1726, was as follows, viz:

YEAR	POPULATION	SLAVES	FREE COLORED	QUAKERS
1726	668			
1730	1,004	42		
1745	1,185			54
1790	2,571	141		
1800	3,066	98		
1820	3,532	81		
1820	4,265	28	205	
1830	4,934	3	225	
1840	5,324		218	
1850	6,433		247	
1855	6,735		297	
1860	7,130		273	
1865	7,625			
1870	8,250		435	
1875	8,190		554	
1880	9,765		570	
1885	10,774		591	
1890	11,268			
1895	12,855		897	

EVERYNAME INDEX

ABBETT, Gov 288 293 380
ABBOTT, Benjamin 217
ABRAMS, Adam 338 340 Charles 332 335 Enoch T 348 Skidmore 332 335 348 Thomas 203
ADAMS, 257 Albert 463 George O 478 Harry B 477 John Quincy 256 257 Jonathan 77 Thomas 211
AKINS, John 476
ALLEN, 178 Charles 202 Ethan 177 John 91 Robert 311
ALONZO, Willis 339
ANDERSON, John I 200 William C 384
ANDROS, Edmund 28
ANEHOOPEON, 18
ANNE QUEEN OF ENGLAND, 40 60
ARGALL, 23
ARMSTRONG, 195 Evan 336 337 Gen 194 195 William 332 335
ARNOLD, 178 Benedict 177 214 Gen 193
ARTHUR, 378 Chester A 436 Pres 365 369 385 386
ASHFIELD, Richard 95
ASHMEAD, Frank S 467
ASHTON, 70
ASTON, 70
ATKINSON, Isaac 197
AUMACK, George 348 Richard

AUMACK (continued) Jr 348
B, Capt 320
BACON, Jeremiah 70
BADCOCK, John 212 Jos 84 Jose 179 Joseph 53 104 187
BAILEY, James T 373
BAILY, John 53
BAKER, 447 John 179 205 206 450 L R 447 Latimer R 479 Philip P 447 Philip Pontius 446
BALL, Josiah 287 Sophia 287
BALLENGER, Benjamin 206
BANCROFT, 29 Ephraim 136 John 113 N P John 132 Samuel 85 98 113 Thomas 53 85 113
BANCROFTS, Elizabeth 73 Thomas 73
BANER, George 336 338 Isaac 114 134 Jacob 236 Joseph 467
BARBER, Francis 200
BARD, Peter 63
BARKER, Benjamin F 479
BARNES, Charles 85 George W 435 459 Samuel 336 338 348
BARNETT, Furman 333 334 467 Hetty 408
BARROWS, Walter A 303 305 440
BARTON, Samuel C 435
BASNETT, Richard 32 Richd 32
BASS, Elizabeth 73 J 63 Jeremiah 41

BASS (continued)
    48 61 79 450 Richard 73
BASSE, 63 Jeremiah 39 51 64 79 80
    Peter 32
BATE, William J 303 William T 452
    460-462
BATEMAN, 421
BATTS, Elijah D 348
BAUER, Abraham 84
BAYARD, James A 271
BAYMORE, Joseph 245 Robert Jr
    269
BEARDWOOD, Matthew 474
BEAVER, Gov 341
BECK, A 273 C 273 G 273 H 273 J M
    273 Jacob W 272 273 L 273
BECKWITH, Thomas 333 334
BEEKMAN, Director 26
BEER, Jonathan 58 60
BEESLEY, Dr 21 25 26 29 40 53 61
    68 99 103 105 125 184 198 219
    225 289 290 Jonathan 289 Maurice
    10 29 115 229 250 272 280
    289 290 363 383 451 464 Theophilus
    290 Thomas 141 248 289
    290 302 363 371 452 Thomas H
    290 355
BELCHER, Gov 281
BENEZET, Alderman 109 Alfonso
    430 Anthony 377 430 John H 430
    474 William H 303 377 463
BENNET, John 93-95
BENNETT, 265 Aaron 265 405
    Abraham 186 193 212 213 Abram
    180 Cornelius 233 362 Eliza 422
    George 247 284 Henry 340 349
    James C 475 Jeremiah 422 John
    475 Stephen 302 422 Stephen D
    303 306 William 473 475
BERKELEY, 27 28 John 27 107
BERNARD, Gov 125 126
BIDDLE, Capt 329 Wm 32

BISHOP, Samuel 453
BLACKBURRY, William 53
BLACKMAN, Constantine 236
BLAINE, James G 393 Mr 341
BLAKE, John W 473 474 476
BLATTNER, William G 479
BLENKOW, Capt 332 David 332
BLINN, George W 469
BLIZZARD, Charles H 470
BLOCK, Aariaen 15
BLOEMMAERT, 20 Mr 19 Samuel
    18 19
BLOEMMART, 17
BLOOMFIELD, Joseph 221
BOLSHER, Elizabeth 73
BOLTON, Mr 407
BOND, Thomas 191 Thoms 192
BONEY, Morris 398
BONNEL, Isaac 110
BONNELL, Isaac 110
BONNS, Richard 70
BOOTH, George 84
BORDEN, Jonathan 336 338 Thomas
    141
BORIE, Edward Jr 478
BOURGEOIS, E A 477
BOWEN, Seth 114
BOWKER, Jerome 332 335 Joseph
    236
BOYD, George W 442 Mr 168
BOYLE, W H 385
BOYS, Capt 213
BRADDOCK, Gen 117 John 236
BRADNER, John 45 74 98 Mr 75
BRADY, Thomas 311
BRAINARD, John 115 140
BRAME, Mrs 33
BRAN, Joseph 197
BRANDERETH, Timothy 51 58 60
    463
BRANDITH, Timothy 48
BRANDRETH, Tim 74 Timothy 41

483

BRANDRETH (continued)
   48 49 52 59 72 84 464
BRAU, Joseph 205 206
BRAY, Thomas 448 472
BREWTON, Albert F 333 Albert S
   334 Joseph 332 335 Joseph H 479
BRIDGES, Charles 462 479
BRIGGS, Charity 221 Elizabeth 73
   James 73 John 37 53 Keziah 73
   Margery 73 Martha 73 Mary 73
   Sarah 73
BRIGHT, William H 479
BRIGS, James 85
BRISTOW, Benjamin 364
BRODERICK, Col 322 Lt Col 322
BRODHEAD, Mr 20
BROOKEBANK, Joseph 94
BROOKS, Capt 210 Clarence R 403
   Dr 424 Elizabeth 408 Emma T 7
   360 Isaac Jr 73 Loraina 359 Mr
   359 360 Samuel 359 Seth 70
   Thomas 359 Thomas R 359 360
   403 Thomas Rezo 359 Timothy 70
BROOKSBANK, Joseph 93-95
BROTHER, Dr 192
BROWER, Chauncey M 467 Hewlett
   460 472 Platt 470 Tabitha 467
BROWN, Henry 338 340 348 Rev Mr
   318 Robert 209 Thomas 197 205
   206 William B 470
BRYANT, William R 466 478
BUCHANAN, Pres 356 377 421
BUCK, 203 Abagail 71 Crawford
   459-462 Howard C 469 Isaac W
   473 Jason 468 Jeremiah 203 John
   73 84 Thomas 104
BUDD, 35 42 James 35 John 40
   Thomas 40 William 32
BULL, Richard 79
BULLITT, 434 John C 398 428 431
   Logan M 397 398
BUNNELL, Eli 454

BUNNER, A 184
BURCH, 314 David D 314 Eliza 408
   Wm 170
BURNET, Aaron 43 Esther 43 Hester
   99
BURNETT, Gov 96
BURNS, James 303
BURNSIDE, 319 Gen 317 322
BURRELL, W H 377 William H 466
BURTON, 239 Capt 239
BUSH, Thomas 305 307
BUTCHER, Thos 32
BUTLER, 82 Gen 321
BUZBY, John L 336 338
BYLLINGE, 39 42 Edward 39
BYLLYNGE, 28 Edward 28
CABOT, 13 27 John 12 Sebastian 12
CAIN, M 423
CAKE, George B 436 474 J Frank 386
   431 Jacob F 406 428 Jacob Frank
   378 Mr 378 Mrs 378 Pauline 378
CAMBEL, Robert 206
CAMELLE, Robert 205
CAMERON, 191 Alan 192 Allen 190
   191 Simon 316
CAMP, David 236 Eli 236 Elias 332
   335 Jaen 110 John C 348 Mary
   110
CAMPANIUS, 22 26
CAMPBELL, Ellen 110 George 205
   206 Henry 110 Peter 126 Robert
   110 197
CANFIELD, Frederick P 462
CAREY, Deborah 471
CARLL, Margaret C 469
CARMAN, 30-32 Caleb 29-32 43 48
   49 52 72 Daniel 53 Elizabeth 52
   James 72 James H 435 Jno 30
   John 12 43 47-49 52 Jonathan 84
   Joshua 53 84
CARMANS, Elizabeth 57 Joshua 56
CARPENTER, Thomas P 380

CARR, Robert 27
CARROLL, Herbert M 469 Mark A 263 465
CARTARET, George 107
CARTERET, 27 28 George 27 28
CARTWRIGHT, Peter 53
CASEY, 331 332
CASSEDY, Albert J 303 William 408 455 473 477 William F 474 475 477
CATTELL, A G 364 Alexander G 371
CHALKLEY, 96 Thomas 96
CHAMBERS, Daniel 335 338 340 James 348 James F 338 340 348 John 332 333 335
CHAMPION, Ira S 477 John 126 Mary 74 Robert 74 Smith 467
CHANCE, John L 468
CHAPMAN, James T 478
CHARLES KING OF ENGLAND, 28
CHARLES II KING OF ENGLAND, 40 107
CHARLES, Symon 32
CHATTEN, James A 467 Joseph D 281 467
CHATTIN, John S 212 Joseph D 456
CHEEVER, 359
CHESTER, Hiram 197 206 J Monroe 466 James 338 340 John 113 136 Lewis S 478
CHEW, Ann 73
CHILL, 434
CHRISTIANSEN, Hendrick 15
CHURCH, 362 Christopher 70 85 86 136 139 Daniel 236 Edward 113 Isaac 408 419 422 Isaac M 408 421 422 424 472 Isaac Miller 419 Jeremiah 85 407 John K 408 422 472 473 476 John Kake 422 Judith 420 Mr 419 420 422 Mrs Webster 239 Rebecca H 408 Theodore 333 334

CLARK, 155 Aaron B 336 338 Abraham 186 Charles 421 Charles G 373 Edwin P 373 Eliza 422 James 420 465 472 James V 435 Mr 421 Owen S 303 307 311 Thomas D 474
CLAY, 271 Harry 271 Henry 257 262 270-273 Mr 272-274 276
CLEMENT, John 41 Mr 126
CLEMENTS, Jacob 132
CLEVELAND, Grover 448 Pres 391 437
CLIFTON, Thomas 53
CLINTON, Henry 199 213 214
CLIVER, Jonathan 336 338
CLOUTING, Charles H 478
CLYMER, 82 Wm 89
COCHRAN, James 205
COCKIUS, James N 399
COFFIE, Barnabas 282
COFFIN, James A 273
COLE, Christopher 244 Edward 241 Eugene C 391 452 Eugene Conrad 390 John S 336 337
COLEMAN, Belle S 469 Bishop 426 Stephen T 469
COLLINGS, Zebulon 236
COLLINS, 99 Elisha 234 John 336 338 Joseph 336 338
COLOGNE, Mr 249 250
COLUMBIA, 434
COMBURY, Lord 62
COMPTON, Ichabod C 469
COMRANS, Capn 132
CONDICT, Lewis 257
CONE, John 187
CONNELL, 221 John 221
CONOVER, Benjamin 339 340 John 236
COOK, Charles 191 Mark 336 337 William W 336 337
COOKE, 191 Charles 190 192 Francis

COOKE (continued)
 285 Jacob 192
COOKS, William 107
COOMBS, Charles H 336 337
COOPER, Alfred 381 Frederick 311
 George B 381 Maj 310 Richard M
 256 257
CORNBURY, 62 63 Edward 60
 Edward Viscount 62 Gov 64 Lord
 80 Lord Viscount 62
CORNWALLIS, 200 216 Lord 194
COROSN, David 207
CORSON, 39 76 314 Aaron 236 242
 Abner 207 Alexander 339 452
 458-462 Allen 241 242 Amos 236
 451 453 Amos S 456 Andrew 113
 Baker 381 470 Charles H 336 338
 Charles S 336 Charles W 336 338
 Christian 38 68 Cornelius 187 197
 241 Cornelius Jr 236 Daniel 454
 Darius 187 197 203 David 113
 114 187 197 205 241 Davis 205
 Eleanor W 469 Elijah 236 246
 Elva 463 Enos 241 243 Ezra 243
 455 George W 338 340 German
 345 346 Harrison J 471 Henry T
 460 Jacob 38 68 113 187 197 202
 205 211 237 303 Jacob S 348
 James H 469 James M 472 Jesse
 187 197 205 207 John 33 38 39 52
 54 68 114 197 237 John Jr 38 68
 John W 332 333 335 Joseph 104
 113 128 130 134 135 141 144 171
 174 179 205 233 Joseph E 301
 302 328 Judith 228 Levi 187 197
 455 Lucien B 336 338 Luther 469
 Martha 55 74 McBride 236 Miles
 454 Nathan 228 Nathaniel 237
 Nicholas 197 336 338 Parmenas
 187 197 222 451 453 Peter 38 39
 46 52 54 68 76 104 205 207 287
 450 471 Peter Jr 38 68 Rem 187

CORSON (continued)
 197 205 207 Remington 356 380
 381 463 470 Samuel D 314 Seth
 242 Seth W 469 Somers 241
 Sylvanus 355 457 458 Theophilus
 461 462 Thomas 472 Willets 345
 Willitts 346 Youngs 460
COSTON, John 57 65 Peter 84
COWEN, R B 364
COX, Abram 203 Daniel 38 79 Danl
 34 Gideon 299 Mr 132
COXE, 42 Col 66 Daniel 39 40 43 61
 62 69 79 Dr 33-35 40-43 45 52 57
 66 114 Jno 133
CRADOL, Frederick W 332
CRAFFORD, Elizabeth 49 George 66
 John 56
CRAFTON, John 197 205 206
CRAIG, J F 302 Joseph F 314
CRANDALL, John 84
CRANDELL, John 85
CRANDOL, Franc's 114 Frederick
 335 Frederick W 348 James 338
 340 435 Jonathan 241
CRAWFORD, 38 Capt 169 Eleazer
 113 202 211 469 George 53 65 98
 John 46 52 56 58 59 Jonathan 234
 Joshua 98 236 243 244 Page R
 338 340 Richard 468
CREAMER, Daniel 336 338 Ezekiel
 237 Frederick 336 337 Reuben
 336 338 Thomas M 332 335
CREESEY, John 60
CRESS, Amos 190
CRESSE, 39 Amos 196 213 215
 Anthony 237 332 333 335 Arthur
 39 46 49 51 52 70 72 113 136 207
 Arthur Jr 53 74 Arthur Sr 74
 Daniel 113 206 Daniel Jr 244
 David 85 243 454 455 Ezekiel 136
 George 233 George S 332 335 J
 Alvin 359 Jacob 190 197 James

CRESSE (continued)
　　53 113 136 John 53 73 85 190 194
　　196 213 John Jr 84 85 Jonathan
　　136 Joseph 348 Lewis 85 113 118
　　Lewis H 303 306 Mary 71 Moses
　　86 Mrs Nathan 227 Nathan 227
　　Richard F 244 Robert 85 105 113
　　136 Stephen 115
CRESSEE, 65 David 206 John 65
　　Lewis 207 Zebulon 206
CRESSEY, Philip 171 Robert 84
CRESSIE, James 84
CRESSIS, Arthur 60
CRESSY, Moses 85
CRESY, John 79
CRISSY, 356
CROELL, Samuel Jr 84
CROFFORD, Benjamin 85 George 84
　　John 84 Joshua 85
CROMWELL, Barnebas 67 Oliver
　　349
CROSBY, Robert 53
CROSSLE, Jonathan 53
CROWEL, Samuel 48
CROWELL, Aaron 238 Anne 73
　　Barnabas 84 98 113 Barnebas 67
　　Daniel 205 206 Daniel F 332 335
　　Edward 73 Elisha 113 Hannah 281
　　Jacob 84 206 James 217 362
　　Jeremiah 73 Joseph 73 Josiah 73
　　85 98 207 Mary 73 Page 459 460
　　Samuel 41 48 51 52 84 85 113
　　Yelverson 55 98
CUMMINGS, Jonathan 466 Leonard
　　466 Samuel S 332 335 William L
　　458
CURWITH, John 52
DAGG, Jeremiah 237
DALBEY, Moses S 467
DAN, 319
DANIEL, James 96 Mr 24
DANIELS, Clement 104 Jeremiah 197

DANIELS (continued)
　　206 233 John 237
DARE, Robert M 336 338
DAVENPORT, Francis 58
DAVIS, 30 31 83 Evan 30 31 Israel
　　203 James L 349 John B 435
　　Matthew L 273 Mr 74 Parker S
　　311 William 197 206 William H
　　478
DAWSON, Capt 209 Isaac W 471
　　Michael 176
DAY, John 32 Thomas 198 205 206
DAYTON, Col 183 Jacob 49 52 53 58
　　59 84 John 336 338 Ruth 48
DEACON, George 60 79
DEAN, Mr 274 Nicholas 273 Ruth 71
　　William 53
DECATUR, Capt 219 Cmdr 226 227
　　264 405 Com 227
DECATURE, Capt 219
DEDRICK, William E 479
DENIZOT, 434 Victor 475
DENNIS, Jno 31 John 12 53
DENNY, William 127
DERMER, 23
DERROM, Col 341
DEVAUL, Elwood 333 334
DEVER, Roger 449
DEVERRAZANI, John 12
DEVITT, Charles J 460-462
DEVRIES, 21 23 Pieterson David 20
DICKINSON, John 184 201 233 376
　　John Jr 245 Joseph E 338 340
　　Nathaniel 242 Philemon 193
　　Wade 246 247
DIMMICK, Mrs 393
DIVERTY, Deborah 288 James 287
　　468 Jesse 379 Jesse H 287 288
　　451 William 287
DIXON, William 51
DOAK, James J 435 442 475-477
DOCKMINIQUE, Charles 93-95

DOCMINIQUE, Charles 95
DONK, Vander 14
DONNELLY, P J 435
DOOLITTLE, Henry F 473 475
　William 375 469
DOUBLEDAY, Wm 85
DOUGHERTY, Adj 311 Charles H
　439 475 477
DOUGLAS, Samuel E 340
DOUGLASS, H Freeman 373 473
　Harry S 465 John 234 Joseph Jr
　472 Samuel E 338 339 348
　Thomas 237 458
DOWNES, Capt 97 Richard 73
DOWNS, 102 Capt 84 Charles 455
　473 Richard 72 86 90 102 463
DPTY SEC OF NEW JERSEY, 161
DUBOIS, 33 Jedediah 392 John 32
DUBOLDY, William 53
DUBROIS, 33 34 42 John 32 34 42
　Mr 33
DUBROISE, 34 35
DUDLEY, Thomas H 365
DUKE, Francis K 435 439 475-477
　Louisa 439
DUKE OF YORK, 13 27 28
DUKE OF YORKE, James 107
DUNCAN, Elizabeth 73
DUNGAN, 299 Charles B 286 299
DUNN, Lewis L 470
DUPONT, Admrl 350
DUTCH, Billy 298
EAGLESFIELD, George 58 70 405
EARL OF HILLSBOR-
　OUGH, 160
EARLY, William 338 340
EARNEST, Frank 469 Mauldare 237
EATTON, Thomas 133
EBERAD, Capt 33
EBRAD, Isaiah 34
EDMONDS, Downes 113 Richard
　207 Robert 222

EDMUND, Sir 24
EDMUNDS, Albert S 333 334 Downs
　136 171 180 205 293 371 375 451
　453 Downs Jr 292 293 298 451
　455 Eli D 349 Enoch 279 438 451
　463 474 Enos S 479 Evan 332 335
　Herbert W 373 Hugh 333 334 J
　Henry 472 James H 285 439 475
　James Henry 438 Jonathan 53 Mr
　293 359 403 N Perry 359 Perry
　404 Richard D 370 438 452 456
　458 463 464 467 473 474 476
　Robert 223 243 250 279 370 425
　466 Thankful 425
EDWARD, David 196 Joseph 197
EDWARD III KING OF ENGLAND,
　285
EDWARDS, 212 Abiah 12 Amos 237
　Anne 239 Daniel 205 David 187
　190 192 Elmer 338-340 Ephraim
　72 85 113 James 86 113 136 John
　203 Jonathan H 332 335 Joseph
　104 105 125 171 178 180 201 202
　205 212 Josiah 113 Lemuel 110
　Lewis 460 Morgan 70 103 104
　109
EGLESFIELD, Anne 73
ELBERSON, Joseph 338 340
ELDREDGE, 39 Aaron 180 205 206
　224 225 234 369 464 467 Daniel
　113 338 Daniel C 439 458 Eli 171
　176 178-180 183-185 216 450 463
　464 Ezekiel 39 48 49 98 205 207
　450 463 Ezekiel Sr 66 George H
　332 Henry H 479 Jacob 219 237
　James 136 James S 332 Jeremiah
　142 195 225 246 450 451 464
　Jeremiah L 364 John 113 Jonathan
　207 Joseph 467 Joseph C 459 460
　467 Judith 228 Levi 207 450
　Louisa 439 Mr 407 Nelson T 364
　463 Samuel 98 99 113 142 171

ELDREDGE (continued)
   246 Sila 205 Thomas 243 247
   William 228 451 473 William B
   303 316 324 435
ELDRIDGE, 28 187 Daniel 340 Eli
   187 196 Ezekiel 52 58 65 66 79
   84 Ezekiell 31 George 348 468
   George H 335 Jacob 234 James S
   335 John 28 Joseph 206 Levi 171
   Samuel 84 85 97 William 85 97
ELDRIG, Samuel 79
ELDRIGG, Ezekiel 79
ELLIOTT, Clark 332 335 Joseph 332 335
ELMER, Eli 196
ELSE, John 53
ELWELL, Charles S 338-340 William H 477 Willim H 477
ENDICOTT, Owen 332 335
ENGLAND, Daniell 31
ENGLISH, B 478
ENTRIKIN, Lewis T 461
ERICKSON, Moses 198
ERIXON, Moses 206 Samuel 189
ERIXSON, Moses 205
ERNEST, Seely 332 335
ERRICKSON, George 339 340 John 339 340 Lizzie N 471
ERRICSON, E S 471
ESTEL, Daniel E 298
ESTELL, James 348
EVELIN, Master 25
EVELYN, 24 Master 23 Robert 23
EWING, George 203 James 233 332 335 Jeremiah 246 Jeremiah Jr 237 Livingstone 332 335 Samuel E 461 462 479
FACKLER, H W 478
FALKENBURG, Joseph 453 454 Somers 241
FALKENBURGE, 240 Joseph 40 240 451

FALKINBURGE, Joseph 452
FARROW, 339 385 436 J Henry 385 458 John 259 465 John Henry 373 477 Mr 385 William 259 340 373 435
FENLIN, 434
FENNER, A 273
FENTON, Mr 385 W H 385
FENWICK, 28 29 John 28
FIDLER, John 217 Jonathan G 333 334
FIFIELD, Jonathan 362 Joseph 242 465
FILKIN, Edward 303
FILKINS, Edward 306
FINLEY, Howard 459 Mr 104 Samuel 104
FISH, John 53
FISHER, 434 Elnor 408 Hendrick 107 Henry 114 Robert 446 477
FITHIAN, 421
FLANNAGAN, Samuel 200
FLAVEGER, James 311
FLOWER, William 113
FLYNN, 318 321 323 Capt 318 319 321 324
FORCUM, William E 478 479
FOREMAN, John 74 84 Jonathan 49 53 85 105
FORMAN, Gen 195
FORSTER, Capt 196 Nathaniel 188
FORTESCUE, Richard 85
FORTESKUE, Richard 73
FORTESQUE, Richard 74
FOSTER, 317 Capt 197 Charles P 476 Christopher 113 Constantine 207 248 Edward 84 Jacob 233 Jeremiah 243 John 206 John Y 308 Joseph 248 339 340 Levi 233 Levy 464 Mr 392 Nathaniel 85 102 104 113 131 135 136 140 174 221 Reuben 238 332 333 335 342

FOSTER (continued)
453 466 Robert E 244 466 Salanthial 194 196 Salanthiel 128 178 190 205 218 Salathiel 188 Samuel 85 113 Samuel P 392 Stephen 207 237 Thomas 53 Thomas S 332 335
FOURMAN, Jonathan 113
FOX, William S 398
FRAMBERS, Nicholas 336
FRAMBES, Nicholas 338
FRANCINE, Col 310 311
FRANKLIN, Benjamin 119 176 Dr 120 Gov 143 150 151 160 169 281 Morris 273 Mrs Benjamin 119 120 William 135 139 176 Wm 158 161
FREAS, Joseph 371
FREEMAN, 82
FRELINGHUYSEN, Frederic T 365
FRENCH, Howard M 336 338 Robert 53 Thomas 237
FRETWELL, 61 John 61 Peter 60 450
FRYER, 434
FURMAN, Jonathan 98
GALLOIS, Samson 32
GAMBLE, Calvin 198
GAMMAGE, Mr 273
GANDY, Amos T 469 David 237 George E 336 338 John 279 470 Reuben 454 Thomas 52 84 206 Thomas R 336 337 Uriah 205 207
GANETSON, Daniel 7 206
GARFIELD, Pres 393
GARLICK, Elizabeth 45 Hannah 48 John 53 85 Joshua 85 Mrs 45
GARLOCK, John 85
GARRETSON, Aaron 408 409 423 473 474 Aaron Sr 285 Daniel 7 233 463 Elijah 206 Elizabeth 77 Joshua 10 205 207 237 Rebecca 96 Rem 52 54 68 Samuel 74

GARRETSON (continued)
Townsend W 459-462
GARRISON, Benjamin B 314 Elizabeth 110 J Swain 477 Jacob 109 Jeremiah 314 John C 314 Jonathan S 466 Joseph 332 335 Katharine 110 Noah 104 Robert 348
GARRON, Thomas 336 338
GASKELL, Joseph H 440
GASKILL, John 237
GATES, Gen 200
GAUL, J W 273
GAVINSON, Deborah 73
GECKLER, John 311
GEORGE KING OF ENGLAND, 105
GEORGE II KING OF ENGLAND, 125
GEORGE III KING OF ENGLAND, 147, 191
GERRY, Robert 255
GIBBON, Nicholas 105 118
GIBSON, Robert 473
GIFFORD, Capt 197 James H 336 338
GILBERSON, Lubbart 53
GILBERT, John 33
GILE, Augustus C 435 476
GILMORE, Harry L 316 325
GILMOUR, Harry L 303
GILPIN, Hood 399
GISBORSEN, Lubbart 84
GOAFE, John 85
GODFREY, 33 39 Andrew 85 Benjamin 33 34 39 47 52 54 65 Edmund Y 339 Elijah 222 Elijah Jr 237 Hezekiah W 298 452 454-456 Jacob 463 James 105 114 130 141 171 187 198 205 218 James Jr 205 207 Jesse S 333 334 John 237 Joseph 174 Nicholas W 332 333 Philip 205 207 213 218 Thomas 188 218
GODYN, 17 18 20 Mr 19 Saml 18 19

GOFF, 39 Ashbury 470 Daniel 237
  Elbridge G 332 335 Howard 471
  John 39 55 114 227 234 241 John
  F 332 333 335 Joseph 241 243
  Rettie M 469 Silas 113 William
  134 136
GOFORTH, John 365
GOING, Thomas 53
GOLDEN, 100 101 Deborah 86
  Eleazer 127 John 198 Joseph 100
  141 William 52 65 68
GOLDENS, William Sr 54
GOLDIN, 210 249 John 187 202 205
  207 210 Mary 110 Samuel 198
  206 William 109
GOLDING, Rem G 68 William 58
GOODEN, Lewis 345 346
GOODWIN, Thomas 53 84
GOOF, John 207
GORDON, 21 23 195 Charles C 271
  Thomas 67
GORGE III KING OF ?, 134
GOULDEN, William 49
GOULDER, William 64
GOULDING, William 52
GOV OF NEW JERSEY, 215 302 315
  331
GOV OF PENNSYLVANIA, 153
GRACE, Albert 333 335 Anna H 467
  Charles 345 346 James A 333
  James S 335 Jesse 339 340 John
  199 200 201
GRADY, John 457
GRANGER, 259
GRANT, 378 Gen 364 Pres 364
GRAY, Henry 53
GREELEY, Horace 271 273
GREEN, Jacob 184
GREENE, Gen 195
GRICE, Francis 202
GRIFFING, Moses 187 198 Sarah 198
GRIFFINGS, Moses 198

GRIFFITHS, Thomas 70
GRINNELL, Capt 217 Richard 216
GROOM, Ann 110 Peter 110
GRUFF, William 336 337
GULICKSEN, Joshua 98
GUSTAVUS ADOLPHUS KING OF
  SWEDEN, 17
HACKET, William 237
HAINES, John 235 245 246
HALL, Clement 100 Isaac H 306
  Joseph 473 Matthew W 333 335
  Sarah 100
HALPIN, John 398 476
HAMBURGER, Judge 434
HAMILTON, And 52 Andrew 51 80
HAMLIN, 341 Hannibal 364
HAMMOCK, 39
HAMPTON, Jeremiah 333 335 Mr 74
HANCOCK, Mr 126 O E 364 William
  107
HAND, 68 119 427 Aaron 237 Aaron
  D 362 Aaron W 359 403 464 479
  Abraham 53 65 70 84 114 Absa-
  lom 207 Absolom Jr 243 Albert E
  348 Ann 73 Anna M 397 Benja-
  min 52 70 73 85 97 Benjamin Jr
  53 73 Capt 212 350 362 Charles
  136 343 464 Christopher 234
  Christopher Smith 349 Constant
  206 Constantine 198 206 Cornelius 74 84 85 198 206 Daniel 53 55
  84 109 113 137 213 463 David
  188 190 193 197 David E 333 334
  Dr 397 Eleazer 113 198 206 222
  451 463 Elias 339 340 Elihu 136
  Elijah 239 Elijah Jr 349 Elisha
  102 192 Elizabeth 71 Enoch 362
  Enoch W 314 315 427 476 Ezekiel 84 113 205 Ezra 207 Franklin
  302 371 452 454 458 459 464
  George 43 84 98 105 Henry 113
  119 136 139 141 171 174 178-180

HAND (continued)
183 189 191 196 205 244 427 463
473 476 477 Henry W 285 349
Henry Walker 349 Isaac 53 73 84
Isaiah 113 Jacob 73 113 118 135
136 141 171 174 239 Jacob G 460
461 James 113 Jane 281 Japhet
187 198 Jehu 98 Jeremiah 53 61
84 98 103 104 113 117 118 198
222-224 242 244 261 287 453 463
464 465 469 Jeremiah Jr 223
Jeruthy 71 Jesse 178-181 183 186
190 196 206 208 216 218 219 450
464 John 43 64 84-86 92 97 114
179 188 193 196 201 John Jr 180
John M 465 John W 345 346
Jonathan 176 184 185 218 267
268 395 450 Jonathan 3rd 267
Jonathan Jr 233 267 464 Jonathan
Sr 464 Joseph 53 84 303 362 427
475 476 Josiah 118 Levi 206
Mark 349 Matthew 219 Miller 237
243 Mr 219 303 403 Mrs Jesse
288 Nathan 134 179 193 196 207
Nathaniel 84 85 463 Peter 85
Philip 333 335 408 463 Philip Jr
473 Pocianci 73 Recompence 98
113 236 267 427 Recompense 136
198 Return 74 Robert E 400 403
452 460 461 463 Robert S 462 S S
471 Samuel 333 335 Sarah 267
Sarah H 408 Seth 222 223 225
Seth L 333 335 349 Shamgar 38
44 46 48 49 52 55 58-60 64 65 84
98 113 136 137 267 Shamgar Jr
53 84 Shamger 51 Sheriff 222
Silas 113 Stephen 225 455 456
Stillwell 437 Thomas 7 43 49 52
53 58 73 84 113 128 171 191 205
207 228 267 Thomas H 333 335
Thomas Jr 84 Thomas P 333 334
Timothy 113 205 Zelopead 85

HAND (continued)
Zelophead 73
HANES, Joseph H 387 452 475-477
HANKINS, Benjamin A 348 Eleazer
F 348
HARCOURT, Daniel 122
HARDIE, Elizabeth 45
HARDY, Gov 281
HARLAN, 435
HAROO, Richard 53
HARRIS, Dr 201 Robt 205 William S
459 460
HARRISON, 253 259 367 Benjamin
372 399 441 Gen 394 395 437
Martin L 479 Mrs 393-395 Mrs
Pres 393 Pres 245 341 393-395
HART, Charles A 442 M G 273
Thomas 406
HARTSHORN, Hugh 180
HARVEY, Gov 24
HARWOOD, L 423 Lilburn 298 Mr
407 William 48 53
HASE, John 113
HASSLER, Simon 386
HATCH, Brig Gen 350
HATHORN, Hugh 183 187 195
HATTON, 148 155-158 168 170 218
John 143 147 148 150 151 160
161 167 218 John Jr 168 Jr 158
Mr 148-156 158-166 169 Sr 158
HATTOWELL, Benj 170
HAUTENOAN, Don Joseph 89
HAWTHORNE, James 85
HAYES, Abraham 336 338 Charles S
303 Maj 196
HAYNE, Senator 257
HAYNES, A L 302 Albert L 461 462
475 476
HAYS, Elijah 237
HAYTHORN, Hugh 185 450
HEARON, Samuel 314
HEATON, Rev Mr 109 Samuel 72

HEBENTHAL, William 298
HEDGES, David 205 James 113
HEISLER, Charles 335
HEISLES, Charles 333
HEMINGWAY, Washington 466
HEMLOCK, Edward 58
HENDERSON, Clark 263 James 458
HENDRICK, 14
HENDRICKS, Thomas A 365
HENDRICKSON, Cornelius 16 23
HENRY, Bennett 338 Joseph P 476 Joseph T 476 Mr 75 Wm 133
HERITAGE, Isaac 348 Job 314 Richard 314 William H 348
HEWES, 180 Humphrey 43 72
HEWET, Thomas 136
HEWIT, Joseph 74 113 Randal 52 Reuben 113 Shamgar 205 Thomas 53 105 114
HEWITT, 38 39 Aaron 339 340 Artis 243 Daniel 207 Dorothy 52 E Ellsworth 472 Edwin S 472 Freling F 339 340 George 340 Henry Y 362 Humphrey 263 John 339 340 Jonathan 236 Jonathan Jr 454 Randal 58 Randall 39 Shamgar 233 Thomas 454 455 Thomas Jr 246 463 William 247 467
HEWS, Humphrey 66
HEYSET, Pieter 20
HEYSSEN, 23 Peter 18
HICKEY, Job 237
HIGBEE, Joseph S 333 335
HIGGINS, Andrew 216 Eliakim 32
HIGGINSON, Francis 285
HIGH, John 314 Jonathan 53 Malachi 338 340
HILDRETH, 434 440 A Carlton 452 461 462 Alvin P 387 426 440 452 459 460 474 476 477 Daniel 136 David 85 113 207 227 338-340 David Jr 243 E Swain 476

HILDRETH (continued)
Ephraim 226 243 246 453 454
George 362 407 426 431 James 114 136 237 465 James Jr 206
James M E 398 399 440 441 472
Jonathan 207 463 Joseph 113 134 136 180 244 450 463 Joshua 113 226 247 376 Josiah 85 Mayor 441 Mr 440-442 Surrogate 376
Theodore F 349 William 234 244 375 464 468
HILGERT, 382 J 382 Mr 382
HILL, George W 371 Mr 70 Philip 70 Robert C 373
HILLYER, Capt 310
HINTS, Anne 74 Hester 74 Joseph 74 Thomas 74
HISCOX, Sarah 71
HITCHNER, Enoch J 462
HOAG, Lewis 311
HOBART, 404
HOFFMAN, 315 J Durell 461 462 James 244 John T 333 335 Silas 315 William 348
HOGBURN, William 237
HOLDEN, Benjamin 85
HOLES, Charles K 280
HOLLINGSHEAD, George 104 206
HOLLINSWORTH, 435
HOLMES, 38 240 362 Capt 197 Charles K 471 Elizabeth 329 Gabriel H 339 340 Hugh H 472 John 202 207 Joseph 303 Joseph H 338-340 345 346 Judge 302 362 Nathaniel 212 247 250 255 276 329 452-455 465 Nathaniel Jr 276 451 Richard 362 Richard C 284 362 426 455 Robert H 240 451 Robert M 262 464
HONDOIN, Joseph 84
HONN, Samuel 333 335
HOOKER, 308 311 Gen 308 Joseph

HOOKER (continued)
305 308
HOOPER, 290 Abagail 290 Col 200 Ir
 S 95 William 290 William S 291
 292 303 305 307 407 444 456
 459-461 463 473 477 William
 Smith 290
HOOTON, Lew 66
HORNER, Isaac 32
HORTON, Mahlon 336 338
HOSKINS, Caesar 7 52 60 84 85 463
 Thomas Caesar 7 43
HOSSET, Gillis 18 20
HOSSETT, 23
HOULDEN, Joseph 41 48
HOULDING, Joseph 51 52
HOW, Gen 193 194
HOWEL, Edmund 59
HOWELL, Edmund 463 Edward 53
 John 53 Joshua 53 Richard 199
HUBARD, John 53
HUBBARD, James 109 John 54
HUDDELL, G H 371
HUDDLE, Commr 25
HUDSON, 14 15 17 21 23 Hendrick
 15 16 Henry 14
HUES, Isaac A 478
HUFFMAN, John B 464
HUGES, Capt 88
HUGG, Mr 132
HUGHES, 39 253 257 383 Aaron 234
 246 Abigail 238 Albert 238 Archd
 205 Capt 88 227 237 Christopher
 79 Constant 84 98 102 207 463
 Constant Jr 84 Constantine 88
 Daniel 467 Daniel B 170 Daniel L
 342 389 Elijah 84 136 179-181
 183 185 195 223 450 Elijah Jr 464
 Elijah Sr 104 464 Ellis 105 206
 224-228 254 255 405 465 Ellis Jr
 207 George W 421 465 Henry A
 383 Hugston 98 Humphrey 39 52

HUGHES (continued)
 57 72 73 90 92 98 138 237 238
 383 450 463 Humphrey Jr 84
 Jacob 104 113 136 223 228 234
 237 463 James R 369 375 Jedediah 74 Jedekiah 136 Jeremiah 84
 Jesse 207 John 73 113 Joseph 233
 406 Joseph B 244 333 335 453
 454 465 476 Joseph E 282 355
 368 369 457 464 466 473 474
 Joseph H 477 Judge 368 Judith
 138 Matthew 336 338 Memucan
 109 180 187 207 Memucum 196
 Mennican 229 Moses 237 Mr 91
 181 257 Robert E 475 476 Spicer
 250 455 463 Thomas 406 451
 Thomas B 408 457 473 474
 Thomas H 225 226 250 255 256
 405 406 451 463 Thomas P 254
 451 453 463 William 237 405
HUGHS, Elijah 102 Humphrey 86 97
 102
HUGLINGSWORTH, Levi 202
HUIT, Randall 84
HULING, Jacob 61 450
HULTON, Hen 170
HUMFREYES, Alexander 30
HUMPHRIES, Alexander 37 53 John
 79 Joshua 32
HUNLAK, Edward 32
HUNLAKE, Edw Jr 32
HUNLOCK, Edward 60
HUNT, Dr 188 John Jr 205
HUNTER, 62
HUNTLEY, Uriah H 478
HUSTED, 203 Ephraim 203
HUTCHINSON, Rhoda L 469 Robert
 469
HUWES, Memucan 218
INGERSOL, Jaen 110 Joseph 109
INGERSOLL, David T 336 338
 Richard 336 338

INGLES, John 110
INGOLDSBY, Richard 66
INSELL, Samuel 187 198
IRELAND, Elijah 359 470 Joseph W 303 306 Mary 110 Thomas 109 110 Townsend 307 Townsend T 303
IRISH, Ambassador 276
ISARD, 362 Isaac 362 John 114
ISZARD, Abraham L 298 John Jr 241 Michael 113
IZARD, John 205 207 Simeon 207
JACKSON, 257 Andrew 256 262 Pres 262 394
JACOBS, T Fletcher 303 Thomas Fletcher 306
JACOBY, Henry 460
JACOCKS, Jas 85 William 49
JACOKS, 58 William 52 57
JACOX, William 84
JACQUES, Joseph 213
JAMES, Edward 237
JAMES KING OF ENGLAND, 13 27 68
JAMES I KING OF ENGLAND, 13
JAMIESON, David 40
JANNCEY, 87
JANNEY, Capt 87
JANQUENO, 18
JARMAN, Jonathan 465 Richard 336 337
JARVIS, 48 John 41 47 48
JENKINS, 109 Capt 196 197 Easter 71 Esther 71 Jonadab 113 Jonan 205 Jonathan 171 178 180 189 190 196 203 206 221 450 463 464 Mr 70 71 90 91 N 73 Nathanael 63 90 104 109 Nathanael Sr 104 Nathaniel 70 71 73 90 178 Nathaniel 2d 71 Nathaniel Jr 113 Nathl 450
JENNINGS, Mary 71 Samuel 60

JERVIS, John 51-53 84
JOHNS, Miss 272
JOHNSON, 48 278 325 Amos 113 Andrew 286 437 Benjamin 55 85 104 113 Capt 127 Charles T 409 473 476 Col 284 Daniel 53 84 206 David 54 206 220 221 451 Dr 114 115 130 Ebenezer 84 113 463 Eldredge 476 Eldridge 438 475-477 Jacob 237 Jacob E 316 325 James W 468 Jeremiah 224 233 468 John 125 Joseph W 303 305 307 Joshua 333 335 Levi E 306 Ludlam 223 Mr 129 438 Nathan 114 Oliver 34 47 49 53 84 Pres 286 Reuben T 471 Samuel 84 Thos 114 William 49 52 55 65 84 Wm 48
JOHNSTON, Ebenezer 139 Samuel 98
JONES, Alphonso A 333 335 Esther 71 Henry 205 John 470 Richard 53 Samuel 139 Sylvia 139
JUET, Robert 14
JULIEN, Rev Mr 340
KATES, George W 472 Martha G 468
KATTS, Francis 339 340
KEACH, Elias 70
KEARNEY, Philip 303
KEELER, William H 459
KEEN, Nicholas 202
KEENAN, Thomas 306
KELLONY, John 198
KELLY, Aunt Judy 393 394 Uncle Dan 393 394
KELSEY, John 205 206 Mr 109
KENNEDY, Charlotte R 424 Dr 424 425 Henry A 425 J S 425 James S 409 424 457 473 474 477
KENT, Gideon 207
KERN, William H 386
KERNS, Patrick 303

KERRICK, Adam 336 337
KIDD, 59 Capt 59
KILSEY, John 198
KIMSEY, David 454 David T 306
    James H 333 John W 303 306
KING, 434 Daniel 237
KING OF ENGLAND, 13
KING OF GREAT BRITAIN, 206
KINSEY, David 453 454 James H 335
KIRBY, William H 306 311
KIRLAND, Col 158
KNIGHT, Edward C 383 Joseph 53
KRAMER, Andrew 345 346
LACKE, Wm 211
LAIB, Frederick 311
LAKE, Ezra B 377 James E 377
    Samuel Wesley 377 William 53
    377 452 460 461
LAMBERTON, George 23
LAND, Benjamin 84
LANDIS, Charles K 385 398 448
LANGLEY, Henry 333 335 Thomas
    84 85
LANSING, John L 475
LARNING, Thos 147
LAUGHTON, Benjamin 113
LAURANCE, 33 Andrew 32 33 Mary
    32
LAURENCE, 33 Andrew 33
LAWRENCE, 33 62 107 Andrew 32
    Chairman 107 Daniel 139 140 142
    James 62 Joseph 62 May 241 Mr
    140 Robert 107
LAWRIE, Gawen 28
LAWRISON, Peter 32
LEACH, Alonzo L 443 Col 341 El-
    bridge G 285 Elizabeth 285 Frank
    Willing 365 J Granville 332 333
    339 340 365 Joseph S 280A 284
    285 299 340 342 356 365 408 409
    431 443 457 458 465 473 474
    Joseph Smallidge 287 Josiah

LEACH (continued)
    Granville 340 Lawrence 285
    Lemuel Jr 285 Lemuel Sr 285 Mr
    285-287 356 357 365 366 Mrs J
    Granville 281 Sanford 285 Sophia
    287 William 285
LEAMAN, Charles H 479
LEAMING, 39 46 76 78 106-108 116
    119 128 134 137 179 183 184 214
    Aaron 46 55 76 79 80 84 92-96 99
    101 105 107 108 113 116-118 125
    126 128 129 132 141 171 172 174
    175 178 180 187-190 193 202 204
    214 215 250 339 340 384 450 463
    Aaron 1st 44 90-92 99 450 464
    Aaron 2d 90 91 98 106 114 138
    227 248 250 259 352 450 Aaron
    3d 250 Aaron Jr 85 106 450 C F
    303 Christopher 39 43-45 85 98
    109 138 139 180 207 221 242 352
    473 477 Christopher 1st 44 Chris-
    topher 2nd 44 Coleman F 214 302
    303 343 353 355 457 464 Deborah
    138 Deborah Hand 138 Elizabeth
    44 100 Esther 43 Esther B 44
    Furman 234 451 Hannah 44
    Humphrey 464 473 474 Israel 407
    423 473 J F 303 James 428 474
    475 James Jr 474 Jane 44 Jere 113
    Jeremiah 84 91 116 118 136 200
    259 263 300 353 451 Jeremiah
    2nd 44 Jeremian 99 John D 339
    340 Jonathan 190 191 207 223
    224 450 463 Jonathan F 261 302
    303 352 353 376 389 451 452 464
    Joseph F 284 Lydia 99 Mary 408
    Matthias 100 Mr 91 129 180 195
    260 Parsons 209 Persons 202 222
    227 249 259 451 Richard S 328
    331 353 367 371 379 452 456-458
    Sarah 139 Sen 379 Sheriff 250
    Spicer 222 453 Spicer Jr 237

LEAMING (continued)
   T 144 148 Thomas 45 55 66 74 84
   85 92 113 117 135 140 141 143-
   145 165 171 174 179 183 184 196
   218 220 Thomas 1st 44 Thomas H
   471 Thomas Jr 178 183 184 Thos
   85 147 Thos Jr 180 Walter S 389
   390 452 476 477
LEAMYENG, Aaron 63 Christopher
   43 51 52 99 Esther 43 Hester 99
   Thomas 53 99
LEAMYING, Aaron 86 Christopher
   205
LEAYEMAN, Christopher 49
LEBAKE, Isiah 33
LEBORE, Peter Carson 65
LECHE, John 285
LEE, 321 324 327 345 Abel 187 198
   237 Alphonso D 333 335 Francis
   269 Gen 320 323 James W 461
   462 478 John W 337 Joseph W
   336 R H 478 Robert E 320 321
   323 348
LEECH, J 273
LEEDS, Japhet 77
LEEK, Mr 124
LEMEN, Aaron 180
LEMING, Aaron 86 Thomas 86
LEMMON, Thomas 435
LENNIG, F 272
LEONARD, 65 145 Aaron 85 Henry
   113 J 144 148 Jo 145 John 104
   105 113 117 135 141 143 144 147
   165 174 Thomas 65
LESTER, George W 345 346
LETART, Judeth 78
LILLIES, David 34
LINCOLN, 278 341 Mr 301 Pres 286
   301 316 329
LIPPINCOTT, Levi E 336 338
LISTON, Edmond 88
LITTLE, Albert B 477 James 336 338

LITTLE (continued)
   John 244
LIVINGSTON, William 199 204
LIVISTON, Gov 193
LLOYD, Charles 336 338 David 348
   John 336 338 Leaming 336 338
   Richard F 333 335
LOCK, William 110
LOGUES, Abraham 126
LONGSTREET, 310
LORD, George 189
LORE, Deborah 110
LOVELACE, Lord 62
LOVETT, George L 477
LOWRIE, 28
LUCAS, 28 33 Augustus 32 33 Daniel
   32 Daniel Sr 33 Nicholas 28
LUDLAM, 38 39 46 54 Albert H 407
   Anthony 46 53 54 83 85 97 237
   Charles 12 302 Christopher 178
   190 196 218 219 222 227 241 242
   453 Clinton H 284 329 343 456
   457 Coleman F 332 333 335
   Edwin 332 335 Furman L 401 452
   George 244 George L 423 473
   474 Henry 190 196 220 222
   Hudson 449 Isaac 54 85 Jacob Jr
   103 James 221 225 227 233 James
   J 244 263 Jeremiah 130 136 180
   Jesse D 380 452 459 Jos 180
   Joseph 39 46 53 54 57 65 84 186
   205 207 234 245 Joseph Jr 102
   Joseph Sr 53 Mr 271 273 290
   Norton 237 Providence 85 Reuben
   127 141 171 174 205 478 Richard
   362 Richard S 234 263 406 408
   451 455-457 Richard Smith 241
   270 290 407 Sammuel R 475
   Samuel 54 Samuel R 303 426 474
   475 Thomas 189 469 Thomas E
   388 398 459 478 Thomas Jr 237
LUDLON, Joseph 83

LUDLOW, Joseph 84
LULDAM, Isaac 114
LUMMIS, 203 Joseph 203
LUMUS, Edward 84
LUPTON, Christopher 113
LYCETT, John W 473
LYNCH, Dennis 52 64
LYONS, John 423
MACHEY, John 114
MACKENZIE, Alexander 465
MACKEY, John 54 125 134 141 171 174 178 179 187 188 193 195
MADDEN, Hosea F 470 Jennie 470 Martin 470 Otis 470
MADDISON, Allen 191
MADISON, James 231
MAGEE, John 336 338
MAGONAGLE, Mary E 356 Mr 356 358 Mrs Samuel R 358 S R 303 341 Samuel R 286 303 305 329 356 421 452 465 472 474
MAGONIGLE, Mr 284 Samuel R 284
MAGRATH, Christopher S 284 285 373 435 474-476 Mr 285
MAGUIRE, James 260 466 467
MAGWAY, John 201
MALHERBE, Nicholas 33
MANNERY, Furman 336 338
MARCY, 372 406 Dr 425 429 Harry B 467 Matthew 255 455 456 468 S S 423 Samuel 429 Samuel S 242 328 372 408 421 425 426 456 457 465 473 474 Thankful 425 V M D 277 371 398 429 Virgil M D 371 372 426
MARKLEY, 356
MARPOLE, George 126
MARSH, Daniel 218
MARSHALL, Benjamin H 460 Edward 53 Ellis H 470 Frederick 336 338 James 32 53 Randolph 454

MARTINEAU, Nicholas 53
MARTINES, Nicholas 34
MARY QUEEN OF ENGLAND, 68
MASON, Mr 407 William 43 52 59 60 65
MATHEMEK, 18
MATHEWS, Capt 73 Elijah 237 Richard 197 Saml 32 Samll 31 Samuel 51 58-60 65 72 85 Tho 31 Thomas 31 84 Wm 85
MATIKETT, Isaac 34
MATTHEW, William 136
MATTHEWS, 39 Elizabeth 73 Isaac 207 John 74 98 Mary 73 Moses W 305 307 Richard 178 190 207 Samuel 39 43 44 46 49 52 55 242 261 452 453 463 Samuel Jr 53 Thomas 53 William 84 98 113
MAYPS, Mary 74
MCCANE, James 246
MCCARTNEY, James 465
MCCARTY, John W 345 346 Joseph 339 340 Joseph A 345 346 William Sr 362
MCCLAUGHAN, Capt 127
MCCLELLAN, Gen 308
MCCLOSKY, John 217
MCCOLLUM, Jesse 476 Peter 474
MCCONNELL, 434
MCCOOK, Edward 365
MCCORMICK, Isaac W 345 346
MCCRACKEN, Mr 273
MCCREA, John 40
MCDONALD, Maj 133
MCGINNIS, Dr 188
MCKAIN, Elizabeth 408 Thomas 408
MCKAY, John 179
MCKEAG, William H 339 340 345 346
MCKEAN, Alexander 453 William V 393
MCKENZIE, Alexander 405

MCKINLEY, 404
MCMACKIN, B 423 Benjamin 407 J 423 Joe 407 John 407 Mr 405
MCMICHAEL, Marshal 386
MCPHERSON, Maggie A 471
MCQUAY, John 198 201
MEASY, John 460
MECRAY, 406 Dr 429 J E 434 James 398 408 409 423 429 430 473 474 477 James Jr 349 474 475 477 James Sr 474 Jeremiah 227 407 Jeremiah E Jr 477 John 303 307 435 440
MEKOWETICK, 18
MELVIN, 435 F 437 Frederic J 473 Frederick J 435 466 472 Mayor 386 432 436 437 Mr 436
MENINGAULT, Elizabeth 32
MERCER, Dr 275 Robert J 371
MESSICH, William W 435
MEY, 15-17 23 Capt 16 Cornelius Jacobsen 15 17
MICKEL, Hollis 336 338 James 127
MICKLE, 49
MIDDLETON, Edward 470
MILLER, 378 Aaron 328 398 452 456-458 463 468 Burr 378 Eliza 434 James 114 James T 468 Jeremiah 53 Jonas 377 406 407 465 Jonas S 380 Joyce 13 Lafayette 380 Lemuel E 379 382 398 452 475 477 Mr 126 302 378 Pauline 378 Richard T 380 Seth 243 246 468 Simeon B 477 Thomas 43 53 Vincent 44 Vincent O 386 464 W B 302 456 W Burr 406 438 Waters B 298 302 303 328 343 365 378 408 431 451 452 456 457 459 466 472-474 Waters Burrows 377 William C 477
MILLS, 144-146 150 151 162-164 Charles 303 Charles G 338-340

MILLS (continued)
Ephraim 406 407 Jedediah 147 Jedidiah 148 Jeremiah 136 Jonathan 136
MINUIT, Peter 20
MITCHELE, Robert 93
MITCHELL, John 200 227 Robert 94 95 William 227
MITCHILL, Robert 95
MIXNER, Edward J 467
MONCHERON, 14 Balthazer 13
MONJOY, 33 James 32
MONROE, Jas 231
MOORE, Adam 336 338 Amos C 234 236 453 454 Gainer P 446 477 John M 395 Nathaniel 236 Sarah 267 William G 437
MORGAN, Abel 104 Mr 104
MORRIS, 133 Anthony 34 John S 466 Lewis 40 93 96 Robert 190 191 Rockliff 468 Samuel 336 338
MORTON, 367 Levi P 342 Thomas 333 334
MOTT, James 218
MOUSSEL, Thomas 81
MULFORD, Enos 237 Ezekiel 85 Isaac W 345 346 Lewis 84 Stephen 408 William 85 98
MULLER, Robert S 478
MULLERY, Lt 311
MULLINER, Henry C 298
MULLIS, Jacob 126
MUNRO, Peter J 472
MURCH, 156-158 168 John 156 168 Mr 168
MURPHY, Bernard 466
MURR, Mr 132
MURRAY, Nicholas 371
MUTCHMORE, S A 371
MYERS, William 32
NEGRO, Jethro 221
NEVILL, Speaker 108

NEWBOLD, Joshua 61
NEWELL, William A 363
NEWTON, Caleb 113 124 Ebenezer
 99 113 451 464 Eleazer 98 Isaac
 113 205 John 178 180 190 196
 John 2d 188 Nathaniel 459 460
NICHOLS, Charles E 391 463 465
NICKERSON, James 237
NICKKOLLS, William 85
NICKLESON, John 206
NICKOLS, William 85
NOBLE, George 53
NORBURY, Joseph 244
NORCAULT, Eleazer 98
NORTON, Albert 348 Caleb 86
 Daniel 85 Danl 86 David 339 340
 348 Ebenezer 86 Ezra 269 George
 207 236 Jeremiah 237 Nathaniel
 85 98 Uriah 348
NOTT, Richard 339 340
NOTTINGHAM, Jacob 236 Jonathan
 234 244
NUMMY KING OF THE LENNI-
 LENAPES, 9
NUTON, Ebenezer 85
OGBOURNE, Samll 32
OGDEN, Aaron 199 George 303
 Robert 115 William 338 340
OLDEN, Gov 268 301 302 316 317
OLDMIXON, 10 66
OLIPHANT, William 467
ORAM, Samuel Jr 237
OSBORN, J B 478 Jennie L 467
 Jonathan 84 Joseph 229 Mary 71
 Nathan 86
OSBORNE, Ananias 105 Annanias
 113 Jonathan 43 48 52 59
OSBORNES, Abiah 74 Ananias 74
 Bezabeel 74 John 74 Nathan 74
 Ruth 74
OSBOURN, Jonathan 60
OSSET, Gillis 20

OTO, Dr 188
OTTO, Frederic 178 218
OWEN, Benjamin 263
PAGE, John 52 67 72 96 Mr 133
 Thomas 113
PAIGE, John 73 Peter 85
PAINE, Clinton P 442
PAKAHAKE, 18
PALMER, Gideon 236 Joseph Jr 425
 William K 469
PANCOAST, L M 460 461
PANKTOE, 12
PARKER, Alvin H 260 George 32
 James 188 Joel 315 Joel E 368
PARSON, Lydia 73 Robert 141
PARSONS, John 52 55 84 86 98 99
 John 3d 45 Lydia 99 Robert 113
 135 205 224 225 Robert 1st 45
 Robert Jr 196 199
PARVIN, David 203 Jeffrey 203
PATTERSON, F E 308
PAUUW, 17 20
PEACOCK, Albert T 469
PECK, 31 John 31
PEMHAKE, 18
PENN, 28 William 28
PENNINGTON, William 236
PEPPER, Amos 237
PERDRAIN, 33 Elizabeth 32 Mr 32
 Peter 32 33 35
PEREMAN, Robert 84
PERIMAN, Abner 206
PERSONS, Elizabeth 45 John 45 John
 1st 45 John 2nd 45 Lydia 45 Mr
 45 Robert 190 Robert Jr 188
PETERSON, 434 Jacob L 478 Samuel
 206 Walter S 333 335 William
 237 William L 449 459
PETIT, Charles 150 Chas 150 Mr 150
PETTIT, Mr 144
PETTITT, Thomas W 336 338
PEYRARD, James 33

PHARO, Eliza 278 Timothy 278
PHILPOT, 203 Abraham 203
PIERCE, 400 Franklin 284 Richard 399
PIERSON, David 409 473 David W 473 Isaac 257 John 237 Ludlam 463 Stephen 303 306 Thomas 237
PINE, Abigail 52 Jonathan 12 29 48 49 53
PITMAN, Charles 255
PLANTAGENET, 10 23 Beauchamp 23
PLOWDEN, 23 Edmund 23
PLUMER, James 206
PLUMMER, James 198 206
POINSETT, Benjamin F 476
POLK, 271 Pres 421
POLLEY, Clark 407
POLLOCK, James 371
POLLY, Clark 282
POWELL, Capt 24 336 Charles R 336 Josiah 333 335
PRENTISS, William 479
PRES OF THE UNITED STATES, 320 331 344
PRESTON, 203 Abijah 203 Charles M 472 Ebenezer 201 Isaac 203
PRICE, 277 Edward 467 Eliza 278 John 246 277 408 John T 468 Kezia 277 Keziah 408 Lt Col 310 311 Millicent 110 Nathan C 442 474 Theophilus Pharo 278 Theophilus Townsend 277 William 277 408
PRITCHARD, William L 333 335
PRYOR, James E 446 477
PYNDE, 30 Edward 30
RALEIGH, Walter 13
RALFE, John 86
RALPH, John 80
RAME, Mrs 32 33
RANDOLPH, E T 428 James Fitz 257

RASH, Jonathan 339 340
RAYNOR, Morris 53 Theirs 53
READ, Charles 115 163 Mr 132 148
RECEAVER, Ulysses 306
RECHTER, Edward 93
REDHEFFER, Benjamin 303
REEVES, 292 Abijah 199 239 293 Abijah D 332 335 Abraham 239 293 303 455 Abram 292 451 455 Adonijah 239 Andrew H 456-458 Benjamin F 428 C B 459 David 246 298 David Jr 303 306 George H 479 George W 373 John 39 46 49 52 54 55 74 305 307 479 John N 435 466 John W 333 334 452 458 460 461 Rachel 428 Swain S 303 305 307 311 William H 479
RELFE, John 159
RENDARD, 33 Peter 33
RENEY, 119 James 119
REVEL, 61 Thomas 61
REVELLE, Tho 52
REX, Nathaniel 98
REYBURN, John E 399 442 Mr 442
REYNOLD, Mrs 407
REZNOO, J P 371
RICARD, Frederick 352
RICE, Edward 242 Edward L 395 464 Leaming M 395 452 458-461
RICHARDS, 32 Philip 32 Robert 54
RICHARDSON, 385 436 Benjamin 84 F L 437 Furman L 384 452 466 474 475 477 Jacob 113 118 207 Jehu 98 Jeremiah 207 John 43 52 Jonathan 84 Joseph H 469 Samuel 84 85 William 53
RICHE, Miss 272
RICHIER, Edward 93-95
RIDMAN, Joseph 237
RIEBENACK, Max 442 Mr 442
RIEL, Charles P 333 335
RITCHIE, James Jr 478

ROBB, Thomas 398
ROBENSON, William 113
ROBERTSON, 408
ROBINSON, Charles 85 Douglass J 462 Elijah 453 James 218 John B 333 334 Mr 385 R Curtis 385 460 466 William 85 113 114
ROBISON, Charles 70 71 Elizabeth 71
RODAN, David W 477
RODNEY, C A 231
ROSCO, Nathaniel 85
ROSEMAN, George 474
ROSS, 119 Edmund L 400 452 464 James C 467 Marcy 113 119 Thomas 105 William 303
ROYAL, William J 470
ROYALL, William B 331
RUCHIER, Edward 94
RUDMAN, 26
RUDOLPH, 434 A J 478 Henry 339 340 348 349
RUGGINS, Benjn 189
RUSH, Richard 257
RUSLING, Sedgewick 255
RUSSEL, Oliver 52
RUSSELL, John 339 340 John M 467
RUTHERFORD, Henry S 476 William C 333 335
RUTTER, George 236
RYAN, Reuben W 471
SABSOVICH, H L 396 Professor 396
SACOOCK, 18
SAINT, Daniel 405 407 David 263
SALAWAY, Justice 34
SANDGRAN, Charles 435 473 477 Mitchell 435
SAPP, Clayton G 339 340
SAVAGE, Joseph 55 109 141 171 174 180 183 185 450
SAWOWONWE, 18
SAWYER, 316 318 320 321 323 474

SAWYER (continued)
Capt 317 318 321-324 Col 324 H W 320 398 Henry W 301 316 319 323 386 390 435 474 475 Henry Washington 316 318 Mr 302 316 317
SAYERS, Thomas D 339
SAYRE, Jeremiah 227 Mrs Jeremiah 227
SAYRES, Lemuel 110
SCHELINKS, Cornelius 113
SCHELLENGER, Aaron 243 246 408 Aaron Jr 473 474 477 Aaron Sr 477 Cornelius 98 Daniel 458 459 Enos 212 Henry 136 206 Isaac 407 Jeremiah 473 474 Jeremiah B 474 John 234 Joseph 457 458 473 474 477 Joseph M 477 Louisa M 408 Virgil D 332 335 William 206 473 William S 474
SCHELLINGER, 39 Cornelius 43 Daniel 452 Henry Jr 468
SCHELLINKS, Cornelius 39
SCHENCK, J H 448
SCHEUCH, Gen 427
SCHICK, Charles S 478
SCHILLENGER, James 198
SCHILLINGER, Cornelius 72 Cornelius Jr 72 Mary 72
SCHILLINKS, Enos 124
SCHILLIUX, Cornelius Jr 85
SCHILLUX, Lydia 73
SCHMOELE, Dr 298 Henry 298 William 298
SCHULL, Daniel 198 206 Hezekiah 85
SCHURCH, Samuel 478
SCHUYLER, Peter 125
SCOT, 86 Walter 86
SCOTT, James T 236 Thomas 187 198 Thomas Jr 205 Thomas Sr 205

SCOVEL, Alden 330 Catherine 330
SCRAF, 212
SCULL, 76 126 Abel 237 Abigail 110
    Daniel 206 Franklin 348 Isaac 110
    John 77 104 110 113 Tabitha 110
SEAGRAVE, Artis 72 William 70 73
    84 97
SEAGREAVES, William 74
SEAMAN, Henry P 435
SEARS, Samuel 82
SEARSE, George M 336 338 Reuben
    336 338
SEC OF WAR, 320
SECY OF STATE, 230
SEELEY, Thomas M 470
SEIGMAN, W V L 359 375 464
SELOVER, Martin 339 340
SERVANT, Margrett 31
SESPINE, 33 Heter 33
SEWELL, Gen 442 William J 347 399
    428 431 442
SHARP, Anthony 209 Isaac 80
    Thomas C 470 Zebulon 53
SHARSWOOD, George 53
SHARWOOD, William 53
SHAW, Alexander A 408 Charles A
    474 475 Charles T 333 335
    Edmund 72 Elijah 207 Harvey 245
    246 269 James H 460 Jane E 408
    Jeremiah 237 John 43 48 52 65 73
    86 114 118 136 198 205 206 463
    John F 307 Jonas 469 Joseph 60
    Joshua 73 84 86 113 Lemuel A
    473 Lydia 71 73 99 Nathan 73
    Nathaniel 136 Richard 73 85 113
    Silaw 118 Thomas 218 220 W
    Frank 476 William 53 60 65 66 73
    74 84 99 207 William A 479
SHELDON, Francis W 333 335
SHELLINKS, Cornelius 43
SHELLMIRE, Maj 322
SHEPPARD, A R 365 Dickison 70

SHEPPARD (continued)
    John G 348 Mr 109
SHERMAN, Gen 350 William
    Tecumseh 393
SHIELDS, Edward 383 Edward P 386
    464 Henry B 383 Joanna D 383 W
    S P 442
SHIMP, Richard D 472
SHIVERS, Edward M 462 472
SHOEMAKER, James 359 457 458
    James Jr 463 John W 336 338
SHORT, Nathan 43 Nathaniel 52 84
SHUTE, Nathaniel 84
SHUTTON, Isaac 85
SICKLER, Augustus H 478
SIDDALL, Frank 448
SILVER, Charles J 303 307
SIMKINS, William 136
SIMPKINS, William 53 84 113
SIMPSON, 203 C 459 James 203
SKELINGER, Cornelius 84
SKELLINKS, Cornelius 52
SKENE, Jno 30 31 John 32 Justice 34
SKINNER, Atty Gen 149 Cortd 150
    Cortland 150 Mr 148-151 Thomas
    93-95
SKULL, Daniel 187
SLAVE, Hughes 144 146 148 161 163
    166 Jethro 221 Ned 148 Troy 133
SLOAN, Smith 237
SMALLIDGE, Elizabeth 285 Joseph
    285
SMALLWOOD, Gen 195
SMART, 434
SMITH, 134 Abagail 290 Abijah 233
    270 451 464 Abraham 53 70
    Abram 73 Capt 313 Carman 113
    Christopher 220 225 Constantine
    227 Daniel 136 205 David 72 218
    David T 456 464 Deborah 270
    288 Elias 110 Elihu 113 134
    Elothes 71 Enoch 205 Frank E

SMITH (continued)
461 462 467 478 479 Frank E
Smith 478 George W 303 305 312
313 343 373 470 473 474 German
242 Griffin 467 Herbert C 478
Isaac 233 235 437 Isaac H 437
474 475 477 Jacob 114 205 207
242 Jacob G 234 241 267 453 454
464 468 James L 242 243 269 270
276 302 451 453-455 James T 303
305 307 312 Jesse M 474 476
John 85 113 114 237 263 452-455
John H 479 John L 242 Jonathan
109 113 135 136 Joseph C P 461
462 Levi 233 Lewis S 462 Margery 71 Micajah 459 460 474 475
Mr 126 Mrs Enoch 227 Reuben
338-340 Richard 64 74 85 113
Samuel 78 108 118 Socrates J 348
Thomas 105 114 134 136 141 312
463 Uriah 113 210 233 237 W S
272 Walter G 470 Wesley C 477
William 52 70 84-86 92 97 102
140 171 174 229 290 312 313 339
340 William F 333 335 William Jr
102 Wm 114
SNELL, Capt 210
SNOW, Capt 248 249
SNYDER, Aaron H 466 William 333
335 Willoby 7 338
SOMERS, 126 185 362 Col 196 Jesse
212 John 49 76 Judeth 78 Richard
76 78 186
SOUDER, Jacob 241 242 453 468
Peter 463 464 Webster 236 Willoby 7 Willowby 340
SPALDING, 314 Augustus 314 John
338 339
SPEACE, John D 435
SPENCER, John 479
SPICER, 29 44 63 66 67 76 79 80
106-108 115 116 119 124 125

SPICER (continued)
127-129 133 134 137 139 2d 139
Col 84 Deborah 138 139 Elisha
121 Enoch 55 Esther 44 Jack 121
Jacob 12 29 44 48 52-55 60 63 64
66 67 72 79 80 84 86 90 92 97 98
102 105 107 108 113-115 117 118
120 125 128 134 135 137-139 450
Jacob 1st 464 Jacob 2d 105 114
115 137 450 Jacob 3d 248 Judith
121 138 139 Maj 67 Michael 44
Mr 129 Samuel 44 Sarah 44 138
Sylvia 138 Thomas 44
SPOFFORD, James P 461
SPRINGER, Alexander 471 Alexander W 466 Alexander Whilldin
371 Benjamin 126 247 Edward D
349 Francis G 345 346 Jesse 234
236 Jonathan J 362 452 454 Mr
362 Samuel 243 261 263 302 362
453 454 463 Samuel R 236
STACY, Mahlon 61
STANCLIFF, John 72 103
STANFIELD, James 52
STANFORD, Thomas 53 59 60
STANTON, Edward M 324 M Hall
371
STARR, Richd 31
STATES-GENERAL OF NEW
NETHERLANDS, 18
STATES-GENERAL OF HOLLAND,
15
STATES-GENERAL TO ENGLAND,
28
STEEELMAN, 202
STEELE, John 53
STEELMAN, 126 211 Anthony 359
458 459 463 Harry G 446 477 478
James 80 Jonas 359 Richard 203
STEINMEYER, Lewis 466
STEPHEN, Charles H 340
STEPHENS, 83 Charles H 339

STEPHENS (continued)
  Gen 195 Henry 85
STEPHENSON, Eli 233 James 54
STEVENS, Andrew H 457 David 203
  Elizabeth 128 Ezekiel 235 453
  454 467 Henry 85 187 197 202
  206 375 Isabella 408 James H 371
  John 129 Jonathan C 303 305 307
  311 Lewis T 444 476 477 Mr 130
  303 Richard 129 Stephen 198 205
  206 Thomas S 303 William T 332
  333 335 375 376 439 444 452 461
  462 473-477
STEVENSON, Ezegiel 338 Ezekiel
  336 Richard 207 Richard C 460
  461
STEWART, James Jr 315 John 366
STILES, Hannah 73 Henry 72 73 82
  Henry Jr 72 Mary 72 William 279
  467
STILL, Isaac 126
STILLWELL, Capt 198 Elizabeth 71
  Enoch 171 178 179 190 193 215
  John 46 53 70 84 85 141 Maj 190
  Nicholas 74 100 108 135 140 141
  144 171 178 179 193 196 198 205
  209 216 450 Richard 113 Sarah
  198 William 43 53
STILWELL, Enoch 202
STIMSON, Stephen 235
STITES, 38 39 55 69 101 Abigail 84
  Benjamin 55 84 98 190 205 Benjn
  188 Dr 127 Esaiah 113 Esaroh 84
  George 113 136 237 Hannah 71
  Henry 39 43 46 48 52 55 57 69 70
  84 91 97 102 104 139 205 463
  Humphrey 196 207 216 225 Isaiah
  55 100 104 205 463 Israel 205
  207 237 Jacob 206 John 55 102
  205 206 303 451 454 John K F
  421 465 473 474 477 Jonathan 84
  136 Maurice B 336 337 Nathaniel

STITES (continued)
  229 Philip 243 247 Richard 55 84
  97 102 113 Richard B 302 458
  Samuel R 332 333 335 426 473
  475 476 Sarah E 431 Thomas 136
  196 Thos 205 Townsend 55 455-
  457 William 113 431 477 Zebulon
  229
STOCKTON, John P 358
STONEBANK, Thomas 85
STONEMAN, 308
STORY, John 36 53
STRATTEN, Isaac 71
STRATTON, Abigail F 408 George
  408 473
STRONG, Charles 237
STRONGHAM, David 66
STRYKER, Adj Gen 179 195 Gen
  179 200 202
STUART, George H 371 John 475
STURMER, John J 472 John J Jr 468
STURTEVANT, John 407
STUYVESANT, 26 Gov 26
SULLIVAN, Gen 195 200 John M
  476
SUMERS, Richard 97
SUMMERS, Richard 80
SUMMIS, Edward 53
SURRAN, Gabriel G 336 Samuel T
  336 337
SURRANN, Gabriel G 338
SUTTON, Emma T 7 James 109 110
  John 72 John P 333 334
SWAIN, 277 362 Aaron 206 Charlotte
  R 424 Daniel 118 141 171 174
  237 277 David E 333 334 Ebenez-
  er 43 54 70 102 104 113 118
  Edward Y 283 464 Elemuel 54
  Elihu 84 Henry 230 231 269 283
  302 380 464 Humphrey 229 Isaac
  Jr 468 Jacochs 205 Jacocks 220
  229-231 269 John 222 302 303

SWAIN (continued)
  John W 457 459 467 Jon 85
  Jonathan 54 70 86 Joshua 54 230
  231 269 282 283 380 451 463
  Joshua Jr 242 282 283 298 360
  451 463 464 Kezia 277 Lemuel
  455 474 477 479 Lemuel Jr 473
  476 Lemuel Sr 424 Luther M 468
  Mary 71 Mr 269 428 Nezer 113
  207 450 Nicholas T 303 305
  Rachel 428 Return B 371 428 474
  Reuben 54 74 207 Richard 54 113
  Ruth 71 Silas 54 136 171 205 207
  Zebulon 54 180
SWAINE, Daniel 113 Ebenezer 84
  105 James 85 Jonathan 84 Richard
  84 Samuel 85 Silas 84 Zebulon 85
  113 205
SWAN, Joseph 198 205 206 Samuel
  257
SWANE, Daniel 135
SWIFT, John 272 Mr 151
SWING, Michael 461
TALLMADGE, Recorder 273
TARRESAN, 82
TATHAM, 34 John 34 Mr 33 34
TAYLOR, 51 70 Bayard 439 Benjamin 463 Capt 210 Deborah 73
  Elizabeth 71 73 74 Elmer 339 340
  George 34 35 41-43 47-49 51 52
  56 60 70 73 74 84 113 114 130
  180 205 206 464 George Jr 53
  Hannah 71 James E 397 398 477
  Jeremiah 74 John 52 65 70 72-74
  84 92 130 206 463 464 468 472
  John Jr 85 Lydia 73 Margery 73
  130 Mary 73 74 Samuel 74 237
  Thomas 114 Thomas H 345 346
  W W 439 Wallace 237 William 73
TECHEPEPEWOYA, 18
TELFORD, John 478
TENNIS, Edward A 398

TEQTS, John 33
THOMAS, Gabriel 57 James 237
THOMPKINS, Dr 472 Sarah D 468
  William A 468
THOMPSON, 124 Catherine 330 Col
  330 Elizabeth 329 Harry C 473
  John W 466 Judith Swayne 420
  Mary 356 Richard 235 244 255
  260 277 284 329 356 406 451-453
  455 463 464 Richard 1st 239
  Richard Jr 250 466 Richard R 379
  473-475 Richard S 329 Robert P
  467 William 246
THORN, R Howard 466
THORNTON, John 336 338 345 346
THROP, 31 Jno 31
TIASCONS, 24
TIBBLES, Ewing W 336 338
TINDALL, M B 408 Mary E 356 N B
  282 356 Richard T 303 306
TINICUM, Printz 22
TIRANS, 24
TODD, Chester J 468
TOMBS, Samuel 330
TOMLIN, Almain 246 Andrew J 349
  401 463 Benjamin Jr 269 Deborah
  270 J 227 Jedediah 236 John F
  338-340 345 401
TOMLINSON, Justice 67
TOMSEN, Nathaniel 244
TOMSON, John 85
TOOMBS, Samuel 309
TOWNSEND, 29 37 38 76 78 315
  Capt 196 197 Charles W 339 340
  Cornelius 459 Cresse 233 463
  Daniel 113 David 205 207 220
  463 David S 345 346 Edward F
  348 476 Edward L 338-340 Eli 55
  221 222 455 Elijah 180 205 222
  223 225 232 362 450 451 464
  Elijah Jr 292 465 Embury 339 340
  Enoch 225 F Sidney 439 444 473

TOWNSEND (continued)
475-477 Henry 190 194 196
Henry Y 195 450 463 Henry
Young 196 200 205 209 215 253
375 Isaac 105 114 Israel 253 407
451 454 455 Israel S 333 335
James 114 201 205 464 Jehu 464
Jeremiah H 473 John 29 37 38 49
51 52 54 58 59 64-66 72-74 76
82-84 140 141 174 225 232 254
451 454 463 John Jr 205 227
Jonathan 206 222 Joshua 236 241
253 254 375 444 451 Judge 67
Mrs John Jr 227 Phebe 37 Reuben
222 451 Richard 29 53 64 66 76
77 84 96 97 205 330 450 451 463
Richard H 315 330 Richard Jr 83
84 Richard S 336 338 Robert 53
66 85 86 92 97 102 463 Samuel
113 206 451 459 464 Shamgar C
345 346 469 Silvanus Jr 114 205
Smith 328 456 Socrates 407 Stillwell H 463 Swain 267 453 463
464 Swaine 234 Sylvanus 54 463
Sylvanus Jr 179 Thomas 457
Thomas T 300 William 473-475
William H 456 457 William S 328
342 452 454-457 Zebulon 237
TRADER, George 336 338
TREEN, 212 Capt 211 William 210
212 Wm 211
TROUT, John 333 335
TURNER, Capt 318 322 Nathaniel 23
Peter 470 William 393
TYLER, 253 Jeremiah F 333 334 John
458 459
UNCLE ABE, 293
USSELINX, William 17
VANDERBILT, Cmdr 281
VANEMAN, Daniel 237 Richard 198
205
VANGELDER, Abraham 187 Isaac

VANGELDER (continued)
187 Jeremiah 187
VANGILDER, Abraham 54 114 198
Ezekiel 236 Hannah 471 Isaac 198
James 243 Jeremiah 198 205 John
54 113 220 Smith 242 Thaddeus
381 471 Thomas 455 463 William
R 471
VANGILDERS, Richard 38 Robert 38
Sylvanus 38 Thompson 37 38
VANHOOK, Lawrence 198
VANHORN, Burgher V 479 Peter
Peterson 72 Rev Mr 109
VANHOUTEN, Martin 311
VANNAMAN, Theophilus 336
VANNEMAN, Theophilus 337
VANRENSELAER, 17 20
VANTWILLER, 20 Wooter 18
VANVALIN, Franklin J 478
VANWRINKLE, Thomas L 305
VAUGHAN, Benjamin 120
VEACH, Hezekiah 337 Hezekiel 336
VENIMON, Richard 206
VERHULST, William 17
VERRAZANI, 13
VOSS, Edgar 345 346 Ezekiel 332
333 335
WAGGONER, John S 477
WALES, 440 Dr 360 E L B 440
Edmund L B 372 Edmund Levi
Bull 360 Eli B 361 407 Eli L B
284 Roger 360 405
WALKER, 119 Albert 329 330 J
Newton 371 Thomas 119
WALLACE, John 460
WALTON, Henry H 478
WANAMAKER, John 371 393 Mr
393 Postmaster Gen 393
WARD, Gov 270 James 269
WARE, 427 Daniel C 354 423 429
473 474 George S 473 476 J Stratton 458 474 James W 423 John

WARE (continued)
  221 John G W 328 354 409 423
  429 472-474 Joseph 222 237 284
  298 328 354 379 407 423 429 455
  465 466 472 473 477 Marshel 427
  Mashel 7 423 Maskel 7 328 354
  429 458 459 473 Samuel F 243
  328 335 342 452 455-457 473
  Samuel F Jr 333 Samuel Fithian
  276 328 423 455 Uncle John 429
  W S 303 W W 319 Walter S 303
  Wilmon W 328 354 355 423 429
  451 452 458 473-476
WARNER, 28 Caleb 303 Caleb L 316
  325 Edmund 28 John H 316 325
  Maurice V 333 335
WARWICK, Alfred 345 346 Samuel
  237
WARWIN, John 32
WASBROUGH, Capt 82
WASHBOURNE, John 285
WASHBURN, W H 479
WASHBURNE, Col 341
WASHINGTON, 182 185 193 194
  199 203 215 Gen 186 193-195
  200 215 216 George 178 267
WATERS, James 467
WATSON, 252
WATT, James 141 220 Mr 142 Pastor
  220
WAY, James P 449 478
WAYNE, Gen 195
WEATHERBY, Benjamin 336 338
  Leaming 333 335
WEATHERILL, Christop 32
WEAVER, Catharine 110
WEBB, Phoebe 408
WEBSTER, Daniel 257
WEEKS, Andrew 452 461 Andrew S
  461 Charles H 303 305 307
  George T 333 335 James 339 340
  John 333 335
WEGTON, 31 Abraham 31 Mrs
  Abraham 31
WELDON, Jeremiah 333 335 Joseph
  52 67 72
WELES, David 72
WELLES, Gideon 402
WELLS, Daniel 74 Martin 460 478
WENTZELL, N N 301 302 Nicholas
  A 465
WERTS, George T 440 Gov 370 380
WEST, Capt 301 John 298 301 303
  406 474 Richard M 81
WESTCOTT, 212 Ebenezer 298
  Edwin F 470 Elva E 335 345 346
  Ephraim 470 Eva E 333 Marietta
  470
WESTON, Abraham 37 53
WETHEREL, 133
WETHERILL, John 107
WHEATE, Bery 32
WHEATEN, Josept 190
WHEATON, Daniel 346 Daniel H
  345 346 478 Jonathan 237 Joseph
  187 197 237
WHEELER, J H 398
WHELDEN, James 85
WHELDING, Joseph 73 Mary 73
WHILDEN, Isaac 84 James 140 141
  143-145 147 165 171 174 Jas 143
  Joseph 84 Joseph Sr 85 Justice
  165 Seth 171
WHILDIN, Joseph 58
WHILDING, Joseph 86
WHILLDEN, 39 James 147 450
  Joseph 39 73 Matthew 206 219
  450 451
WHILLDER, 83
WHILLDIN, Alexander 370 371 Capt
  281 282 319 320 406 David 128
  Hannah 44 281 Isaac 113 J 148
  James 109 113 117 136 180 193
  205 281 Jane 281 John G 282

WHILLDIN (continued)
   John Galloway 282 Jonathan 281
   Joseph 44 52 228 281 463 Mary
   281 Matthew 193 228 298 299
   474 Mr 228 370 Seth 196 Wilmon
   304 Wilmon Jr 282 Wilmon Sr
   281
WHITAKER, James 298 338 340
   Joseph 333 335 Joseph W 348
   Joshua 346 Josiah 333 335 345
WHITE, 83 Daniel H 333 335 H 272
   Peter 77
WHITLOCK, William 49 51 52
WHITNEY, George 385 466
WHITTINGTON, Thomas 461
WIBLE, Thomas 467
WICKWAUS, Samuel 189
WIGGINS, Daniel 73
WILDAIR, Hannah 71
WILDOW, 83
WILEY, James 467 John 302 304 375
   464 Samuel W 459
WILIETTS, James Jr 196
WILKS, B 273
WILLARD, Richard 128
WILLDIN, James 191
WILLET, James 194 John 114 Moses
   241
WILLETS, 39 Amos 192 Capt 198
   Enoch 205 Hope 55 202 James
   134 James Jr 189 John 39 54 113
   229 450 Nicholas 229 233 307
   451 Reuben 451
WILLETT, Amos 198
WILLETTS, Capt 196-198 Elmer 339
   340 Enoch S 336 338 Henry Y
   332 333 335 Isaac 114 J Howard
   307 329 James 201 James S 469
   John 135 Jonathan 339
WILLEY, John 284
WILLIAM KING OF ENGLAND, 68
WILLIAMS, Abigail 238 Barlow 360

WILLIAMS (continued)
   Enos R 338 339 439 475 Francis
   468 George H 364 George L 339
   340 345 346 Inspector 167 J 160 J
   Ashton 433 473 John 255 453 454
   470 Joseph Q 379 426 430 432
   439 457 472-477 Lewis S 336 338
   458 Loraina 359 Mackey 263 451
   467 470 Mr 168 431-433 439
   Sarah E 431 Stephen 336 338
   Thomas 302 328 342 343 452 456
   457 470 Thomas B 333 335
   Townsend S 336 338 William 238
   William F 374
WILLIAMSON, M 297 Moses 260
   261 272 277 285 303 375 384 Mr
   260 272 285 Thomas H 285 439
   440 475 477
WILLIMIN, Richard 240
WILLING, 133
WILLIS, Alonzo 339 340 John 85
WILLIT, John 212
WILLITS, Amos 187 Capt 212 Isaac
   55 Jacob 55 205 James 55 190
   James Jr 178 179 187 John 55 74
   Martha 55 74 Reuben 451
WILLKISS, John 73
WILLS, Daniel Sr 32 Danll 32 John
   79
WILLSON, Thomas H 398
WILSON, 9 Bell P 470 H R 371
   James 193 John 268 355 463 470
   Sarah 267 Stacy M 333 335
   Stephen B 476
WINDER, 321 324 Capt 323 Gen 317
   318 321 322 J H 319 Provost Gen
   319
WINTZELL, Sarah 227
WITHERSPOON, John 186
WOERTZ, John G 478
WOLDREDGE, John 48 53
WOLFE, 434 Charles S 366

WOLLY, John 53
WOODRUF, R 227
WOODWARD, Capt 117
WOOL, Gen 329
WOOLMAN, S G 423 Samuel 423
WOOLSON, Aaron 235 244 John 255
WORLEDGE, 42 John 41
WORLIDGE, Jno 74 John 40
WORTH, Jos 82 Joseph 83
WRIGHT, Amnon 466 Elias 298
WVOYT, 18
YARD, Joseph 115
YATES, John 237 William 205 207
YORK, Stites 476
YOUNG, 39 Alexander 342 368 452 457 458 Dr 368 Enoch 233 Henry 39 43 54 56 84 86 91 92 97 102 104 105 111 118 135 136 138 139 187 197 205 368 390 450 463 464 Hugh H 241 Job 220 John 205 John W 459 469 Judge 54 Millicent 134 Sallie 469 Stephen 114 187 198 205 263 452-455 Stephen H 469 Uriah 187 198 Wilbur E 472

www.ingramcontent.com/pod-product-compliance
Lightning Source LLC
Chambersburg PA
CBHW060312230426
43663CB00009B/1680